LONDON

APA PUBLICATIONS
Part of the Langenscheidt Publishing Group
L

About This Book

Editorial

Editor
Roger Williams
Editorial Director
Brian Bell

Distribution

UK & Ireland
GeoCenter International Ltd
The Viables Centre, Harrow Way
Basingstoke, Hants RG22 4BJ
Fax: (44) 1256-817988

United States
Langenscheidt Publishers, Inc.
46–35 54th Road, Maspeth, NY 11378
Fax: (1) 718 784-0640

Canada
Thomas Allen & Son Ltd
390 Steelcase Road East
Markham, Ontario L34 1G2
Fax: (1) 905 475 6747

Australia
Universal Press
1 Waterloo Road
Macquarie Park, NSW 2113
Fax: (61) 2 9888 9074

New Zealand
Hema Maps New Zealand Ltd (HNZ)
Unit D, 24 Ra ORA Drive
East Tamaki, Auckland
Fax: (64) 9 273 6479

Worldwide
Apa Publications GmbH & Co. Verlag KG (Singapore branch)
38 Joo Koon Road, Singapore 628990
Tel: (65) 865-1600. Fax: (65) 861-6438

Printing

Insight Print Services (Pte) Ltd
38 Joo Koon Road, Singapore 628990
Tel: (65) 865-1600. Fax: (65) 861-6438

First Edition 1989
Ninth Edition 1998
Updated 2001

CONTACTING THE EDITORS
We would appreciate it if readers would alert us to errors or outdated information by writing to:
Insight Guides, P.O. Box 7910, London SE1 1WE, England. Fax: (44 20) 7403-0290. insight@apaguide.demon.co.uk

www.insightguides.com

This guidebook combines the interests and enthusiasms of two of the world's best-known information providers: Insight Guides, whose titles have set the standard for visual travel guides since 1970, and Discovery Channel, the world's premier source of nonfiction television programming.

The editors of Insight Guides provide both practical advice and general understanding about a destination's history, culture, institutions and people. Discovery Channel and its Web site, www.discovery.com, help millions of viewers explore their world from the comfort of their own home and also encourage them to explore it firsthand.

How to use this book

The book is carefully structured both to convey an understanding of the city and its culture and to guide readers through its sights and activities:

◆ To understand London today, you need to know something of its past. The first section covers the city's history and culture in lively, authoritative essays written by specialists.

◆ The main Places section provides a full run-down of all the attractions worth seeing. The main places of interest are coordinated by number with full-colour maps.

◆ The Travel Tips listings section provides a point of reference for information on travel, hotels, restaurants, shops and festivals. Information may be located

EXPLORE YOUR WORLD
Discovery CHANNEL

Above: entertainer in Covent Garden.

quickly by using the index printed on the back cover flap – and the flaps are designed to serve as bookmarks.

◆ Photographs are chosen not only to illustrate geography and buildings but also to convey the moods of the city and the life of its people.

The contributors

This new edition was edited by **Roger Williams** and builds on the original edition produced by **Andrew Eames**, later executive editor of many Insight Guides, and **Brian Bell**, who is now editorial director of the series. All three have worked for Britain's national newspapers and they bring a journalist's sharp observation to bear on this endlessly stimulating capital.

The editors sought out writers with the ideal combination of affection for, and detachment from, their subject that defines Insight Guides. Several were associated with *The Times*: **Tim Grimwade**, who wrote on the West End, the bright heart of the city; **Srinivasa Rao**, who described the melting pot of races in the city; **Allison Lobbett**, who researched and wrote the chapter on London's financial quarter, The City; and **Lynne Truss**, now a successful novelist, who profiled that object of many anecdotes, the London cabbie.

Other writers included literary journalist and author **Brian Morton**; **Victor Bryant**, a lecturer on ceramic history and a trained tourist guide lecturer on London; the prolific **Roger St Pierre**, whose 17 books range from the *Book of the Bicycle* to the *Illustrated Encyclopedia of Black Music*. The history section was written by **Roland Collins**, an accomplished writer, photographer and artist. The fact-packed Travel Tips section was assembled by **Andrea Gillies**, the first female editor of the *Good Beer Guide*, **Beverley Harper** and book editor **Clare Griffiths**.

Many of the pictures in this book are the vision of **Richard T. Nowitz**, a *National Geographic* photographer based near Washington DC. Other shots came from **Glyn Genin**, who returned to photography after many years as a national newspaper picture editor, **David Gray**, a market researcher with a passion for photographing London, and **Neill Menneer**, who has exhibited his Images of London. Picture research was by **Hilary Genin**, who contributed the shopping feature, and further research was by **Lesley Gordon**, who also wrote the text on Brixton.

Map Legend

----	County Boundary
	National Park/ Nature Reserve
	Underground
	Airport
	Bus Station
P	Parking
	Tourist Information
	Post Office
	Church/Ruins
	Mosque
	Synagogue
	Castle/Ruins
★	Place of Interest

The main places of interest in the Places section are coordinated by number with a full-colour map (e.g. ❶) and a symbol at the top of every right-hand page tells you where to find the map.

CONTENTS

Maps

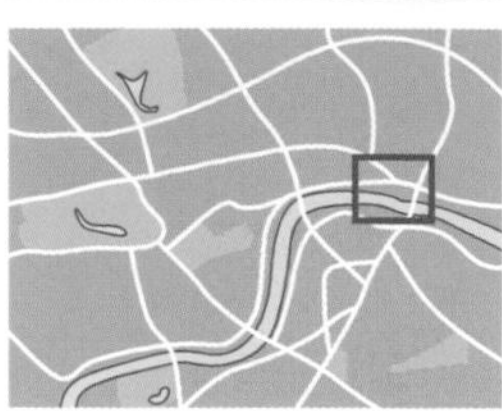

Interior plans of Westminster Abbey, St Paul's Cathedral and the Tower of London face the inside back cover.

The London Underground map is on the back flap

Introduction

History

People

Features

Formality and fun mix in a City of London festival

Insight on....

Information panels

Travel Tips

♦ **Full Travel Tips index is on page 261**

Places

DOMINE
DIR

BANHAM
ALARMS
01-584 3566
43
K C
P
permit
holders
only

41

FINANCIAL TIMES
South Africa imposes tougher regulations on black townships

THE STREETS OF LONDON

Nobody ever planned London. Its growth was propelled by great events and great individuals, and its history is vividly reflected in its street names

Threadneedle, Throgmorton, Bread and Milk Streets; Yukon Road, Zampa Road, Zander Court and Cosmo Place; Manchuria Road, Morocco Street, Max Roach Park and Bohemia Place: all are street names of London which portray some part of London's history, some snippet of world events, of empire building, of television fashions, or simply of the street planner's own politics. They are names that can reveal more than the buildings: whole areas are named after colonial leaders, regions of Australia and highpoints in the Boer War. There are 12 Churchills and four Dallases.

There is no single underlying logic behind street naming. The multifarious nature reflects the city itself and something of its fascination. Taxi drivers probably learn more English history from these names than they did at school.

An unplanned city

London is not uniform. It is patchy, unplanned, organic. This is not a city of grand vistas, but everyone finds his or her own favourite holes and corners. While it has a long and venerable past, that past is often not visible. Over the centuries the ripples of history have repeatedly destroyed parts of the city and the subsequent rebuilding has resulted in a cocktail of streets that combine many different tastes.

Queen Boadicca burnt the the city the Romans had built here in AD 61, but this was just the first of many serious setbacks. The plagues of 1665 claimed the lives of 100,000 Londoners and a year later the Great Fire, started in Pudding Lane, destroyed much of the city. In the bombing blitz of World War II, 29,000 Londoners were killed, and 80 percent of buildings in the City (the financial area) were damaged, a third completely destroyed. A hurricane in October 1987 tore down 15 million trees in the southeast of England, and another fierce storm in 1990 wreaked even more havoc.

In this process of change, something good has usually emerged from each disaster. So dark and narrow were the streets in the old City of London, for example, that shopkeepers had to erect mirrors outside their windows to reflect light into the shops. The heavy bombing of World War II eventually provided the opportunity for widening and lightening; slums disappeared and the level of street crime declined.

PRECEDING PAGES: riding the London Eye, erected for the millennium; upstream from Tower Bridge; Houses of Parliament; smart southwest London address. **LEFT:** City types. **RIGHT:** Cockney Pearly Queen.

Village London

To most residents, the city is a collection of communities or villages, once independent but long since swallowed up, along with much of the surrounding countryside, by the expanding metropolis. At the centre of this patchwork city is a common area of shared London, a London of work and play. This book deals primarily with shared London, the essential London of the West End, City and South Bank, but there is a section on some of the more interesting local "villages" such as Hampstead, Notting Hill, Islington, Greenwich and Brixton.

It would be misleading to suggest that this is the city that true Londoners know, that this is where they participate in a morass of entertainment into the small hours, taking boat trips and visiting museums at every opportunity. The fact is that, as in most cities, the residents do not take sufficient advantage of their inheritance. Londoners seldom go to fringe theatre productions, rarely go to the West End and have not visited St Paul's since they went in a school party. But this is London: it is all here, waiting for anyone to dip in and discover something to entertain, fulfil or delight. Henry James described the capital as a "giant animated encyclopaedia with people for pages". With all its variety and history, it's hard to know where to start as a tourist, but James's emphasis is a good one. The people and the culture matter as much as the buildings. Left in the hands of tourist organisations, any city can become a string of tourist buildings. On the following pages we present interesting places to visit as well as the main tourist sites.

Try the balcony of the Royal Festival Hall (on the South Bank) after dark for a glorious view of lights along the Thames; a round trip on the Docklands Light Railway in order to view the

Some Vital Statistics

London accounts for 15 percent of Britain's gross domestic product and its £17 billion economy is larger than that of Greece, Finland or Portugal. More of Europe's 500 largest companies have their headquarters in London than in any other city, and more of the world's top 500, after Tokyo.

London is not one of the world's most dangerous or violent capitals but there are a number of street robberies (more than 20,000 a year). It is said that in Petticoat Lane the pickpockets are so fast that you can buy your own handkerchief by the time you reach the end of the market stalls. And yet this is the city where milkmen can leave pints on doorsteps in relative safety.

London is tremendously dominant within the United Kingdom, and always has been. In 1605, 6 percent of the of the country's population lived in the city. Today the population of the 610 sq. mile (1,580 sq. km) metropolis stands at 6.7 million (with a slight majority of women), 12 percent of the country's total population.

London is still the largest city in Europe. It caters for 18 million tourists a year and 25,000 street-people sleep within its confines. London's weather is by no means as bad as Londoners make out. Over a year, the city averages three hours and 20 minutes of sunshine a day. New York's rainfall is double – London's just seems greater because it falls more slowly and lingers longer.

revitalisation of what was the warehouse of the world, and what is now becoming a tourist attraction; and tea dances at the Waldorf Hotel. For a spectacular view of London, go to the top of Westminster Cathedral (not the Abbey) spire, or alternatively view the City's worker ants from the top of the Monument, the striking 202-ft (61-metre) Roman Doric column built by Sir Christopher Wren to commemorate the Great Fire of 1666.

LONDON CALLING

More countries can be dialled directly from London than from any other city.

Have lunch at Fortnum and Mason's on Piccadilly, or take in an open-air performance of Shakespeare in Regent's Park theatre, which you might precede with a cruise along the Regent's Canal. On the South Bank, splash out on a drink at the Oxo Tower, or better still, the restaurant at Shakespeare's reincarnated Globe.

Have a drink at the Grenadier public house on Wilton Row, off Knightsbridge; amble around Harrods; enjoy a meal at the Roof Garden in Derry Street, off Kensington High Street; visit Camden's trendy market on Saturday or Sunday, and earthier Brick Lane market on Sunday. Try a fringe theatre production or a late-night cabaret; stroll through Leicester Square and Covent Garden at night for the international flavour of the city. Walk around the City and the East End at the weekend when offices are closed, and sense the history of the Square Mile from street names – Crutched Friars, Half Moon Court, Frying Pan, Magpie and Hanging Sword alleys, Knightrider Street and Sermon Lane.

Bus and boat rides

The best way to see London properly is by walking. Another good way to get a glimpse of the real London is to sit upstairs on a double-decker bus and travel from the centre to the perimeter. You can also get your bearings from a trip up or down the River Thames.

When public transport first began to operate, only the rich could afford to commute, leaving the poor to settle in central London. In recent years that trend has reversed, and house prices have pushed the lower-paid out into the suburbs. This "gentrification" of inner London terraces has halted. The past decade has seen some grand developments along the banks of the river, which is at last becoming more of a feature of daily life, and this trend should continue as architects and planners search for ways to mark the dawn of the 21st century: bridges, glass bubbles and funfairs have all been proposed.

Meanwhile, the broad brushstrokes of London's image remain the same. This is the city where exiles gather in favourite haunts, and where charity functions revive Cockney Pearly Kings and Queens in suits made of buttons, where clubs are exclusive, judges wear wigs and a coach-drawn royalty eschews the common touch. It's where paparazzi stand on pavements outside the better discos and the taxi drivers, fount of all knowledge about the streets of London, tell you about the famous people they've had in their cabs.

In these pages you will learn about all of this and more: when the first public lavatory opened in London; where to buy jellied eels; why taxi drivers don't like their passengers to interrupt; and how to find the hidden police station in Trafalgar Square. Here, in short, is all the variety of the city *Newsweek* magazine recently dubbed the coolest place on the planet. ❑

LEFT: on the world's oldest Underground system, reading daily newspapers replaces conversation. There are 10 national newspapers to choose from. **RIGHT:** reflection in a Covent Garden market stall.

Decisive Dates

Roman: AD43–410

AD43: Londinium settled during second Roman invasion; a bridge is built over the Thames.
61: Boadicca, Queen of the Iceni tribe in East Anglia, sacks the city before being defeated.
c. 200: Three-mile (5-km) city wall built, encompassing fort, forum, amphitheatre and temple.
410: Troops are withdrawn to defend Rome.

Saxon: 449–1042

AD449–527: Jutes, Angles and Saxons arrive in Britain, dividing it into separate kingdoms. Attacks by Vikings.
604: St Paul's Cathedral founded by King Ethelbert.
c.750: Monastery of St Peter is founded on Thorney Island, to become Westminster Abbey.
8th century: Shipping and manufacturing flourish on the riverbank near today's Strand.
884: London becomes capital under Alfred the Great.
1042: Edward the Confessor moves his court from the city to Westminster and rebuilds the Abbey.

Norman: 1066–1154

1066: William I, Duke of Normandy and descendant of the Vikings who settled in northern France, conquers Britain and is crowned in Westminster Abbey. The Normans introduce French and the feudal system.
1078: Tower of London's White Tower built.

Plantagenet: 1154–1399

Descendants of the French House of Anjou.
1176: London Bridge built of stone.
1191: The City elects its first mayor.
1220: St Paul's Cathedral rebuilt.

Lancaster and York: 1399–1485

Rival royal houses resort to civil war, dramatised by Shakespeare in *Richard III*.
1444: Guildhall rebuilt.

Tudor: 1485–1603

Of Welsh descent, the Tudors preside over the English Renaissance, under Queen Elizabeth I.
1514: Hampton Court Palace begun.
1532: Henry VIII builds Palace of Whitehall, the largest in Europe. It catches fire in 1698.
1534: Henry VIII declares himself head of the Church of England and dissolves the monasteries.

English Monarchs since the Norman Conquest

Norman
William 1066-87
William II 1087-1100
Henry I 1100-35
Stephen 1135-54

Plantagenet
Henry II 1154-89
Richard I 1189-99
John 1199-1216
Henry III 1216-72
Edward I 1272-1307
Edward II 1307-27
Edward III 1327-77
Richard II 1377-99

Lancaster
Henry IV 1399-1413
Henry V 1413-22
Henry VI 1422-61

York
Edward IV 1461-83
Edward V 1483
Richard III 1483-85

Tudor
Henry VII 1485-1509
Henry VIII 1509-47
Edward VI 1547-53
Mary 1553-58
Elizabeth I 1558-1603

Stuart
James I 1603-25
Charles I 1625-49
[*Commonwealth 1649-53 Protectorate 1653-60*]
Charles II 1660-85
James II 1685-89
William and Mary 1689-1702
Anne 1702-1714

Hanover
George I 1714-27
George II 1727-60
George III 1760-1820
George IV 1820-30
William IV 1830-37

Saxe-Coburg-Gotha
Victoria 1837-1901
Edward VII 1901-10

Windsor (from 1917)
George V 1910-36
Edward VIII 1936
George VI 1936-52
Elizabeth II from 1952

1536: St James's Palace is built.
1550: Somerset House is built.
1588: William Shakespeare (1568–1616) begins his dramatic career in London.

Stuart: 1603–1714

The arrival of the Scottish kings unites the two kingdoms. Religious intolerance continues.
1605: Guy Fawkes tries to blow up Parliament.
1620: The Pilgrim Fathers set sail for America.
1642–49: Civil war between the Cavalier Royalists and the republican Roundheads. Royalists are defeated. Charles I is executed.
1660: Monarchy is restored under Charles II.
1660–69: Samuel Pepys (1633–1703) writes his diary chronicling contemporary events.
1664–66: The Great Plague kills one-fifth of the 500,000 population.
1666: The Great Fire destroys 80 percent of London.
1675: Sir Christopher Wren (1632–1723) starts work on St Paul's Cathedral.
1694: The Bank of England is established.
1699: St James's Palace used as a royal court, and continues to be so for 138 years.

Hanover: 1714–1837

The House of Hanover is ushered in by Georges I, II, III and IV. The Architectural style is known as Georgian.
1724: St Martin-in-the-Fields is built.
1732: George II makes 10 Downing Street available to Sir Robert Walpole, Britain's first Prime Minister; it is established as the home of future Prime Ministers.
1744: Sotheby's auction house is founded.
1764: The Literary Club founded by Samuel Johnson, compiler of first English dictionary.
1783: Last public execution at Tyburn.
1811–20: The Prince Regent, later George IV, gives his name to the Regency style.
1820: Regent's Canal is completed.
1824: The National Gallery is established.
1829: Police force is established by Robert Peel.
1834: The Houses of Parliament are built after the Old Palace of Westminster is destroyed by fire.

Saxe-Coburg-Gotha: 1837–1917

The height of of Empire: building programmes over all parts of the capital. Queen Victoria (1837–1901) is declared empress of India.
1840s: Trafalgar Square laid out on the site of royal stables to commemorate Nelson's victory.
1851: The Great Exhibition held in Hyde Park.
1859: A 13-ton bell, Big Ben, is hung in the Clock Tower of the Houses of Parliament.
1863: First section of the Underground built between Paddington and Farringdon Street.
1888: Jack the Ripper strikes in Whitechapel.
1890: First electric railway to be built in deep-level tunnels, between the City and Stockwell.
1894: Tower Bridge built.
1903: Westminster Cathedral built.
1909: Victoria and Albert Museum opens.
1914: World War I begins. First air raids on the city.

Windsor (so named from 1917)

1922: British Broadcasting Company transmits first programmes from Savoy Hill.
1939–45: World War II. Children evacuated, London heavily bombed. 29,000 civilians killed and 1.75 million London homes destroyed.
1951: Festival of Britain; new concert halls are built on South Bank near Waterloo.
1976: National Theatre building opened.
1982: Thames Barrier is completed.
1986: The Greater London Council is abolished.
1996: Shakespeare's Globe, a replica of the original theatre burnt down in 1599, opens on Bankside.
2000: Ken Livingstone becomes London's first elected mayor. Tate Modern opens on Bankside. ❑

PRECEDING PAGES: *Trafalgar Square by Moonlight* by the 19th-century artist Henry Pether.
LEFT: shopping at a lamp-maker's around 1700.
RIGHT: London Bridge before the Great Fire.

BEGINNINGS

The Romans chose their site well. The river was the key to London's strategic importance and it would remain so through the centuries

Did London begin in Creffield Road? During the Stone Age, this now undistinguished street in the West London suburb of Acton was home and workshop to prehistoric flint workers. They left 600 worked flints, and the discovery is one of the few on which our knowledge of pre-Roman London is based. Together with the scant evidence of a hand-axe from Piccadilly Circus, the Acton locations are sites on an archaeologist's map through which an ancient river flowed and created gravel banks in the clayey basin on its way to the North Sea.

Not until AD 43 does the story of London begin, when the invading Roman army chose gravel banks between Southwark and the City as the site of their bridge. Roman London, the Celtic "Llyn-din", the fort by the lake, quickly took shape, but suffered a setback 17 years later when British guerrillas under Queen Boadicca attacked and burned areas around Lombard Street, Gracechurch Street and Walbrook.

A rebuilt Londinium, as the Romans called it, had by AD 100 supplanted Colchester as the capital and military and trading centre of Britain. It had a timber-built bridge, quays, warehouses and domestic buildings. Wattle and daub were faced with plaster; Kentish ragstone was brought by boat for public buildings and the necessary defensive wall constructed to resist raids by Saxons from the Continent. Roads radiated to Colchester, York, Chester, Exeter, Bath and Canterbury.

Decline and fall

By AD 288 the settlement's importance had been recognised by Rome. It was given the proud name Augusta, but that pride went before a fall. In 410, threatened by the Germanic races from the north, Rome had no alternative but to recall its garrison from England. Culture withered and the very fabric of Londinium crumbled.

Under the Saxons, it recovered its importance. And in the early 8th century the literary monk, the Venerable Bede, called it the "Market of the World". South of the original wooden London Bridge, the Borough came to independent existence.

By 900, Alfred, King of Wessex, had resisted Danish invasions, but subsequent attacks ended

with Sweyn as King of England. After his death Canute was crowned in the palace of the Saxon kings which the City's Aldermanbury district near Guildhall is thought to perpetuate.

Two miles (3 km) up river on Thorney Island, the Monastery of St Peter, later the great West Minster, had been established. Following his accession in 1042, Edward the Confessor moved his court from the City to Westminster, thereby creating the division of royal and mercantile power which had a profound effect on the character and growth of London. Edward, in lieu of his pilgrimage to Rome, set about rebuilding the Abbey, where succeeding kings were crowned, married and, until George III (d.1820), buried.

LEFT: an artist's impression of Roman London.
RIGHT: Bacchus riding a tiger, from a mosaic pavement found under Leadenhall Street.

City landmarks

In 1066 William the Conqueror brought the laws of Normandy to England, but promised London privileges that are still honoured today. Self-direction in local affairs was satisfied by the election of a first mayor in 1192, with aldermen and a court. A new St Paul's Cathedral was started and the great keep of the White Tower completed in 1097. Westminster Hall, the largest building of its kind in Europe, followed. By 1176 work had begun on a stone London Bridge, houses had appeared on it and the suburb on the south bank was growing. The Roman wall, with six gates, formed the city boundary,

but that part on the river bank had been replaced with wharves.

Trading ships sailed up the Fleet and Walbrook rivers to quays now long buried but remembered in local street names. Narrow lanes between manors and religious houses within the city wall set the pattern for the later congested, haphazard arrangement of streets and alleys that has persisted to our time. The only surviving landmark is Crosby Hall, a typical merchant's mansion built originally in Bishopsgate and then re-built on Chelsea Embankment.

Along the riverside road from the City to Westminster, fine houses with gardens running down to the water brought early ribbon development. Bridewell Palace at Ludgate was built alongside a bishop's palace at Salisbury House near St Bride's. In the Strand, the Palace of the Savoy stood next to Durham House.

London was now home to more than 25,000 people, worshipping in more than 100 parish churches within the walls and almost within the shadow of a medieval St Paul's.

Union and plague

By the 14th century the city's merchants had joined together in craft associations for protection and trade promotion and built their "gild" halls. The 15th-century Guildhall followed, and fire, bombing and restorers have failed to diminish it as one of the City's key buildings.

Lawyers now got together in Inns west of the City and bishops further afield in palaces at Lambeth, Holborn, Fulham and Southwark. London still had farms, smallholdings and marshy wastelands an archer's shot away from its walls.

The city had grown to 50,000 by the time of Geoffrey Chaucer, the "father of English poetry". This in spite of the "Black Death" of 1348, when, in one day alone, 200 dead were taken outside the city and buried in mass graves. The smaller population gave peasants a better bargaining hand and in the ensuing Peasants' Revolt of 1381, led by Wat Tyler and Jack Straw against a new tax, London was briefly occupied, and the Palace of Savoy burned. Richard II promised to abolish serfdom but when he was back in control, he reneged on the promise and brutally suppressed the movement.

London stopped growing in the 14th century. The City (now with a capital C) quite simply had no ambitions to get any bigger. Had it wanted to expand, it would have had to change its character, perhaps endangering in the process its hard-won privileges and sacrificing its unique position as a major European market and port. Whatever was happening outside the walls, the City maintained a blinkered detachment that was not disturbed for centuries – not, in fact, until Queen Victoria's reign. ❑

Left: Wat Tyler, leader of the Peasant's Revolt, is beheaded by the Lord Mayor of London, watched by Richard II. **Right:** Charles d'Orléans, captured at the Battle of Agincourt in 1415, was held in the Tower of London for 25 years. In the background of this early picture of the city is London Bridge, with houses.

THE GOLDEN AGE

The Tudor and Stuart monarchs presided over a cultural renaissance. But it was fire that changed the face of London forever

The much married and celebrated divorcé Henry VIII (1491–1547) almost qualifies as the "father" of modern London, though the changes he brought about were the accidental outcome of a bid for personal freedom from the power of the Church.

In 1536, after the Pope had refused to annul his marriage to Catherine of Aragon so that he could marry Anne Boleyn, Henry decided to cut all ties with Roman Catholicism. He pronounced himself head of the Church of England, persuading Parliament to authorise the dissolution of the monasteries. Their property and revenues were granted to the Crown, and Henry either gave them to close supporters or sold them. Cardinal Wolsey's house was added to an expanding palace in Whitehall. Hyde Park and St James's were enclosed as deer parks.

New uses for old churches

When foreign visitors commented on the depressing ruins of the churches and monasteries, the areas were redeveloped. The City took on the church's humanitarian work, buying St Thomas's to care for the sick and elderly, Greyfriars for orphans, Bridewell for criminals and beggars, and Bethlehem (which later became corrupted to "Bedlam") to house lunatics.

Convent (now Covent) Garden and Clerkenwell, Stepney and Shoreditch, Kennington and Lambeth all expanded, taking London's population from 50,000 in 1500 to 200,000 by the end of the century. Today, little survives of Tudor London's typically wood-framed houses with their oversailing upper storeys. A fair idea of the character of the old street scene can, however, was preserved in the Old Curiosity Shop at 13 Portsmouth Street, near Lincoln's Inn. A lasting monument to the era is Henry VIII's Hampton Court Palace, southwest of London.

Henry's daughter, Elizabeth I, whose mother, Anne Boleyn, had been beheaded for supposed adultery, came to the throne in 1558. She was truly London's queen and the "Golden Age" began, not only in a commercial sense, but also in education and the arts. She presided over the English Renaissance and her court was enlivened by music and dance.

William Shakespeare, a Londoner by adoption, was far from adulated by the authorities. When the Lord Mayor banned theatrical performances from London, Shakespeare and his fellow playwright Ben Jonson moved outside his jurisdiction to new sites on the south bank of the Thames, an area notorious for bear pits, brothels and prisons.

LEFT: Henry VIII, destroyer of monasteries and builder of palaces. **RIGHT:** his daughter, Queen Elizabeth I, who ruled in a Golden Age of the English Renaissance.

Revolution and style

Being childless, the "Virgin Queen" Elizabeth chose James VI of Scotland to succeed her as James I of England, thus launching the Stuart dynasty. Religious conflict continued, and a Catholic faction attempted to blow up Parliament in the infamous "Gunpowder Plot". On

5 November 1605, Guy (Guido) Fawkes was caught about to ignite barrels of gunpowder in the cellars beneath the House. Fawkes was executed, but 5 November, Guy Fawkes Day, is still marked with fireworks, and his effigy is burned.

Against a background of conflict between King James and Parliament, London responded to a new influence: the Italian architecture of Palladio as seen through the work of Inigo Jones. The purity of Jones's style is best seen in the Queen's House at Greenwich, begun in 1613. Six years later came the Banqueting House in Whitehall, the first time Portland stone was used in London. Throwing gothic to the winds, he designed the little-known Queen's Chapel at St James's Palace.

His most significant contribution to the new city was his work on the old Convent Garden for the Duke of Bedford. The great Piazza he created there was the prototype for the most loved and typical feature of the city, the London square. On the east side, behind a massive portico is "the handsomest barn in England": his St Paul's church.

Water, pestilence and fire

At the beginning of the 17th century, London's rapidly expanding population began to make demands on water supplies that the city could no longer satisfy. Private, though necessarily self-interested, benefactors set up conduits in various streets and restrictions were put on brewers and fishmongers to prevent waste.

By 1600 a source of pure water was vital, and for one man, Hugh Myddleton, an obsession. A Welshman, goldsmith and banker, he conceived the idea of bringing a "New River" to London from springs near Hertford. At his own expense he started work on the man-made river in 1609 and brought it as far as Enfield before his money ran out. He turned to a former customer, James I, who became his partner with a half-share in the profits. By 1613 the New River Head in Finsbury, just north of the City, was reached.

Great tragedies lay ahead for London. In 1665 the still inadequate water supply and lack of sanitation brought the dreaded plague to the overcrowded city, and before it ran its course 100,000 inhabitants died. The Great Fire, less than a year later, came as if to cleanse the stricken city. From a baker's shop on Pudding Lane, Eastcheap, the flames raged for five days, reaching as far west as the Temple.

Miraculously, only half a dozen people died. The disaster was chronicled by Samuel Pepys (1633–1703), an Admiralty official and the most famous diarist of his time. He watched from the attic of his house in Seething Lane near the Tower as, under the Lord Mayor's direction, houses were pulled down to stop the fire spreading. Most people busied themselves removing their belongings to the stone churches or to boats on the river. Pepys dug a pit in his garden to save his wine and "parmazan" cheese. He saw "St Paul's church with all the roof fallen", and watched the fire crossing the Bridge to Southwark. After the fire, 13,000 houses and 87

parish churches lay in ruins, but rebuilding was immediately planned.

Wren's dream

Christopher Wren, Surveyor General to the Crown, returned from Paris, his mind filled with new ideas. London, too, he thought, should have *rond-points*, vistas and streets laid out in a grid pattern. But people wanted homes quickly and traders wanted to carry on their businesses, so Wren's best ideas were never realised. Expediency dictated that the new should rise on the sites of the old, with one prudent difference: new buildings were made of brick, not wood.

Wren turned his inventive powers to rebuilding 50 of the City's damaged churches. His achievements lie in the individuality of their soaring towers and steeples which rise above the rooftops. In 1675 work began on his masterpiece, a new St Paul's Cathedral. People sensed that St Paul's had a symbolic importance to the City which Samuel Pepys movingly described in his diary. There is a story that, when Wren asked a workman to fetch him a stone in order to mark the precise centre of the cleared site, the man brought a fragment of an old tombstone. On it was inscribed the single word *Resurgam*, "I will arise again".

By 1700 City men were beginning to commute from fashionable suburbs such as St James's, and from Soho and Mayfair in the west and Holborn and Clerkenwell in the north. Only a quarter of the regional population (674,000) lived in the old City. A tax was raised in 1710 to provide "fifty new churches in and about the cities of London and Westminster and Suburbs thereof" but few were built. James Gibbs built St Mary-le-Strand and St Martin-in-the-Fields, but it was Nicholas Hawksmoor, Wren's right-hand man, who expressed his art most nobly in St Anne's, Limehouse, St George-in-the-East, St Mary Woolnoth, St George in Bloomsbury Way and Christchurch, Spitalfields.

LEFT: an unknown artist painted Old St Paul's burning in the 1666 Great Fire, which devastated the city. **ABOVE :** *The Frozen Thames* by Abram Hondius: the city's climate used to be considerably cooler.

Ripples of growth

House building spread through the green fields beyond Soho towards Hyde Park and across the Tyburn road. As the ripple of this 18th-century building ring moved outwards, the older centre was coming to the end of its useful life. The need for better communications, now becoming a priority, brought demands for another river crossing. Westminster Bridge was completed in 1751, but nearly 20 years passed before the City had its own second bridge, at Blackfriars.

Whitehall was now beginning to take on its 20th-century character. The palace of kings was replaced by the palaces of government, with office blocks for the Admiralty and Treasury, and William Kent's faintly incongruous barracks for the Horse Guards. As the century proceeded, the work of two Scots had far-reaching effects. Heavyweight William Chambers and lightweight Robert Adam came out fighting for the title of most influential architect. Adam's Adelphi, begun in 1768, and Chambers' Somerset House of 1776, both set between the Strand and the river, aptly contrast their styles. ❑

SPLENDOUR AND SWEATSHOPS

The Victorian era saw Britain creating the largest empire the world had seen. Many Londoners became rich – but a new impoverished class was born

By 1800 London was poised on the brink of a population explosion without parallel anywhere in the world. In the next 35 years it was to double in size – and the railways were yet to come.

While Britain was at war with Napoleonic France, work on public buildings necessarily withered, but housing statistics swelled with the increases in civil servants. Paddington and Marylebone, Camberwell and Kensington, Bethnal Green and Hackney, Knightsbridge and Chelsea forged their identities and hastened to join hands in the family of London. It was certainly becoming an affluent family, prompting the Emperor of Russia on a visit in 1814 to ask "Where are your poor?"

Growing pains

The Emperor, however, had not been east of the Tower of London. Unlike the West End, the East End suffered ribbon building along the roads to Essex. Whitechapel High Street was "pestered with cottages", and Wapping with mean tenements. It was an area vulnerable to the impact of new developments in commerce following the Industrial Revolution. Canals had already linked the Thames with the industrial Midlands. Docks cruelly dismembered the riverside parishes. In 1825, 1,250 houses were swept away for St Katharine's Dock alone. The inhabitants were compressed, sardine-style, into accommodation nearby. The character of the modern East End was in the making. "Sweat shops" and the labour to go with them multiplied in this fertile soil of ruthless competition, poverty and immigration.

The Thames had always been the natural gateway to London, and the East End the natural landfall for the foreigner. In 1687 alone, 13,500 new Londoners had arrived from the Continent fleeing persecution. The Huguenots settled in Spitalfields, planting mulberry trees in their gardens to feed the silkworms that produced the silk to feed the looms in their attics. These were the elite of immigrants. The Polish and Russian Jews who came to Whitechapel in the 19th century were less privileged, producing clothing, boots and shoes and cheap furniture in living and working conditions that became London's "slums".

By the 1830s the Industrial Revolution was making its impact on the Thames below Wapping. The marshy pools of the Isle of Dogs, long dedicated to the rural pursuits of duck-shooting and hunting, were deepened to make the West and East India Docks. Wharves and shipyards lined the banks of the river itself in Blackwall, Deptford and Greenwich. The workers doubled the population and whole new parishes were formed. London was now the centre of Britain's industry; its trades literally "housed" in the older areas outside the City. Coach makers gathered in Covent Garden's Long Acre; furniture

LEFT: a painting by Phoebus Leven, dated 1864, shows Covent Garden as a bustling market.
RIGHT: Gustav Doré chronicled the 19th-century growth of the capital's slums.

makers in the straggling Tottenham Court Road. Vauxhall, Battersea and Wandsworth came up smelling of soap, paint, chemicals and varnish.

With all this activity, London's air was dense with smog – although this word had not yet been coined. The earliest photographs of London's streets show them disappearing into a "fog" after a few hundred yards, even on a good day.

The growth of residential London to the north and west was reflecting not only the new prosperity, but also the recognition by dukes and speculators of the enormous potential of their estates so close to the centre. The big houses were razed and the streets and squares of Portland and Portman, Berners and Bedford, Southampton and Somers rose in their places in the rather severe pattern associated nowadays with Georgian London.

DICKENS'S FOGGY VIEW

"Fog everywhere. Fog up the river, where it flows among green aits [islands] and meadows; fog down the river, where it rolls defiled among the tiers of shipping... of a great and dirty city."

The world metropolis

One estate, old Marylebone Park, shaped like a balloon with a string stretching down to the Strand, reverted to the Crown in 1811. Its development was to display the growing political, cultural and commercial importance of London as the "world metropolis". The genius whose inspired proposals for a garden city linked by a new road to the Prince Regent's Carlton House met with such ready acceptance was John Nash (1752–1835). His ideas were allowed to materialise only in part. Just eight villas were built, half a circus at Park Crescent, and the Regent's Canal, brought in for picturesque effect, was banished to the outer perimeter. Though closer inspection of both design and workmanship can be a disappointment, the famous stucco terraces are undeniably superb scenery. An appreciation of these palaces need not be impaired by the knowledge that today's renewed domes are made of glass fibre.

Nash's Regent Street, completed in 1823, carved an inspired path between Soho and Mayfair that defined and isolated the character of both areas effectively. A quarter turn brought the new street to Piccadilly and on line for Carlton House. Unfortunately it was replaced by Carlton House Terrace when George IV considered Carlton House no longer grand enough for a monarch and ordered Buckingham House to be upgraded to a Palace. There followed a replanned St James's Park, improvements in the Strand, and the creation of a new open space, Trafalgar Square.

The pity is that Nash's work at Buckingham Palace lies buried beneath the façades of later and lesser architects. The saying goes: "But is not our Nash too, a very great master? He found us all brick, and leaves us all plaster." An architect's most telling epitaph?

Congestion and crime

London, in the early 19th century, used its new-found power and a vast amount of public money to grapple with the problems of its own making.

The City was becoming very congested, so bridges were built at Waterloo (1811–17) and Hammersmith (1824–27). London Bridge was rebuilt (1823–31) and foot passengers given a tunnel under the Thames at Wapping.

Courts of law and prisons responded to rising crime, while gentlemen's clubs met the Regency passion for gambling. In Bloomsbury's Gower Street, London University was born, and a fruit and vegetable market came to Covent Garden. Great collections were housed in the British Museum and National Gallery, and a lesser one in Sir John Soane's exquisite building at Dulwich.

Londoners were on the move. In 1829 Mr Shillibeer introduced them to the omnibus, and the first steam train arrived with the London & Greenwich Railway of 1838. Terminal stations followed at Euston, King's Cross and Paddington by 1853; at Blackfriars, Charing Cross and St Pancras by 1871. The tracks elbowed their way through built-up areas to the fringes of the city and destroyed thousands of homes en route. At the same time, Londoners gave up "living over the shop" and travelled out to dormitories in ever more distant suburbs.

The city was about to embark on a programme of renewal that was to bring the most significant changes since the rebuilding that followed the Great Fire.

LEFT: *Gin Lane*, an engraving by the moralising William Hogarth, shows 18th-century squalor.

ABOVE: Regent Street, an integral part of John Nash's Grand Design for London.

The Great Exhibition of 1851

"All London is astir, and some part of all the world." So John Ruskin wrote in his dairy on the morning Queen Victoria opened the Great International Exhibition in Hyde Park. Joseph Paxton's Crystal Palace, marrying iron and glass, was inspired by the Great Conservatory at Syon House and the conservatory at

Chatsworth. The lightweight, light-admitting structure was made for speedy erection and perfectly suited to its purpose of displaying Britain's skills and achievements to the world. Transported south of the Thames to Sydenham in 1852, it gave its name to a new Victorian suburb, Crystal Palace – although the building itself burned down in 1936.

Hub of the Empire

A staff of 125 at the Colonial Office, 12 Downing Street, administered an Empire covering a fifth of the world.

With money taken at the turnstiles of the Great Exhibition, Prince Albert, Queen Victoria's husband, realised his great ambition: a centre of learning. Temples to the arts and sciences blossomed in Kensington's nursery gardens. The Victoria and Albert Museum was followed by the Queen's tribute to her husband: the Royal Albert Memorial, the Albert Hall in 1871, museums, colleges and a large block of flats.

At Westminster, work was proceeding after the destruction by fire of the Houses of Parliament in 1834 – caused, ironically, by an overheated furnace. Charles Barry and Augustus Pugin's Gothic extravaganza rose phoenix-like from the ashes; the House of Lords by 1847, the Commons and Clock Tower by 1858 and the Victoria Tower by 1860. Shortly afterwards, it was discovered that, because of defective sewers, the whole place was sitting on a cesspool.

Cleaning up the Thames

By this time, the "sights" of London had dropped into place. The British Museum gave a home to the Elgin Marbles in 1816, and Trafalgar Square gave a hero's welcome to Nelson's column. The City Corporation, meanwhile, was making determined efforts to unlock the congested streets, cutting swathes through Holborn's houses and cemeteries for the viaduct to bridge the Fleet valley. Fleet Street, the Strand and Whitehall were by-passed by the grand boulevard of the Victoria Embankment, and Cheapside by Queen Victoria Street.

Further upstream, the Chelsea Embankment savaged the artists' riverside village. The Tower of London suffered when a new river crossing opened in 1894 and stole its name: Tower Bridge. Steel dressed up in stone, but an acknowledged engineering feat, Tower Bridge has become a symbol for London, rivalling St Paul's.

By 1859 another problem had arisen, serious enough to cause the adjournment of the House of Commons: the unbearable stench from the Thames. Londoners still depended largely on the river for drinking water, and at the same time disposed of all their sewage in the river. Outbreaks of cholera were common until the City Engineer, Joseph Bazalgette, devised a scheme to take the sewage well downstream to Barking in Essex and release it into the river after treatment. His scheme, which involved creating the embankments, was in operation by 1875 and is still the basis of the modern drainage system.

London was also at last waking up to the problems presented by a polarised community. Throughout the East, there was poverty and overcrowding, and throughout the West, affluence and spacious living. The twain met where pockets of slums in older areas co-existed with the city's greatest treasures, such as Tom-All-Alone's next to Southwark Cathedral.

Dickens and social reforms

The great Victorian novelist Charles Dickens described the resort of down-and-outs and penny-a-nighters in *Bleak House* (1853). Jo, the crossing sweeper, lived in Tom-All-Alone's, as one of "a crowd of foul existence that crawls in and out of gaps in walls and boards; and coils itself to sleep, in maggot numbers where the rain drips in". Public conscience was aroused by the writings of Dickens and the social reformer Henry Mayhew. This encouraged both political action and private philanthrophy.

The railways did some of the reformers' work for them. The hovels of Shoreditch were destroyed for a terminus at Bishopsgate in 1843. St Pancras Station dispatched the squalor of Agar Town, which Dickens called "an English Connemara" because of its Irish population. Soon London's clerks and lower-paid workers began colonising the new world at the city's edge, opened up by the first suburban railway, the Metropolitan, in 1863.

The road builders did even better. St Giles's "Rookery" disappeared beneath New Oxford Street and Shaftesbury Avenue, and much of Wapping High Street was taken for road widening. The insanitary dwellings of Clare Market and Drury Lane were to survive until the Aldwych development in 1900. Some slums persisted, for example the homes of immigrant communities such as the Jews in Whitechapel, the Lascars in the West India Dock Road and the Chinese community in Limehouse. It was left to an American philanthropist, George Peabody, not just to destroy the wretched, insanitary hovels, but to provide a decent alternative. Peabody Trust dwellings for the working classes of London, along with the later Guinness Trust, made a positive and lasting contribution to relieve the suffering of London's poor. The Peabody Trust continues to operate today.

LEFT: 19th-century horse-drawn congestion.
ABOVE: the world's first underground railway system.

A new county is created

The example of these public-spirited people led to the granting of wider powers for local authorities to deal with overcrowding and derelict property. Greater changes were imminent. The administration of the City's square mile was separated from the 117 sq. miles (303 sq. km) of the new County of London, and in 1889 London's government was vested in London County Council, which was housed in the palatial County Hall, across the river from the home of the central government at Westminster.

By the end of the 19th century, the city was throbbing with life, pulling the strings of "puppet states" within the Empire and unloading the Empire's fortunes across its wharves. Its docklands were called the warehouse of the world.

Then came the 20th century, which would change just about everything. ❑

NEWS OF THE WORLD
WAR DECLARED
OFFICIAL

A MODERN METROPOLIS

Economic recession, aerial bombing, urban blight... London survived everything the 20th century had to throw at it and emerged stronger than ever

Few nations are proud of the vistas their entry points present to visitors. Arrival at Heathrow airport is no exception. From here the M4 motorway, often congested, passes through the broken dreams of 20th-century planners. The move out of the city began with such Utopias as Hampstead Garden Suburb before World War I, and suburbia, the promise of a semi-detached home with a garage and garden, caused ribbon building and expanded outlying towns such as Staines and Slough.

Traditionally the prevailing westerly wind has dictated that the foulest, grimiest industries, such as tanning, were set up in the east end of London, so their unpleasant smells might not blow over the richer residents who lived in the west. In the 20th century, when cleaner industries such as electronics arrived, factories were set up on the west side of the city, where they could promise workers the prospect of decent new housing, and throughout the 1930s suburban homes mushroomed, the best of them in Art Deco style, painted white with curved windows looking like ships' bridges. The factories, too, had some style, spreading out down such arteries as the Great West Road and the A30, the alternative road to London when the M4 is blocked. But there was also a depressing sameness about much of this building, and during the Blitz of World War II Sir John Betjeman, subsequently the Poet Laureate, felt obliged to urge: "Come friendly bombs and fall on Slough."

Business corridor

In more recent times, American and Japanese companies have set up business at the head of the "M4 Corridor", their glass gleaming alongside the road into town. The sophisticated Stockley Park, a 100-acre (40-hectare) architects' showpiece, is five minutes from the airport. As the city-bound traffic slows to a crawl over Hammersmith flyover, the eye is drawn by the startling irregularity of the London Ark; this glass creation, rented to Seagrams, laid claim to being Britain's first ecologically sound office block, but it has set up wind and sound tunnels that have enraged local residents.

Britain's capital has evolved piecemeal over centuries, without any great overall plans. Twice in its history, however, it has had to be rebuilt. On the first occasion, in 1666, it was a moment of carelessness in Thomas Farrinor's bakery which led to the Great Fire. On the second, 275 years later, it was the bombs and rockets of the Third Reich which killed 29,000 civilian Londoners and changed the face of the City.

St Paul's Cathedral straddles the two eras. Perhaps the most famous home-front photograph of World War II shows Sir Christopher Wren's great dome looming indomitably out of a swirl of smoke and ash. In more recent years, St Paul's has become a symbol of a rather different sort, a bulwark rather than a phoenix. All around it, on the sites that were blazing in the

LEFT: "Read all about it!" England declared war on Germany on 3 September 1939.

RIGHT: newsvendors are still a part of street life.

famous wartime photograph, have sprung up some of the less happy examples of modern architecture in the capital. The more conservative of the clerks and clerics who walk through the charmless concrete precincts of Paternoster Square, famously condemned by that amateur architecture critic, Prince Charles, like to say that modern town planners and architects have done more damage than the Luftwaffe did.

Instances such as this have helped to focus attention on past mistakes and there has been a move back to more "traditional" values in city architecture and planning. The tendency to see London as a whole, rather than as a massive jigsaw of parts, meant that "policy" has often won over common sense. So far, the process has been only defensive; a spate of renovations and refittings in place of the old demolish-and-build policy. In architecture, you have to live with your mistakes for a very long time.

But "policy" has been a restrictive measure. Planning permissions are hard won in London, which prevents dreamers from making bold plans for the city. Modern architects are not held in high esteem and many people side with Prince Charles and his pleas for traditional buildings on a "human scale".

The city has had no equivalent of Baron Haussman, who laid out modern Paris, nor has it been subject to the whims of presidents or prime ministers in search of immortality through grand monuments. There is simply too much bureaucracy to make such things work.

Skyscrapers from the ashes

Of all the European cities devastated during the war, London is the least skyscraped. With so many bombsites available in the centre and with only the rather notional boundary of the protected Green Belt on the periphery, there was still more than enough scope for the planners to spread outwards rather than upwards. The effect has been to highlight the few genuine skyscrapers around, which are instantly recognisable on the horizon.

The highest building in 1964 was the 580-ft (177-metre) British Telecom Tower, an honour which was relinquished first to the moodily black tower of the National Westminster Bank in Bishopsgate, EC2, and then to the massive Canary Wharf in Docklands, which became Britain's tallest building. There are a couple of "media towers" on the South Bank (housing London Weekend Television and the giant IPC magazine publishers). But today, most of the high-rise building is residential, like the Chelsea Harbour development, and is located well away from the city centre, where even the National

Westminster Bank found it more economical to move out of its landmark block.

The trend towards towers was far from problem-free. Along the busy spine of Holborn, High Holborn and New Oxford Street is Centre Point, 350 vertical feet (107 metres) of offices, built in 1965 and largely unoccupied until the 1980s. Property prices and ground rents elsewhere in London had risen so much by the time it was completed that, for many years,it was uneconomical to lease it out. It was a symbol of a new London economic downturn, and for a long time many of its floors remained deserted; it was not until the mid-1990s that it was anything like almost full. Several national newspapers, physically escaping the old technology of Fleet Street, came here, attracted by the prospect of low rents. The development, described as being 1930s Chicago in scale, became high-profile enough to attract the attention of those modern gangsters, the IRA, who detonated a massive bomb here in 1996.

BLAME THE BOMBERS

Since an IRA bomb exploded in Docklands in 1996, Canary Wharf Tower has been barred to visitors.

The boom of the 1980s also resulted in more

and a potent image of the architects' dilemma and fate, a building only ever known from the outside design, absolutely inescapable but generally unloved.

In a similar vein a quarter of a century later, a tower arose in Docklands at Canary Wharf, at 850 ft (260 metres) a massive focal point for the office development designed by the Argentinian Cesar Pelli. The completion of this symbol of the City's wealth was again marked by an

LEFT: during World War II Underground stations functioned as air raid shelters.

ABOVE: the 1951 Festival of Britain brought optimism to post-war London and created the South Bank complex.

imaginative low-rise architecture in the capital, though strict planning laws kept many flights of fancy at bay, in particular grand plans for the City dreamed up by Peter Palumbo. Robert Venturi expanded the National Gallery and Terry Farrell brought impressive new designs to Charing Cross Station and the Secret Service's headquarters south of the river at Vauxhall Bridge.

Among many bold strokes in the City, which was showing off and riding high, was Richard Rogers' Lloyd's of London building off Fenchurch Street. The architect of the Pompidou Centre in Paris brought his "inside out" style to bear on a building loved by architecture students for its bold use of stainless steel but initially disliked by many of the insurance brokers who had to spend their working lives in its uncomfortable cathedral-like interior.

With many of the traditional East End homes and factories destroyed in the Blitz, the planners decided to turn the idea of the old residential street on end and move it out to Essex or across the river to Peckham and Camberwell. The phrase "vertical street" was elegant and the idea worked well on paper, but it turned into a messy tragedy in practice. The fatal collapse in 1968 of a residential tower block at Ronan Point in Hackney underlined a nagging doubt that was beginning to develop about the technical and social problems of high-rise living.

Owner Occupiers

In 1910, 10 percent of London's properties were owner-occupied. This has increased to 90 percent.

Living in the sky

Although the high blocks built on the devastated Barbican site (now the Barbican Centre) attracted social prestige, high-rise living became associated with poor-quality housing and a welter of social problems. It was all too convenient to concentrate the poor and less well adjusted into multi-storey flats or sardine-tin estates.

Housing in all forms has seen many changes. In 1910 only about 10 percent of all dwellings in the country were owned by the people who lived in them. By contrast, today only 10 percent are now privately rented, and Victorian terraces are now often sub-divided into flats. The result has been to force the traditional Londoner further and further into the suburbs, where house prices are usually cheaper. Inner London has been converted and colonised by the new Londoner, who has migrated from the corners of the country or from overseas.

This colonisation has been accused of destroying London life, and nowhere more so than in Docklands, where the local environment of the Eastenders has been transformed in recent years by the arrival of computer-driven trains and communications centres.

The truth is that the development of Docklands has seen the destruction of some old properties, but it has also seen the creation of many new ones, and the developers have been forced to sell some of their houses at "affordable prices" to the residents of the area. The high premium of houses in this area allowed some of the more unscrupulous locals to buy affordable housing and re-sell it instantly at a much higher market price. The arrival of sky-high interest rates at the end of the 1980s did much to restore realistic property values – though prices began to rise again in the late 1990s.

Docklands also provided a focus for architects, who, frustrated by decades of converting old properties, were able to create a new waterfront city of myriad shapes and sizes. Will it ever cohere visually? Only time will tell.

Who runs London?

There has always been tension in London, as in any great city, between localism and corporate municipal values. With a resident population of 6.8 million and a working and visiting population that is far higher than that, Greater London is like a small country with the traditional conflict between national and local government. Since 1888 and until it became the Greater London Council (GLC) in 1965, the London County Council (LCC) oversaw all the planning policy and urban amenities within its 117 sq. miles (302 sq. km) of authority.

In the immediate post-war years, not even a mood of optimism (compounded of two parts relief, one part genuine forward looking) could ignore the fact that the social and political tide had turned. Central government was more powerful than ever before, but under Labour governments the commitment to planned municipal progress was not what it had been. A uniform, authority-planned city was out of favour.

The LCC's great post-war achievement and symbol was the Royal Festival Hall, centrepiece of the current South Bank Centre and of the arts complex that includes the Queen Elizabeth Hall, National Theatre and National Film Theatre. The modernist architect's plans may have looked promising in the fireworks' glare of the 1951 Festival of Britain, around which time it was built, but has since come in for increasing criticism for its austere concrete looks, though plans to turn it into a glass "crystal palace" failed to attract a Millennium grant.

Popular suspicion of a planned society was something that the Greater London Council never quite overcame. The authority was also greatly at odds with Margaret Thatcher's government in the 1980s and hung provocative banners highlighting the rising unemployment figures outside County Hall headquarters, designed to be read easily across the river from the terraces of the Houses of Parliament. Under its Labour leader, Ken Livingstone, the GLC, behaving like a last outpost of the Peace and

LEFT: high-rise housing was a feature of the 1960s: this is around the Oval cricket ground, south London.
ABOVE: County Hall workers before the GLC was scrapped.

Love movements of the 1960s, did everything possible to infuriate Mrs Thatcher. A Buddhist Peace Pagoda arose in Battersea Park, a statue to Nelson Mandela appeared on the South Bank at a time when he was still imprisoned and Mrs Thatcher was strongly opposed to the introduction of economic sanctions designed to weaken apartheid in South Africa. Fares were cut on London's Underground and buses, which attracted more passengers but flew in the face of the government's anti-subsidy policy.

By 1986, Margaret Thatcher had had enough. With a breathtaking disregard for grass-roots democracy, she forced through legislation disbanding the GLC, and sold the historic County Hall to a Japanese corporation which converted the building into an entertainments complex housing an aquarium, a video games arcade, a Dalí museum, two hotels and a McDonald's. The government argued that, by restoring final authority to the various borough councils, London's bureaucracy would be streamlined.

Return to village life

Without the central control of the GLC, London reverted to its village sub-structure, based around its 33 boroughs. Naturally, their concerns are local, and outsiders are surprised to hear councillors in Wandsworth or Lewisham, Blackheath or Southall, talk of "London" as if it were a separate place. It had been the GLC's job to make the diverse communities work as one, to the advantage of all.

The Thatcher government insisted that the new boroughs should run more efficiently and that all local services be put out to tender (being given, usually, to the cheapest operators). Central government grants were dependent on local government "efficiency", and each borough was allowed to set its own property taxes.

Hand in hand with these policies went the government's policy to sell public rented housing to its tenants. The effect was that those who could afford to buy, did, and the more desirable the property, the more easily it was sold. Soon more than 70 percent of the nation were home-owners. Those buying their homes were also likely to vote for the government, while those without homes in an unsympathetic borough were often forced to move on. Charges of gerrymandering were laid at the feet of some councils, including Westminster, whose council leader, Dame Shirley Porter, had become famous for selling off a cemetery for £1. In 1996, auditors found her guilty of unlawful practice in favouring certain areas for electoral purposes and she and her team were ordered to pay back £31 million.

Those who could not afford to buy their own homes often lived on estates of such unpleasantness that, however cheap the price was, the property was hardly worth the money. A kind of underclass started to form.

When it had been reconstituted in 1965, the GLC inherited massive social problems not of its own making, and most of them not susceptible to central planning. Moreover, the actual trends were opposite to the political agenda. Political issues became wider, but people's lives were once again being increasingly concentrated on specific communities, either geographical, ethnic or social, each with their own particular circumstances and problems.

London's housing problem

One tried, but equally controversial, alternative to the high-rise approach to public housing was the creation of small but densely concentrated estates, often quite separate from the surrounding streets, with raised walkways and split-level entrances. These estates were a bid to restore the old community spirit of the East End, but the random concentrations of people often merely led to tension. In place of neighbourliness and co-operation, there grew a mixture of hostility and tribalism. Racial attacks most common in such communities. People became territorial.

A further instance of this movement away from traditional communities is the growth of custom-built shopping centres in place of local shops and pubs. People are being forced to travel further and further from home in order to shop, eat and drink. This led to increased transport problems. A motorway ring road, the M25, was built around the city in the 1980s to take traffic away from London, but in fact it has made the capital more accessible to many on its perimeters. The result: traffic in the centre has increased, and its speed has declined.

A major investment in the ageing Underground system, denied during the 1980s by government insistence that funding must come from private sources, is now being made in the hope that improvements may lure people back to public transport. But progress is slow: overcrowding, signalling failure and escalator breakdowns are daily occurrences and those with a coveted parking space at work see no reason to abandon their cars. Plans to charge vehicles for entering the central area are being discussed, along with more effective policing of car-free bus lanes.

LEFT: traditional tourist attractions such as Portobello antiques market continue to flourish.
RIGHT: fashionable restaurants such as Pharmacy, in Notting Hill Gate, are meeting places for celebrities.

Dating streets by names

If it's hard to escape the sense of history in any important city, it's particularly hard in London. Science fiction writers like to fantasise about what would have happened if England had been conquered in 1942; would Piccadilly have become "Adolf Hitlerstrasse" and Trafalgar Square "Hindenburgplatz"? Street signs are still

the best fossil trace of a city's past. It's possible, even without a knowledge of architectural style, to date rows of streets by their names: Scutari, Therapia and Mundania Roads in Forest Hill declare their origins in the Crimean War; in Shepherd's Bush, the signs say Bloemfontein, Mafeking and Ladysmith, suggesting Victorian struggles overseas. Today in Brixton a park is named after a jazz drummer, Max Roach. An industrial estate is dedicated to the black American revolutionary Angela Davis, and there are Nelson Mandela streets, squares and houses.

Change continues and brings with it the predictable mixture of enthusiasm and fear. The Prince of Wales, who made his first impact on the city's architectural community by referring to Norman Foster's proposed ultra-modern National Gallery extension as a "carbuncle", has since led the way in condemning the more outrageous projects. Suspicions about modern architecture, long held by the man and woman on the street, have been taken up by the their leaders. But, although the architects and planners are largely in retreat, they've also never been busier. The riverside has a new ribbon development as the old disused warehouses and wharves of a past industrial age are demolished or renovated, both in Docklands and in upmarket areas such as Chelsea, Battersea and Fulham. The new rail link from St Pancras to the Channel Port of Dover has highlighted development towards the Thames estuary where the city is doing its latest sprawling.

The coolest place on the planet

Labour's landslide victory in the 1997 general election was welcomed by most Londoners. Tony Blair, who had played in a pop group in his youth, seemed more in tune than recent prime ministers with the pop stars, fashion designers and film makers who were enjoying their greatest international success since the 1960s. London was pronounced by oracles such as *Newsweek* magazine to be "the coolest place on the planet" and the tourism industry duly benefited. A strong economy turned white elephants such as the gargantuan Canary Wharf office complex in Docklands into sell-out successes. Visionary architects such as Sir Richard Rogers dreamed up grandiose plans for modernising the city, whether by encasing the arts complex of the South Bank in a giant bubble or creating a pleasure ground the length of the river – though financing proved elusive in most cases.

The downside was that the cost of housing, hotels, food and transport soared, making London more expensive than most other European capitals. Employers found it harder to recruit junior staff, who could neither afford to live in central London nor afford to commute into it.

Millennium madness

Britain took the millennium seriously, setting up a commission and making £1.6 billion ($3 billion) available from the national lottery to invest in projects to celebrate the start of the next thousand years. In London, plans focused on creating an exhibition site at Greenwich, recalling the Great Exhibition of 1851 and reminding the world that the world's time zones are based on Greenwich Mean Time. A gigantic dome covering 20 acres (8 hectares) and rising to 50 metres (164ft) was erected on the 50-acre (20-hectare) site of a disused gasworks, and promised a Disneyworld of delights about the state of the world and its future. The Millennium Dome looked like a spectacular flying saucer from the outside, but its various exhibits – Life Zone, Spirit Zone and so on – were widely criticised as being worthy rather than exciting, the sort of thing one might expect to be concocted by a government committee. The 12 million visitors predicted for the exhibition's 12-month lifespan failed to materialise – fewer than half that number of paying customers showed up – and recriminations flew as costs soared towards the £1 billion mark. The composer Andrew Lloyd Webber suggested blowing up the Dome, with a competition being held to decide who should press the plunger.

In stark contrast, another millennium project, a giant observation wheel called the London Eye *(see page 194)* became a great success, promising that, on a clear day, you could see for 25 miles (40 km). The 450-ft (135-metre) wheel, the world's largest, was erected beside the imposing County Hall without much effort at achieving visual congruity. Riders could look down on the area immediately to the east and imagine that all of London's builders were employed here, for the long neglected south bank of the Thames, where Shakespeare first staged his greatest plays and Dickens mined the material for many of his novels, was rapidly regenerating itself as the entertainments centre it had been 400 years previously. In front of Waterloo station, the homeless were cleared out of a concrete wasteland to make way for an imposing IMAX cinema. By the river, close to where a replica of Shakespeare's Globe Theatre had been constructed in the late 1990s, a disused power station was transformed into Tate Modern, a mammoth museum of modern and contemporary art which became an instant success. The Millennium Bridge, the first new river crossing in central London for more than a century, enabled pedestrians to walk from St Paul's Cathedral to Tate Modern in just seven minutes – though, two days after it opened, it had to be closed for several months to enable engineers to eradicate its excessive swaying.

LEFT: the Millennium Bridge being built in 2000; in the background is Shakespeare's Globe.

ABOVE: Leadenhall, one of the old wholesale markets now turned into a mix of stylish shops and restaurants.

A mayor emerges

Even more significantly, the new Labour government decided to restore a measure of self-government to the capital by creating a new and unprecedented post for the city: an elected mayor (as distinct from the largely ceremonial post of Lord Mayor, whose role is confined to the financial "square mile" of the City of London). The election was dominated by the populist politician Ken Livingstone, the man who had controversially led the Greater London Council abolished by Margaret Thatcher; rejected as a mayoral candidate by his own party (Labour), "Red Ken" stood as an independent and won decisively. As head of the new Greater London Authority, the mayor's top challenge was to tackle the capital's chronic traffic congestion, and his first battle was to oppose the Labour government's plans to sell off parts of the increasingly decrepit Underground system to private companies.

Whatever hopes the new authority might have for improving London, it seemed likely that, for the most part, the city would continue to resist the ambitions of planners and go on growing in its traditional organic – that is, haphazard – way, as it always had done. In truth, it is this lack of tight central control that has given London its principal allure: infinite variety. ❑

The Architectural Legacy

Central planning played no part in London's development, but men of genius such as Christopher Wren, John Nash and Inigo Jones made their mark

Little remains to be seen of Roman Londinium, and even less of the subsequent Saxon Lundenwic. Last glimpses of the city wall the Latin settlers raised, with 13,000 barge loads of stone imported upriver from Kent, can be seen at Tower Hill, while lowly foundations of the Roman Temple of Mithras have been laid out in Queen Victoria Street.

The Saxons built mostly in timber, but they were grateful for the Roman stones. All Hallows-by-the-Tower has a shallow-curved Saxon arch, built with Roman tiles and masonry. Otherwise, they left little trace.

Norman to Gothic

The Norman conquest of 1066 brought firmer resolution to the city, notably in the White Tower, the central building of the Tower of London. It was built as a sturdy box that showed the natives who was in control. Construction began around 1078 and much of the stone was imported from Caen in Normandy. Within it is St John's Chapel, a compact, robust chamber with squat pillars and rounded arches that were the hallmark of Norman architecture – what in Europe would be called Romanesque. Only one other example of this style can be seen in the city, and that is at St Bartholomew the Great, which was founded in 1123.

Medieval London grew from Gothic architecture. Imported from France in the 13th century and remaining in vogue until the middle of the 16th century, it evolved in stages. Much more delicate than Norman, it made outer walls thinner by supporting them with exterior buttresses. This allowed lancets and larger windows, which featured the Gothic pointed arch. Rib vaulting was a feature of Early English Gothic: its simple, unadorned geometric shapes can be seen at Southwark Cathedral, a former priory. This style was developed by adding carved bosses and capitals, and more extravagant tracery in windows. The result was Decorated Gothic. The round Temple Church, off Fleet Street, dates from this time. Westminster Abbey, begun in 1245 in Early Gothic style, was enhanced in the late 14th century by Henry Yevele (1320–1400), the royal mason and London's first known architect. He also built the Jewel Tower and Westminster Hall, a vauntingly ambitious space, 240ft by 60ft (73 by 18 metres) with a wonderful hammerbeam roof, supporting 660 tons, designed by the carpenter

Hugh Herland. It remains the heart of the Houses of Parliament

In England, Gothic's final phase was Perpendicular, in which arches became flattened and widened, and the vertical lines of their tracery continued to the lintel to give support.

Tudor London

The finest piece of Gothic architecture in London is Henry VII's Chapel in Westminster Abbey, one of the most lavish and exuberant pieces of church architecture in the country. It was completed by his son, Henry VIII, who otherwise went about destroying religious houses in his draconian Reformation. These monarchs were great builders and "the king's works" stretched along the banks of the River Thames as overseas trade and exploration grew.

A hallmark of the Renaissance buildings of Tudor times, often described as "Elizabethan" after Henry VIII's daughter Elizabeth I, is the use of half-timbering and red-brick. Staple Inn in High Holborn (*pictured on page 207*) is a sole survivor from the period, while the George, a galleried coaching inn south of the river in Southwark, though not built until 1687, would have been typical of this time. The Elizabethan era also saw the building of permanent theatres, such as Shakespeare's Globe, now reconstructed on its original Southwark site.

Brickwork was confined to the rich. Warm and appealing, it provided flexibility to produce octagonal towers and fancy chimneys as well as making patterns from its colours and shapes. Palaces were built like this: at Greenwich, Hampton Court, St James's, Lambeth and Westminster, where a vast pleasure complex, one of the grandest in Europe, had tennis courts and a fighting cock pit. A style called Jacobean, taking its name from the kings James, developed from Elizabethan, though only one example in the city remains: Prince Henry's Room (1610–11), facing on to Fleet Street above the entrance to the Middle Temple. Its original moulded plaster ceiling, with interlocking geometric patterns, is still in place.

GOTHIC HEIGHTS

The finest Gothic work in Britain is Henry VII's chapel in Westminster Abbey.

Inigo Jones and the Italian style

Prince Henry died prematurely, leaving the throne to his younger brother, Charles I, who brought a new elegance to the city in the shape of Inigo Jones (1573–1652). The court architect had travelled to Italy and he brought Italian Classical Renaissance to Britain in the fine Banqueting Hall in Whitehall Palace, and Queen Mary's House in Greenwich, both still standing, and the Palladian Covent Garden, set out, with the classic church of St Paul's, around London's first square.

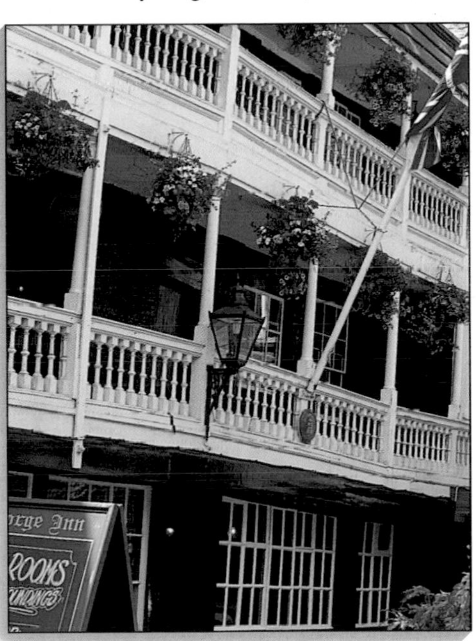

LEFT: sturdy Norman pillars in St John's Chapel.
ABOVE: Tudor brick in St James's Palace.
ABOVE RIGHT: pre-Great Fire vernacular: the George Inn.

Wren and the Great Fire

Sir Christopher Wren (1632–1723) is undoubtedly the architect of the City, but if there had been no Great Fire in 1666, his name would not be so well known today. The fire burned for three days and 80 percent of London's buildings were destroyed. In spite of all precaution (no thatching was allowed and distance between houses was regulated), the half-timbered buildings burned easily. Among the disastrous losses were the Guildhall and Old St Paul's, one of the finest medieval churches in Europe, as well as more than 100 churches in as many parishes, more than any other city in the world.

Sir Christopher Wren was a scientist and self-taught architect. His plans for the rebuilding of London were rejected, but he managed 52 churches (26 remain) as well as St Paul's. In particular, as Surveyor General for some 50

years (he lived to be 92), he was not allowed to place his churches where wanted, but had to rebuild on the old, cramped sites, inspiring the cheering wave from elegant spires in unlikely corners that gave the city its skyline until they were drowned by post-war rebuilding.

These peculiarly English classical Baroque monuments eschewed the Catholic buildings of the past. Their windows bathe white and gold interiors with light, dramatically highlighting the stained wood box pews and balconies. All the mystery and mysticism of the medieval church is banished in favour of this comfortable, almost domestic style. (His successor, Nicholas Hawksmoor, would go further, deliberately plotting his buildings to provoke devil worshippers who had divined meaning in the angles and geometry of earlier, Catholic churches.)

In the reformed Protestant religion, Wren believed churches should be "fitted for Auditories with Pews and galleries... and all to hear the Service, and both to hear distinctly, and see the Preacher." As for St Paul's, with a classical facade and spectacular dome, based on St Peter's in Rome, it has remained symbol of the nation's faith and glory.

Wren's mastery of harmonising baroque with classical design also left its mark further afield, on the unimpeachable Greenwich and Chelsea naval and military hospitals, and on the royal palaces, including the palace at Kensington, newly acquired by William III.

John Nash and Georgian London

John Nash (1752–1835) is the man who gave the West End style. Bankrupt by a speculation in Bloomsbury, he was destined for obscurity when, in 1811, as he approached the age of 60, the Prince of Wales assumed the Regency. Nash's wife was a former mistress of the Prince Regent, the future George IV, who proved to be an outstanding town planner. A royal lease was up on Marylebone Farm, and Nash designed some 50 elegant, formal villas in the classical style, in what is now Regent's Park. He added great theatrical terraces, with Doric and Corinthian colonnades and sculpted pediments, which it was hoped would run from the park down Portland Place and Regent Street to Carlton House Terrace by The Mall.

His Grand Design remains the greatest piece of urban planning in London, even though, in 1848, a colonnade of cast iron columns that ran down Regent Street was removed as they had become a haunt of prostitutes.

Nash was building for a new landed class, and half a century after his death there was a boom in the Georgian style. New visions of planning were being inspired. The Adams brothers, Scottish devotees of the classical style who espoused "Etruscan", are better known for their exquisite interiors, particularly their ornate fireplaces. But they also planned Bedford Square and made Portland Place wide enough to keep open the views. Bedford Square's houses are typically Georgian, a style of simple elegance: uninterrupted brick terraces houses with long sash windows and elaborated porticoes.

As Italian influence waned, curiosity of all things Greek became the vogue. Sir Robert Smirke (1781–1867) built Covent Garden Theatre as a replica of the Temple of Minerva in Athens before going on to erect the monumental British Museum to house Lord Elgin's plunder from the Parthenon. William Wilkins (1778–1839) was another Hellenophile, and his designs were carried out on University College and the National Gallery in Trafalgar Square. Decimus Burton (1801–81) crowned his Atheneum Club with a gold statue of Pallas Athenae, and even Christian churches were built like temples to the pagan Greek gods.

POINTED REVIVALIST

Augustus Pugin, a Catholic convert, thought it time to get back to pre-Wren basics: Gothic was to be the style of the Houses of Parliament.

Victorian revivals

A Parallel between the Noble Edifices of the 14th & 15th Centuries and Similar Buildings of the Present Day; Shewing the Present Decay of Taste was the title of a pamphlet by Augustus Pugin (1812–52). It was Pugin's contention that church architecture had now become too pagan and it was time to return to the "True Principals of Pointed or Christian Architecture". By "pointed" architecture, he meant Gothic architecture, and his chance to lead a Gothic Revival came on 16 October 1834, when the Old Palace of Westminster burned down.

Pugin's design for the new Houses of Parliament, carried out with the architect Charles Barry (1795–1860) went back to basics: it took for its inspiration the Henry VII chapel in Westminster Abbey and was planned down to the last coat hook.

Gothic Revival was the cornerstone of Victorian architecture. It made the main hall of the Royal Courts of Justice in the Strand by G.E. Street look like a the nave of a church, and it produced a most distinctive Tower Bridge. Gothic Revival was a cause espoused by the aesthete John Ruskin, who advocated the use of colour, and emphasised ornamentation rather than structure. In his theories, he was joined by William Morris, the towering figure of the Arts and Crafts movement, which took a romantic, backward look at the medieval world, inspiring various manifestations of Art Nouveau throughout Europe.

LEFT: St Bride's, Wren's original "wedding cake".
RIGHT: Victorian Tudor revival at Lincoln's Inn.

Another of the great Gothic Revivalists was Sir George Gilbert Scott (1811–78) who turned St Pancras Station into a temple of the art and built the elaborate memorial to Prince Albert in Hyde Park. His designs were tempered for the Colonial Office in Whitehall, which he described as "a kind of national palace". Gothic was not the only art to be revived: the eclecticism of Victorian architecture was infinite. There was a Tudor Revival, as in the New Hall at Lincoln's Inn, and a style known as "Queen Anne", a sort

of Georgian Dutch, was taken from the time of Wren and used by such architects as Norman Shaw (1831–1912) in building superior residences in Chelsea and West London. He also built New Scotland Yard (1890), the headquarters of London's Metropolitan police until 1967 and now renamed the Norman Shaw Building and used by Members of Parliament.

London remains predominantly Victorian, but the additions of the past 50 years have not been unadventurous. Among the modernists is Denys Lasdun, whose National Theatre buildings on the South Bank complex have been reviled by traditionalists – as Wren's and Nash's works were in their own lifetime. ❑

TRAFFIC WARDEN
10175

A MELTING POT

There have been racial tensions, even riots. But London has absorbed its latest waves of immigrants and is now a truly international metropolis

Saris and sarongs; mosques and mandirs; calypso and chopsticks; turbans and tandooris. Somewhere in London there's something of everything and someone from everywhere. Whereas the nation's non-white population is 4.4 percent, the figure for inner London reaches 20 percent, and more than a quarter of central London's population wasn't born in the UK. Colour is an easy way to tell where someone's family is from; what's less clear is where the thousands of white immigrants have dispersed. The city is a cultural melting pot, which residents tend to take for granted.

Any metropolis is a mix of nations. Celts, Romans, Saxons, Angles, Jutes, Danes and Normans were the first to tumble into London's melting pot. They came across the Channel and over the North Sea. The first trading agreement in English history was in 796, between Charlemagne and the English king Offa. Trade then was mainly in cloth, and the North Sea trade continued for many centuries, bringing Flemish weavers.

The first Asian immigrants to arrive in Britain were resident by 1579. Some 10,000 of Indian origin arrived at about the time the missionary Thomas Stephens became the first Briton to set foot in India. Religious intolerance also caused migrations and in the 17th century Huguenots – Protestants hounded from France – settled in Spitalfields in east London where they became silk weavers. The chapel they built here in 1743 became a Jewish synagogue in the 19th century and is now the London Jamme Masjid, a mosque, reflecting the changes in just one area of the city.

Century of immigration

In the 19th century the port of London was the largest in the world, and clippers such as the *Cutty Sark* had races to bring the year's first tea crops home from China. The Chinese community was in Limehouse, where Sherlock Holmes went to mull over his latest conundrums in the relaxing atmosphere of the opium dens. Ming Street, Peking Street and Mandarin Street are the sole legacy of the community that was heavily bombed in World War II. Today, Chinatown, called Tong Yan Kai (Chinese Street), is around Gerrard Street in Soho. Here resident Chinese opened restaurants during the war years to cater for British and US forces. Chinese herbalists and medicines are also sought out in Chinatown. Although the streets and annual New Year's festivities mark this out as the centre of London's Chinese population of 55,000, they also live in all parts of the capital.

The traumas of 19th-century Europe led to the mass exodus of Jews, and East London became England's Staten Island, with half a dozen refugee ships arriving every day. The Jews settled around the East End, giving it a dominant character. Since then, the community of around 250,000 has dispersed – to Stamford

PRECEDING PAGES: Anglo-Saxon punk; Commonwealth wallpainter. **LEFT:** everyone's friend, the traffic warden. **RIGHT:** London Central Mosque, Regent's Park.

Hill, Golders Green and Finchley – and in 1996 Blooms, East London's most famous kosher restaurant, closed its doors.

Jews had been in England since Roman times, but subsequent conflict resulting from their moneylending activities reached a head in the 13th century when Christians decided that they could be moneylenders, too. Some 5,000 Jews were expelled, and weren't allowed to return until the Resettlement in 1656. Over the following century came Sephardic Jews – prosperous merchants from Iberia – and poor Yiddish-speaking Ashkenazi Jews from Central Europe. In 1797 Nathan Meyer Rothschild arrived from Frankfurt and seven years later founded a bank in the City and in 1847 a descendant became the first Jewish MP. The most famous Jewish parliamentarian was Benjamin Disraeli, Prime Minister in 1868 and 1874–80.

CHANGED ALLEGIANCE

In 1847 Baron Lionel de Rothschild, head of the family City bank, became an MP and refused to swear the Christian oath to enter parliament. The law was subsequently changed.

The 19th century also brought the railways and a demand for labour. The Irish responded, settling in Camden and Kilburn, north of the rail termini at Euston and King's Cross. The Irish had been coming to Britain since the Anglo-Norman invasion of Ireland in the late 12th century. Mainly Catholic, they suffered for their faith in the Gordon riots of 1780, a dozen years before St Patrick's Catholic Church, which today holds services in Spanish and Cantonese, was built in Soho.

Irish immigration during the 19th-century was largely brought about through the great famine of 1846–48, and many who came spoke only Gaelic. Throughout the 20th century the Irish have continued to be a significant force in the building industry. The 256,000 population is scattered today across north and west London. The Fleadh, the London Irish Festival, takes place on the first Sunday in July at Roundwood Park in Willesden.

European settlers

Following the German invasion of Poland in 1939, the 33,000-strong Polish military in exile settled as a state-within-a-state in Mayfair and Kensington. Their pilots shot down one in seven German planes in the 1940 Battle of Britain, and their soldiers fought on every front. At the end of the war 150,000 were settled in London, where a small community had already existed around the Polish Roman Catholic church in

Devonia Road, near the Angel in Islington. Their presence in Earl's Court in the 1960s led to it being dubbed the Polish Corridor, but today their numbers have fallen to about 50,000, scattered through north and west London. A daily Polish-language newspaper, *Dziennik Polski*, is still published and the Sikorski Museum – named after the Prime Minister killed in an air-crash during the war – which gives an account of the former Polish Government in exile, is in Princes Gate.

Poles had been coming to London since the political upheavals of the 19th century, arriving at about the same time as the Italians, who first settled around the church of St Peter's in Clerkenwell, in an area known to the residents as The Hill and to Londoners as Little Italy. The population was at its height from 1900 to 1930, but wartime internment sealed the area's fate. Gazzano's in Farringdon Road and Terroni's in Clerkenwell Road, both delicatessens, are among the few survivors .

When Italians living in Britain were interned during World War II, their role as restaurateurs was taken over. In Charlotte Street their places were taken by Greek Cypriots, who had been filtering into Britain since the 1920s. Disruptions on Cyprus caused further immigration in the 1950s and 1960s, with Greek and Turkish Cypriots amicably settling side by side in north London. Today there are 100,000 Cypriots in London – about 20 percent of these are Turkish, the same ratio as on the island. The densest Greek community is around Green Lanes in Harringay, north London, where traditions are maintained in male-only cafés behind net curtains – members of the community play *tavli* (backgammon) and drink their own strong coffee and brandy.

Seasonal Arabs

In summer, when Middle East temperatures become too hot for comfort, London attracts many Arabs, who spend much of their time enjoying the coolness of the parks and the breadth of shopping opportunities. The revenues generated by the oil price hikes of the mid-1970s first brought Middle Eastern Arabs to London in significant numbers, and funded a mosque in Regent's Park, which can hold 1,800. They are fragmented and come from all walks of life; the largest communities are from Egypt, Iraq and Morocco, with a total of around 50,000. Most live in Kensington and Bayswater, and they are very visible in Edgware

LEFT: Chelsea Pensioners, veteran soldiers who reside in the Royal Hospital, Chelsea.
RIGHT: different times, different uniforms.

Road, north of Marble Arch, where their restaurants and shops shine into the night. London is one of the largest Arab media centres.

Commonwealth immigrants

The 20th century has seen immigration mostly from the Commonwealth, and the resulting ethnic influence extends as far as Heathrow. The airport itself was largely built by construction workers from India's Punjab. At the height of the 1950s post-war boom, when London was experiencing a shortage of semi-skilled labour, a retired British Indian Army major hit upon the idea of enticing sturdy Sikhs.

After the Sikhs came the Caribbeans, who found work on London's buses and Underground railway network. In the prosperous textile mills of Yorkshire and Lancashire, Pakistanis kept the machines rolling round the clock. As the corners of the British Empire collapsed, the immigrants holding British passports claimed their rights to continue living in Great Britain. Many of them settled in ghettos around the city which are now communities in their own right.

The largest of the non-white ethnic groups are the Indians (689,000), followed by Afro-Caribbeans (500,000), Pakistanis (406,000),

Chinese (122,000), Africans (102,000) and other smaller groups. Today, Britain's Asian population of more than 1 million, including East African Asians, Bangladeshis and Vietnamese boat people, is the largest in Europe.

There are many sub-sections within the major groups: Sikhs, complete with *kirpans* (small swords) and unshorn hair, live in Southall, not far from Heathrow; the Bangladeshis dominate the rag trade in the less affluent East End of London, which was once the home of Russian and Jewish tailors and bootmakers; and the entrepreneurial Patels, the original *dukanwallahs* (shopkeepers), are just about everywhere with their late-opening corner shops. The Patels

LOCAL CELEBRATIONS

The **Italian** community in Clerkenwell each year holds the Procession of Our Lady of Mount Carmel on the Sunday following her saint's day, 16 July. It starts outside St Peter's church and for 45 minutes winds its way through the adjoining streets.

In February, the **Chinese** community in Soho's Gerrard Street ushers in the Chinese New Year with dragon-dancers and street parades.

Anyone in London during the last weekend of August shouldn't miss the Notting Hill Carnival. The entire **Caribbean** population takes to the streets in Europe's biggest street carnival, which lasts for three days.

made the best of three worlds. Born in job-starved India and angered by the rampant caste system, they gladly responded when the British, at the height of the Raj, asked for volunteers to work in East Africa on the coastal railways. There they learned English to deal with their bosses, mastered Swahili to get on with their African "boys", and scrupulously retained their own language, customs and culture. When African nationalism struck in the 1960s, they fled from Kenya, Uganda and Tanzania to what they regarded as their final home: Great Britain. In the capital they settled in the north London suburb of Brent, which became known as Little Gujarat. Schools in Brent, the home of many newcomers, list 200 languages as the mother tongues of their students, ranging from Sinhalese to Serbo-Croatian, Cantonese to Canarese.

MANY CHIEFS

The name Patel is "village chief" in Gujarati. More than 700 are listed in the London business phone directory.

Domestic help

About half a million foreigners, mainly refugees and displaced persons from Europe, entered Britain after the war. In the 1960s, the British Ministry of Labour lured Spaniards and Portuguese with work permits. The final wave of immigrants started in the 1970s with workers arriving from countries such as the Philippines, Morocco and Latin America. They came to find jobs in hospitals and hotels, often filling positions in catering and domestic work.

Domestic work had been the order of the day for the young African slaves brought back to England in the 1570s. In Elizabethan England, there were black entertainers at court. Black people were once used as payment for the return of English prisoners from Spain and Portugal. Adorned with pearls and silver bobbin lace, black people often paraded in the Lord Mayor's Pageant.

Although the numbers involved were very small, the blacks were noticeable enough to attract the disfavour of Queen Elizabeth, who in 1601 issued a proclamation stating that she was "highly discontented to understand the great numbers of negars and Blackamoores which (as she is informed) are crept into this realm". However, her banishment of all blacks was not very effective.

LEFT: the police attempt to bridge the culture gap.
ABOVE: Sikh priests lead a procession in Southall.

Two hundred years ago, ahead of the rest of the world, the MP William Wilberforce formed the anti-slavery society, which still functions today. He introduced a bill which in 1834 resulted in the abolition of slavery in the British Empire.

In the late 19th century, Indian princes sent their sons to public schools and universities in Britain: Jawaharlal Nehru, the future president of India, went to Harrow and Trinity College, Cambridge, and then to the Inner Temple. The middle classes, too, sent their sons to the Inns of Court to become lawyers: they would be the elite who oversaw India's independence.

Colour bar

While London likes to think of itself as a multicultural society, it has very few administrators or top civil servants from what it euphemistically calls the "New Commonwealth". Americans, accustomed to seeing blacks, Hispanics and Amerasians as their mayors, state governors, ambassadors to the UN, or even presidential contenders, are astonished by the lack of varied races in the higher echelons of Whitehall or other government departments. You can pass through the City or the Inns of Court or Docklands without meeting a business tycoon, leading lawyer or top editor from the settlers' communities. Many blame discrimination, others cite the language barrier, weak academic qualifications, and the relatively advanced age at which the ethnic professionals attain their skills. Until the general election of 1987, there were no ethnic minority members of Parliament; that situation has begun to change.

London has not proved a place of opportunity for many of the immigrants unless they are prepared to make sacrifices. As newsagents, the Patels work enormously hard, starting at 5am with the delivery of the morning newspapers and working well into the evening. Outside the central area of the city, a non-Asian newsagent has become a rarity.

Street bazaar

Petticoat Lane market, a stone's throw from Liverpool Street railway station, is the nearest thing to an oriental bazaar this side of the Suez Canal. Hundreds of stalls do a roaring business every Sunday, selling everything from cut-price French food processors to Taiwanese word processors, handloom Indian batik dresses to intricately hand-woven Pakistani carpets featuring the Pope or the peacock.

Petticoat Lane attracts Arabs in flowing *djellabas* and Indian women in shimmering six-yard silk saris, which cover the entire body save the waist. According to Indian males, the waist is considered to be the sexiest part of the female anatomy.

Indoors, ethnic interests are also well served in London's plethora of museums and galleries. The Commonwealth Institute on Kensington High Street offers insights into life in developing countries, with stunning model recreations of village environments. It covers 49 Commonwealth nations. The Museum of Mankind (in Burlington Gardens) spreads its net of exhibitions even wider.

London welcomes every type of visitor. Karl Marx and Mahatma Gandhi studied here. Charles de Gaulle lived in exile here. Writers such as Paul Theroux, Salman Rushdie and V. S. Naipaul chose to work here. People from every corner have settled here, and people from all over the world come to visit. Even Harrods, the quintessentially English store, has been owned by an Egyptian since 1985, and it sells 40 percent of its merchandise to tourists. ❑

LEFT: young Londoners out and about in Brixton.
RIGHT: the thriving Chinese community in Soho.

LOON FUNG
Chinacrafts
TEL: 437 1922
FULL-TIME VACANCY
APPLICANT MUST BE
誠聘职员
Loon Fung

THE ROYALS

Who they all are, and where you might catch a glimpse of them

Almost every day of the year, a member of the Royal Family appears in public somewhere in London, pursued by battalions of royalty watchers, professional and amateur. As patrons of various societies, the members of the family are in demand to open buildings, give prizes and visit hospitals. The Court Circular, published daily in major national newspapers, details their engagements, while the tabloid press relishes their marital disengagements. There are easier ways to see the Royal Family.

On the second Saturday in June when the Queen's birthday is officially celebrated, she travels by carriage to Horse Guards Parade for the ceremony of Trooping the Colour. In November, she is transported by state coach to Westminster for the State Opening of Parliament, escorted along the Mall by the Household Cavalry and greeted by a fanfare of trumpets. This is the only time she wears the monarch's traditional robes and crown. Also in November, she attends the Service of Remembrance at the Cenotaph in Whitehall. In July a member of the family takes the salute at the Royal Tournament, a military show at Earl's Court.

The Queen cannot intervene directly in government affairs, but she is thought to make her views known in weekly audiences with the prime minister and, since her experience of reading state documents dates back to 1952, when some of today's Cabinet were not even at school, her views are taken seriously. Much is implied from sentences in the press that begin: "The palace is understood to disapprove of..."

A government mouthpiece

At the opening of each Parliament the Queen reads a speech announcing the government's plans for that parliamentary session, whether she agrees with them or not. Her only other major utterance is her Christmas TV speech, which carries a caring but apolitical message.

LEFT: the Queen plays a central role in public ceremonial life and still draws the crowds.

ROYAL DISCONTENT

A great deal is implied from sentences in the Press that begin: "The Palace is understood to disapprove..."

Outside the UK, her interests are sometimes more obvious, as demonstrated in the 1987 Fijian coup, where she sent personal messages to the deposed governor and the Fijian people. Prince Charles, on the other hand, takes a more active role, sometimes steering a controversial course which is often interpreted as either criticising or endorsing the moves of government. A majority in Britain still supports the monarchy, though the grief shown after the 1997 death of Diana, Princess of Wales, suggested that they preferred the "people's princess" style to the formality of the Windsors.

Several shops in London have royal warrants, identified by a Royal crest. These honours are granted by senior royals who use the shops regularly. The Queen buys perfume, for example, from J. Floris (Jermyn Street) and Prince Philip has his hair cut by Truefitt and Hill, Bond Street.

Family of horse lovers

The family is known for its love of horses, and several members go in June to Epsom in Surrey for the Derby, the year's most prestigious flat race. They also go to Royal Ascot, a four-day meeting in June at a racecourse owned by the Queen in Berkshire. The Queen is a significant racehorse owner and her daughter Anne, the Princess Royal, participates in equestrian events. At the Windsor Horse Show in May, Prince Philip has competed in four-horse carriage racing. Prince Charles plays at the Guards' Polo Club at Smith's Lawn near Windsor.

The Queen spends April, Ascot week and Christmas at Windsor, January at Sandringham in Norfolk, early July at Holyrood House (Edinburgh) and September at Balmoral (Aberdeenshire). Kensington Palace is the London home of Princess Margaret, the Duke and Duchess of Gloucester and Prince and Princess Michael of Kent. The Queen Mother lives at Clarence House, behind St James's Palace, where the Duke and Duchess of Kent have an apartment. Prince Andrew has rooms at Buckingham Palace, the main residence of Prince Edward. ❑

THE COCKNEY

Meet the real Londoners, though not all are born within the sound of Bow bells

Being a Cockney is as much a state of mind as it is a turn of phrase, and it is not exclusively genetic. The original definition of a cockney – someone born within the sound of Bow bells, the clarion of St Mary-le-Bow in Cheapside in the City – would today exclude most Londoners. The resident population of the City (London's financial area) is tiny, and the sound does not penetrate far.

Cockneys no longer need to be white and Anglo-Saxon; there are Italian, West Indian, Jewish and Pakistani cockneys. Nor do they necessarily have to be Londoners; the high cost of living has driven many out, and neighbouring towns such as Stevenage have large cockney populations. So what then makes a cockney? Certain traditions, being a member of an identifiable urban group, a distinctive language – and a quick sense of humour. Ask a cockney taxi driver if he was born within the sound of Bow bells and he'll probably say something like: "Yes, pal, but my mother had the radio on loud at the time."

Rhyming slang

Cockney is a London accent, widely broadcast by 'Enry 'Iggins in the musical *My Fair Lady*. It has no use of the aspirant "h", the "t" in the middle of words such as "butter", or the final "g" in words ending "ing". Cockneys traditionally speak in a rhyming slang which supposedly originated among barrow boys who didn't want their customers to understand what they said to each other. A "whistle" is a suit, short for whistle and flute, "north and south" means mouth. It is a language that is still being developed. Cockneys are constantly recreating their slang, and different groups of friends have different sets of ever-changing expressions. Some have longer lives, such as "bugs bunny" (meaning money) and "trouble and strife" (meaning wife).

Cockneys are concentrated in the East End of London, and are popularly portrayed on the television soap, *EastEnders*. Newsvendors and market-stall traders are usually cockneys – they are shrewd, street-wise people, who prefer to work for themselves and who value freedom more than wealth. The aristocracy of the cockneys are the pearly kings and queens, whose suits are embroidered with mother-of-pearl buttons.

Pubs play a large part in the community and each community jealously guards its pub and its patch. A good pub landlord arranges group excursions; dads bring their dressed-up sons to the pub on a Sunday morning, and members of a group of regulars at one pub don't go to drink in another unless they're looking for a fight. Cockneys drink "Forsyte saga" (lager); they eat pie and mash with green parsley sauce and seafood. "A cockney wedding with no eels is a poxy wedding," says one.

It has become fashionable for middle-class people to affect something of a cockney accent, and linguists have detected a new London sound: Estuary English. This is the dialect, they say, that is now spoken from the West End to Essex, levelling off the modern London accent somewhere between cockney and middle-class English. ❑

LEFT AND RIGHT: cockneys are kings of the street markets.

THE BOBBY

Police officers in London still have a relatively benign image

Britain's bobbies, unlike most cities' police forces, have an avuncular image. They don't usually carry guns (nor, when balloted, do they indicate any desire to do so) nor do they wear dark glasses. Somewhere within their clothing are a truncheon (baton), a puny whistle and a pair of handcuffs. This lack of personal arsenal reflects the fact that London, considering its size, is a relatively safe city.

A low annual murder rate of around 200 in the metropolitan area was helped by a ban, in 1997, on the possession of hand guns. Minor assaults are the most common felony. Oxford Circus Underground station is a black spot for pickpockets, and bag snatchers. Bag snatchers also operate in busy pubs in the West End and the centre of town.

Street robbery

The police have a good record for solving the more serious crimes. The clear-up rate for murders is around 80 percent, compared to less than 20 percent of around 1 million notifiable offences in the city each year. One of the largest categories affecting the visitor is street robbery, with more than 20,000 instances a year.

Today there are more than 28,000 officers in the Metropolitan police department (the Met). The force was started in 1829 when the old watchmen were abolished by the Home Secretary, Sir Robert Peel, who gave his name to the force, first as "Peelers", then as "Bobbies". They were such a welcome novelty, but they initially spent much of their time chasing out of-town criminals on behalf of wealthy landlords. In the 19th century the force was often supplemented by "special constables" for such occasions as the Chartist demonstration of 1848, which was policed by 4,000 regulars and 17,000 specials. Today the Met has 1,500 specials and, despite being unpaid, volunteer, part-time officers, they have the same uniform and the same powers as a regular bobby. This type of force is unique to the UK. In addition to the Met, the City has its own distinct force of 1,000 officers, which functions within the confines of the financial square mile. They are distinguished by red-and-white markings on their uniform and a similar tall helmet with a combed top-piece.

Basic qualifications for the force are being of good character, being able to swim 100 metres and having good eyesight. There may also be an aptitude test. The Met has abolished minimum height qualifications, but the City force still sets

high standards: male officers must be over 5ft 11in (1.8 metres). Police officers don't have the right to go on strike and their brief extends to the community at large, to helping the public in emergencies and in difficulties.

For most visitors to London, a police officer will be a source of advice and information. Although there has been recent evidence of racist prejudice in some parts of the force, the image of the police, particularly to visitors, has always been a good one. This has been helped by positive media coverage. Television programmes in particular have promoted the image of the fundamentally caring but rather overworked hero of the street. ❑

LEFT: a dancing partner at the Notting Hill Carnival.
RIGHT: keeping a watchful eye out in Whitehall.

TUW 260S

THE CABBIE

Friend or foe? Nobody's neutral about the London taxi driver

There are plenty of cliché characters in London: Beefeaters, Chelsea Pensioners, red-jacketed Horseguards, and seriously pierced punks. However, the average Londoner doesn't stumble across a Beefeater all that often and has probably never taken a photo of a Horseguard. But visitors and Londoners alike do regularly come face to face with one city character: the taxi driver.

Taxi drivers, or cabbies, are true Londoners. They are experts on London, and are essential to its life, coursing through the city's veins in their little black cells. (Not that all the cabs are black any more: advertising has turned some of them into garish perambulating billboards.)

The Knowledge

A London cabbie is thoroughly immersed in his profession. He takes pride in it, knowing that nowhere else in the world does a taxi driver need to know so much in order to qualify for a licence to work. Would-be drivers must register with the Public Carriage Office and then spend up to four years learning London in minute detail (called "doing the Knowledge"). They do this by travelling the streets of the metropolis on a moped, whatever the weather, working out a multitude of routes from a clipboard mounted on the handlebars.

"The Knowledge" sounds like a philosophical absolute, and in a way it is. Once qualified, the London cabbie is his (or, occasionally, her) own boss, a condition that spells heaven to many British people.

About 20,000 drivers work in London, of which half are owner-drivers. The others either hire vehicles from the big fleets or work night shifts in someone else's cab. In all, there are more than 15,000 vehicles. The classic cab, known as the FX4, was launched in 1959 and some models are still going strong. The newer Metrocab has taken a while to find the same place in customers' and cabbies' affection.

Each driver and each cab is licensed by the Public Carriage Office, and there are strict regulations controlling both. Cabs must be in perfect working order (they are checked once a year, and are expected to have a working life of around 10 years) and they must be clean. Having acquired "the Knowledge", a driver must also pass a special driving test.

Legislation regarding taxis – officially Hackney Carriages – has existed for 300 years, on the presumption that a driver with a licence would be less likely to assault his passengers. It states that the taxi driver is obliged to take a passenger wherever he wishes to go within the Metropolitan Police District or City of London, provided the journey doesn't exceed six miles. He is also obliged to go by the most direct route in distance and/or time. If a driver says, "I'll just go this way to avoid Oxford Street", it means that he is taking a route that he believes, given traffic conditions, will be quicker.

LEFT: "being my own boss" is every cabby's dream.
RIGHT: usually cheerful, often talkative, and with a proven knowledge of the city.

The most common complaint from passengers is that drivers take roundabout routes. In reality this is unlikely, since it is not in a cabbie's interest to keep a passenger (or a "fare") in the cab a moment longer than is necessary. It is more profitable to get rid of one passenger and pick up another hire fee.

A more just complaint is that increasingly taxis travel around (particularly late at night) with their "For Hire" lights on, but pick and choose their passengers, saying to those they refuse, "Sorry, I'm heading east", meaning that they are only interested in work that takes them part of their way home. Many will make excuses to avoid having to leave the city centre.

On the other side of the coin are the taxi users who complain that cabs do not detour as often as they used to. The residents of every city complain bitterly about congestion and traffic and London is no exception. Private car ownership in the UK has tripled since the early 1960s, and 70 percent of London households are car-owning households, despite the extensive public transport networks. The result of all this is jams, and the result of jams is an eternally-ticking meter and an eternally growing fare. Expert cab travellers contend that the average cabbie (if such a person exists) is no longer keen to follow back streets and short cuts, but for the sake of a quiet life is happy to sit in the city's main arteries and quietly earn his living going nowhere.

Taxi driving in London is still very much a male profession. Only a small proportion of drivers are women, though the number is rapidly increasing. It is also very much a white, working-class occupation, and traditionally a large percentage of drivers are Jewish (which can make it hard to find a cab on Jewish New Year).

In practice, taxi drivers are a class unto themselves. In many ways they have a uniquely levelling attitude to the English class system. They know that they are as good as anybody because they have the opportunity to compare themselves to all types of people passing through their cabs. They meet people from all walks of life and of all nationalities – more than the Foreign Secretary does, probably. And they meet more British people than the Home Secretary.

PUBLIC AND PRIVATE TRANSPORT

The average speed of morning rush-hour traffic in London is around 10 mph, somewhat less than it was when horse-drawn carriages were used in the capital. In the 1970s speeds were higher, at 14.2 mph.

London also has the most comprehensive bus network in Europe and more miles of Underground track per head than Paris or Berlin. A million commuters use public transportation daily into Greater London, with another 250,000 travelling independently. Overall, the Underground network (the oldest in the world) carries 750 million passengers a year and the buses 3 million a day.

- ☛ Black cabs can be booked in advance. Tel: 0171 272 0272.
- ☛ Women who would prefer a woman driver can call the minicab service Ladycabs. Tel: 0171 254 3501

Tips for the traveller

From a practical point of view, here are a few hints on travelling by London taxis. First, throughout the city, and especially outside hotels and stations, there are taxi ranks where taxis wait for passengers. At Heathrow airport there is also a separate rank for taxis operating a cab-share scheme: passengers pay a standard fare for a trip into central London (the amount payable depends on how many other people share the cab).

Within London it is fairly easy to hail a cab by shouting or waving. It is usually worth hailing taxis on the opposite side of the road just for a quick demonstration of how London taxis can "turn on a sixpence", and of how the drivers are impervious to the sound of screeching tyres and elbows on horns all around them.

These are the easy bits; the difficult choice confronts you after settling into your seat. Do you try to strike up a conversation?

Most London taxi drivers, particularly the older ones, love to talk. London social gatherings are a forum for anecdotes about taxi drivers. The reason is not because the drivers can negotiate the rabbit warren under the Barbican Centre; it's because, given the chance, cabbies never stop talking. Traffic, foreign policy, famous people they have chauffeured, where to eat in the Canary Islands, why the wife has walked out, are all topics of conversation.

Having a two-way conversation is almost out of the question. For one thing, the passenger can see only the back of the driver's head (whereas the cabbie can see the passenger in his rear-view mirror) and, for another, the driver can't hear much because of the engine. What tends to happen is that he shouts a monologue over his shoulder through the statutory six-inch gap in the glass partition, while the passenger makes feeble (and ignored) attempts to join in. Most cabs carry a notice that reads: "Thank you for not smoking". A cartoon in the satirical magazine *Private Eye,* which had a long-running column supposedly written by a cabbie, amended this notice to read: "Thank you for not interrupting".

When the conversation or journey (whichever is the longer) is over, there is the matter of paying the fare. Displayed on a meter, it is shown usually as two separate amounts: an amount for the trip (calculated on a combination of distance and time), plus a second amount for any "extras" (additional passengers, luggage, travelling at certain times of day or at weekends).

Drivers don't expect enormous tips (in cabbie lore, tips supposedly stands for "To Insure Prompt Service"), though they claim they are taxed on an expectation of receiving 15 percent above the fare. They generally prefer a rounding-up of the fare by about 10 to 15 percent to the nearest 50p or £1 and they will occasionally huff about having to give change at busy periods, as it takes up their time. It is worth having the right money ready.

ABOVE: the classic black cab, designed in 1959 and still going strong.

Cabs and minicabs

The London taxi is an institution that is also a brilliant working proposition. It is emphatically a trade and not a public service. Economic pressures on the cabbie and regulations for the protection of the passenger mean that the public is efficiently served – even more so since most taxis are radio-controlled.

"Minicab" firms are another matter entirely, and it is worth emphasising here that minicabs have absolutely nothing in common with London taxis, and do not have the black cabs' ability to pick up people in the street. A minicab is often simply a private car, and some minicabs are not only unlicensed as Hackney Carriages but also not adequately insured.

Minicabs are cheaper than taxis for long distances, but there is no cast-iron guarantee of safety from the minicab firm. Moreover, the minicab driver can be useless to a stranger to London. There is nothing worse than settling into the back seat, warily eyeing a rusty hole in the floor under your feet, and saying, "Oxford Street, please" and having the driver ask brightly, "Oxford Street? Where's that?" ❑

The New
GERSHWIN
musical comedy
CRAZY FOR YOU
Prince Edward
Theatre
12
Oxford Cir. Whitehall
Elephant Camberwell
Peckham Dulwich
TRAFALGAR SQUARE
CRAZY TO MISS IT!
JACK TINKER
DAILY MAIL
Prince Edward
Theatre
7.5T
CUV 302C
G740 YLU

THE DOUBLE-DECKER

No matter what happens, the big red vehicle just won't go away

The red double-decker bus is to London what the cable car is to San Francisco, or the gondola to Venice. It's part of the fabric of the city. But it's rather more than that: in the form of the traditional Routemaster, it is a mechanical miracle, introduced in 1959 with an expected lifespan of 17 years and still on the road. Of 2,825 originally built, 900 are going strong.

They've been threatened with the scrap heap many times. In 1970 London Transport decided to phase out conductors. This meant phasing in pay-as-you enter buses with driver-operated doors, thus eliminating the joys of hopping on and off the platform of a passing vehicle and of chatting with the conductor.

Conductors survived, though in fewer numbers, and are still appreciated: indeed, in 1994 the Queen gave Dominican-born Tony Severine, a conductor on the No 12. route from Dulwich to Shepherd's Bush, an MBE (an honour standing for Member of the British Empire) for "outstanding service to the travelling public". (This didn't mean, of course, that she had taken the bus herself.)

Safety first

In 1996 the European Union pronounced that the open platforms were dangerous and that Routemasters should be banned because of instability. Hypothesis rather than statistics supported this assertion. In a bid to prove their safety, London Transport staff filled the top deck of a bus which was then cornered at a tilt of 40 degrees. It didn't topple over.

Routemasters have undoubted charisma. TV documentaries have been made about them, a 1963 feature movie starred one (*Summer Holiday*, with the singer Cliff Richard) and they have crossed deserts and continents to continue life in all corners of the world. They are simply built with aluminium panels that can be bolted on and off, and mechanics so simple that an engine change takes only seven hours. In 1992 a £10 million refurbishment programme began, to ensure Routemasters were kept alive into the 21st century. A single innovation was a flexible roof – the only part to be made abroad, in the US – which would stand up to falling trees, a fear caused by recent storms. Two years later, when privatisation of bus services threatened to change the vehicles' livery, the Transport Minister had to bow to public pressure and intervene, promising to keep the vehicles red.

Perhaps he had learned from British Telecom who had to make a hasty U-turn after they began replacing the much-loved red phone box.

Londoners, valuing tradition above comfort, went on humming the tune of versifiers Michael Flanders and Donald Swann:

Its tickets cost a pound apiece,
why should you make a fuss?
It's worth it just to ride inside
that twenty-foot long by ten-foot wide,
inside that monarch of the road,
observer of the Highway Code,
that big six-wheeler, scarlet-painted,
London Transport, diesel-engined,
97-horse-power omnibus. ❑

LEFT: the Routemaster, monarch of the road.
RIGHT: good views from a sightseeing bus.

THE CITY OF CEREMONIES

Fairytale coaches and medieval costumes all play a part in the rich pageants that brighten the capital's calendar

Where else can you see judges in wigs, guards in bearskin "busbies" and a monarch with diamonds as big as the Ritz? Many events that celebrate the country's institutions have cheerfully failed to take account of the arrival of the 20th century. Daily routines such as Changing the Guard at Buckingham Palace and the Ceremony of the Keys at the Tower of London are the unchanging fabric of the city's life. Cavalry officers in Hyde Park, dressed as if for an epic film of the 19th-century Crimean War, fire a 21-gun salute on the Queen's real birthday (21 April) when cannons also fire in the Tower of London. The Queen is at her fairytale best in November when she rides in a royal carriage from Buckingham Palace down the Mall for the state opening of Parliament. Other events include the commemoration in January of Charles I when royalists dress up in Whitehall. Charles II founded Oak Apple Day in May for the red-coated Chelsea pensioners.

▽ PEARLY MONARCHS
Cockney kings and queens wear suits sewn with buttons and appear mainly at charity functions. On the first Sunday in October at St-Martin-in-the-Fields, Trafalgar Square, they attend the Costermongers' Harvest Festival.

DOGGETT'S COAT AND BADGE ▷
The Worshipful Company of Fishmongers organise this July race, from London Bridge to Cadogan Pier, to find the Thames's top oarsman. It was started in 1716 by an Irish comedian, Thomas Doggett, for a prize of a coat and badge (right).

▽ **TROOPING THE COLOUR**
The "colour" is a regimental flag, and at Horse Guards Parade, Whitehall, on the Saturday nearest10 July – the Queen's official birthday – a flag of one of five regiments of Foot Guards is marched past the Queen, who wears a brooch with the insignia of the relevant regiment. This is one of the most colourful military ceremonies in London. It began as an exercise to show troops which flag they should rally round in battle.

GREAT PAGEANTS FROM THE PAST

London's love of pageantry was never better demonstrated than at the Diamond Jubilee of Queen Victoria in 1897. Britain was then at the height of Empire, and its military might was in full display. On a sunny June day, the Queen set off in the state landau drawn by eight cream horses, heading an unprecedented parade from Buckingham Palace to St Paul's (above) where a service was held on the steps outside. The procession included all the crowned heads of Europe and regiments from every part of the Empire. There was a detachment of Maoris from New Zealand, African riflemen and, most colourful of all, turbanned Indian lancers, Sikhs and Pathans in red, ochre and blue, whom the Queen insisted form her personal escort.

The Silver Jubilee of Queen Elizabeth II in 1977 was less dramatic, but it nevertheless drew crowds to the capital, and left a series of walks through the capital marked by "Jubilee Walk" plaques in the streets.

Coronations, royal weddings and funerals all need the ceremonial touch. The military nature of the processions is reinforced by the fact that members of the royal family all have regimental connections. Thus the gun carriage – rolled out for every departing monarch, as well as public figures such as Winston Churchill – bore Princess Diana to Westminster Abbey in 1997. The bearer party was from the Welsh Guards, to whom she had been commander-in-chief.

△ **LORD MAYOR'S SHOW**
The Company of Pikemen and Musketeers form a bodyguard around the 200-year-old gold coach of the newly elected Lord Mayor as it is driven from Guildhall to the Law Courts on the second Saturday in November. A senior alderman is elected annually for the post.

BEATING THE BOUNDS ▷
This Ascension Day ceremony is a City tradition from Reformation times. Choirboys assert their rights to their parish by beating its boundaries with willow wands. Today lead markers on buildings show where the boundaries lie.

NIGEL PATRICK
PHYLLIS CALVERT
MAXINE AVICE
AUDLEY LANDON
RICHAR &
BRIER
PRESENT LAUGHTER
BY NOEL COWARD
NIGEL PATRICK
PHY
CAL
MAXINE AVICE
AUDLEY LANDON
PRESENT LAUG
BY NOEL COWA
QUEENS THEATRE
UBY 262

THEATRELAND

From Shakespeare to Sondheim, Wilde to Lloyd Webber, the best – and the worst – of plays and musicals turn up in the West End

The opening of Shakespeare's Globe on Bankside has been seen as a triumph of culture over commercialism. Here, for the price of a ticket, you can sit on rock-hard benches, squint through the sun slamming in over the thatch roof, peer around pillars to try to catch lines from the acoustically challenged stage, and even, if the youthful director Mark Rylance is to be taken at his word, cat-call and lob the occasional tomato if a performance is not to your liking.

This is theatre heritage to appeal to the tourist as well as the purist, an Elizabethan playhouse risen from the rubble of time. And even if its location, at the south end of London Bridge, is a bit off the beaten track, many will make for its doors simply to savour the unique experience. The brainchild of American actor and director Sam Wanamaker, who didn't live to see it completed, the theatre is a replica of the 1599 auditorium in which William Shakespeare had shares and where he staged many of his plays. Like many theatres over the years, the original Globe was destroyed by fire.

Topical issues

London's theatrical history goes back to a playhouse opened at Shoreditch in 1576 by James Burbage, the son of a carpenter and travelling player, and its development encompasses a strong tradition of taking side-swipes at social issues. In the *Roaring Girl* of 1611, for example, playwright Thomas Dekker dwelt at some length on London's traffic jams.

In modern times, live theatre was supposed to succumb first to movies, then to television, yet it is still one of those essential attractions that every visitor to London is supposed to experience. It remains a mystery, however, what cultural sustenance coachloads of Japanese and American tourists derive from a convoluted Alan Ayckbourn farce or an imaginative production of Shakespeare set in a variant of the Third Reich. More cautious visitors play it safe and opt for one of the blockbuster musicals.

In the days when *Oklahoma!* and *Guys and Dolls* dominated the musical theatre, no-one would have guessed that the West End would hijack the genre from Broadway. Yet it happened with surprising speed. First, Tim Rice and Andrew Lloyd Webber demonstrated the possibilities of the cunningly crafted rock-musical form with *Jesus Christ Superstar* and *Evita*. Then, leaving Rice to indulge his passion for cricket and aptitude for writing Oscar-winning tunes for Disney cartoons, Lloyd Webber focused his fanaticism for the stage musical by composing *Cats* (a collaboration with the late T. S. Eliot), *Phantom of the Opera, Starlight Express* and *Sunset Boulevard*.

LEFT: Shaftesbury Avenue, heart of the theatre disctrict.
RIGHT: *Cats* helped make London's name for musicals.

Scoff though some serious critics might, the shrewder theatrical brains quickly realised that revenue from musicals could be used to underwrite more serious work. In particular, Trevor Nunn, who had banished all personal financial worries by directing several of Lloyd Webber's musicals, including *Cats*, masterminded the Royal Shakespeare Company's 1985 production of *Les Misérables*. Despite a tepid critical welcome at the time, "*Les Mis*" went on to conquer the world, making millions in the process for the Royal Shakespeare Company. Nunn was eventually forgiven for such populism when he accepted the top-drawer post of director of the Royal National Theatre.

Perhaps, despite his detractors (who compared him unfavourably with Stephen Sondheim), Andrew Lloyd Webber did after all have the skills of a Svengali: he even employed Prince Edward, the Queen's youngest child, before the prince set up his own production company. Many tried to emulate Lloyd Webber's success, but the trick was harder than it looked. The ignominious failure of a Norwegian musical, *Which Witch*, almost caused a diplomatic incident between Britain and Norway. *City of Angels*, which had run on Broadway for more than two years, closed in London after four months with losses of £20,000 a week.

Traditionalists claimed that the mania for musicals was squeezing out new drama productions. Yet a glance at the theatre listings in *Time Out* magazine doesn't entirely bear out this

THE BEST WAY TO BUY TICKETS

Despite the prevalent notion that everything in London is so successful that it sells out fast, most shows have some seats. It's the more expensive tickets – generally for musicals – that are usually hardest to obtain.

Unlike New York, where most of the ticket-buying is done through agencies, in London tickets can be purchased at the box office, cutting out the fee (sometimes extortionate) of the middle-man. There are, however, a number of good, reliable ticket agencies, which sometimes have more to offer than the theatre itself. A day or so before the performance, they return their tickets to the box office. These tickets are then sold to students, pensioners and the unwaged.

On the day of the performance, unsold tickets are also available from a booth in Leicester Square selling at around half-price. The cheapest performances are matinees, but understudies may then replace the stars. Tickets at the Royal National Theatre are considerably cheaper if bought on the day.

Tickets are offered outside theatres by touts or "scalpers" for anything up to 10 times their face value. There's nothing illegal in this, but it is good sense to ask the face value of the ticket on offer, and the exact position of the seat.

claim. Classics continue to be staged at the Royal National Theatre and the Barbican, new writing is still put on at the Royal Court and the Bush, experimental work and alternative comedy are mounted at the fringe theatres, and playwrights such as David Hare, Tom Stoppard and Terry Johnson do not lack an audience. What's more, favourite thespians such as Alan Bates, Michael Gambon, Ian McKellan, Maggie Smith, Diana Rigg and Judi Dench can virtually guarantee to attract a full house.

FRANKLIN SPEAKING

"In London you have plays performed by good actors. That, however, is, I think, the only advantage London has over Philadelphia."
– BENJAMIN FRANKLIN, 1786

Fringe Venues

In addition to the 50 central theatres, there are around 60 recognised fringe venues in the capital, while theatres outside the centre, in Hampstead, Richmond and Wimbledon, are used as proving grounds for West-End runs. Fringe productions range from standard Shakespeare on a low budget to the latest shows by minority groups keen to put across political or social messages, though much of the new young writing is dark and funny and well-observed.

Established fringe venues include the Young Vic (in The Cut, near the Old Vic), the Almeida (in Islington) and the Half Moon (in the East End). Lively pub theatres include the King's Head in Islington and the Gate Theatre at Notting Hill Gate. There's even one fringe group which is so fringe it doesn't have a venue, but will come and perform in your own front room.

Time Out can be relied on for good weekly information, with potted reviews, ticket prices and so on, and the range of national newspapers in Britain denies any single critic the influence attributed to the drama critic of the *New York Times*. This is just as well, because sometimes they are wildly at variance with public taste. The RSC's *Nicholas Nickleby*, which went on to a couple of revivals and a New York transfer, received grudging, lukewarm reviews when it first opened. *Les Misérables* managed only a couple of good reviews from the national press.

Actors tend to take more notice of criticism than the public. Bad reviews drove Racquel Welch out of town after a short tour in Shaw's *The Millionairess* and provoked the British comic actor Stephen Fry into going to ground on the Continent and contemplating suicide after a difficult opening in 1996.

LEFT: queueing for cut-price tickets, Leicester Square.
ABOVE: rehearsals at Shakespeare's reincarnated Globe.

A seat in history

London's long theatrical tradition can be appreciated in the fabric of the buildings themselves. Each has some grand historical association: the Phoenix with Noel Coward, the Royal Court with the heady days of John Osborne and the angry young men, the Arts with *Waiting for Godot,* the Savoy with Gilbert and Sullivan, Drury Lane with Edmund Kean, the Criterion with Terence Rattigan's *French Without Tears,* the Theatre Royal Haymarket with Oscar Wilde. Some buildings are associated with sensational events: outside the Adelphi in 1897, the tragedian William Terriss was stabbed to death; and inside the Garrick the ghost of a former manager is supposed to appear. The Haymarket organises regular tours of the theatre, as do several other theatres – but don't take too seriously the tales of haunting and ghosts

Most of the present buildings were built during the 50 years from 1880 to 1930, though thankfully many have now been renovated as new managements realise that patrons expect higher standards of comfort these days. When the Canadian entrepreneur Ed Mirvish bought the Old Vic (near Waterloo station), for instance, he spent £2.5 million on refurbishing it. The Maybox Group waved a similar wand at the ailing Whitehall Theatre, restoring it to its art-deco splendour. The Lyceum in Covent Garden reopened in 1996 half a century after it was last used. It is a trend that is likely to continue, as theatres that were turned into part-time television studios or radio show theatres once again find an eager audience for live drama.

WHERE TO SIT

It's important to know the terminology of English theatre layout. What in America is called the "Orchestra" (the seats at the lowest level) is in England called the Stalls; then, in ascending order, come the "Dress Circle" (or "Royal Circle"), and the "Upper Circle" (or "Grand Circle"). The "Gods" refers to the very top, and the seats are not recommended to anyone with vertigo or a hearing impediment. Some theatres allow standing in the Gods.

If in a party, consider asking for a box, which can sometimes work out cheaper than seats in the stalls. You can doze off more privately, too.

National companies

One of the most important features of London theatre is the presence within it of two major subsidised companies: the Royal National Theatre and the Royal Shakespeare Company, both of which seem to stagger from one financial crisis to the next. In terms of audiences, both are successful and originate many productions which transfer into the mainstream theatre of the West End.

The National, on the South Bank, is the more congenial building, despite its intimidating concrete exterior. It holds the record for the longest interval, one hour, necessary for a very complicated scene change. The Barbican, which is the RSC's London home for part of the year (its main base is Stratford-upon-Avon), opened in 1982 and has a splendid and comfortable main auditorium, but the bars and concourses are dingy and impersonal. It also has a small-scale auditorium, The Pit, which according to rumour was hastily converted from a rehearsal room before anyone noticed it had no ventilation. Nevertheless, the Pit has seen some of the most exciting productions in London.

The National, with its three auditoria, has a stronger sense of a working organism than the Barbican. National Theatre audiences arrive early to enjoy a drink. Barbican audiences dive in at the last moment, having had pre-show drinks in neighbouring pubs. The National also has a good restaurant on the mezzanine and is part of the whole South Bank complex, which includes the Royal Festival Hall and Queen Elizabeth Hall concert venues, where art exhibitions and free foyer concerts are part of the atmosphere. The terrace cafés and bars with views across the river will all be affected when it becomes enclosed in a glass bubble in a new project designed to make the site less bleak.

Back-stage tours

The National Theatre also runs an interesting back-stage tour, which imparts information and anecdote in equal measure: "Why are the seats in the Olivier theatre lilac-coloured? Because that was Lord Olivier's favourite colour." Almost every National production is worth seeing.

There is open-air theatre in Regent's Park (usually Shakespeare), and less frequently in Holland Park and Covent Garden. Riverside Studios in Crisp Road, W6, attracts experimental plays and visiting companies. Corin and Vanessa Redgrave once took it over for a month to present their own plays. The Redgraves, like the Richardsons, are the aristocracy of British theatre, but they have yet to have a West End theatre named after them: the accolade recently fell to Sir John Gielgud, for whom The Globe in Shaftesbury Avenue changed its name.

Finally, any visitor interested in theatre ought

LEFT: Prince Edward, the royal theatrical, graces the 5,000th performance of *Starlight Express.*
ABOVE: the theatre as a temple of the arts.

to see the Theatre Museum in Tavistock Street, Covent Garden, and visit French's Theatre Bookshop in Fitzroy Square.

Movie Theatres

British actors, a versatile breed, are well used to appearing before the cameras during the day, then treading the boards in the evening. It's appropriate, therefore, that Theatreland shares its main West End turf with the cinema. The biggest names in lights are in Leicester Square, closed to traffic except when stretched limos are depositing stars at the doors of the Odeon or Empire (a former music hall) for a premiere. Leicester Square is now the pounding heart of the West End, wide awake until the small hours with late-night screenings. Giant cinemas, such as Warner Village West End, and the Odeon Mezzanine, pack up to 10 screens under one roof.

There are also several independent houses and most current releases can be found within walking distance of Leicester Square. The Swiss Centre, Curzon and Lumière are good for foreign and art-house films. The Prince Charles, just off Leicester Square, is one of the cheapest in the West End, and screenings change throughout the day. Cinemas often have cheap days on Mondays and for programmes that start before 6pm.

Outside the West End, cinemas such as the Everyman in Hampstead have films in repertory, while others, such as the Ritzy in Brixton, offer mainstream and art-house movies on different screens.

On the South Bank is the National Film Theatre (NFT), which has seasons of themed films and often hosts talks by actors and directors. It is also the focus for the London International Film Festival every November. The British Film Institute, which opened a huge IMAX cinema nearby in 1999 (*see page 195*), is redeveloping its South Bank site: the much praised Museum of the Moving Image is being extended and will reopen in 2003, along with a new four-screen NFT. ❑

RIGHT: The Royal Shakespeare Company's *Les Misérables* became a massive international success despite poor reviews.

SHOPPING

Just about any item you ever wanted can be found in London. The trick lies in knowing where to start looking for it

There are some things real snobs wouldn't be seen dead doing. Shopping in Harrods is one of them – it's far too full of tourists, you know – although they might just sneak into its Food Hall on the basis that it serves as their local corner grocery shop. Visiting Oxford Street, even in a Rolls-Royce, is another. As for a souvenir shop, they wouldn't even be carried there after *rigor mortis* had set in. But of course, these are exactly the places visitors to the city want to go. And they should.

Oxford Street stretches from Tottenham Court Road, centre for hi-fi gear and computers, to Marble Arch at what was once the less fashionable west end, where Tyburn gallows stood. But the roles have now been reversed. At the Tottenham Court Road end, Virgin Megastore occupies one of the former stores in Ladies Mile, the part of the street that the respectable went to in Edwardian times to find the bold new department stores. Let your eyes rise above the tawdry trinkets of the current shops and you will see the fine façades that held the aspirations of those golden shopping summers.

The department stores that remain form ranks in the more upmarket stretch, west of Oxford Circus: Dickens & Jones, Debenhams, D. H. Evans, John Lewis, Selfridges, their cosmetic halls smelling sickly sweet and staffed by

SPOILED FOR CHOICE

The two major food emporia in London are at Fortnum and Mason's in Piccadilly and Harrods in Knightsbridge, which has 20 bars and restaurants, and seven food halls. On a random day, Harrods has in stock:

- 350 different cheeses.
- 250 kinds of bread.
- 1200 wines.
- 50 kinds of wet fish.
- 25 kinds of smoked fish.
- 48 varieties of jelly bean.
- 20 types of salami.
- 12 kinds of melon.

thickly caked alchemists, their upstairs galleries piled with bolts of cloth rolled out by the last few people on earth who know how to sew. Designers have their niches in many of these stores, which try to be all things to all people and, like trendy grandmothers, are desperate to appeal to the young.

Distinctive stores

The two most distinctive stores are John Lewis and Selfridges. John Lewis thrives on eccentricity. It is a "partnership" in which all employees have shares, and which is "never knowingly undersold". Selfridges, the neo-classical building owned by Sears, has the largest cosmetics and perfumery stall in the world, but it also struggles to be all things to all shoppers. If you are coming to the store by car, leave it in the garage with an attendant who, for a small fee, will have it washed and cleaned by the time you return with your bulging bags.

At Marble Arch, you can find out what Arab women wear under their *hijabs* and *haiks*: in Marks & Spencer they pile trolleys high with woollens as well as underwear by the armful. M&S used to be Britain's favourite clothing chain, but it has been finding it increasingly tough to compete with more specialist stores.

The nearest the county set may get to an Oxford Street store is Liberty in Regent Street, or Fenwick's on Bond Street, where women in woollen skirts and headscarves, with some taste and some money, hunt for gifts for aunts and uncles who are so hard to please. Less hard to please are children at Hamleys, the world's largest toy store, near Liberty. Michael Jackson has neen known to shop here.

Streets off Oxford Street – St Christopher's Place, South Molton Street, Bond Street and South Audley Street – are completely acceptable places to shop, even if most of the nation can only stand and stare.

Bond Street is where art and fashion conspire to relieve customers of large sums of money. Sotheby's, the art auctioneers, leads the arts crowd, fashion is represented by Ralph Lauren, Louis Vuitton, Hermès, Gucci, Joseph, Versace and Christian Lacroix, as well as English stalwarts Church Shoes and Mayfair Trunks, luggage suppliers to HM the Queen. At chocolate makers Charbonnel et Walker, buy Highgrove Peppermint Creams bearing the imprimatur of the Prince of Wales. At Agnews, long associated with the philanthropic publisher Naim Atallah, you can buy what you like, so long as it is made

LEFT: a Harrods doorman, an eye on customers' dress.
ABOVE: Tottenham Court Road, home of hi-fi.

out of silver. The Royal and Burlington Arcades are further diversions. If you still have money to spend, go down to Berkeley Square and see if a Rolls-Royce is to your liking in Jack Barclay, the principal London distributor.

Piccadilly possesses one of the city's smartest food destinations in the Fortnum and Mason department store. Traditional English fare includes Gentleman's Relish, pots of Stilton cheese, pickled walnuts and a variety of preserves. They have their own-brand of tea and supply food hampers for days out at the races or at Glyndebourne opera. It's not a bad place to drop in for tea if your weary legs won't quite take you another hundred yards or so further down Piccadilly to the Ritz.

Men's requisites

St James's, south of Piccadilly, is a male preserve, where obsequious tailors and wigmakers once pandered to the royal court. Today bespoke folk go in for Thomas Pink or Turnbull and Asser shirts, Foster boots and Lobb shoes. This is where the unreconstructed English Gentleman has a decent wet shave, pays £300 for a Dunhill lighter or wafts into Davidoff's for submarine-sized cigars or Black Russian cigarettes. "Thank you for smoking," a sign says.

GOOD DEALS

The cost-conscious in search of cut-price factory outlets will head for East London in search of Burberry (29–53 Chatham Place, Hackney) and Nicole Farhi (75–83 Fairfield Road, Bow). More convenient are Next to Nothing, which has surplus stock from Next stores (Unit 11, Waterglades Centre, Ealing Broadway) or Joseph Sale Shop (53 King's Road, Chelsea).

For electrical goods, head for Tottenham Court Road. This is one of the few places in London where you can bargain: most will match any other price you can get in the street for hi-fi, computer and telecommunications equipment.

Piccadilly leads down into Knightsbridge where Harvey Nichols – "Harvey Nicks" – is *the* only store anyone would dream of shopping in, darling. It's a cultish place for a certain kind of woman (rich) and its fifth-floor restaurant is where the gossip flies. Christmas window dressings are eye-catching, but the ordinary shopper may see this rather clinical emporium as just another upmarket department store.

Down the road is Harrods. Everything, supposedly, is available here. Ask and it shall be yours. But don't leave without visiting the Food Hall, the most splendid cathedral to the culinary arts in, quite probably, the world. The building has a 1,650-ft (500-metre) perimeter and 72 windows which at Christmas an 84-strong design team helps to dress. Beside Harrods is Rigby and Peller, *corsetière* to both the Queen and the Queen Mother – not the image one is looking for, perhaps, when contemplating one's swim-wear and nightwear. Better to go to exotic lingerie specialist Janet Reger just beyond, in Beauchamp (pronounced *Beecham*) Place. This is a pleasant street of restaurants and boutiques, where prices are high and customers well-groomed.

LATE-NIGHT SHOPPING

Shops stay open late – until around 8pm – Thursdays in Oxford Street, Wednesdays in Kensington. A few stores, such as Tower Records in Piccadilly, are open every night until midnight.

from Museum Store. Also in King Street is The Irish Shop. In New Row, Naturally British shows the nation at its most traditional. Anything else you want is all within reach: statues of Egyptian gods from the British Museum Cast Service in Bloomsbury Street; antique cameras at Classic Collection in nearby Pied Bull Yard; anything electrical in Tottenham Court Road. There is theatre memorabilia in Dress Circle in Monmouth Street, just down from Obsessions at Seven Dials,

Fun shopping

For the sheer exuberance of shopping, Covent Garden shouldn't be missed. Over-hyped, maybe, but there are always shops to pop into, such as Paul Smith's, the smart designer's in Floral Street. And while you're here, you might just see what's in the boutiques and speciality stores. Buy anything oriental in Neal Street, and anything herbal or vegetarian in Neal's Yard. In King Street, browse six floors of Dr Martens, which has come a long way since the black boot, in the Piazza get a blow-up Mona Lisa

LEFT: Hermès for fashions, New Bond Street.
ABOVE: West End haute couture and hats.

where gadgets and gizmos are worth a browse. Cinema memorabilia can be had in the Vintage Magazine Shop in Brewer Street, just along from Anything Left-Handed, the shop that sells left-handed versions of tools and implements. Book buyers should head for Long Acre and Charing Cross Road.

Trophy hunters will visit the Scotch House in Knightsbridge for woollens, Burberry in the Haymarket for overcoats, the Vintage House in Old Compton Street for malt whisky, Caviar House, next to the Ritz, for Sevruga, Oscietre or Royal Black caviar.

Everything you ever wanted is in London. All you need bring is the cash. ❑

Markets

Selling high-priced antiques, tawdry trinkets and bric-a-brac, London's markets are full of life and a magnet for browsers

The sign reads: "Billy buys almost everything". Billy's selection of "almost everything" is piled high within a six-foot-square cubby hole in one corner of Camden Lock Market, beside Regent's Canal in Camden. Billy himself is tiny and stands on two milk crates so that he can see over shoppers' heads to watch his junk. Around him an enormous variety of vendors whose accents come from all parts of the globe, not just London, sell earrings made out of innards of clocks, hand-painted shoes, and even life membership to the Finsbury Park Insect Club.

Fly-pickers (illegal traders selling from suitcases) appear and disappear like shadows on the pavements outside, according to whether or not a policeman is in sight. Camden Lock (best Saturday or Sunday) catalogues the charivari of English domestic life from the war years onwards, as well as amassing state-of-the-art crafts of the 1990s, but it isn't cheap. And, like so many other areas of London, parts have attracted the attention of the redevelopers.

On the other hand, stall-holders in Petticoat Lane and Brick Lane in the East End would claim their prices are rock bottom, although goods here (clothes, bric-a-brac, electronic goods) could be "dodgy", meaning either acquired below the counter (illegally) or liable to go wrong. There is a popular saying that, by the time a tourist has walked the length of the Petticoat Lane market, he could be sold his own handkerchief by the last stall.

Dubious merchandise

Brick Lane market starts very early in the morning. While the Camden markets reflect the hidden riches of the city, Brick Lane reflects the hidden poverty. In the side-streets, Eastenders spread their wares on the wet, grey pavement, within a few hundred yards of the Stock Market. Here the latest CD player retails at a bargain price, unchipped despite "falling off the back of a lorry". There are tremendous bargains for the brave, and tremendous rip-offs for the unwary or unlucky.

The West End's Covent Garden is well known, and neighbouring Jubilee Market has gimicky craft stalls, but in fact it is the City which has hosted London's major markets. Billingsgate, the home of fresh fish and foul language, has since been moved from the City to Docklands; Smithfield meat market still functions although there are plans afoot to move it; Spitalfields organic produce market has expanded to include crafts; Leadenhall (so called because of its original lead roofing, at a time when other markets were thatched) has been revived, and now provides market shopping for City workers; ironically, most of the produce sold here is trucked in from the surrounding countryside but ends up being eaten in the suburbs near where it was grown.

Londoners' liking for fresh food has led to a resurgence in the fortunes of Borough Market, near the south end of London Bridge, whose history can be traced back nearly 1,000 years. Although "London's Larder" is primarily a wholesale fruit and vegetable market supplying restaurants and hotels, many of its traders have started selling directly to the public, with retail markets on Friday (noon–6pm) and Saturday (9am–4pm).

Antique markets are widespread throughout the capital. Chelsea's enclosed markets, Chenil Galleries and Antiquarius, are networks of tiny, stall-crammed passages on King's Road, staffed by experts but rather stuffy.There is a better chance of picking up a bargain at Portobello Road, near Notting Hill Gate, where dealers do their shopping. Its many antique shops spill their wares out onto market stalls on Saturdays, attracting huge crowds (mainly tourists). Stall-holders here may seem almost unaware of what they have on their stalls and more concerned to perpetuate their images as street "characters" – but don't be fooled. They know exactly what they have, and what their neighbours have, and what it's worth.

TAKE A CHANCE

"There are tremendous bargains for the brave and tremendous rip-offs for the unwary or unlucky".

Islington's Camden Passage market is strong on (quite pricey) antiques, and features bric-a-brac on Wednesdays and Saturdays.

LEFT: horns of plenty – antiques in Portobello Road.
ABOVE: a busy weekend at Camden Lock, north London.

Outside the central areas of London in the local boroughs – the areas of home life rather than work and play – the local market remains a feature of community life. One of the best all-round markets in London is the weekend market in Greenwich. This is always lively and there is a village atmosphere among shops and stalls around Church Street and the High Road.

Most of London's 70-odd street markets are not arty, crafty or creaking with antiques like the big central markets, but are largely composed of fruit and vegetable vendors offering less variety than supermarkets but at lower prices.

Local markets are an interesting microcosm of London life, with the vendors being old Londoners (both old in terms of age and in tradition) and the shoppers being a mixture of both old and new residents. The Berwick Street market in Soho, even though it is in the centre of the city, is a good example. One thing to watch is that customers are not supposed to touch the fruit and vegetables, which are often served not from the stall but from boxes at the back.

Brixton is more a market for atmosphere than for shopping, although amongst a lot of unremarkable merchandise there is a good assortment of tropical fruit and other West Indian foods and spices that aren't usually available in other markets.

The Pearly tradition

Pearly Kings and Queens are popularly associated with the markets of the East End. Named because of the pearl-like buttons they wear on their costumes, they supposedly came from market-vendor stock.

The first Pearly was Henry Croft, an orphan and a road sweeper, who started to collect buttons from his stretch of road and applied them to a suit in 1880. He supposedly then sold the suit to raise money for a children's home, thus beginning the fund-raising role of the Pearlies which persists. Today Pearlies are ceremonial figures. Their positions are inherited, not elected, and a Pearly generally opens fêtes, does advertising work for charity, and appears regularly at local markets. Visitors can see Pearlies in large concentrations at the Pearly Harvest Festival in October and the Lord Mayor's Show in November. ❑

Was it not a Dainty Dish to set before a King

RESTAURANTS

New restaurants open as frequently as new movies and are just as subject to the whims of fashion. So how do you tell the good from the bad?

London is a great place for dining out and its 12,000 restaurants offer some of the world's most memorable gastronomic experiences. This may come as news to people who have not been here for some years, for the last occasion on which the words "London" and "cuisine" were convincingly linked was at the turn of the century when Auguste Escoffier wielded his rolling pin at The Ritz.

Today the city is straining under a bombardment of accolades, not least – or least, depending on your point of view – more Michelin stars than any other city in Europe bar Paris, which only just scrapes into the lead. There is choice as well as quality. You can eat nachos and noodles, tapas and tempura, balti and bhajis; you can try pizza with Japanese toppings, choose from nearly 200 Thai restaurants or even eat English, a privilege reserved until a few years ago for diners at greasy-spoon cafés, the last remaining eel-and-pie shops and, more tastefully, Simpson's in the Strand.

The foodie revolution

The starting point for this current excellence began in the 1980s when the restructuring of financial institutions produced a legion of footloose brokers and currency traders looking for places to spend their skyrocketing salaries. Exciting restaurants, like designer labels, were avidly sought out, and if a place became popular and trendy, the clients had enough money to ensure it stayed that way. Even pubs began to realise the advantages of serving up more than just sausages, baked beans and bowls of encrusted shepherd's pie.

This was the age of style as much as content, where personalities became cults, and the *nouveaux gourmets* began banging the table and calling for the chef to step out of the kitchen heat and into the limelight to take a bow.

Until this point it was *de rigueur* for the chef to be French, and probably the country's best-known were Albert and Michel Roux of Le Gavroche. Anton Mosimann, the chef at the Dorchester, was Swiss-born, but his accent sufficed, and he became a personality chef on television. But neither the Roux brothers nor Mosimann had the headline-hitting qualities required for real superstardom. This fell to

LEFT: old-fashioned fare at Simpson's in the Strand.
RIGHT: equally old-fashioned, an eel-and-pie shop.

Marco Pierre White, whose style of tetchy talent had hitherto been more associated with football heroes. His kitchen steamed, his rages roared and customers were evicted if they upset him. Remarkably, this feisty temperament belonged to a Briton, though his mother is Italian. He opened his restaurant, Harvey's, on the edge of Wandsworth Common, in 1987, and at the age of 33 became the youngest chef to have won a two-star Michelin rating. In 1995 he became the first British chef to win a three-star rating, for The Restaurant, the premises he had taken over at the Hyde Park Hotel.

Harvey's was just one top restaurant to open in what seems now to have been a crucial year on the culinary scene. It was also the year that Rose Gray and Ruth Rogers, wife of the architect Sir Richard Rogers, opened their River Café in the architect's warehouse in Fulham, West London. This was Tuscan Italian cooking at its pinnacle. Within weeks businessmen calling from Los Angeles found they couldn't get a table for six months.

That same year Terence Conran, the style-maker who had invented Habitat stores and brought the earthy kitchenware of Provence to Britain, opened the Bibendum restaurant in the splendid art-deco Michelin tyre factory building in Fulham Road. Conran, no longer part of Habitat, kept his Sabatier honed on the cutting edge of taste. Having secured his immortality by establishing the Design Museum in Butler's Wharf near Tower Bridge, he returned to the business of eating. Conran started with a successful small restaurant in the building, Blue Print Café, which was followed by the nearby, classier Le Pont de la Tour.

Conran's arrival on the scene began a shift of emphasis away from the chefs and towards the restaurateurs. The man whose products at Habitat had embodied the intimate bistro, made a bold leap into the 1990s, when the recession brought demands for lower prices by people who had acquired a more sophisticated taste. His first move into catering for the masses was with Quaglino's, in Bury Street near Green Park, where flunkies, cigarette girls and a pianist recalled another restaurant of the same name that had been fashionable in the 1930s. This was more than food: it was entertainment, too, and the empire did not stop there. In 1995, in a building in Wardour Street occupied by the Marquee Club where an unknown group called the Rolling Stones once played, he opened Europe's largest eatery, Mezzo, seating more than 700 and catering for 2,000 a day. This was a supermarket-sized operation, employing 100 chefs, covering two floors, with a large restaurant, fast food canteen, café, bakery and patisserie. The menu was also good, and people flocked in.

The hotels catch up

Meanwhile the big hotels and institutions, traditional bastions of good cookery, could no longer afford to rest on their laurels. Marco Pierre White was called in to shape The Restaurant at the Hyde Park Hotel. Nico Ladenis, a Briton born in Kenya to Greek parents and an established 1980s star chef, took over Chez Nico at Ninety Park Lane in the Grosvenor Hotel. Conran did a makeover on the restaurant in Selfridges and the popular young TV chef and British food enthusiast Gary Rhodes was called in to consult on The People's Palace restaurant at the Royal Festival Hall.

Rhodes was one of the new school of Anglo-food fans, whose greatest practitioner was Alastair Little, patron of the Soho restaurant of the same name. A former archaeologist, Little brought a great eclectic flair to his dishes, developing what some called "the new British style". In the quest to find fresh tastes and flavours, he went back to dishes long-since discarded as boring and British, and made them into something much more appetising than anyone ever remembered them being. Sweetbreads, brains, oxtail and suet all emerged from post-war larders to be savoured again.

MEMORY LANE

Rules, in Maiden Lane, dates from 1789. Famous former clients included Charles Dickens and Graham Greene.

Another star of this new British regime is Antony Worrall-Thompson, who surfaced as chef in the Menage à Trois where, skipping the "intercourse", he served up only starters and desserts. Worrall-Thompson moved on to Bistrot 190 in Kensington and into management, launching such restaurants as the Café Dell'Ugo, named after his favourite Italian olive oil, the Atrium near the Houses of Parliament, and his Mad-Max-style Thunder Road in the Trocadero. Conran took up the new note of Englishness with the Butler's Wharf Chop House, to which Anton Mosimann responded across the river at St Katharine's Dock with an up-market fish-and-chip shop archly called M. Fish.

The result of all this bubbling activity has been a melting pot of dishes and ideas. Though the business will always have a mercurial element, and recommendations one day can be cancelled out the next, competition has been welcomed by both diners and owners, and the money is now rolling in.

Meanwhile there are stalwarts which have steered a steady course through these upheavals, absorbing new trends or sticking steadfastly to what they believe their clients want. The River Café remains inviolate, Kensington Place is fun for chatterers, The Ivy and Le Caprice are popular with the rich and famous, Langan's with the would-be famous, the Gay Hussar with journalists and left-wing politicians, the Savoy Grill with businessmen, Le Gavroche with unreconstructed gourmands. ❑

LEFT: Albert and Michel Roux of Le Gavroche.
ABOVE: Mezzo's maestro, Sir Terence Conran.

Pubs

The beer may sometimes be warmer than the welcome and theme pubs are not always dream pubs. But the real thing still exists

Much has been said and written about public houses (as *The Times* traditionally insisted on describing pubs), especially by some of London's literary forefathers, many of whom were particularly partial to a pint or two. Suffice it to say here that, like most other things in a city this size, it is impossible to generalise about the 5,438 pubs in London. Some have live music, some stage striptease, some are genteel and some rough, many are Victorian (a strange product of such a morally critical age) and some were opened last week, perhaps part of a chain such as The Slug and Lettuce – commerce is no respector of traditional names. Every Londoner has a favourite, the choice of which depends as much on the people that frequent it as on the decor.

The Punch and Judy in Covent Garden is typical of pubs in the central entertainment area; it is packed and vibrant with young people who come to meet their friends and stay all evening. Not so in the City, however, where not all pubs are as quaint as Ye Olde Cheshire Cheese (frequented by Dr Samuel Johnson) in an alleyway at 145 Fleet Street. Everywhere is packed at lunchtime in the City, and by 6pm thirsty workers are spilling on to the streets, though many pubs close by mid-evening when the workers have left for home.

Country atmosphere

In the East End the pub retains some of its country role as the centre of a community, and a good landlord knows the names of all his regulars and even organises weekend excursions. Pubs such as the Duke of Edinburgh in Wanstead welcome everyone: the family, children and all. One of the East End's most famous haunts is the atmospheric Prospect of Whitby, but its fame – and the Docklands development – has turned it into something of a tourist haunt.

The King's Head in Islington is one of several theatre pubs. Here a variety of plays are put on against a background of clinking glasses and ringing tills. The actors know they've captured the audience's attention when people stop nipping off to order another pint of beer.

From Richmond to Greenwich, the banks of the Thames are lined with pubs, many of which open directly on to the river's towpath. The Dove in Hammersmith is one such (and is jam-packed with people on a balmy summer's evening) and is the venue where the patriotic anthem *Rule Britannia* was composed. In Southwark the Mayflower is a typical riverside pub. The ship of that name moored here in 1672 before taking the Pilgrim Fathers on their voyage to Plymouth, Massachusetts.

PERFECT PARTNERS

"What two ideas are more inseparable than Beer and Britannia?"

– REV. SYDNEY SMITH

London has several pubs that date from the 17th century, and many retain the atmosphere of that era. One of the best examples is The George in Southwark, the only original galleried coaching inn in London. Rebuilt in 1676, it has remained largely unchanged. The galleries were once the entrance to the inn's rooms.

A fine example of the explosion of pubs during the Victorian era (known for their engraved mirrors, grand central bars and dark velvet upholstery) is the Duke of Cumberland in Fulham, complete with Grecian urns.

The traditional drink in a pub is English beer (ale or bitter). The genuine article is drawn up by hand pump and served at the temperature of the cellar; chilling literally kills it, as beer continues to ferment in the barrel. Pubs used to brew their own beer on the premises, but few still do so; one of these is The Ferret And Firkin In The Balloon Up The Creek, situated in Lots Road, Chelsea, where you can sample their own Ferret Ale or Dog Bolter. Another is the delightful Jerusalem in Clerkenwell. Many pubs are owned by large brewers, selling only their own brands.

Many pubs are open from 11am to 11pm, though within those hours they can choose their opening times. But there are other drinking venues, such as Burlington Bertie in Shaftesbury Avenue, which have extended licences, and if you arrive after 11pm you can get in for a small fee at the door and drink until much later.

However, London's licensing hours may soon be liberalised, and the rush to the bar triggered by that shout of "Last orders, please," at 10.50pm could soon be a forgotten ritual. ❑

LEFT: a distinctive example of a Victorian pub.
ABOVE: traditional beer, drawn from barrels by hand pumps on the bar, arrives at cellar temperature.

The STATE of Independence
MASCO
BY MR HOWARD
400
G861 XML

HMV
OAKLAND
OAKLAND
501
G27 VYE
D255 FYR
11136

PLACES

A detailed guide to the city, with the principal sites clearly cross-referenced by number to the maps

For a cosmopolitan city of 6.7 million people, London is quite parochial. Each neighbourhood, each street corner, is proud of its own identity. Central London is the shared London of all these groups and of 19 million visitors a year as well. Symbols of London – the Beefeaters, the bobbies, the cabbies, the cockneys, the pageantry, the Royal Family, the Houses of Parliament – all are here, along with the stock market, motorcycle messengers, dirty air, and crawling traffic.

But the slow traffic should not be a deterrent. After an initial tour by boat or on an open-top bus to orient yourself, the best way to see Central London is on foot. Although Greater London sprawls for 610 sq. miles (1,580 sq. km), the central area is surprisingly compact. Walkers have time to appreciate the infinite variety of architectural detail that traces the city's long development. What's more, they will be treading in the footsteps of some of history's most celebrated citizens – to aid the imagination, blue plaques (*see page 173*) show where the great, the good and the notorious once lived.

We begin the Places section with a chapter on the River Thames; London grew up around the river and one of the best ways to understand its organic growth is to take a boat trip upstream to Hampton Court or downstream to Greenwich. Next, we focus on the royal and ruling heart of the city, Parliament and Buckingham Palace. The ensuing chapters take in the outer areas of the city, which need a bus or Underground train ride to explore, and finally, on the capital's latest mode of transport, the Docklands Light Railway, there is the story of the new developments in the East End. Village London (*page237*) tours some of the most interesting local communities, and Day Trips (*page253*) suggests a range of excursions most easily made from London.

All the sites of special interest are numbered on specially drawn maps to help you find your way around.

As a visitor, you may be one of the 72 percent who visit the Tower of London, or the 92 percent who make their way to Piccadilly Circus. But you will probably also be one of the millions who find some small, distinctive corner of the city to be enthusiastic about. ❑

PRECEDING PAGES: Sir Christopher Wren's Naval Hospital at Greenwich; the City, from Blackfriars Bridge; shoppers in ever-crowded Oxford Street.
LEFT: Nelson's Column in Trafalgar Square looks down Whitehall to Big Ben.

Northwick Park
Watford Road
Fryent Way
Brent Reservoir
Edgware Road
Hendon Way
GOLDERS GREEN
Hampstead Heath
Northolt Road
East Lane
WEMBLEY
Wembley Stadium
Dudden Hill Lane
CRICKLEWOOD
HAMPSTEAD
Keats House
Finchley Road
Whitton Avenue
Harrow Road
North Circular
Freud Museum
Grand Union Canal
Willesden Lane
WILLESDEN
KILBURN
Greenford Road
London Central Mosque
Western Avenue
Edgware Road
Lord's Cricket Ground
Park Rd
Harrow Road
Scrubs Lane
Paddington
(M40)
Hanger Lane
Wormwood Scrubs
Westway
PADDINGTON
NOTTING HILL
ACTON
Wood Lane
Bayswater Road
Hyde Park
Kensington Gardens
EALING
Holland Park Ave
Gunnersbury Ave
Goldhawk Rd
Holland Rd
KENSINGTON
Gunnersbury Park
Warwick Rd
Cromwell Rd
CHELSEA
(M4)
Chiswick High Road
Osterley Park House
Osterley Park
Strand on the Green
Great West Road
HAMMERSMITH
King's Road
CHISWICK
Castlenau
Great West Road
Chiswick House
FULHAM
Syon House
Kew Gardens
Kew Road
KEW
Mortlake Rd
Fulham Road
New King's Rd
Thames
BARNES
Fulham Palace
River
ISLEWORTH
Upper Richmond Road
Upper Richmond Road
Battersea Rise
HOUNSLOW
Twickenham Rugby Ground
RICHMOND-UPON-THAMES
Roehampton Lane
PUTNEY
High Street
Road
Road
West Hill
Chertsey Road
TWICKENHAM
Marble Hill House
WANDSWORTH
Trinity Road
Great
Richmond Park
Ham House
Wimbledon Park
All England Lawn Tennis Club
Petersham Road
HAM
Robin Hood Way
Wimbledon Common
WIMBLEDON
Richmond Road
Bushy Park
Hampton Court Rd
NEW MALDEN
Morden Rd
KINGSTON-UPON-THAMES
Cannon Hill Common
MITCHAM
Hampton Court Palace
Hampton Court Park
RAYNES PARK
Hampton Court Way
Portsmouth Road
Malden Way
Morden Park
SURBITON
MORDEN

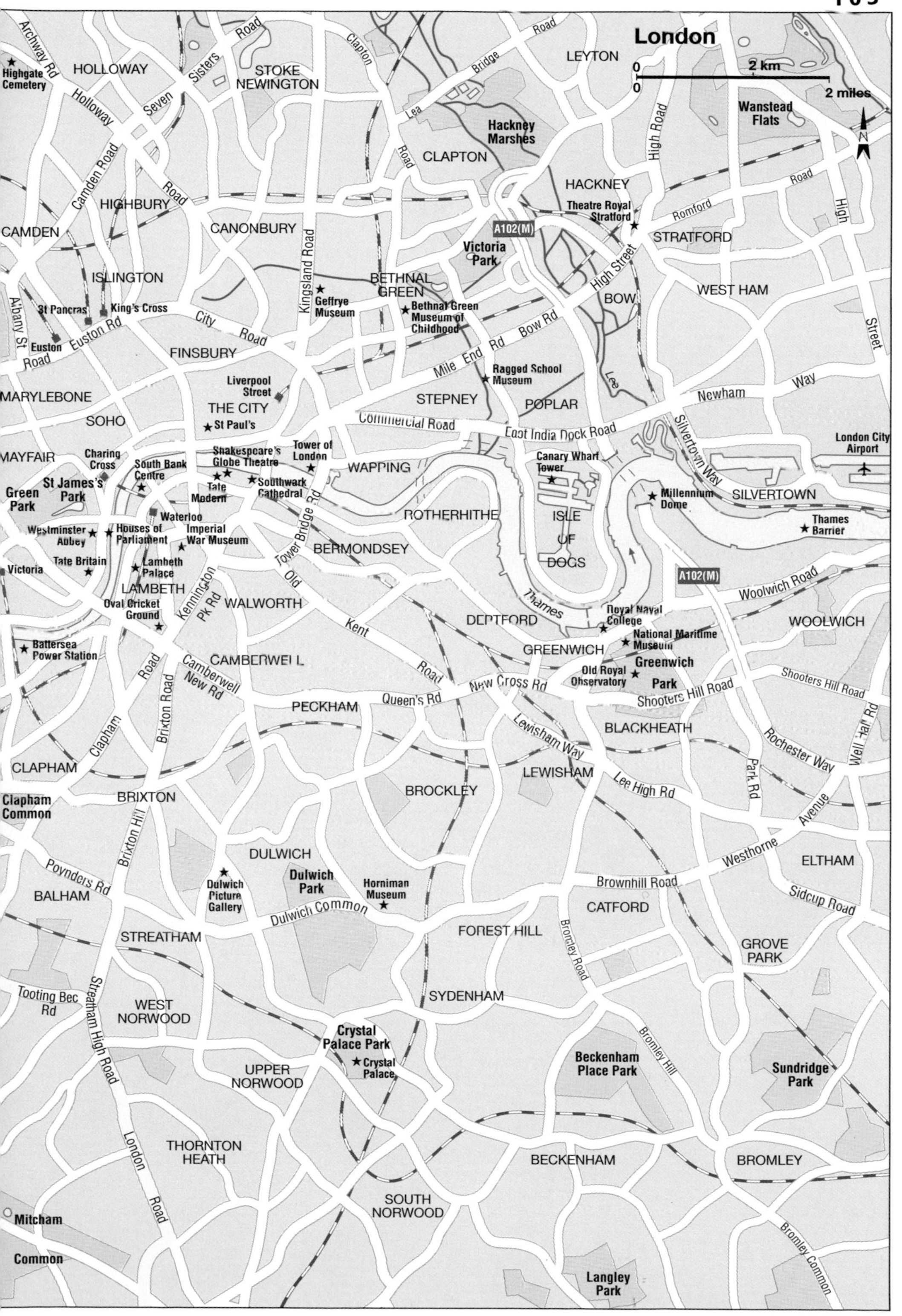
London
0 2 km
0 2 miles
N
Highgate Cemetery
HOLLOWAY
STOKE NEWINGTON
LEYTON
Wanstead Flats
Hackney Marshes
CLAPTON
HIGHBURY
HACKNEY
Theatre Royal Stratford
CAMDEN
CANONBURY
A102(M)
Victoria Park
STRATFORD
ISLINGTON
BETHNAL GREEN
BOW
WEST HAM
St Pancras
King's Cross
Geffrye Museum
Bethnal Green Museum of Childhood
Euston
FINSBURY
Ragged School Museum
Liverpool Street
MARYLEBONE
THE CITY
STEPNEY
POPLAR
SOHO
St Paul's
London City Airport
MAYFAIR
Charing Cross
Shakespeare's Globe Theatre
Tower of London
WAPPING
Canary Wharf Tower
South Bank Centre
Green Park
St James's Park
Tate Modern
Southwark Cathedral
Millennium Dome
SILVERTOWN
Waterloo
ROTHERHITHE
ISLE OF DOGS
Thames Barrier
Westminster Abbey
Houses of Parliament
Imperial War Museum
BERMONDSEY
Victoria
Tate Britain
Lambeth Palace
LAMBETH
WALWORTH
Oval Cricket Ground
DEPTFORD
Royal Naval College
WOOLWICH
Battersea Power Station
National Maritime Museum
CAMBERWELL
GREENWICH
Greenwich Park
Old Royal Observatory
PECKHAM
BLACKHEATH
CLAPHAM
LEWISHAM
Clapham Common
BRIXTON
BROCKLEY
DULWICH
ELTHAM
Dulwich Picture Gallery
Dulwich Park
Horniman Museum
BALHAM
CATFORD
STREATHAM
FOREST HILL
GROVE PARK
SYDENHAM
WEST NORWOOD
Crystal Palace Park
Crystal Palace
UPPER NORWOOD
Beckenham Place Park
Sundridge Park
THORNTON HEATH
BECKENHAM
BROMLEY
SOUTH NORWOOD
Mitcham Common
Langley Park
Archway Rd
Holloway Road
Seven Sisters Road
Clapton Road
Lea Bridge Road
High Road
Camden Road
Romford Road
High Street
Albany St
Euston Rd
Euston Road
City Road
Kingsland Road
Bow Rd
Mile End Rd
Lee
Newham Way
Commercial Road
East India Dock Road
Silvertown Way
Tower Bridge Rd
Old Kent Road
Woolwich Road
Thames
Kennington Pk Rd
Camberwell New Rd
Road
Brixton Road
Queen's Rd
New Cross Rd
Shooters Hill Road
Lewisham Way
Rochester Way
Well Hall Rd
Clapham Road
Lee High Rd
Park Rd
Avenue
Brixton Hill
Westhorne
Poynders Rd
Brownhill Road
Sidcup Road
Dulwich Common
Bromley Road
Tooting Bec Rd
Streatham High Road
Bromley Hill
London Road
Bromley Common

Hampstead
Euston Station
Camden Lock
British Library
Camden Town Hall
Argyle St
Swinton St
Acton St
King's Cross Road
REGENT'S PARK
EUSTON
Eversholt Street
Euston Road
Judd Street
Outer Circle
Albany Street
Hampstead Road
Euston Mosque
Holy Cross
ST PANCRAS
Inner Circle
REGENT'S PARK
Upp. Woburn Pl.
Woburn Pl.
British Medical Association
Gray's Inn Road
St Anne
Euston Tower
EUSTON SQUARE
Tavistock Square
Thomas Coram Foundation
Doughty St
Madame Tussaud's
Holy Trinity
Euston Centre
Percival David Found. of Chin. Art
Brunswick Sq
CORAM FIELDS
PARK SQ GARDENS
WARREN ST
University College Hospital
Gower Street
University College
Bernard St
Guilford Street
Dickens House
Royal Academy of Music
Marylebone Road
Euston Rd
REGENT'S PARK
Park Crescent
Fitzroy Square
Tottenham
Charlotte St
RUSSELL SQ
University of London
Russell
Gt Ormond St Hospital for Sick Children
St Marylebone
Portland
Great Portland St
Telecom Tower
American Church in London
RUSSELL SQ GDNS
Square
Southampton Row
Road
MARYLEBONE
St Charles
GOODGE ST
Gower St
BLOOMSBURY
Theobald's
Marylebone High St
Wimpole Street
Harley Street
Place
Pollock's Toy Museum
Court
Goodge St
British Museum
HOLBORN
Broadcasting House BBC
Bedford Square
Bloomsbury Square
Vernon Pl.
Street
Road
St George
Bloomsbury Way
High Holborn
Wallace Collection
All Souls
Langham Pl.
Mortimer
Bloomsbury St
HOLBORN
Sir John Soane's Museum
Thayer St
Wigmore Hall
TOTTENHAM COURT RD
New Oxford St
Lincoln's Inn
LINCOLN'S INN FIELDS
Street
Regent
High Holborn
Kingsway
Cavendish Sq
Street
Wigmore
Oxford
Charing Cross Road
St Giles High St
Soho Square
John Lewis
OXFORD CIRCUS
Phoenix Theatre
Endell St
Great Queen St
Old Curiosity Shop
Selfridges
Street
Palladium Theatre
Monmouth St
Neal St
Drury Lane
Oxford
New
Berwick St
Wardour St
Dean Street
Frith St
Aldwych Theatre
St Clement Danes
BOND ST
Hanover Square
Liberty
Bow St
Street
Carnaby St
Old Compton St
COVENT GDN
Royal Opera House
Theatre Museum
Aldwych
St Mark
Bond
St George
St
SOHO
Ave
The Market
Bush House
Grosvenor
Conduit
Regent Street
Shaftesbury
LEICESTER SQ
St Martin's Lane
Long Acre
London Transport Museum
Courtauld Institute
Roosevelt Memorial
St
Brewer St
Chinatown
St Paul
Somerset House
COVENT GARDEN
Square
US Embassy
London Pavilion
Trocadero Centre
Leicester Sq
London Coliseum
Lancaster Pl.
Gilbert Collection
MAYFAIR
Berkeley Square
Piccadilly Circus
PICCADILLY CIRCUS
National Portrait Gallery
Strand
Adelphi Theatre
The Savoy
Mount Street
Faraday Museum
Old Bond St
Royal Academy of Arts
Haymarket
St Martin-in-the-Fields
Waterloo Bridge
Immaculate Conception
National Gallery
VICTORIA EMBANKMENT GARDENS
Grosvenor Chapel
Piccadilly
St James
Trafalgar Square
CHARING CROSS
Victoria Embankment
National Film Theatre
Fortnum & Mason's
Nelson's Column
Dorchester Hotel
Jermyn St
ST JAMES'S
Charing Cross Station
EMBANKMENT
Queen Elizabeth Hall
Park Lane
St James's St
Mall
Admiralty Arch
Northumberland Ave.
The Ritz
Whitehall Theatre
Royal Festival Hall
SB
Curzon St
GREEN PARK
Duke of York Column
ICA
Hayward Gallery
Hilton Hotel
Shepherd Market
Chapel Royal
Pall
The Admiralty
Whitehall
Old War Office
Hispaniola
Achilles Statue
Marlborough House
Mall
Horse Guards Parade
Banqueting House
Embankment
Tattershall Castle
Piccadilly
Bandstand
St James's Palace
Guards Memorial
Lane
Christ Church
The
Ministry of Defence
London Eye
JUBILEE GARDENS
Wellington Museum Apsley House
GREEN PARK
Clarence House
Horse Guards Road
Lancaster House
Downing St
Foreign Office
Cenotaph
HYDE PARK CORNER
Wellington Arch
ST JAMES'S PARK
Parliament St
Victoria
London Aquarium
County Hall
York Road
Queen Victoria Memorial
Constitution Hill
Cabinet War Rooms
Treasury
WESTMINSTER
Grosvenor Cres.
BUCKINGHAM PALACE GARDENS
Buckingham Palace
Birdcage Walk
Gt. George St
Central Hall
Big Ben
Westminster Bridge
Florence Nightingale Museum
Grosvenor
Wellington Barracks
Guards' Chapel & Museum
WESTMINSTER
Broad Sanctuary
St Margaret St
Belgrave Square
Queen's Gallery
Buckingham Gate
ST JAMES'S PARK
Houses of Parliament
Thames
St Thomas' Hospital
Road
Royal Mews
Westminster Chapel
Buckingham Gate
New Scotland Yard
Victoria Street
Westminster Abbey
Jewel Tower
Abingdon St
Place
Belgrave Pl.
Hobart Pl.
Grosvenor Gdns.
Westminster City Hall
Church House
VICTORIA TOWER GARDENS
Lambeth Palace
LAMBETH
Lower Belgrave St
Buckingham Palace Rd
Street
St Matthew
Great Peter St
BELGRAVIA
Victoria
VICTORIA
Westminster R.C. Cathedral
Depts. of Transport & Environment
Millbank
Lambeth
Lambeth Palace
King's Road
Eccleston St
Victoria Station
St John's Concert Hall
Lambeth Bridge
Horseferry Road
Tate Britain
Museum of Garden History

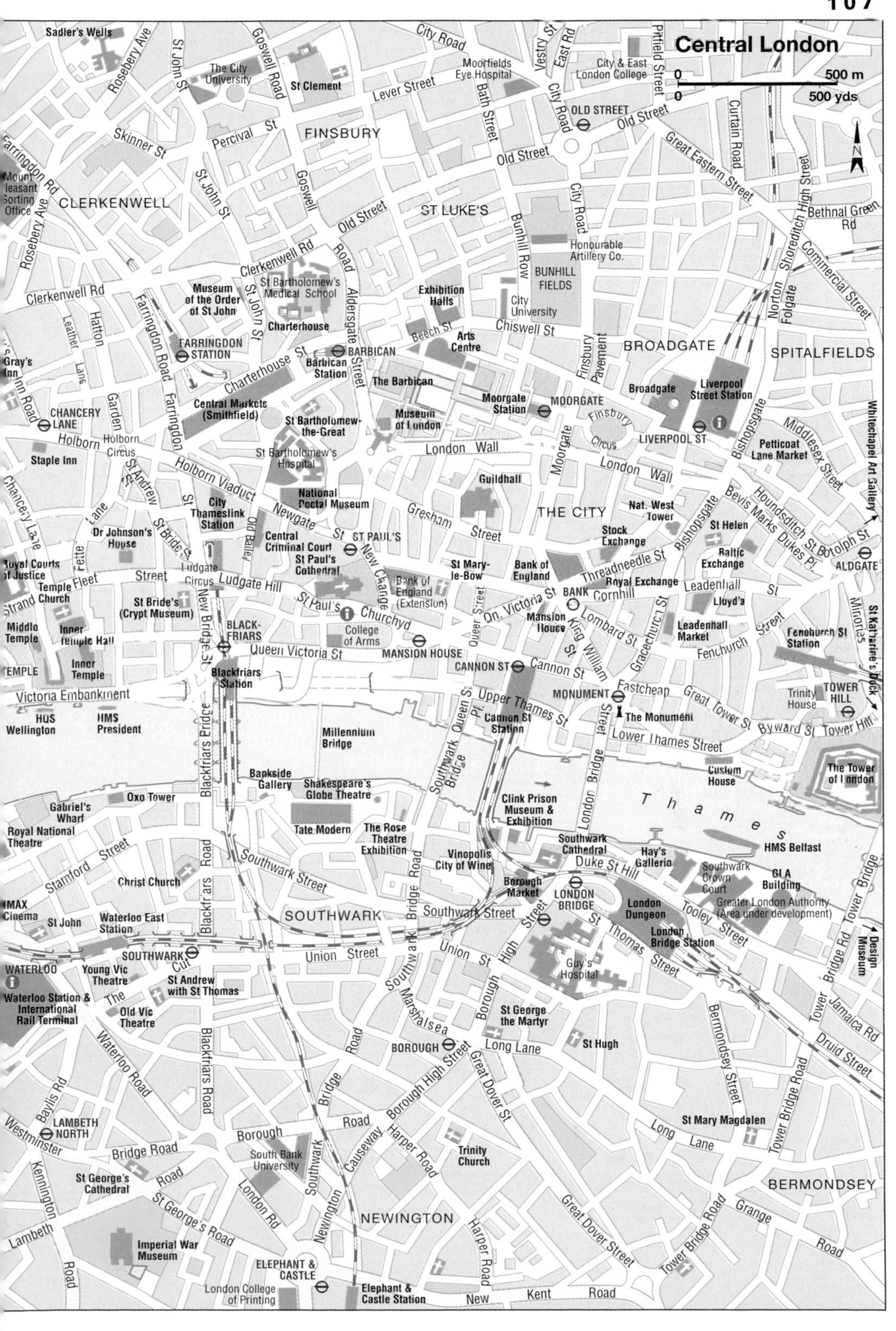
Central London
0 500 m
0 500 yds
Sadler's Wells
Rosebery Ave
St John St
The City University
Goswell Road
St Clement
City Road
Moorfields Eye Hospital
Lever Street
Vestry St
East Rd
City & East London College
Pitfield Street
Bath Street
City Road
OLD STREET
Old Street
Curtain Road
Skinner St
Percival St
FINSBURY
Farringdon Rd
Mount Pleasant Sorting Office
CLERKENWELL
St John St
Goswell
Old Street
ST LUKE'S
Bunhill Row
City Road
Great Eastern Street
Shoreditch High Street
Bethnal Green Rd
Commercial Street
Rosebery Ave
Clerkenwell Rd
St Bartholomew's Medical School
Road
Honourable Artillery Co.
BUNHILL FIELDS
Clerkenwell Rd
Museum of the Order of St John
St John St
Aldersgate
Exhibition Halls
City University
Norton Folgate
Leather Lane
Hatton
Farringdon Road
Charterhouse
Beech St
Arts Centre
Chiswell St
Finsbury Pavement
BROADGATE
SPITALFIELDS
Gray's Inn
FARRINGDON STATION
Charterhouse St
BARBICAN
Barbican Station
Street
The Barbican
Moorgate Station
MOORGATE
Broadgate
Liverpool Street Station
Gray's Inn Road
CHANCERY LANE
Garden
Farringdon
Central Markets (Smithfield)
St Bartholomew-the-Great
Museum of London
Finsbury Circus
LIVERPOOL ST
Bishopsgate
Middlesex Street
Petticoat Lane Market
Whitechapel Art Gallery
Holborn
Holborn Circus
St Bartholomew's Hospital
London Wall
Moorgate
London Wall
Staple Inn
Holborn Viaduct
Guildhall
Chancery Lane
St Andrew
National Postal Museum
Gresham Street
THE CITY
Nat. West Tower
Bishopsgate
Bevis Marks
Houndsditch
Fetter Lane
Dr Johnson's House
City Thameslink Station
Newgate
Old Bailey
Central Criminal Court
St PAUL'S
New Change
Stock Exchange
St Helen
Dukes Pl
St Botolph St
Royal Courts of Justice
St Bride St
Ludgate Circus
St Paul's Cathedral
St Mary-le-Bow
Bank of England
Threadneedle St
Baltic Exchange
ALDGATE
Strand
Temple Church
Fleet Street
Ludgate Hill
Bank of England (Extension)
Royal Exchange
Leadenhall St
Minories
St Bride's (Crypt Museum)
New Bridge St
St Paul's Churchyd
Queen Street
Qn. Victoria St
BANK
Cornhill
Lloyd's
Middle Temple
Inner Temple Hall
BLACK-FRIARS
College of Arms
Mansion House
Lombard St
King William St
Gracechurch St
Leadenhall Market
Fenchurch Street
Fenchurch St Station
St Katharine's Dock
TEMPLE
Inner Temple
Queen Victoria St
MANSION HOUSE
CANNON ST
Cannon St
Blackfriars Station
Victoria Embankment
Upper Thames St
MONUMENT
Eastcheap
Great Tower St
Trinity House
TOWER HILL
HMS Wellington
HMS President
Millennium Bridge
Queen St Pl.
Cannon St Station
The Monument
Byward St
Tower Hill
Lower Thames Street
Blackfriars Bridge
Southwark Bridge
London Bridge
Custom House
The Tower of London
Bankside Gallery
Shakespeare's Globe Theatre
Oxo Tower
Gabriel's Wharf
Clink Prison Museum & Exhibition
Thames
Royal National Theatre
Tate Modern
The Rose Theatre Exhibition
Southwark Cathedral
HMS Belfast
Stamford Street
Southwark Street
Vinopolis City of Wine
Hay's Galleria
Duke St Hill
Southwark Crown Court
GLA Building
Tower Bridge
Christ Church
Blackfriars Road
Borough Market
LONDON BRIDGE
Greater London Authority (Area under development)
IMAX Cinema
Waterloo East Station
SOUTHWARK
Southwark Street
London Dungeon
Tooley Street
St John
Southwark Bridge Road
High Street
St Thomas Street
London Bridge Station
Design Museum
SOUTHWARK
The Cut
Union Street
Union St
WATERLOO
Young Vic Theatre
St Andrew with St Thomas
Guy's Hospital
Bridge Rd
Waterloo Station & International Rail Terminal
The Old Vic Theatre
Marshalsea Road
Borough
St George the Martyr
Tower Bridge Rd
Jamaica Rd
Waterloo Road
Blackfriars Road
BOROUGH
Long Lane
St Hugh
Druid Street
Bermondsey Street
Borough High Street
Great Dover St
Tower Bridge Road
Baylis Rd
LAMBETH NORTH
Westminster Bridge Road
Borough Road
St Mary Magdalen
Long Lane
Causeway
Harper Road
Trinity Church
South Bank University
Southwark Bridge Road
St George's Cathedral
BERMONDSEY
Kennington Road
St George's Road
London Rd
NEWINGTON
Newington
Grange Road
Great Dover Street
Tower Bridge Road
Lambeth Road
Imperial War Museum
Harper Road
ELEPHANT & CASTLE
London College of Printing
Elephant & Castle Station
New Kent Road

PRINCESS
POCAHONTAS

OLD FATHER THAMES

The River Thames is London's main artery: a trip up and down this historic highway is the best way to get acquainted with the city

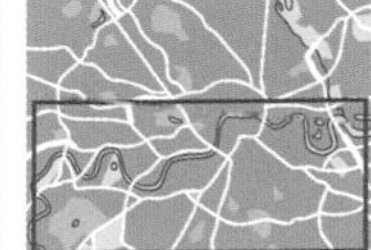

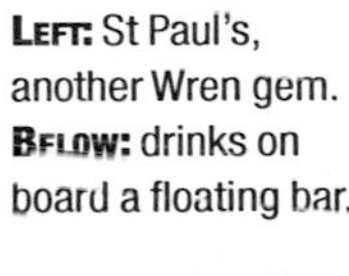

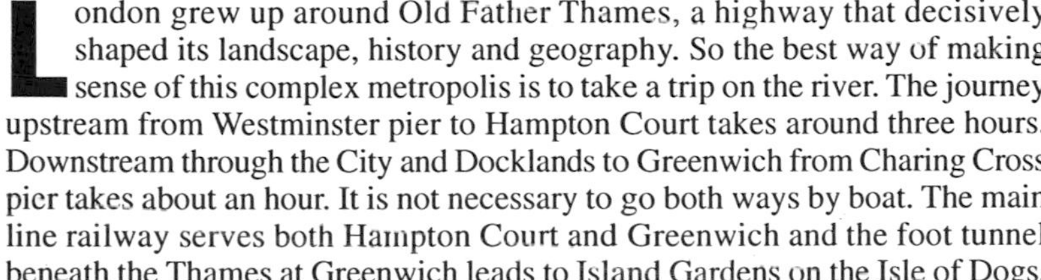

London grew up around Old Father Thames, a highway that decisively shaped its landscape, history and geography. So the best way of making sense of this complex metropolis is to take a trip on the river. The journey upstream from Westminster pier to Hampton Court takes around three hours. Downstream through the City and Docklands to Greenwich from Charing Cross pier takes about an hour. It is not necessary to go both ways by boat. The main line railway serves both Hampton Court and Greenwich and the foot tunnel beneath the Thames at Greenwich leads to Island Gardens on the Isle of Dogs, the last stop on this branch of the Docklands Light Railway.

Ribbon of history

Grain Spit, Deadman's Point and Mucking Flats witnessed the arrival of all those people who have contributed to the composition of the English – the Celts, Romans, Angles, Saxons, Jutes and Danes. In the Thames estuary Shoeburyness, Sheerness and Sheppey watched the Elizabethan explorers sail out centuries later to stake their claims in far-off corners of the world. Pilgrims boarded here for the New World, convicts for Australia.

Its banks were lined with palaces, gardens, orchards and estates. Westminster Abbey and all the royal palaces from Greenwich to Hampton Court via Whitehall and the Savoy rose beside it, as did the palaces of the bishops of London, Canterbury, Winchester and York. Golden barges transported royalty, showed off the City guilds and held waterborne pageants. In 1717, 50 musicians drew alongside George I's royal barge and performed a work by George Frederick Händel. His *Water Music* so enthralled the king and his mistress, Madame de Kilmanseck, that two encores were demanded.

The British navy at its height built ships in the great naval yards of Deptford, Woolwich and Chatham, and trained its officers in Sir Christopher Wren's magnificent buildings at Greenwich, which he designed as a twin to his riverside army hospital in Chelsea. Pleasure gardens were laid out in the 18th century, at Vauxhall, Ranelagh and Battersea.

Between 1860 and 1900, when London reaped the harvest of the Empire and its docklands were the warehouse of the world, the river became the dark and poverty-stricken highway described by Charles Dickens, where the most wretched of Londoners scavenged for flotsam and jetsam in the mud. Their numbers were added to by refugees escaping pogroms and poverty in Europe, who disembarked in their thousands to start new lives in the East End.

Decline began in the first half of the 20th century and was hastened in World War II when the Thames acted as a flight path for German bombers. Today helicopters

LEFT: St Paul's, another Wren gem.
BELOW: drinks on board a floating bar.

For details of places on the South Bank, see *South Bank* chapter, page 195.

are allowed to fly low over the river, and flights heading for Heathrow airport are guided by its route.

These days, at regular intervals stories appear in the newspapers to show how clean the river is getting, how salmon have been caught, how seals have entered the estuary, how otters have returned to the upper reaches. It is all a far cry from the 19th century summer sitting of Parliament which had to be abandoned because of the unbearable stench of its polluted waters. There are also sporadic stories about starting up regular commuter passenger services on the Thames. Attempts in the past have not lasted, the most recent being in the development of Docklands when piers from Chelsea Harbour to Canary Wharf were added.

Much of the riverbank can now be walked, particularly on the south bank, where the **Thames Walk** ensures access to the whole length of the London river. Though London south of the river is poorly served by local transport, all places are also within easy reach of the centre by Underground, bus or rail. Westminster and Charing Cross are the nearest Underground stations for the departure piers.

Upriver: from Westminster Pier to Hampton Court

On a corner of the bridge just above **Westminster Pier** ❶ is a statue of **Queen Boadicca**, the native warrior who sacked Roman London in AD 61; the statue's critics included an archaeologist who described it as an "armoured milkfloat". **Westminster Bridge** was dramatically opened in 1863 with a 25-gun salute at 3.45am, marking the hour of Queen Victoria's birth and the number of years she had been on the throne. **The Houses of Parliament** on the far side of the bridge are best seen from the river. Between the building and the water's edge is a hidden terrace where MPs take tea and entertain guests. During the Great Stench

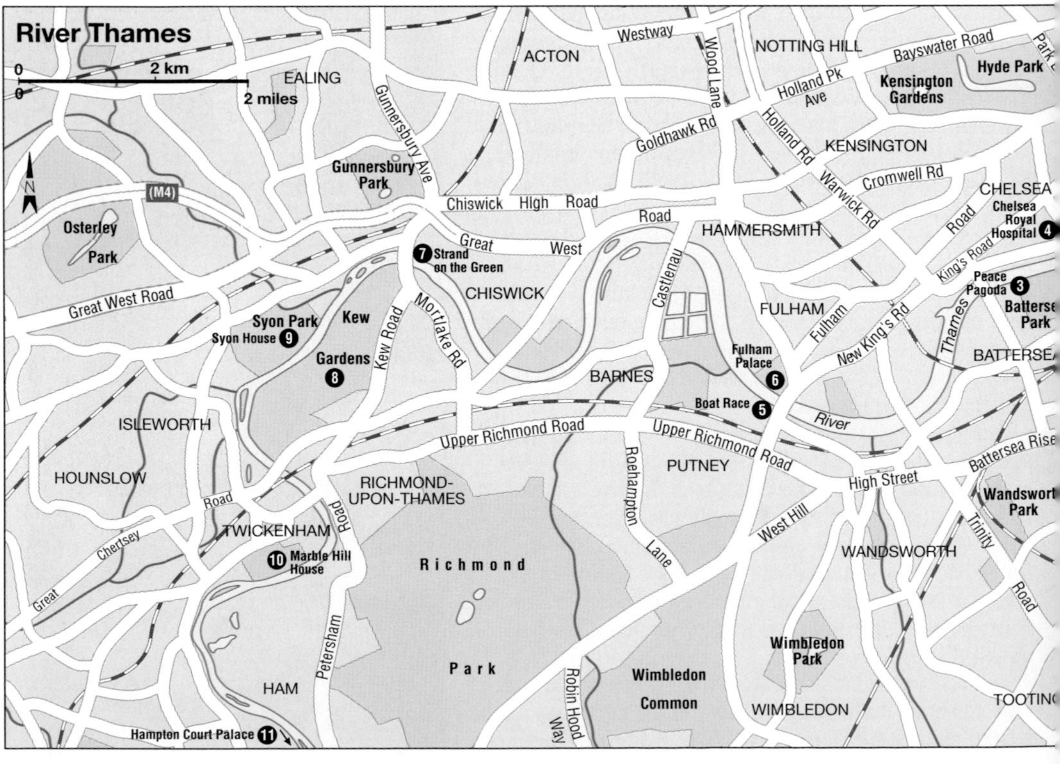

River Thames

0 2 km
0 2 miles

ACTON
EALING
Westway
Wood Lane
NOTTING HILL
Bayswater Road
Hyde Park
Kensington Gardens
Holland Pk Ave
Holland Rd
Gunnersbury Ave
Goldhawk Rd
KENSINGTON
Gunnersbury Park
Warwick Rd
Cromwell Rd
(M4)
CHELSEA
Chelsea Royal Hospital ❹
Chiswick High Road
Osterley Park
Road
HAMMERSMITH
Great West Road
❼ Strand on the Green
King's Road
Peace Pagoda ❸
CHISWICK
Castlenau
Battersea Park
Great West Road
FULHAM
Syon Park
Kew
Fulham
Syon House ❾
Kew Road
Mortlake Rd
New King's Rd
Thames
Gardens ❽
Fulham Palace ❻
BATTERSEA
BARNES
Boat Race ❺
ISLEWORTH
River
Upper Richmond Road
Upper Richmond Road
Battersea Rise
HOUNSLOW
Roehampton
PUTNEY
RICHMOND-UPON-THAMES
High Street
Wandsworth Park
Road
TWICKENHAM
Road
West Hill
Trinity
Chertsey
Lane
WANDSWORTH
❿ Marble Hill House
Richmond
Road
Great
Petersham
Wimbledon Park
Park
Robin Hood Way
Wimbledon Common
HAM
WIMBLEDON
TOOTING
Hampton Court Palace ⓫

of 1858, caused by a powerful mix of industrial and sewage pollution, sheets soaked in chloride of lime were hung over the windows but that was not enough: parliament was abandoned. Opposite, on the south bank, are St Thomas's Hospital and the Archbishop of Canterbury's residence, **Lambeth Palace**. It is close to **Lambeth Bridge** where stone pineapples sit on plinths in recognition of John Tradescant (1570–1638) who brought exotic fruits to England and is commemorated in a garden at Lambeth. When the bridge was built in 1802 the archbishop was paid handsome compensation for loss of earnings from the horse ferry that had been a good source of his income.

Millbank Tower, a government building, is the modern block on the right, once the tallest in London. Next to it is the **Tate Britain** ❷ (*see page 129*), founded by the sugar tycoon Sir Henry Tate and built on the site of the massive Millbank penitentiary. Early in the 19th century, prisoners sentenced to deportation to Australia embarked from here. Opposite is **Vauxhall Cross**, the hush-hush green and cream MI6 building designed by Terry Farrell; this secret services HQ is built in a "Faraday Cage" which stops electro-magnetic information passing in or out of the building. A terrorist rocket fired at it in 2000 did little damage.

The eight demure figures above the piers on **Vauxhall Bridge** represent, on the downstream side, Fine Arts, Local Government, Science and Education and, on the upstream side, Engineering, Pottery, Architecture (holding a miniature St Paul's) and Agriculture. Beyond on the left is **Nine Elms**, where Covent Garden fruit and flower market was unromantically sited after being uprooted from the West End in 1974, and the disused four-chimneyed **Battersea Power Station**, which may be developed as a hotel and entertainments complex.

Battersea Park lies on the left after Chelsea Bridge, marked by a **Peace**

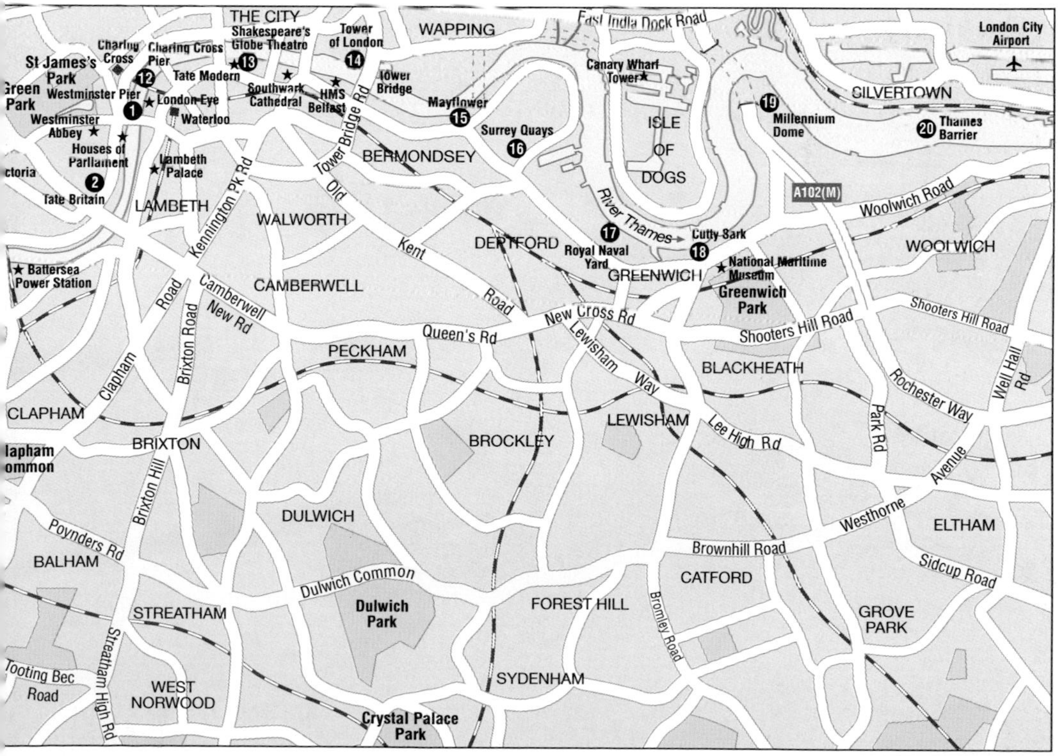

Millbank prison was a model of liberality when it opened in 1821. Inmates were allowed to work, making mailbags, which British prisoners still do.

The Peace Pagoda in Battersea Park, erected by Japanese Buddhists.

Pagoda ❸ erected by Japanese Buddhist monks to commemorate the Year of Peace in 1985. Another pleasure garden, Ranelagh, on the Chelsea bank, was popular in the 19th century, and next to it is **Chelsea Hospital** ❹ for old soldiers, built by Christopher Wren in 1694. **Cadogan Pier**, on the Chelsea end of the attractive Albert Bridge, marks the end of the watermen's annual rowing race, the Doggett's Coat and Badge. This is a single-scull event from London Bridge raced on rough water against the tide, but the number of true watermen has dwindled, and only half a dozen or so take part. On the north end of **Battersea Bridge** is the largest collection of houseboats moored on the river. Just beyond are the chimney stacks of Lots Road Power Station, built to provide an independent electricity supply for the Underground network. Alongside is **Chelsea Harbour**, with a marina, smart restaurants, a large car park and a gymnasium that paparazzi made famous in their pursuit of the late Diana, Princess of Wales. A sphere on the spire of its apartment block rises and falls with the tide.

Leafy streets and old riverside pubs

Leafy **Putney** is the start of the **University Boat Race** ❺, an annual competition between the universities of Oxford and Cambridge in March. The race between the two opposing rowing eights, in dark and light blue, was started in 1829 and still attracts media attention. It is rowed upstream, with the tide. In early days the race was umpired from a rowing boat manned by Thames watermen, who managed to keep pace with the university gentlemen.

Here, though still in London, the banks are named after the counties to which they once belonged before the city encroached: Surrey on the south side, Middlesex on the north side. On the opposite side from Putney in Fulham is **Bishop's**

BELOW: a victorious Cambridge crew in the University Boat Race.

Park and **Fulham Palace** ❻, official residence of the Bishop of London. Its grounds and walled garden are open to the public.

The waterside becomes increasingly green further upriver. Bomb damage from World War II was limited here, and riverside malls at Hammersmith and Chiswick remain unspoilt, with some of the most elegant housing in London. **Strand on the Green** ❼ has a fine pair of waterside pubs, the **Bull's Head** and the **City Barge**, both more than 350 years old and ideal for a riverside drink.

The trees of **Kew Gardens** ❽ (*see page 247*) line the southern bank beyond Kew bridge to Richmond, matched by the gardens of **Syon House** ❾, designed by Robert Adam in 1761, on the north (Wed–Sun,11am–4.15pm; Oct–Dec 14, Sun only, closed Dec–Apr; entrance fee). The bridge in this elegant outer London community dates from 1774, and is the oldest still in use on the river. The 18th-century **Marble Hill Park** and **House** ❿, beyond Richmond, are open to the public (daily 10am–6pm, Oct–Mar 10am–4pm Wed–Sun, admission fee), although most riverboat passengers who get this far will finally disembark at **Hampton Court Palace** ⓫ (*see page 253*).

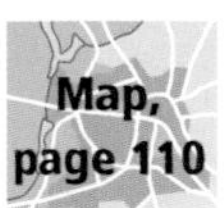

ABOVE: The painter J.M.W. Turner, Chiswick's most famous resident.
BELOW: Vauxhall Cross, the bug-proof spy building.

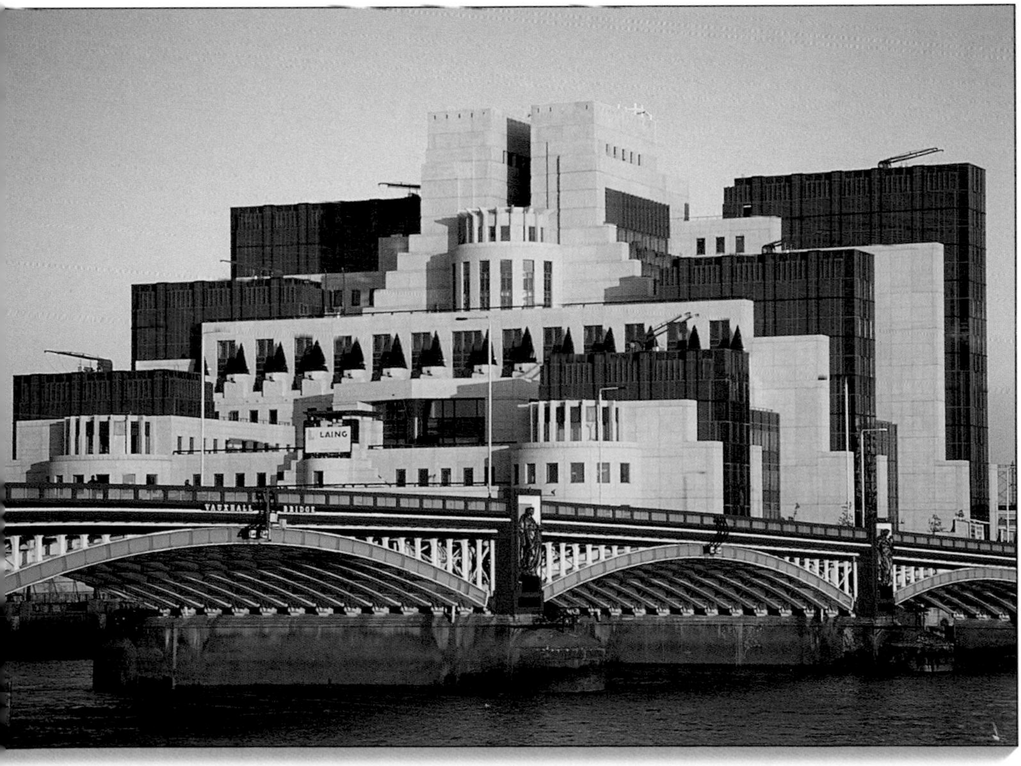

Downstream: Charing Cross to Greenwich

The starting point for trips downriver is **Charing Cross Pier** ⓬, on **Victoria Embankment** by Embankment Underground station. The Embankment runs from Blackfriars to Westminster. It was designed and built in 1870 by the engineer Sir Joseph Bazalgette to solve two problems: the increasing congestion of the city and the overwhelming stink of the river. It covered the mudflats, carried the Underground lines as well as sewage pipes and provided a thoroughfare and gardens.

One of the first time capsules was buried beneath Cleopatra's Needle when it was erected in 1878. It contains photographs of the 12 most beautiful women of the day.

BELOW: the Shell building downriver from Victoria Bridge.

Beside the pier is **Cleopatra's Needle**, made in 1450 BC and a gift from the viceroy of Egypt. It was erected after the Embankment's completion in 1878, after an adventurous sea voyage from Egypt which cost six sailors' lives. Opposite Charing Cross Pier is the South Bank complex, built for the 1951 Festival of Britain. On the right is **Hungerford** railway bridge with a pedestrian walkway. There have been recent plans to enhance this walkway, or even add a new pedestrian bridge, perhaps incorporating shops and stalls, which the original London Bridge had. Beyond **Waterloo Bridge** and Temple Pier are two moored ships: the *Wellington*, the Livery Hall of the Honourable Company of Master Mariners, and *HMS President*, involved in youth training. Opposite are **Gabriel's Wharf** with crafts shops, and the **Oxo Tower** where the smart set dine.

In between the Blackfriars road and rail bridges are the stranded piers from the former rail bridge of the London, Chatham and Dover Railway, its huge crest adorning the south end of the wide bridge. The former Bankside Power Station, now transformed into the cutting-edge art gallery, **Tate Modern** *(see page 196)*, is on the right just before the thatched white drum of the replica of **Shakespeare's Globe** ⓭ *(see page 197)*. Boats pass under the elegant **Millennium Bridge**, the first new river crossing in central London for a century. The 18th-century **Anchor pub** is a good watering hole here, with a riverside terrace.

Beyond **Southwark Cathedral** and **Cannon Street** railway bridge is **London Bridge**, an unprepossessing construction but one with the most historic connections. Freemen of the City of London still have the right to drive sheep across it. It is the fifth bridge to be built on this site. The first, dating from AD 43, marked for 1,700 years the only place where the river was spanned. Its replacement, built in 1176, was heavy with nearly 200 shops and houses, and

Map, page 110

the tax paid by the occupants kept the bridge open. It also acted as an effective dam for the river, which became so slow-moving that it regularly froze over in winter. Frost Fairs were held on its surface. Unfortunately, the slow movement of the river could not cope with the increasing drainage demands made on it, and in summer it smelt strongly of sewage. The last bridge, by John Rennie, was exported and re-erected in Lake Havasu City, Arizona, in 1973.

Towering landmarks in the Pool of London

Between London Bridge and **Tower Bridge** is the **Upper Pool of London**, lorded over by the great fortifications of the **Tower of London** (*see page 224*). Traitors' Gate in the embankment wall was the river entrance to the Tower, for delivering prisoners to their fate. The Pool of London was once a hive of water-borne trade. **Billingsgate Market** on the north bank is signalled by a golden fish weather vane on its roof, but it moved down to Docklands in 1972. **Hay's Galleria** marks the first of the **Surrey Docks** on the south bank. ***HMS Belfast,*** a World War II cruiser, is moored here as a museum (open daily 10am–6pm; Oct–Apr 10am–5pm; entrance fee). Tall ships came into the Pool for the last time in the 1980s: a new bridge downriver at Dartford has put paid to their visits.

Tower Bridge ⓮, a masterpiece of Victorian Gothic architecture dating from 1894, has become a symbol of London. During the days when the capital was a flourishing port, it opened several times a day. In 1954 a bus driver was awarded a medal for putting his foot on the accelerator when, to his horror, he saw the bridge yawn open before him. The bus leapt a 3ft (1m) gap.These days the bridge opens around 500 times a year to let large ships pass under; it takes 90 seconds for the bascules to lift fully. **Tower Bridge Experience** is an exhibition that

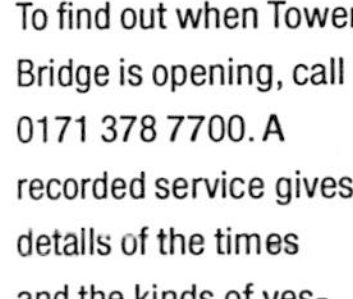

To find out when Tower Bridge is opening, call 0171 378 7700. A recorded service gives details of the times and the kinds of vessels passing through for the following week.

BELOW: the battle cruiser *HMS Belfast* and Tower Bridge.

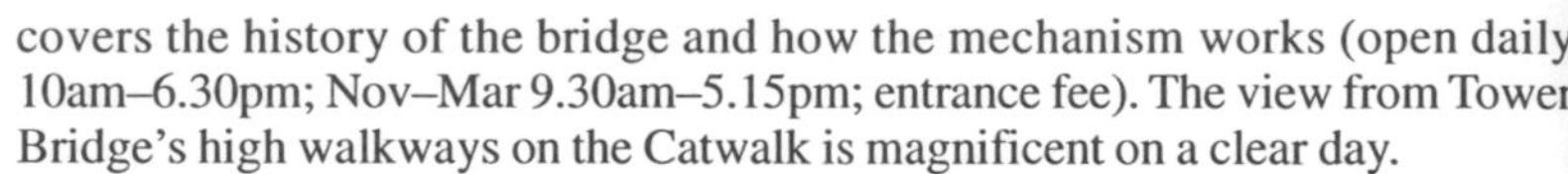

covers the history of the bridge and how the mechanism works (open daily 10am–6.30pm; Nov–Mar 9.30am–5.15pm; entrance fee). The view from Tower Bridge's high walkways on the Catwalk is magnificent on a clear day.

Beyond Tower Bridge is **St Katharine's Dock,** the most accessible of the Docklands developments, which in its heyday imported 400 tons of ostrich feathers a year for Edwardian women's fans and headdresses. On the south bank is **Butler's Wharf**. From here the river widens into the main Pool of London, where warehouses, quays and docks sprawl for miles along either bank. Pirates and thieves abounded among the rich cargoes of the river, and felons were kept in prison hulks in horrendous conditions. Captain Kidd was among the notorious pirates hanged at **Execution Dock** in **Wapping**, where the river police was formed. Among its tasks today are pulling suicides from the river, at the rate of around one a week. **Rotherhithe** lies on the south bank and among its traditional pubs is the **Mayflower** ⓯, where the Pilgrim Fathers moored their ship before sailing to Plymouth and America in 1620. The Anglo-American spirit remains: the pub is allowed to sell US as well as English stamps.

Cargoes to the continent used to be transported in magnificent Thames sailing barges. Some can be seen in St Katharine's Dock and every June they race from the estuary at Gravesend to Colchester in Essex.

The heart of Docklands

At **Limehouse Reach** the river turns south around the Isle of Dogs with the Canary Wharf tower unmistakably at its centre. On the right is **Surrey Quays** ⓰, a large shopping and commercial development and, just beyond it, where **Greenwich Reach** begins, is the huge Royal Naval Yard at **Deptford** ⓱, a place of such renown that Peter the Great of Russia studied here, Henry VIII fitted out his navy here, and in 1581 Francis Drake was knighted by Queen Elizabeth I after his circumnavigation of the world. Nearly 400 years later, in 1967, Queen Elizabeth II repeated the action when, with the same sword, she knighted Francis Chichester after he had completed the first single-handed voyage round the world. His 53-ft ketch, *Gypsy Moth IV,* lies next to the great tea clipper, the *Cutty Sark,* at **Greenwich** ⓲. This historic part of London, with Wren's masterful Royal Naval Hospital, National Maritime Museum and Observatory, plus the Millennium Dome, is often the end of a river trip, and it provides a great deal to explore *(see page 240)*.

River trips may continue, however, sweeping back up the eastern side of the Isle of Dogs to **Blackwall Reach**, around the vast area reclaimed from the Gas Board and cleared at the taxpayer's expense for the **Millennium Dome** ⓳, the focus of the celebratory events that heralded the year 2000. Beyond it is **Woolwich,** once the Royal Navy's dockyards and arsenal.

The dominant structure today is the **Thames Barrier** ⓴, which spans the river by the Royal Victoria Dock, protecting 45 sq. miles (117 sq. km) of London, including the Houses of Parliament, from the very real danger of flooding. In 1953, 300 people died in disastrous floods and, with southeast England sinking at a rate of 12 inches (30 cm) every 100 years, the situation won't improve. The £435 million barrier, finished in 1982, has been closed several times when floods threatened. It has a visitor centre on the south side and you can reach it by boat or bus from Greenwich (open 10am–4pm weekdays, 10.30–4.30pm weekends, entrance fee). ❑

BELOW: Thames Barges. **RIGHT:** the Thames Barrier, ready to save the city from flooding.

8
8

PARLIAMENT AND BUCKINGHAM PALACE

Westminster is the centre of Official London. Parliament meets here, the Queen has her London home here, and national mourning is conducted from Westminster Abbey

Westminster lies a mile or so upstream from the City of London and the two core areas of the capital developed as quite separate communities, keeping a wary eye on each other. Even today the monarch is supposed to ask the Lord Mayor of London for permission to enter his part of town. As the focus of government and the monarchy, Westminster contains within its ancient and easily walked boundaries the nation's policy-making civil servants, the Prime Minister and the Cabinet, and the Queen and her family. Many kings and queens are buried in Westminster Abbey, founded by the last of the Saxon rulers, Edward the Confessor (1042–66), who built the first great abbey and a palace around a Benedictine monastery on what was then a marshy spot beside the River Thames.

The Palace of Westminster was replaced as a royal residence by Henry VIII when he built the magnificent, but now lost, Palace of Whitehall. Church and state evolved as one when the first parliaments sat in the choir stalls of St Stephen's Chapel in the Palace of Westminster, facing each other, as they do today on the same site in the Houses of Parliament.

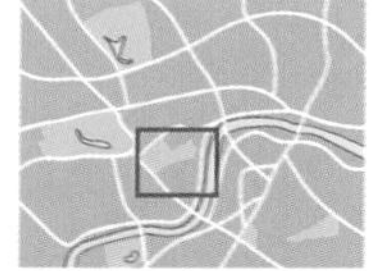

PRECEDING PAGES: the Lords Chamber in the Houses of Parliament.
LEFT: a dismounted Horse Guard.
BELOW: No. 10 Downing Street.

Whitehall's pomp

The corridors of power begin on the south side of **Trafalgar Square**, where a bronze statue of a little man on horseback points towards the heart of Westminster. Le Sueur's 1633 sculpture of **King Charles I** ❶ is the oldest of many excellent equestrian statues in London. and it marks the spot where all distances from London are measured. It has a chequered history. King Charles's dispute with parliament led to a Civil War, which he lost, and as a result he was beheaded in 1642. The statue of the disfavoured monarch was then sold to a scrap dealer, who promised to melt it down for souvenirs, but actually hid it until the monarchy was restored. In 1675 it was placed on a marble plinth facing straight down the broad and unmistakably official thoroughfare called **Whitehall**, a word that has become synonymous with faceless civil servants.

Most buildings along this wide thoroughfare are government offices. Beyond the Whitehall Theatre on the right are the offices of the Armed Forces Commander-in-Chief, known as the **Horse Guards** ❷.Outside this colonnaded building are mounted sentries in fancy uniforms, white gloves, plumes and helmets. These are soldiers of the Life Guards or Royal Horse Guards, guarding the site of the main gateway to what was the **Palace of Whitehall,** used by King Henry VIII in the 16th century and burnt to the ground in 1698. Through

Every hour from 10am to 4pm the two mounted horse guards of the Queen's Household Cavalry are changed. In fact they are guarding nothing. This is the former guardhouse of the Palace of White-hall, where Henry VIII enjoyed his sports of tennis, tilting and cockfighting.

the archway of Horse Guards and opening out on to St James's Park is the huge **Horse Guards Parade**. Here in June the Queen's birthday is honoured by a splendid ceremony called **Trooping the Colour**; the name is derived from the regimental colours which are paraded.

Opposite Horse Guards, on the other side of Whitehall, is the magnificent renaissance-style **Banqueting House** ❸, built by Inigo Jones, the 17th-century architect who introduced this Italian style of architecture into England (open 10am–5pm, closed Sun, entrance fee). It is the only surviving fragment of Whitehall Palace. Inside this huge hall, the ceiling is divided into nine large panels filled with astonishingly rich baroque figure paintings by the Flemish artist Rubens. They were commissioned by Charles I to glorify – or deify – the House of Stuart. Shortly after he finished this work, Rubens was knighted, but the Civil War followed and Charles I was executed on a scaffold outside this building which embodied the divine right of kings.

The **Cenotaph** ❹, the national war memorial designed by Sir Edwin Lutyens, rather unspectacularly breaks Whitehall's monotony. On Remembrance Sunday in November this is the focal point of a service attended by the Queen and political leaders to remember the dead of two world wars and other conflicts.

The Prime Minister's home

London's most famous address, **Downing Street** ❺, is little more than a short terrace of four 18th-century houses in dull brown brick, now sealed off behind a heavy gate as a precaution against a possible terrorist attack. The street is named after the diplomat Sir George Downing who went to America with his parents in 1638 and became the second student to graduate from Harvard

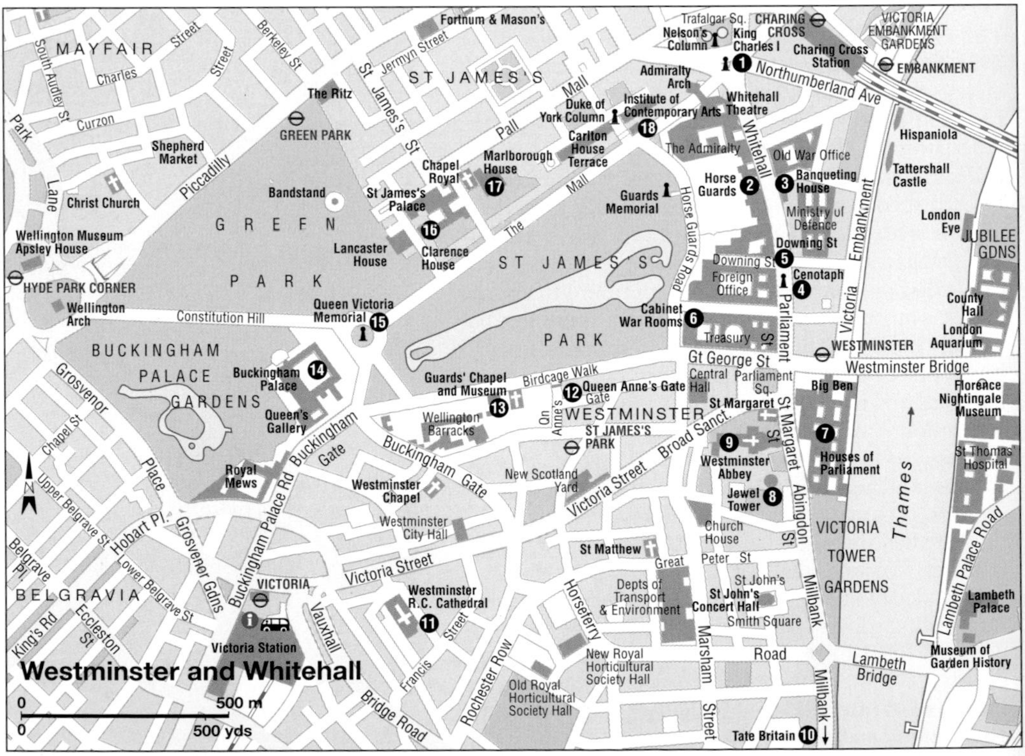

Westminster and Whitehall

0 500 m
0 500 yds

University. He returned to England and fought in the Civil War for Cromwell's republican cause, and bought the land in 1680, where he laid out the street. Four houses remain. No. 10 is the official residence of the Prime Minister, and the venue for Cabinet meetings, which take place in the ground-floor Cabinet Room. The plain black painted door and simple net-curtained windows suggest nothing of its stylish, well-proportioned rooms or of the important state business which goes on inside. Successive prime ministers have lived here since 1732 when King George II offered the house to his prime minister, Sir Robert Walpole.

Adjoining houses are used as official residences by other senior members of government; the Chancellor of the Exchequer, for example, has his official residence at No .11, which has a handy internal adjoining door to No. 10. The Chancellor's accommodation is in fact larger, and in 1997 the incoming Chancellor, bachelor Gordon Brown, gallantly changed places with the Prime Minister, Tony Blair, who needed the space for his wife and three children.

Beyond the Cenotaph, Whitehall becomes **Parliament Street**. The great stolid buildings on the same side as the Horse Guards house the Foreign and Commonwealth Offices, which contained the former Colonial Office from where the Empire was administered. Its designer, Sir George Gilbert Scott, described it as "a kind of national palace". Its south side in King Charles Street, faces the **Treasury** and **Cabinet Offices**, which leads to **Clive Steps** and a statue of Robert Clive (1725–74), a key figure in India. Beside the steps is a small wall of sandbags, the only above-ground sign of the **Cabinet War Rooms** ❻ (open daily 9.30am–5pm; entrance fee). This wartime, bombproof seat of government included the combined office-bedroom used by Sir Winston Churchill.

Map, page 122

At the height of the Empire, more than a quarter of the world was administered by a few dozen civil servants in the Colonial Office in Whitehall.

BELOW: bobbies on royal watch.

Inside the House

The Houses of Parliament consist of the House of Commons and the House of Lords. The Commons, the House of locally elected Members of Parliament (MPs), wields virtually all the power but inhabits only half the building. Jutting out towards Parliament Square is Westminster Hall, with offices, dining rooms and libraries of the Commons stretching behind it to the river. In the centre is the Commons' debating chamber.

To the right of Westminster Hall is the domain of the Lords. Senior judges, bishops and archbishops, dukes, marquesses, earls, viscounts and barons all contribute to the legislature here. Most lords govern by birthright, as descendants of the previous ruling classes, but the voting rights of such hereditary peers are being abolished – a reform which will have a major impact on the parliamentary process. The Lords' main role is to examine and sometimes block bills proposed by the lower house (the Commons), although a measure can be reintroduced. Many members are life peers, ennobled for services to the nation. Former members of the Commons are often rewarded for years of good service – or removed to the Upper House to get them out of the way.

There are 651 elected MPs. The Commons seats only about 450. This is not a problem since MPs attend sessions when they wish. The governing party sits on one side, facing the opposition. Cabinet ministers sit on the front bench, opposite the "Shadow Cabinet".

Major parties represented are the Conservatives, Labour and the Liberal Democrats. General elections are run on the basis of local rather than proportional representation. Therefore a party's presence in the House may not accurately reflect its overall national standing. A party, however, needs an overall majority in the House to push through its bills. The procedure of lawmaking is so complex that a bill usually takes more than six months to be enacted. If it is still incomplete at the end of the parliamentary year, it is dropped. Various techniques are employed by the opposition to delay a bill. For particularly contentious issues, the government's Whips (party members who bring MPs into line) may have to recall MPs from their sick beds to ensure that a difficult bill is passed. The government's Whips are the party members who bring members into line on such issues.

The press can report on Parliament and the business of both houses is televised. A select group of journalists ("lobby correspondents") have informal "background" briefings with ministers or officials. They attribute information from the prime minister's press secretary as "sources close to the Prime Minister".

Parliament meets from October to July. In November, the government's plans for the year are announced in the Queen's Speech at the State Opening, which takes place in the chamber of the Lords. From the Strangers' Gallery, the public can watch the House of Commons at work. The House meets at 2.30pm and Cabinet Ministers answer questions for an hour. Prime Minister's Question Time, recently reduced from two sessions to one a week, usually attracts a full house. ❑

LEFT: statue of the Victorian prime minister William Gladstone in the Central Lobby of the Houses of Parliament.

The Houses of Parliament

Parliament Street empties out into **Parliament Square**, with its tall trees and lawns lined with statues of illustrious statesmen. This, the country's first official roundabout, is surrounded by national landmarks.

The clock tower of the **Houses of Parliament** ❼ has become a symbol of London. Its elaborately fretted stone sides rise up nearly 330 ft (100 metres) to a richly gilded spire above the clock and a 13-ton hour bell supposedly nicknamed **Big Ben** after a rather fat government official called Sir Benjamin Hall who was commissioner of works when the bell was installed. Facing Big Ben is **Portcullis House**, a £250 million office block for members of parliament; its much criticised "chimneys" form part of the air conditioning system.

If you want to climb the clock tower to see Big Ben, you can join a tour: for details, telephone 020-7219 4862.

The oldest part of the Houses of Parliament and one of the oldest buildings in London is **Westminster Hall**, begun in 1078. The thick buttressed walls are spanned with a magnificent hammer-beamed oak roof. This hall has witnessed many crucial events in British history: coronation celebrations, lyings-in-state and treason trials. Among those condemned to death were Sir Thomas More, who fell foul of King Henry VIII; King Charles I, accused of treason against Parliament; and the 17th-century revolutionary Guy Fawkes, who tried to blow up the buildings. The story of the discovery of this bomb plot is still lightheartedly celebrated every 5 November with firework displays all over Britain.

In 1835 a fire achieved what Guy Fawkes had failed to do and most of the ancient rambling Palace of Westminster was destroyed. Westminster Hall and a small crypt chapel survived. Parliament took the opportunity to build a comfortable purpose-built meeting place.The present **Houses of Parliament** were created in an exuberant Gothic style by Sir Charles Barry and Augustus Pugin. The houses have distinctive but simple rectangular outlines which are embellished with gilded spires and towers, mullioned windows and intricate stone carving and statues. The immense **Victoria Tower** marks the southern end of the building, and the grand entrance to the House of Lords. It is also is the entrance used by the Queen when opening a new session of government. Most of this tower is used to store the old records of parliament. A Union Flag (the national flag, colloquially called the Union Jack) flies from the tower when parliament is in session. Night sittings are indicated by a light shining over the clock tower.

The building covers 8 acres (3.2 hectares); there are 11 open courtyards and more than 1,100 rooms. Apart from the ceremonial state rooms and the two main debating chambers, the House of Lords and the House of Commons, there are libraries, dining rooms and tea rooms and also offices and secretarial facilities for government ministers, opposition leaders and ordinary members of parliament.There is nothing spartan about the buildings at all. Many of the walls are covered with heroic Victorian paintings and the woodwork is carved in an intricate Gothic fashion. The construction symbolises some of the contradictions which are evident in British democracy and character: strong, traditional and class-conscious, with an ambivalence to change; diligent, yet comfort-loving.

St Stephen's is the main entrance to the House of

BELOW: the clock tower, symbol of Britain's Parliament.

ABOVE: Rodin's "Burghers of Calais". Their self-sacrifice saved the French city from being sacked by the English in 1347.

Commons, and anyone can watch debates from the visitors' gallery, though there are often queues (when in session, Mon–Thurs from 3.30pm, Wed and Fri mornings, free).Beneath **St Stephen's Hall** is the ancient crypt chapel that survived the fire. Members can take their marriage vows and even have their children baptised here.

Opposite Parliament is the moated **Jewel Tower** ❽, a last relic of the Palace of Westminster, which has a small museum of Parliament Past and Present (10am–1pm, 2–6pm, Oct–Mar 10am–1pm, entrance fee). Beyond the Victoria tower are the **Victoria Tower Gardens**, which contain memorials to Emmeline Pankhurst and her daughter, who were instrumental in winning votes for women, and Auguste Rodin's powerful statue group, *The Burghers of Calais*.

Westminster Abbey: a national shrine

The most historic religious building in Britain is **Westminster Abbey** ❾ (open Mon–Fri 9.15 am, last tickets 3.45pm, Sat 9am–1.45pm; admission fee; regular guided tours from 10am). It is also an outstanding piece of Gothic architecture, which is probably more striking from the detail on the inside than from its outward aspects. Much of the present abbey, the third on the site, was built in the 13th-century in early English Gothic style by Henry III. In the 16th century, Henry VII added on the remarkable chapel at the eastern end of the sanctuary in the late Gothic Perpendicular style. During the 18th century, Nicholas Hawksmoor designed the distinctive towers at the main west entrance.

BELOW: Guardsmen parade for Trooping the Colour.

Until the 16th century the abbey was an important monastery. In addition to their religious duties, the monks translated and copied important books and manuscripts. They also ran a school to teach reading and writing in English and

Latin, starting a long tradition of quality formal education in Britain. Henry VIII dissolved the monasteries in 1534 when he quarrelled with the Pope but Westminster Abbey continued to be used as the royal church for coronations and burials. All but two of the reigning monarchs from William the Conqueror onwards have been crowned here.

The Abbey has always had a special place in national life because of its royal connections. So many eminent figures are honoured in this national shrine that large areas of the interior have the cluttered and confused appearance of an overcrowded sculpture museum. The nave has a fine example of graceful early Gothic vaulting, with tiers of arches on either side and an impressive choir screen, behind which is the choir and sanctuary. The **Tomb of the Unknown Warrior** houses a body brought back from France after World War I, along with the soil for the grave, as an anonymous representative of the countless dead.

Poets' Corner lies beyond the nave in the south transept. Geoffrey Chaucer was the first poet to be buried here, in 1400. Alfred Lord Tennyson is buried here and Ben Johnson is buried standing upright; William Shakespeare, John Milton, John Keats, Oscar Wilde and countless other literary luminaries have only monuments. Behind the sanctuary are magnificent and ornate **Royal Chapels** and tombs. The **Chapel of Edward the Confessor** is the earliest, containing the tomb of the founder of the abbey himself, and that of Henry III, the man who rebuilt it in its present form.

The Abbey also houses the **English Coronation Chair**, built in 1300 for Edward I and still used for the installation of new monarchs. One of the most refined and daring pieces of late Gothic architecture is the **Chapel of Henry VII**. With carved stalls, brilliantly patterned banners and, above all, exquisite

● *An interior plan of the Abbey can be found on the last page of this book.*

ABOVE: the ancient Jewel Tower.
BELOW: Horse Guards progress up a snowy Mall.

fan-vaulting on the roof, it is a breathtaking sight. Looking at its apparently delicate structure, it is difficult to believe that it withstood the blast of a bomb dropped nearby during World War II.

The cloisters are often bustling with people buying or making brass rubbings. Beyond them is the **Chapter House** where early in the morning the medieval monks gathered to listen to their abbot. The inlaid decorated floor tiles are among the best preserved medieval tiles (open daily 10am–5pm). The **Undercroft Museum** in the main cloisters has a collection of effigies and other relics (open daily10.30am–4pm, entrance fee). Passageways lead to **Westminster School**, founded by Elizabeth I when the monks' school was closed. Up until World War I, pupils had to wear top hats. It is still a highly-regarded private school. Hidden nearby is the tiny but delightful **Little Cloister**; the main cloisters lead to **Dean's Yard**, which used to be part of the Abbey gardens.

Close to Westminster Abbey, is **St Margaret's Church,** which is used by members of the House of Commons for official services and for high-society weddings. Sir Walter Raleigh (1552–1618), the dashing sea-captain, poet and favourite of Queen Elizabeth I, who established the first British colony in Virginia and introduced tobacco and potatoes to Britain, was buried here after his execution. William Caxton (c.1421–91), who ran the first English printing presses nearby, is also buried here.

ABOVE: fan vaulting in Westminster Abbey.
BELOW: the north side of the Abbey.

The home of British art

Beyond Westminster Abbey and Victoria Gardens a short street leads into one of London's most unobtrusive but notable concert halls, **St John's Smith Square**. This former 18th-century church has fine acoustics and a reputation for classical music, often broadcast on radio. In the crypt is a good wine bar-cum-restaurant.

A 15-minute walk further down Millbank, beyond Lambeth Bridge, is **Tate Britain ⑩**, founded in 1897 by Henry Tate, of the Tate & Lyle sugar empire, and is today the storehouse for the Tate's collection of British art from 1500 to the present day (daily 10am–5.50pm, admission free). It is complemented by Tate Modern, across the river on Bankside, which houses most of the Tate's modern and contemporary international collection *(see page 196).*

Works are shown in a series of thematic displays, with historical and contemporary pieces exhibited side by side. Among the outstanding British paintings are attractive portraits by Thomas Gainsborough (1727–88), evocative views of the English countryside by John Constable (1776–1837) and intensely dramatic and impressionistic seascapes and landscapes by the prolific J.M.W. Turner (1775–1851) which are housed in an extension designed by Sir James Stirling. These are the paintings Turner bequeathed to the nation on his death, with the stipulation that they should all be hung in one place, and should be available for the public to see, without charge. Notable contemporary British artists represented include Howard Hodgkin, Damien Hirst and Mona Hatoum.

The Tate also stages free lectures and film shows, and continues its reputation for avant garde, with the award of an annual Turner Prize: the winning works are invariably pilloried by the popular press.

Map, page 122

ABOVE: August Rodin's *The Kiss*, is one of the Tate's many exhibits; currently it is on display in Tate Modern.

The Catholic cathedral: inspiration among office blocks

The west door of the Westminster Abbey opens on to **Victoria Street**, important commercially but, since its re-building, a long grey canyon of undistinguished office blocks, with the domed building of Methodist Central Hall guarding its opening. Down this street, close to the Victoria Station end, is **Westminster Cathedral ⑪**, the most important Catholic church in London. Its bold red-and-white brickwork makes it look like a gigantic layer cake. Built at the end of the 19th century in an outlandish Italian-Byzantine style not seen elsewhere in London, it has a 330-ft (100-metre) striped tower incorporating a lift for public use (daily Apr–Sep, admsision fee). The views from the gallery at the top are superb. The interior of the cathedral is spacious, sumptuous and impressive. Many of the chapels are enriched with coloured marble cladding on the walls.

On the north side of Queen Victoria Street behind St James's Park Underground station is **Queen Anne's Gate ⑫**, a small, quiet street which has retained much of its 18th-century atmosphere. It's worth a detour to see the original carved door canopies on the elegant terraced houses, although all but one have now been painted over. Lord Palmerston, who became prime minister in 1855, was born at No. 20, in one of the houses overlooking **St James's Park**. This formal arrrangement of lakes and flora is one of the most delightful in London. Formerly the grounds of St James's Palace, it was layed by the great 18th-century landscape gardener "Capability" Brown, but was later wrecked in a peace celebration gala, designed by John Nash, at the end of the Napoleonic Wars in 1814. It has always had a collection of ducks and water fowl, including black swans,

BELOW: Westminster Cathedral.

In spite of her stuffy image, Queen Victoria was a great admirer of the nude. Among studies of both men and women she acquired was a nude Diana she gave Prince Albert as a wedding gift.

and there have long been pelicans in residence here. They are fed every day at 3pm. Another entertainment is the lunchtime concerts played in the bandstand.

Continuing the ornithological theme is **Birdcage Walk**, which takes its name from an 18th-century aviary, running along the south side of the park from Parliament Square to Buckingham Palace and dividing the park from the drilling ground of the **Wellington Barracks** ⓭, the home of the Royal Grenadier Guards and the Coldstream Guards. Here the **Guards' Chapel and Museum** (daily 10am–4pm, entrance fee) are on the site of a former chapel which was hit by a bomb in 1944, killing 121 members of a congregation. There are five of these aristocratic infantry regiments of Guards, first formed during the Civil War, and their commanders-in-chief are members of the royal family.

Home of the Royals

Buckingham Palace ⓮ has been the main London home of the royal family since Queen Victoria moved here in 1837 when she acceded to the throne. Her grandfather, George IV, employed John Nash to enlarge the building which had been built in the 17th century for a Duke of Buckingham. Nash added two wings later enclosed in a quadrangle and its main facade was designed by Aston Webb in 1913. The sumptuous **State Rooms** are open to the public for a few weeks in late summer when the Queen is not in residence (open Aug–Sept, daily until 4.30pm; entrance fee: tickets at Green Park tube from 9am). These include the Dining Room, Music Room, White Drawing Room and Throne Room, where there are paintings by Vermeer, Rubens and Rembrandt. The tour also allows a glimpse of the 40-acre (16-hectare) Palace gardens where the cream of society mingles with the good and the worthy at the celebrated garden parties. The

BELOW: royal garden party guests.

guests are invited because of some worthy contribution made to the nation, but few of the 8,000 people a year get to shake the Queen's hand. In keeping with many events in the London society "season" of high-class social events, these garden parties – which take place, rain or shine – have long been a quaint way of keeping the right sort of young people in each other's company; guests are requested not to bring their married sons and daughters.

The **Queen's Gallery** in Buckingham Palace Road is open daily (9.30am–5pm, entrance fee). The paintings on view change constantly. The Queen has one of the greatest private art collections in the world – including an exceptional collection of Leonardo da Vinci drawings – and the one-room gallery has had changing exhibitions, usually dedicated to single artists, since it opened in 1952, yet some still remain unseen. The adjoining **Royal Mews** contain royal vehicles, from coaches to Rolls-Royces. The Gold State Coach, built for George III in 1762, is still used by the Queen on major state occasions (open 12–4pm Tues–Thur; Oct–Dec 12–4pm Wed; closed Jan–Mar; entrance fee).

Only the invited get further into the 600-room palace, although one enterprising intruder penetrated as far as the Queen's bedroom one night in 1982. She talked to him quietly while managing to summon palace security. The Queen and the Duke of Edinburgh occupy about 12 of the 650 rooms, on the first floor of the north wing, overlooking Green Park. If the Queen is in residence, the royal standard flies from the centre flag-pole. On great occasions the family appears on the first-floor balcony to wave to the crowds outside the gates. Most of the everyday crowds come to see the **Changing of the Guard** at 11.30 every morning (alternate mornings in winter) outside the palace. The New Guard, which marches up from Wellington Barracks, meets the Old Guard in the fore-

BELOW: the royal standard flying over Buckingham Palace shows that the Queen is at home.

court of the palace and they exchange symbolic keys to the accompaniment of regimental music. The Irish Guards are distinctive for their bearskin hats (now made from synthetic materials). Behind the scenes are more sophisticated protection measures: there is a large nuclear shelter underneath the palace.

The **Queen Victoria Memorial** ⓯, in front of the palace, was built in 1901. It encompasses symbolic figures which glorify the achievements of the British Empire and its builders. The **Mall**, the wide throroughfare leading from Buckingham Palace to Trafalgar Square, was laid out by Charles II as a second course for the popular French game of *paille maille*, a kind of croquet, when the one in Pall Mall (*see page 155*) became too rowdy. The Mall is the venue for one of London's great pageants, the autumn **State Opening of Parliament**, when the Queen rides in a gold stage coach surrounded by more than 100 troopers of the Household Cavalry wearing armorial breastplates. A further eccentricity are the two farriers who accompany the procession, bearing spiked axes to kill any horse that is lamed in the parade and chop off its hooves to prove the horse flesh has not been sold to a butcher.

Palatial buildings on The Mall

The Mall is lined with a succession of grand buildings and historic houses reflecting different styles and periods. The ducal palaces have been used as royal residences: **Clarence House** ⓰ is home to the Queen Mother; at **Lancaster House** Chopin gave a recital for Queen Victoria; and **Marlborough House** ⓱, designed by Sir Christopher Wren, was the home of Queen Mary, consort of George V (1865–1936), until her death in 1953. Now it is a Commonwealth conference and research centre. The brick Tudor **St James's Palace**, which faces on to Pall Mall was the home of Henry VIII and is now used by Prince Charles and by palace and government officials. Beyond it are the two white-painted classical facades of **Carlton House Terrace**, built by John Nash, who was responsible for many of the grander parts of central London.

BELOW: footman to Her Majesty. **RIGHT:** the main entrance to Westminster Abbey.

At the Trafalgar Square end, the terrace incorporates the **Mall Gallery** and the **Institute of Contemporary Arts** ⓲. The ICA gallery, cinema and theatre resides in the restored Nash House. It has always been on the cutting edge of the avant-garde. On the right are the headquarters of **The Royal Society**, a learned body for the promotion of natural sciences. The oldest society of its kind, it was founded in 1660 by a group of scientists and philosophers in Oxford, and was established in London in 1666. Among its distinguished presidents were Sir Christopher Wren and Sir Isaac Newton. Opposite is an example of wartime architecture. The large reinforced concrete structure on the corner of the park is a bombproof shelter built for the Admiralty, which was nicknamed **the Citadel**, or Lenin's Tomb.

Admiralty Arch, at this eastern end of The Mall, leading on to Trafalgar Square, is only three decades older, but aesthetically is much more pleasing. It is part of the old Admiralty Building which adjoins Whitehall. Traffic passes through the two outer arches: the central arch is opened only for state occasions, letting royalty in and out of the city. ❑

SUN ALLIANCE & LONDON INSURANCE
SPONSORED BY
British Gas
North Thames
FOR A
CLEANER CITY

Enjoy
Coca-Cola
Coke
McDonald's
Kodak
Carlsberg
WIMPY

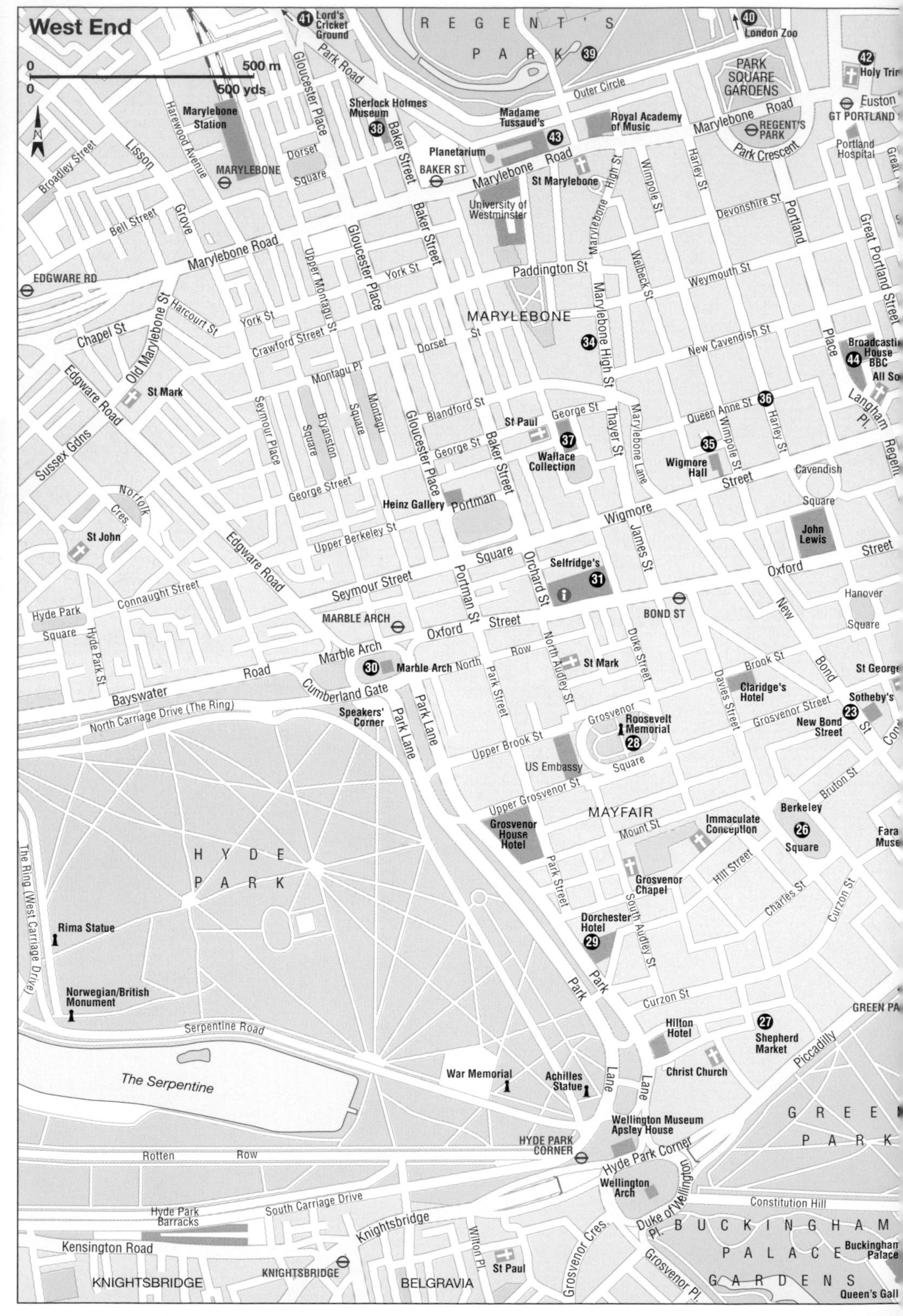
West End
0 500 m
0 500 yds
N
Lord's Cricket Ground
41
REGENT'S PARK
39
40
London Zoo
42
PARK SQUARE GARDENS
Park Road
Gloucester Place
Sherlock Holmes Museum
38
Baker Street
Madame Tussaud's
43
Royal Academy of Music
Outer Circle
Marylebone Road
REGENT'S PARK
Park Crescent
Euston
GT PORTLAND
Portland Hospital
Marylebone Station
MARYLEBONE
Harewood Avenue
Lisson
Broadley Street
Dorset Square
Planetarium
BAKER ST
St Marylebone
University of Westminster
Marylebone High St
Wimpole St
Harley St
Devonshire St
Portland
Great Portland Street
Bell Street
Grove
Marylebone Road
Upper Montagu St
Gloucester Place
York St
Paddington St
Walbeck St
Weymouth St
EDGWARE RD
Harcourt St
Old Marylebone St
Chapel St
York St
Crawford Street
MARYLEBONE
Dorset St
34
Marylebone High St
New Cavendish St
Place
44
BBC
Edgware Road
St Mark
Montagu Pl
Seymour Place
Bryanston Square
Montagu Square
Montagu
Gloucester Place
Blandford St
St Paul
George St
37
Wallace Collection
Thayer St
Marylebone Lane
Queen Anne St
36
35
Wimpole St
Harley St
Langham Pl.
Wigmore Hall
Street
Cavendish Square
Sussex Gdns
Norfolk Cres.
George Street
George St
Baker Street
Heinz Gallery
Portman
Wigmore
St John
Upper Berkeley St
Square
James St
John Lewis
Street
Edgware Road
Orchard St
Selfridge's
31
Oxford
Connaught Street
Seymour Street
Portman St
BOND ST
New
Hanover Square
Hyde Park Square
Hyde Park St
MARBLE ARCH
Oxford
Street
Marble Arch
30
Marble Arch
North Row
North Audley St
St Mark
Duke Street
Brook St
Bond
St George
Road
Bayswater
Cumberland Gate
Park Street
Davies Street
Claridge's Hotel
Sotheby's
North Carriage Drive (The Ring)
Speakers' Corner
Park Lane
Park Lane
Grosvenor
Roosevelt Memorial
28
Grosvenor Street
New Bond Street
23
St
Upper Brook St
US Embassy
Square
Bruton St
Upper Grosvenor St
MAYFAIR
Grosvenor House Hotel
Mount St
Immaculate Conception
Berkeley
26
Square
HYDE PARK
The Ring (West Carriage Drive)
Park Street
Grosvenor Chapel
South Audley St
Hill Street
Charles St
Curzon St
Rima Statue
Dorchester Hotel
29
Park
Norwegian/British Monument
Curzon St
Serpentine Road
Hilton Hotel
27
Shepherd Market
Piccadilly
The Serpentine
War Memorial
Achilles Statue
Lane
Lane
Christ Church
GREEN PARK
Wellington Museum Apsley House
HYDE PARK CORNER
Rotten Row
Hyde Park Corner
Wellington Arch
Duke of Wellington Pl.
Constitution Hill
Hyde Park Barracks
South Carriage Drive
Knightsbridge
Wilton Pl.
Grosvenor Cres.
BUCKINGHAM PALACE GARDENS
Kensington Road
St Paul
Grosvenor Pl.
KNIGHTSBRIDGE
KNIGHTSBRIDGE
BELGRAVIA

British Library
Euston Centre
WARREN ST
University College Hospital
University College
Percival David Foundation of Chinese Art
49
Thomas Coram Foundation
50
CORAM FIELDS
Brunswick Sq.
Gower Street
Gordon Sq.
Woburn Pl.
Bedford Way
Tottenham
University St
Fitzroy Square
Maple St
Torrington Pl.
RADA
University of London
Russell
RUSSELL SQ.
RUSSELL SQUARE GARDENS
Bernard St
Guilford Street
Gt Ormond St Hospital for Sick Children
Great Ormond St
Milman St
Dickens House
Gray's Inn Road
John St
Telecom Tower
45
American Ch. in London
Senate House
48
Square
Southampton
St George the Martyr
Theobald's Road
Cleveland St
GOODGE ST
Court
Store St
BLOOMSBURY
Bedford Row
Jockey's Fields
St Charles
Pollock's Toy Museum
Goodge St
Bedford Square
Bloomsbury
46
British Museum
Great Russell Street
Bloomsbury Square
Vernon Pl.
D. Procter St
Red Lion St
Middlesex Hospital
Street
HOLBORN
Holborn
High
Row
Road
St George
47
Bloomsbury Way
HOLBORN
Mortimer
Berners
Newman St
Charlotte St
Great Russell Street
St
Lincoln's Inn
Great Titchfield St
TOTTENHAM COURT RD
New Oxford St
Sir John Soane's Museum
Eastcastle St
St
Street
High Holborn
Drury Lane
LINCOLN'S INN FIELDS
Oxford
Charing
St Giles
High St
Kingsway
Soho Square
3
St Barnabus
Endell
Great Queen St
Old Curiosity Shop
OXFORD CIRCUS
Palladium Theatre
Noel St
Phoenix Theatre
Shaftesbury Avenue
Cross
Neal St
London School of Economics
Royal Courts of Justice
Great Marlborough St
Berwick Street Market
5
Frith St
Greek St
Monmouth St
St
Drury Lane
Liberty
32
Wardour St
Dean St
Road
Acre
Bow St
Theatre Royal
Aldwych Theatre
St Clement Danes
Broadwick St
Berwick St
Old Compton St
4
COVENT GDN
13
Royal Opera House
Theatre Museum
Bush House
Carnaby Street
Hamleys
SOHO
Peak St
Avenue
Charing
Photographers' Gallery
14
Long
Floral St
COVENT
London Transport Museum
Aldwych
St Mary le Strand
Regent
Gerrard St
6
Chinatown
Cross
St Martin's
Acre
12
The Market
St Paul
GARDEN
Courtauld Institute
King's College
Shaftesbury
LEICESTER SQ.
Garrick St
Somerset House
Savile Row
Brewer St
London Pavilion-Rock Circus
2
Trocadero Centre
7
Leicester Sq.
London Coliseum
Bedford St
Adelphi Theatre
Strand
The Savoy
11
Gilbert Collection
Lancaster Pl
25
33
Cafe Royal
Road
Lane
Street
Piccadilly Circus
1
Eros
Haymarket
Orange St
National Portrait Gallery
William IV St
Embankment
Waterloo Bridge
Museum of Mankind
21
Royal Academy of Arts
PICCADILLY CIRCUS
Regent St
National Gallery
9
St Martin-in-the-Fields
VICTORIA EMBANKMENT GARDENS
Burlington Arcade
Old Bond St
Piccadilly
St James
20
Jermyn St
22
Theatre Royal
Trafalgar
8
Square
CHARING CROSS
Villiers St
10
Victoria
Fortnum & Mason's
Waterloo
Her Majesty's Theatre
Nelson's Column
Charing Cross Station
National Film Theatre
James Street
19
St James's
18
Square
ST JAMES'S
Place
Charles I
EMBANKMENT
Northumberland Ave
Queen Elizabeth Hall
The Ritz
St James's St
King St
Pall
15
Mall
Admiralty Arch
Whitehall Theatre
Duke of York Column
ICA
The Admiralty
Hispaniola
Royal Festival Hall
Waterloo Rd
Hayward Gallery
Chapel Royal
16
Carlton House Terrace
Whitehall
Old War Office
Tattershall Castle
Marlborough House
Mall
Green Park
St James's Palace
17
Guards Memorial
Horse Guards Parade
Banqueting House
Embankment
Thames
London Eye
Ministry of Defence
The
Clarence House
JUBILEE GARDENS
Road
Lancaster House
Horse Guards Road
Downing St
Cenotaph
London Aquarium
Foreign Office
Waterloo Station
ST JAMES'S PARK
York
Queen Victoria Memorial
Cabinet War Rooms
Victoria
County Hall
Treasury
Parliament St
WESTMINSTER
Gt George St
Parliament
Westminster Bridge
Birdcage Walk
Guards' Chapel & Museum
Big Ben
Florence Nightingale Museum
WESTMINSTER
Central Hall
Square
Houses of Parliament

THE WEST END

Piccadilly, Soho, Leicester Square and Covent Garden are the good-time parts of town, where people come to be entertained, to eat, drink and be sociable round the clock

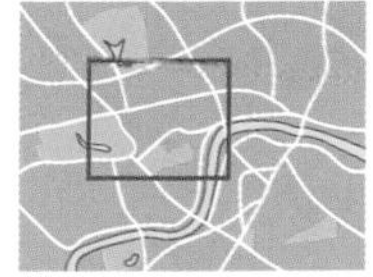

The West End is the entertainment centre of the capital where the lights are brightest, the crowds cheeriest, and the pubs and bars and restaurants buzz till late at night. At its heart is **Piccadilly Circus ❶**, where the first illuminated signs appeared in 1890. A few years later the statue of Eros, Greek god of love, was erected as the Angel of Charity in honour of the philanthropic Seventh Earl of Shaftesbury (1801–85) who drove the broad thoroughfare which bears his name through the squalid slums that had grown up to the northeast.

Adding to Piccadilly's bright lights are the refurbished Criterion theatre on the south side, and a former music hall, the London Pavilion, on the east. This now contains the **Rock Circus**, where you can see a variety of not especially lifelike pop stars in waxwork, and hear their songs (11am–9pm Mon, Wed, Thu, Sun, Fri; 11am–10pm Sat; 12am–9pm Tues; admission fee). Just beyond it is the **Trocadero Centre ❷**, a massive shopping arcade with glass walkways, potted plants, waterfalls, cinemas and cafés, in contrast to its Georgian facade. Its attractions include the seven-storey **Segaworld**, billed as the world's biggest hi-tech indoor entertainment theme park (10am–midnight weekdays, 10am–1am weekends). Planet Hollywood, the trendy American burger restaurant, is on the corner and, on the next block, the super-models' business venture, the Fashion Café.

PRECEDING PAGES: Piccadilly Circus.
LEFT: souvenir badges, brollies, scarves and ties.
BELOW: two girls in a fountain, Trafalgar Square.

Bustling Soho

On the north side of Shaftesbury Avenue lies **Soho**. which has always been popular with immigrants. Flemish weavers, French Huguenots, Greeks, Italians, Belgians, Maltese, Swiss, Chinese and Russian Jews have sought refuge here. Their influence is still felt in the patisseries, delicatessens, restaurants and shops. Four hundred years ago Soho was an area of open fields, and its name is said to come from a hunting cry: "So-ho, so-ho!". **Soho Square ❸** was one of London's best addresses when it was built in the 17th century. In its centre are a statue of Charles II and an elaborate 19th-century mock Tudor gardeners' toolshed from which steps lead down to a vast underground cavern, used as a workshop during the war and still waiting to be put to good use. A hint of the square's former glory can be seen in the 18th-century house of charitable works, caring for the destitute, **St-Barnabas-in-Soho,** on the corner of Greek Street. Its elegant interior has fine wood carvings, fireplaces and plasterwork (open Wed 2.30–4.30pm, Thur 11am–12.30pm).

As the rich moved further west, to Mayfair, Belgravia and Kensington, Soho became fashionable with artists and writers. In the 1950s and early 1960s its coffee bars and jazz clubs made it London's bohemian heart. A host of historic characters has therefore been associated with the area, from the painters Thomas Gainsborough

ABOVE: Soho resident Karl Marx wrote his best-known work above an Italian restaurant.

(1727–88) to Francis Bacon (1909–92), from Casanova (1725–98) to Oscar Wilde (1854–1900). The restaurant at 41 Beak Street was the home of Antonio Canaletto, the Venetian painter, from 1749 to 1751. In 1926 John Logie Baird, the Scottish inventor, transmitted the first flickering television images in the attic of a house, at 22 Frith Street, next door to the house where Mozart stayed as a boy. The house at 26 Dean Street where Karl Marx wrote *Das Kapital* between 1851 and 1856 is now a smart restaurant furnished by the works of the artist Damien Hirst, and no longer called **Leoni's Quo Vadis**. Leoni was the original owner, who ran the restaurant with his family from 1926 (when the film *Quo Vadis* was being shown in Leicester Square) until his death in 1969, and it was he who found a hidden library of Marx's research materials. An outbreak of cholera in the mid-19th century drove out most of Soho's wealthier residents and led to the conditions which spurred Lord Shaftesbury to start his clean-up.

Clubs and clip joints

Soho is where the nightclubs thrive (*see page 142*), and it is also the centre of the sex industry, where all tastes are catered for: "Anything you like, sir" is a phrase still murmured to passers-by. Madame Jo-Jo's for drag artists and transvestites in Brewer Street is just a few yards from Raymond's Revuebar, a nude stage show in Rupert Street that has been running so long it has almost become respectable. At the seedier end of the scale, the notorious "clip joints" might serve a bottle of "Champagne" for £100 and girls may be available for extra-curricular activities, but tourists often end up with empty wallets and not much pleasure had. In the 1980s local residents successfully campaigned to close down many of the sex shops and strip clubs, but they have by no means gone away.

BELOW: West End al fresco.

These days the immoral high-ground has been hi-jacked by gay males, who are much in evidence, and many bars and pubs are now almost exclusively their preserve: one example is the Compton Arms, in **Old Compton Street** ❹. This is Soho's main artery, where a few of the celebrated continental food stores, cafés and specialist shops which once dominated the street, live on. Most have been replaced by modern cafés and more outlandish establishments, such as the body piercing shop.

Wheeler's still dispenses a mean oyster at No. 19, the Café Bohème at No. 13 attracts a younger crowd and the Hungarian Pâtisserie Valerie at No. 44 is the best place to stop for coffee and a cake. Just off Old Compton Street are the French House in Dean Street, centre of the Free French in World War II, an artists' haunt and still fiercely French. At 22 Frith Street, opposite Ronnie Scott's jazz club, is Bar Italia, which serves the best cappuccino in town, while Maison Bertaux at 26 Greek Street, though an excellent coffee house, refuses to serve cappuccino at all.

At the west end of Compton Street is **Wardour Street,** once known as the only street in the world which was shady on both sides. It is still the heart of London's film, advertising and recording industries. Film processing laboratories are open around the clock. A tower is all that remains of Sir Christopher Wren's church of **St Anne's**, bombed in the war, though its gardens are a shady spot. The fruit and vegetable market in parallel **Berwick Street Market** ❺ is well laid out and inexpensive. The traders represent the most dense concentration of cockneys in central London apart from the taxi cafés. Still set in the past, they will frequently refer to "ten-bob notes" (50p) or two-bob bits (10p), and their language is pretty raw.

The best place to watch international football matches is the Bar Italia in Frith Street. The giant screen at the back of the bar is visible from the street.

BELOW: The biggest cinemas are located in Leicester Square.

A Night on the Town

Ah, London! London! our delight,
Great flower that opens but at night.
— Richard Le Gallienne, French poet

The make-up of any major city seems to change at night as offices empty into pubs and trains drain the centre of workers and replace them with players. The West End, a shopping and office centre by day, is the heart of London at night. Soho is still the most fashionable area, and is still the sex centre of London, although smut is on the retreat. Some of the best food and the trendiest clubs are here, including Ronnie Scott's jazz club in Frith Street. Other gathering spots for swingers include Kettners in Romilly Street and the Soho Brasserie in Old Compton Street. These are "gathering spots" because many of the Champagne drinkers go on to a nightclub such as Stringfellow's in Upper St Martin's Lane. London's hippest clubs have all-powerful doorpersons who act as arbiters of taste, letting in those faces and fashions that fit, and excluding those who don't, irrespective of their wallet's weight.

The most successful and biggest discos in town are The Hippodrome (Cranbourne Street), The Limelight (Shaftesbury Avenue), the Wag Club in Wardour Street and the famous gay disco Heaven (Villiers Street).

Londoners get a buzz from being in the company of the countless nationalities that throng Leicester Square, Piccadilly, Trafalgar Square, Covent Garden and the Trocadero Centre. These are the best-known central areas for evening promenading and, for an entrance fee of a few pounds, drinking can continue past the 11pm pub closing time at such places as Burlington Bertie's in Shaftesbury Avenue. Although London may not seem to offer a conducive climate, 84 percent of all overseas visitors describe their evening activities as "just walking around".

Further afield, King's Road in Chelsea, Notting Hill and Westbourne Grove, Camden and Islington can be lively in the evenings. More off-beat places, such as around the former market at Spitalfields and among trendy clubs in Hoxton Square, come in and out of fashion. Others might look for the ethnic: Indian in Brick Lane, or the Spanish bars north of Oxford Street, or the latest sushi gimmicks – Yo! Sushi in Poland Street has robot service and claims to have the longest conveyor food belt in the world. Or they might want to skip to another continent at the Rainforest Cafe in the Trocadero Centre, where a suitably steamy ambience has been created.

The South Bank complex (on the southern end of Waterloo Bridge) may not be appealing to the eye, but it does offer an impressive range of cultural choice from concerts through theatre to film, and some of the best views of central London can be had from the banks of the river. On the concrete promenade of the Jubilee Walkway on a summer's evening, busking jazz saxophonists make the place feel just a little like New York.

For a glamorously old-fashioned evening, head for Mayfair and St James's. Here you'll find discreet restaurants and exclusive nightclubs such as Annabel's in Berkeley Square, appealing to an older, sophisticated crowd who don't need to ask the price. ❑

LEFT: Soho nights: Raymond's classic Revuebar.

Chinatown

On the south side of Shaftesbury Avenue are **Gerrard Street** and parallel **Lisle Street**, home of Chinese grocers, restaurants and stores. Kitsch Chinese street furniture, lamps and archways in Gerrard Street make this the heart of **Chinatown** ❻. The oriental cuisine here is the best in town, and there are many inexpensive restaurants. There are also herbal and medicine shops. On Sundays, a family restaurant-outing day for the city's Chinese, there is a market of exotic foods. Chinese New Year in late January or early February is celebrated in style.

Map, page 136

Cinema centre

Leicester Square ❼, home of the big cinemas, has taken over from nearby Piccadilly Circus as the West End's glittering entertainment centre. Before the 17th century, this was the garden of Leicester House and at the four corners of the garden are busts of famous people associated with the square.

At the centre is the Shakespeare monument (1874), surrounded by brass plates in the ground giving distances to cities all over the world. Facing the bard is a statue by John Doubleday of Charlie Chaplin, born in Lambeth, south London, in 1889. Around the square is a regular contingent of caricature artists, buskers, Bible-thumpers and, on special occasions, a funfair roundabout and amusement rides. Every hour people gather outside the **Swiss Centre**, on the northwest corner of the square, to see the folkloric figurative clock chime.

ABOVE: Chinese New Year celebrations.
BELOW: Chinatown offers a spectrum of Chinese cooking.

Hero of Trafalgar Square

In 1805 the British fleet under Admiral Lord Nelson secured a decisive victory against Napoleon's navy at the Battle of Trafalgar off the Atlantic coast of Spain,

Taller in death than in life: the statue is 12ft (3.6m) high, but Nelson was less than half this height at 5ft 6 inches (1.5m).

establishing Britain as ruler of the waves. Nelson was fatally wounded in the encounter, and in 1842 was remembered in the building of **Trafalgar Square** ❽, designed by John Nash. This monumental space vividly reflects Britain at the height of its power, when its navy was invincible and it ruled more than a quarter of the planet. At the centre of the square is the 167-ft (50-metre) Corinthian column and 12-ft (3.6-metre) statue of Horatio Nelson, battle-scarred with only one arm but without a patch on his blind eye. The four handsome lions (1847) are by Edwin Landseer and around the square Canada House, South Africa House and Uganda House are memories of distant Empire days.

The square has long been the site of public gatherings, political demonstrations and New Year celebrations, when the roads all around are locked solid with traffic. The capital's pigeons, a mangy crew spoilt by tourists, have little respect for such magnificence. More than half a ton of pigeon droppings was removed from Nelson's Column in the last clean-up.

There are oddities in the square. The round stone lamp-post on the southeast corner is actually the smallest police station in England. Its lamp is said to have come from Nelson's flagship, *HMS Victory*. There is also a rumour that the French crown jewels are buried beneath the square, placed there by Madame du Barry, mistress of Louis XV, when the site was part of the old royal mews. Every Christmas a 70-ft (20-metre) Norwegian spruce is erected in the square, a gift from the city of Oslo in recognition of the protection given to members of the Norwegian royal family in World War II.

BELOW: Landseer's lions guard Nelson's Column.

Overlooking the square on the north side is the imposing neo-classical facade of the **National Gallery**, designed by William Wilkins in 1838 with an additional modern wing by Robert Venturi completed in 1991. This is the country's most important art gallery and is home to works of the great British and European artists such as Gainsborough, Rembrandt, Rubens, El Greco, Vermeer and Van Gogh (open 10am–6pm, Wed 10am–8pm, Sun noon–6pm; free; *see page 150*).

The **National Portrait Gallery**, in St Martin's Place behind the National Gallery, has a collection of the nation's illustrious men and women by the nation's illustrious artists and photographers. Some intriguing portraits include the only known portrait of Shakespeare painted while he was alive. Top photographic exhibitions are also held here.

Across the road is the church of **St Martin-in-the-Fields** ❾, the oldest building in Trafalgar Square, built in 1724 by a Scottish architect, James Gibbs, when this venue was literally in fields outside the city. Nell Gwynne, mistress of Charles II, is one of several famous people buried in this parish church of the royal family, which was so fashionable in the 18th century that pews were rented out on an annual basis. The royal box is on the left of the altar. The crypts, which house a soup kitchen for the homeless and a café which serves one of the best cups of coffee in London, were a useful air raid shelter in the bombing blitz of World War II.

In the opposite, southwest corner of the square, **Admiralty Arch** marks the start of The Mall, leading to Buckingham Palace (*see page 130*).

As English as tea and roast beef

The mundane architecture of modern buildings in the Strand, the main thoroughfare connecting the West End with the City, cannot hide the fact that it was once one of the most fashionable streets in London. Here you can dine on roast beef at Simpson's, opened in 1848, or take tea in the Thames Room of the Savoy.

Map, page 136

TIP

Look out for posters advertising candle-lit concerts at St Martin-in-the-Fields, one of the most atmospheric concert venues in London. Lunchtime concerts are free.

HORATIO NELSON

Horatio Nelson (1758–1805) is Britain's greatest naval hero. He was a dashing commander and his "Nelson touch" brought such startling victories that the Admiralty forgave his frequent disobedience. His defeat of the Napoleonic Fleet left Britain to rule the high seas for more 100 years. A diminutive figure, he was partially blinded in his right eye at Calvi in Corsica, had his right arm amputated at Santa Cruz and was pacing the deck of HMS Victory in full uniform, medals gleaming like targets, when fatally shot by a French sharpshooter during an engagement off Cape Trafalgar. He often overstepped the mark, famously putting a telescope to his blind eye at the Batlle of Copenhagen and pretending he could not read an order to disengage from battle. In Italy he helped the Bourbon king and queen escape revolutionaries, whom he hanged from his ship, contrary to assurances he had given. The nation showered honours on him but his reputation suffered after his death when the extent of his friendship with Emma Hamilton, wife of the British Ambassador to Naples, became public knowledge. The three had lived in a *ménage à trois* and she bore him a child, Horatia.

BELOW: pigeons love visitors to Trafalgar Square.

Outside Charing Cross station is a 19th-century replica of the last of 12 crosses set up by Edward I in 1291 to mark the stages in the funeral procession of his queen, Eleanor of Castile, from Nottinghamshire to Westminster Abbey. It was originally sited where the statue of Charles I stands at the top of Whitehall, but was torn down in the Civil War. "Charing" is from "*chère reine*" – dear queen – Eleanor.

Gilbert and Sullivan operas, famous for their complex and funny lyrics are quintessentially British. The Savoy Theatre was built in 1881 to stage the first of their operas, and their profits built the hotel.

In Tudor and Stuart times, the Strand was bordered by the mansions of the aristocracy whose gardens flowed down to the Thames. The restored **Water Gate** in **Victoria Embankment Gardens** ❿ next door to the Embankment Underground station, once marked the river entrance to **York House**, London home of the archbishops of York, birthplace of the philosopher and statesman Francis Bacon (1561–1626) and home of the dukes of Buckingham.

Benjamin Franklin made his home in Craven Street and, for a while, Rudyard Kipling, the Nobel laureate and author of *The Jungle Book*, lived in Villiers Street, where the old **Players' Theatre** music hall ran under the railway arches for more than 40 years. Above it, **Charing Cross railway station** was imaginatively rebuilt in 1991 by the architect Terry Farrell; it incorporates offices and is a new landmark on the river.

The **Adelphi Theatre** in the Strand was opened in the early 19th century and it was quickly followed by others. Richard D'Oyly Carte (1844–1901), sponsor of Gilbert and Sullivan operas at the **Savoy Theatre**, also financed the building of the **Savoy Hotel** ⓫, which opened in 1889 as one of the first in London with private bathrooms, electric lights and lifts (elevators). From the Strand, the Savoy is visually unassertive, but it is grand enough to have its own private forecourt, which is the only road in Britain where traffic has to drive on the right.

BELOW: the Savoy Hotel, where traffic drives on the right.

Map, page 136

Past the silver Art Deco front of the rebuilt theatre, through the revolving doors and into the vast foyer, another world unfolds in the huge lounge that overlooks the private gardens and the river.

D'Oyly Carte is commemorated in a stained-glass window in the **Queen's Chapel** of the Savoy, behind the hotel (open for services). It was founded in the 16th century when the former Savoy Palace had became a hospital. Built by Peter, 9th Count of Savoy, in 1246, the palace had its heyday under John of Gaunt (1340–99), when it was "the fayrest manor in Europe, big enough for a large part of an army". It was burnt down in the 1381 Peasants' Revolt.

Covent Garden

Named after a convent whose fields occupied the site, **Covent Garden** ⓬ was for centuries the principal market in London for vegetables, fruit and flowers, and the workplace of Eliza Doolittle, the flower girl in George Bernard Shaw's *Pygmalion* who later burst into song as *My Fair Lady*. The market moved out in 1974 and, since the early 1980s, the area has seen a transformation that has become a blueprint for turning old commercial buildings into a mall of shops and stalls. Numerous restaurants and cafés, shops and showrooms occupy the old warehouses in the narrow streets and alleyways surrounding the market square. There is a good line in street entertainers who are part of the establishment. Would-be performers undergo rigorous auditions, keeping the standards high.

Many of the streets around Covent Garden have been cordoned off with pedestrian pathways. Cute gift stores and card and poster shops proliferate. **Neal's Yard**, at Earlham Street, with an apothecary and bakery and natural food shops,

BELOW: a modern Eliza Doolittle and a Covent Garden musician.

In his 17th-century diary, Samuel Pepys recorded details of the first Punch and Judy show, which was held in Covent Garden's market square.

is gathered around a tiny square full of potted trees. There are many designer shops around here, and it's a good place to buy a hat.

The main piazza was originally laid out with colonnaded town houses designed by Inigo Jones around 1630, and inspired by the 16th-century Italian architect Andrea Palladio. A small market was established as early as 1661. The terraces and arcades have long since disappeared, although the arcade on the north side, where the **Rock Garden** dispenses equal helpings of American-style hamburgers and live rock music, has been recast.

The portico of **St Paul's**, the actors' church, used as a backdrop in *My Fair Lady* and also designed by Inigo Jones, dominates the western end of the square, on to which it turns its back. The vaults and grounds of this church are said to contain the remains of more famous people than any other church except Westminster Abbey, although the headstones have long been removed. An annual clowns' service is held here.

The old flower market, in the southeastern corner of the square, is now home to the **London Transport Museum,** which has a big collection of horse-drawn coaches, buses, trams, trains, rail carriages, and some working displays (open daily 10am–6pm, entrance fee). Next door to the London Transport Museum, but entered from Russell Street, is the **Theatre Museum**, which contains portraits, costumes, stage sets and much memorabilia (11am-5pm, closed Mon, admission fee).

Neighbouring **Drury Lane** is closely linked with the theatre. Its principal venue is the Theatre Royal; when it opened in 1663, it was only the second legitimate playhouse in the city. Charles II's mistress, Nell Gwynne, depicted by cartoonists and comediennes as a voluptuous orange seller, trod the boards here. It

BELOW: market performers: auditions are tough.

has an imposing facade and its stage is large enough to mount such blockbusters as *Miss Saigon* and *The Witches of Eastwick.*

In 1733, another theatre was established in the northeast corner of Covent Garden, on the site now occupied by the **Royal Opera House** ⓭. The 2,098-seat building was closed down in 1997 for a two-year refurbishment *(see below)*. The fire which destroyed the first building in 1808 consumed Handel's organ and a large number of his works. The highest priced venue in London, the Opera House has had to contend with unimpressed audiences: price riots were common in the 19th century, and in 1809 lasted 61 nights.

Opposite its white Corinthian portico is **Bow Street police station**, home in the 18th century of the scarlet-waistcoated Bow Street Runners, the prototype policemen. On the corner is the courthouse where Henry Fielding, the novelist, wrote part of *Tom Jones* (1749) while serving as a magistrate.

Long Acre runs through the middle of Covent Garden, to the north of the Piazza. Britain's best map and travel bookshop, **Stanford's**, is at No. 12–14. Leading off are Earlham Street and Neal Street, full of specialist shops and the most exciting of the old market streets. Long Acre leads to St Martin's Lane, home of Stringfellows nightclub (lap dancing a speciality) and the English National Opera's London Coliseum, where productions are in English. Opposite Long Acre is Monmouth Street and the **Photographers' Gallery** ⓮, which has regular exhibitions. Monmouth Street leads to **Charing Cross Road**, a centre for rare and second-hand books. London's largest bookshop, **Foyle's**, is a perplexing maze of more than 4 million volumes. **Zwemmer's** is known for its fine art and photography books. Music shops and publishers cluster around Denmark Street, known as **Tin Pan Alley**, a home of early British rock 'n' roll. ❑

Map, page 136

ABOVE: Bow Street Runners, or Peelers.
BELOW: the Royal Opera House.

THE ROYAL OPERA HOUSE

Just in time to mark the millennium, the Royal Opera House opened its doors in December 1999 after a £120 million refurbishment that had closed it for 18 months. Before the renovations, the politics behind the beautiful facade in Covent Garden had been vicious and the back-stage facilities cramped. After the reopening, the politics seemed a little more benign and singers, dancers and musicians all had more space in which to rehearse and prepare for performances. Audiences at last benefited from air conditioning. A fly tower had been added and the stage machinery was much more modern.

On the outside, Inigo Jones's piazza was completed, with colonnades running all the way round this corner of the piazza. Beneath them were two new shopping arcades and a new entrance from the market square. For the first time the Royal Ballet Company now has a base at the Opera House, with six ballet studios and a performance studio which seats 200. A further performance space, a 400-seat Studio Theatre, enables the two companies to give around 100 performances here a year.

An effort was made to provide a greater number of less expensive tickets, but administrators continued to complain that opera in London in grossly underfunded.

THE NATIONAL GALLERY

Dominating Trafalgar Square is one of the world's finest art collections, with masterpieces from the late 13th century to the end of the 19th century

The National Gallery is one of the most accessible of London institutions – and always has been. When Parliament voted in 1824 to help found the museum by buying an important collection of Old Masters, it insisted that the new gallery be open to children – otherwise, the poor, who had no nannies, would find it difficult to pay a visit. During World War II, most of the 2,000 works of art were removed for safekeeping, but the gallery played an important role in boosting Londoners' morale by staging free concerts. Today the National Gallery continues to resist any admission charges.

In the 1980s, controversy came to the gallery from an unexpected source: Prince Charles condemned the modernist architecture of the planned Sainsbury Wing. A more harmonious design was eventually chosen. The new wing is home to a splendid innovation, though: the interactive Microgallery, which provides detailed art historical information at the press of a button.

VIRGIN OF THE ROCKS ▷
The new Sainsbury Wing is an excellent backdrop to the gallery's earliest paintings. Leonardo's unconventional treatment of the Holy Family dates from around 1508.

▽ THE AMBASSADORS
The distorted skull in the foreground of Hans Holbein's two sophisticated Frenchmen is part of the painting's allegory of faith and mortality. Holbein was court painter to Henry VIII from 1536.

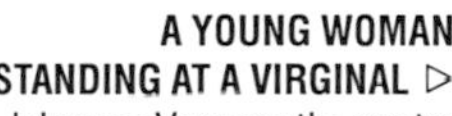

▽ THE CORONATION OF THE VIRGIN
The Gallery's collection of Florentine art is especially strong. This enormous altarpiece by Jacopo di Cione, from 1370, shows the Virgin surrounded by adoring saints.

A YOUNG WOMAN STANDING AT A VIRGINAL ▷
Johannes Vermeer, the master of Delft, painted fewer than 40 pictures. Most are infused with the stillness and extraordinary light of this woman playing a harpsichord.

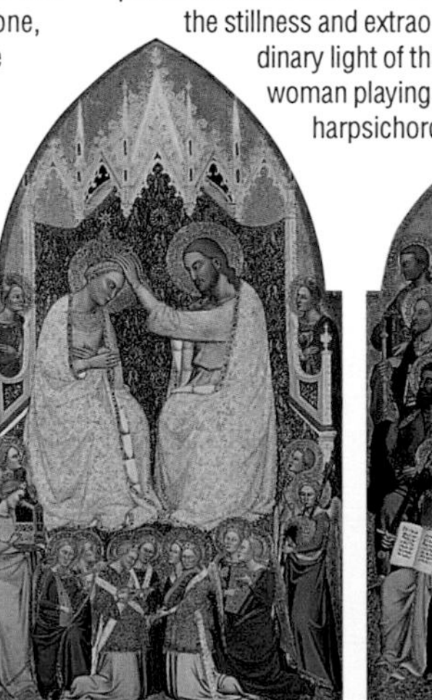

THE NATIONAL PORTRAIT GALLERY

Just around the corner from the National Gallery, in St Martin's Place, is a visual Who's Who of Great Britain: the National Portrait Gallery. Here you will find depictions of the country's most interesting rulers, artists, performers and writers, from around 1400 to the present day (the great English cricketer W.G. Grace, by A.J.S. Wortley, is pictured above). The gallery was founded in 1856 by the 5th Earl of Stanhope, a historian, and occupied various premises around London until the present building opened in 1896.

The collection comprises some 10,000 paintings, drawings and sculptures, plus half a million photographs – only a fraction of which is on display at any one time. Works are arranged chronologically, starting at the top of the building with Holbein's large drawing of Henry VIII, and other Tudor portraits.

Although you may feel that the quality of the art doesn't match the importance of the subject, the collection has some rarities, such as the only authentic portraits of William Shakespeare (by John Taylor) and of Jane Austen (by her sister, Cassandra). There are also self-portraits by the artists Gainsborough, Hogarth and Reynolds, and sculpture by Elizabeth Frink and Jacob Epstein.

Londoners come to the Gallery often for special exhibitions, particularly photography.

THE FIGHTING TEMERAIRE ▷
J.M.W. Turner must have stood beside the Thames as this mighty warship, which had served at the Battle of Trafalgar in 1805, was towed to the scrapyard when steamships replaced sailpower in the 1830s. The finely detailed, elegant *Temeraire*, contrasted with the ugly black tug, expresses the melancholy of the passing of an age. Turner, the son of a Covent Garden barber, left several paintings to the Gallery in 1881.

SELFRIDGES

ST JAMES'S TO OXFORD STREET

Map, page 136

Piccadilly divides the west end of the West End in two: St James's is where purveyors of bespoke goods serve royalty; Mayfair is simply synonymous with money

West of Trafalgar Square and Piccadilly Circus is the smartest part of town. This is where a broom cupboard costs as much as a house in the country, where shoes are hand-made and where life is bespoke. The area is divided in two by Piccadilly. To the south of this famous thoroughfare lies St James's, which grew up around the life of the royal court; to the north Mayfair, the most expensive place to land on the English Monopoly board. The second most expensive, Park Lane, bounds it to the west, while Oxford Street, the capital's most famous shopping street, is on its northern side.

PRECEDING PAGES: St James's Park behind Whitehall. **LEFT:** Gordon Selfridge's 1928 Oxford Street store. **BELOW:** chandeliers in a St James's club.

Gentlemen's clubs

St James's is the epitome of aristocratic London. Along elegant **Pall Mall** ⓯ exclusive clubs mingle with the grand homes of royalty, and their lofty book-lined rooms and elegant, picture-lined dining rooms and chandeliered lounges can be seen from the street. The area has been the haunt of men of influence since the 17th century and it is reassuring to learn that, for the most part, the clubs enjoy a reputation for dull food and boring, snobbish company. However, they do usually have excellent wine cellars. Members are known to be among the more reactionary in the country. In 1889, a workers' demonstration moved along Pall Mall and had nailbrushes and shoes thrown at them from the Reform Club.

It is said that bishops and Fellows of the Royal Society join the Athenaeum, the foremost literary club, while actors and publishers opt for the Garrick. Diplomats, politicians and spies prefer Brooks', the Traveller's, Boodles or White's. Journalists, by contrast, gather at the Groucho Club in Soho. The Reform Club in Pall Mall, the leading liberal club, was the setting in Jules Verne's 1873 novel for Phileas Fogg's wager that he could travel around the world in 80 days. The most famous gaming club was Crockford's, a notorious "den" originally in St James's Street, which was founded in 1828 by a fishmonger from Temple Bar.

Almost all of London's clubs are the near-exclusive preserve of men. Their continuing influence in the social, commercial and political life of the capital cannot be underestimated. Dukes join the Turf Club, while top Tories dine together at the Carlton.

In **Waterloo Place**, at the east end of Pall Mall and the bottom end of Regent Street, the bronze statue of Frederick, the "grand old" Duke of York (whose 10,000 men are fruitlessly marched up and down hill in a popular nursery rhyme), overlooks the Mall and St James's Park from its 124-ft (37-metre) column. The duke cannot

Although St James's has not been a monarch's residence for more than 150 years, foreign ambassadors are still known as "Ambassadors to the Court of St James's".

BELOW: purveyors of traditional style in Old Bond Street.

have been a popular commander: the cost of his monument was met by extracting a day's wages from every man in the armed services. His statue was placed at such a height, it was said, in order that he might avoid his creditors.

Royal terrace

Running in both directions from either side of the Duke of York's Steps is the Georgian opulence of **Carlton House Terrace** ⓰, once the home of the aristocracy and now mainly of government departments. Backing on to The Mall (*see page 132*), it was designed by John Nash and is on the site of Carlton House, the former residence of George IV (1672–1730). Nash was also responsible for the grand plan to connect the royal home to the Prince Regent's new property north of Marylebone Road. This produced the broad sweep of Regent Street. Prime minister William Gladstone (1809–98) lived in a house on the left of Carlton House Terrace from 1856 until 1875.

One building that is unmistakable in Pall Mall is the red-brick **St James's Palace** ⓱ at the western end, built by Henry VIII in 1540 in a style that echoes his palace at Hampton Court. It was, however, never popular with the royals who preferred the grander palace at Whitehall, before it burnt down in 1698. Little remains of the original Tudor palace, which was built on the site of the leper hospital of St James the Less. The state apartments are not open to the public and the chief relic, the **Gatehouse** or **Clock Tower**, one of the finest piece of Tudor architecture in the city, is best viewed from the street.

Henry Jermyn, first Earl of St Alban, laid out the fashionable area around **St James's Square** ⓲ in about 1660. The Dukes of Norfolk had a town house in the square from 1723 until 1938. The same building was used by General Eisenhower when he was preparing to launch the invasions of North Africa and northwest Europe in World War II.

The traditional frontages on **St James's Street** ⓳ includes **Berry Bros and Rudd**, at No. 3, which looks as if it is straight out of a Dickens novel. **James Lock and Co**, at No. 6, is the birthplace of the bowler hat. A few doors up is **Lobb's** who shod the feet of Queen Victoria, among a host of others. A record is permanently stored of every customer's foot.

Jermyn Street ⓴ is another street of fashionable shops, restaurants and hotels and clubs. At its eastern end is the **Haymarket**, running south from Piccadilly Circus, which is home of Burberry's, makers of the beige overcoats that Americans adore, the **Theatre Royal** and **Her Majesty's** (haunted for years by Andrew Lloyd Webber's *Phantom of the Opera*). London's oldest enclosed shopping arcade, Nash's **Royal Opera Arcade,** was once a part of Her Majesty's Theatre until it burnt down and was transferred across the road.

Piccadilly's shops

Court fops and dandies were a source of money-making for London's traders. In the 18th century Robert Baker grew rich by selling them "pickadils", fashionable stiff collars; on the strength of this enterprise he built a mansion on what was then Portugal Street. It became known as **Piccadilly**, and it remains a fashionable street and a favourite location for airline and national tourist offices.

Behind the imposing Renaissance-style facade of **Burlington House** on the north side, there is a handsome courtyard and the **Royal Academy of Arts** ㉑. The Academy stages big, thematic exhibitions all year round and is famous for its Summer Exhibition of both members' and non-members' work. The fun of

Map, page 136

"The parallelogram between Oxford Street, Piccadilly, Regent Street and Hyde Park encloses more intelligence and human ability, to say nothing of wealth and beauty, than the world has ever collected in such a space before."

– SYDNEY SMITH, 1855

BELOW: Beadle and shoppers in Burlington Arcade.

this massive assemblage of paintings is that it ranges from the sublime to the risible; it has even included work by the Prince of Wales.

The **Burlington Arcade** beside the Academy was built in 1819. This Regency promenade of Lilliputian shops, is patrolled by Beadles. In their top-hats and livery, these former soldiers of the 10th Hussars ensure good behaviour, with "no undue whistling, humming or hurrying". Only a Beadle knows what constitutes undue humming. Almost opposite is the **Piccadilly Arcade,** best known for its glass and china ware. The graceful, bow-fronted Regency windows belie the fact that it was built in 1910.

At No. 181 Piccadilly is **Fortnum and Mason's** ㉒, grocers to the Queen and famous for its food hampers and food hall. Shop assistants wear tails. The hourly changing of the guard on the clock face above the shop front is a free attraction.

Further along Piccadilly is **The Ritz**, where afternoon tea in the Palm Court is a tradition and must be booked at least a month in advance (reserved sittings are at 3.30 and 5pm, or join the line at 2pm – no jeans; jacket and tie preferred for men. Tel: 0171-493 8181.) The hotel, built in 1906 as London's first major steel-framed building, was fashionable with London's café society in the 1930s, but lacks the cachet it used to have. In 1995 it was bought for £75 million by the low-profile Barclay brothers, David and Frederick. Its casino, probably the city's classiest, remains popular. The elegant Louis XVI dining room overlooks Green Park.

ABOVE: Fortnum and Mason picnic hamper.
BELOW: tea dancing at the Ritz.

Exclusive Mayfair

The region bounded by Piccadilly and Park Lane, Oxford and Regent Streets, has been synonymous with wealth and power since the early 18th century, when it was first laid out by the Grosvenor family, dukes of Westminster. **Mayfair**

takes its name from the fair which was held annually on the site of what is now Shepherd Market. In the best British tradition, it clings to its exclusivity, although many of the magnificent Georgian homes of business barons and princes of property are now overrun with hotels, apartments, offices, shops and showrooms. The high street of Mayfair is **Bond Street**, divided into Old Bond Street at its southern end leading north to New Bond Street. Here are London's most exclusive couturiers and designer boutiques, jewellery shops, antique stores and art galleries.

The headquarters of **Sotheby's** 23, the auctioneers founded in 1744 and now American-owned, is at No. 34. This is where world record prices for art works are notched up, but not every sale is for millionaires. Admission is free, as long as you look reasonably presentable. Asprey and Fenwick's are part of Bond Street's fabric and are worth checking out. Art galleries proliferate in Bond Street and adjacent Bruton Street, but the best place for galleries is **Cork Street** 24, parallel to Bond Street to the east, with such prestigious premises as Waddington's and the Cork Street Gallery, where Britain's top artists are represented and where museum-quality works are for sale. Just beyond is **Savile Row** 25, home of gentlemen's outfitters, where even "off-the-peg" items are highly priced.

Nightingales rarely sing in **Berkeley Square** 26 as they do in Frank Sinatra songs and, although some of its original buildings remain, this once highly aristocratic square is much spoilt by ugly-looking office buildings. The exclusive Berkeley Square Ball was discontinued in 1989 because of the dreadful behaviour of the guests. In 1774 Lord Clive of India committed suicide at No. 45. The Earl of Shelburne, the prime minister who conceded the independence of the United States in 1783, lived on the site of Lansdowne House, which was pulled

Admiral Horatio Nelson and the Duke of Wellington shared the same taylor in Savile Row – Gieves & Hawkes at No. 1.

BELOW: Sotheby's auction rooms in Bond Street.

The Clermont Club at 44 Berkeley Square is a high-society gambling den, where Lord Lucan lost heavily in 1974 and then disappeared after the murder of his children's nanny and the attempted murder of his wife (above).

BELOW: Oxford Street shopper. **RIGHT:** Park Lane's Dorchester hotel.

down in 1985 to make way for an office block. And **Berkeley Square House** is built on the site of the house where Queen Elizabeth II was born in 1926.

From Berkeley Square, Curzon Street leads to **Shepherd Market** ㉗, Mayfair's "village centre". This small pedestrian enclave is incongruous amid the grand town houses and exclusive hotels. Built in around 1735 by architect Edward Shepherd, it was established to supply the daily needs of the local residents and obliterated the open space which had accommodated the May Fair, whose riotousness offended the well-off residents. Even today it maintains a quaint air. There are small stores and specialist shops, pubs and restaurants, all on a village scale. Among them is a restaurant called Tiddy Dols, named after an 18th-century gingerbread maker who was a well known figure at the May Fairs. At night Shepherd Market is a haunt of upmarket prostitutes.

American connections

A pleasing, friendly statue of General Eisenhower and Winston Churchill having a chat on a bench in Bond Street is a sign of the interest Americans have always had in Mayfair. In 1785 John Adams, the first United States minister to Britain and later the nation's president, took up residence at **9 Grosvenor Square**. No fewer than 31 of the 47 households in the square then belonged to titled families and even now the **American Embassy**, with a defensive "moat" and dominated by an enormous eagle, is the only one in the world that is leasehold. The cost of the statue of **Franklin D. Roosevelt** ㉘ in the gardens was met by grateful British citizens after World War II. The required £40,000 was raised in less than 24 hours. A little more than 20 years later, it was lucky to survive unscathed from the massive anti-Vietnam War demonstrations.

Brook Street, running from the northeast corner of the square to Bond Street, is the home of **Claridge's Hotel**, one of London's premier luxury hotels, mostly in art deco style, though built in 1812. Händel wrote the *Messiah* at the much-altered No. 25 where he lived for 35 years until his death in 1759, and there are plans to open a museum on the premises. Here also is the **Savile Club**, haven of the literary establishment, where the members have voted on the thorny topic of whether or not to allow lay guests at its breakfast table and "mixed-sex lunches" on Saturday afternoons.

Park Lane, running from Hyde Park Corner to Marble Arch, forms the western boundary of Mayfair. Its once magnificent homes overlooking Hyde Park (*see page 190*) have largely been replaced by modern hotels and apartment buildings. These include the **Hilton Hotel** and the **Dorchester Hotel** ㉙, the headquarters of General Dwight D. Eisenhower in World War II, and long popular with film stars visiting London. To the north, the residence of the Grosvenor family (owners of a 300-acre/120-hectare estate covering Mayfair and Park Lane) was knocked down in 1928 to make way for the **Grosvenor House Hotel**. The Great Room of the hotel is London's largest banqueting hall.

Shopping in Oxford Street

A stone slab on a traffic island opposite Marble Arch at the west end of **Oxford Street**, London's principal shopping thoroughfare, marks the spot where a triangular gallows known as the Tyburn Tree stood permanently from 1571 to 1759. Up to 50,000 met their maker here. The site of London's main place of execution took its name from Tyburn Brook, which flowed into the Westbourne River at what is now the Serpentine in Hyde Park. Oxford Street, an old Roman

Map, page 136

George I spoke no English when he arrived in Britain. To make himself feel at home he brought to London a musician whom he had patronised in Germany. George Frideric Händel (1685–1759) soon made Britain his adopted country.

LEFT: the Hilton hotel in Park Lane.
BELOW: style slaves in South Molton Street.

Hanging days at Tyburn were public holidays: the victims dressed in their best, carried nosegays of flowers and took a last mug of ale.

road, was once known as Tyburn Street and the condemned were transported along this street to the gallows from Newgate prison or the Tower of London. In 1850, the **Marble Arch** 30, designed by John Nash and based on the Arch of Constantine in Rome, was placed at Tyburn after being removed from the front of Buckingham Palace because it proved too narrow for the State coaches to pass through.

Crowds first came to **Oxford Street** to see the condemned being taken to Tyburn: this produced a ready clientele for shopkeepers, and stores first appeared along "Ladies' Mile" between Tottenham Court Road and Marylebone Lane, just short of Bond Street Underground station. This was where the first department stores were built, but one of the finest, **Selfridges** 31**,** was built further west by Gordon Selfridge, a Chicago retail millionaire. His huge store opened in 1909, though the present American neo-classical emporium wasn't completed until 1926. It had 130 departments, a roof garden and an ice-cream soda fountain. Marks & Spencer, the drapers, opened their largest store to the west in 1930.

Only buses and taxis are allowed to drive down most of Oxford Street and its widened pavements are usually packed with tourists. Designer shops in St Christopher's Place near Bond Street Underground station offer an escape from the masses, as do Bond Street and South Molton Street on the south side. At Oxford Circus, Oxford Street crosses over **Regent Street** which continues north, part of Nash's scheme to connect the Prince Regent's home at Carlton House with his newly acquired property at Regent's Park. In 1884 the Ladies Lavatory company opened its first public facilities here for the benefit of shoppers. The **BBC** is headquartered in an imposing building at Portland Place (*see page 170*).

In December, Christmas lights are turned on in Oxford and Regent Streets,

BELOW: Oxford Street is for buses and taxis only.

and the thoroughfares become even more crowded. In Regent Street, Christmas decorations go up in mid-October in the overflowing floors of **Hamleys**, the world's biggest toy store, founded in 1760.

Hamleys is in contrast to the heavily timbered, mock-Tudor style of **Liberty** ㉜, around the corner in Great Marlborough Street. Liberty was built in 1924 but founded in the 19th century by Arthur Lasenby Liberty, patron of the arts and expert in foreign silks. The distinctive Liberty designs, which caused Italian Art Nouveau to be called *Stile Liberté*, still continue the tradition. Two notable set-backs for the firm were cancellations of orders from Archduke Ferdinand when he was assassinated in 1914, and curtains that were no longer needed in the Tsar's St Petersburg palace a few years later.

Other stores in Regent Street include jewellers **Garrard's** at No. 112, which maintains the Crown Jewels in the Tower of London. Men may like to visit the fine Art Deco barber's in the basement of the **Austin Reed** clothing store at No. 103. Among several famous restaurants in Regent Street are **Veeraswamy's**, London's first Indian restaurant, and the **Café Royal** ㉝, at No. 68 which was used by *belle époque* figures such as George Bernard Shaw, Oscar Wilde, James Whistler and Aubrey Beardsley. The Café Royal was also a haunt of the high-living Edward VIII and George VI when they were Prince of Wales. Private boxing matches still occasionally take place in the upstairs rooms.

Carnaby Street, on the eastern side of Regent Street, was once the site of a pesthouse and leper colony. For a few brief years in the 1960s, it became the centre of "Swinging London". As quickly as it came into fashion, it fell out again. Laid out as a pedestrian precinct, it is now the home of cheap clothing and souvenir shops catering to tourists. ❑

One of the finest Art Deco rooms in London is the gentlemen's barber's in Austin Reed at 103 Regent Street. For an appointment, call 0171 437 2906.

Left: once-swinging Carnaby Street.
Below: Liberty's distinctive clock.

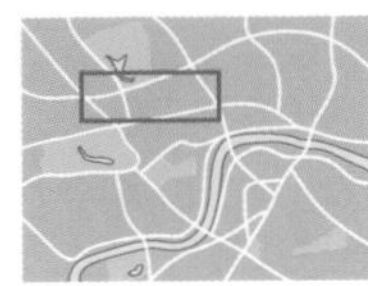

MARYLEBONE AND BLOOMSBURY

North of Oxford Street is London's intellectual area, home of the Bloomsbury set, London University and the British Museum. Regent's Park and London Zoo provide breathing space

"I find Bloomsbury fierce and scornful and stony-hearted, but so adorably lovely that I look out of my window all day long."

– VIRGINIA WOOLF, 1924

PRECEDING PAGES: Nebamun goes hunting, a wall painting in the British Museum. **BELOW:** Regent's Canal, Regent's Park.

Marylebone and Bloomsbury lie beyond Oxford and New Oxford Streets respectively, bounded in the north by Regent's Park and by Euston, St Pancras and King's Cross railway termini. They have a distinct cultural flavour, being the home of Sherlock Holmes, the British Museum, London University, a variety of book publishers and the hallowed Lord's Cricket Ground.

The residential area of **Marylebone** (pronounced *mar-luh-bun*) is largely Georgian, and its streets and squares are named after relatives of the Duke of Newcastle who started the developments here at the beginning of the 18th century. Planning began with the creation of a new road running from Paddington to Islington through the parish of St Mary-by-the-bourne to relieve congestion in Oxford Street. Marylebone has a refined domestic air, although Elizabeth Barrett, who lived in Wimpole Street, had to elope secretly with fellow poet Robert Browning, whom she married in 1842 in Marylebone parish church. The Methodist theologian Charles Wesley (1707–88) and the poet Lord Byron (1788–1824) were baptised in the same church.

Marylebone High Street ㉞ and **Marylebone Lane**, running through the

Map, page 136

centre of the district along the course of the River Tyburn, have a village atmosphere, with small shops and pubs and residential apartment blocks. Crossing Wimpole Street and running parallel to Oxford Street is Wigmore Street, where a number of fashion houses have set up shop. The **Wigmore Hall** ❸❺ is one of the more delightful London concert venues, particularly at lunchtimes and on Sundays. The Art Nouveau building, which has notable acoustics, was erected in 1901 by Friedrich Bechstein, who had a piano showroom next door. Many musicians make their London debuts here.

Harley Street ❸❻, parallel to Wimpole Street, has been the preferred haunt of medical specialists since the 1840s. Although most drugs here are dispensed respectably, one police raid on an expensive holiday apartment netted 50 kilos of cocaine, worth £10 million.

In Manchester Square is **Hertford House**, home of the **Wallace Collection** ❸❼ (10am–5pm, Sun 2–5pm, free). This remarkable display of art wealth ranges from voluptuous 17th- and 18th-century English and European paintings to Oriental armour and Sèvres porcelain. The collection, assembled by the third and fourth Marquesses of Hertford, takes its name from Richard Wallace, illegitimate son of the fourth Marquess. The panelled hall, fine carved staircase and drawing room are as Wallace would have had them in the late 18th century.

At home with Sherlock Holmes

At **Baker Street**, the Underground's District Line platforms were the initial terminus for the Bakerloo railway. Opened in 1906, it was London's first north–south underground line, and ran from Baker Street to Waterloo. The brickwork on the platforms has been restored to its original look. The address in Baker

ABOVE: Sherlock Holmes of Baker St. **BELOW:** the elegant face of Bloomsbury.

Madame Tussaud's

In an age when computer animation routinely fills cinema screens with the miraculous, what impels 7,000 people a day to stand in line breathing in the traffic fumes of London's Marylebone Road in order to gaze at mute, immobile effigies with glass-fibre bodies, wax heads and glass eyes? Knowing the answer to that question has turned Madame Tussaud's into the top tourist attraction in London, beating the Tower into second place.

A key ingredient in the success is that the models are no longer roped off or protected by glass cases. You can stroll right up to them – an impertinence their bodyguards would never permit in real life. You can give Saddam Hussein a piece of your mind. You can be photographed with your arm around Gérard Depardieu. If you haven't brought a camera, a Tussaud's photographer will invite you on entering the exhibition to be pictured alongside Arnold Schwarzenegger and a print will be waiting for you, at a price, when you leave.

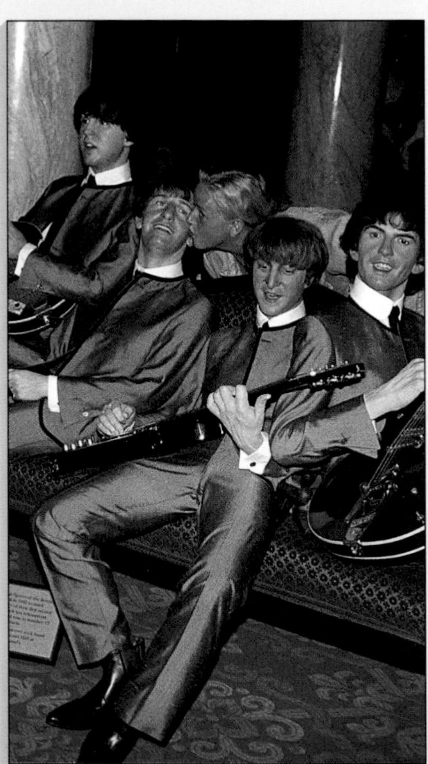

Whatever impulse draws crowds to see a minor television personality declare open a supermarket is at work here in overdrive, and the reactions are similar. Is Mel Gibson really that short? Doesn't Joan Collins have at least one wrinkle? Perhaps the greatest surprise, though, is that quite a few of the likenesses really aren't all that good. Most of the Royal Family are poor, and the essence of Marilyn Monroe and Margaret Thatcher is missed.

The story began during the French Revolution in 1789 when Marie Grosholtz, trained by a doctor in modelling anatomical subjects in wax, was asked to prepare death masks of famous victims of the guillotine. Although she married a French engineer, François Tussaud, in 1795, she left him in 1802 to spend the next 33 years touring Britain with a growing collection of wax figures. Today those gory beginnings are echoed in the waxworks' Chamber of Horrors, which contains the blade that sliced off Marie Antoinette's head and re-creates various none-too-scary tableaux of torture. Vlad the Impaler acts as doorman.

In 1993 the exhibition finally embraced audio-animatronics, populating a new "Spirit of London" ride with moving and speaking figures ranging from William Shakespeare ("To be or not to be") to contemporary street hawkers. Visitors are carried past the historical tableaux in miniature sawn-off taxis; the quality of the effects is uneven, but some of the speaking figures are astonishingly lifelike.

If you like the idea of getting close to celebrities without the remotest chance of being snubbed or ignored, Madame Tussaud's will probably appeal – but, unless you like queueing, buy a ticket in advance or get there when it opens (9.30am in summer, 10am in winter). There are some sobering intimations of mortality, particularly on the shelves of heads discarded from the main displays – how would Lyndon Baines Johnson feel, one wonders, about his decapitated waxen head being plonked unceremoniously between those of Rudolph Nureyev and Nikita Krushchev? If, on the other hand, you are interested in the achievements and motivations of human beings, a London museum – just about any London museum – will provide infinitely greater insight. ❑

LEFT: waxing lyrical with the Beatles.

Street where Sir Arthur Conan Doyle set Sherlock Holmes up in residence, at No. 221B, is in fact occupied by the Abbey National bank, which employs someone full-time to deal with the letters Holmes still receives. Those relating to alleged crimes are referred to the Metropolitan Police. The **Sherlock Holmes Museum** 38 is actually at No. 239 (daily 9.30–6pm, entrance fee). It re-creates the Victorian home of the detective, with pipe, violin and other props.

Map, page 136

Regent's Park

Baker Street, Marylebone High Street and Portland Place all lead to **Regent's Park** 39, an elegant 470-acre (190-hectare) space surrounded by John Nash's handsome Regency terraces, though a lack of funds prevented his full vision of being carried out. The gardens are formally planted, notably the roses in Queen Mary's Garden at the heart of the Inner Circle and not far from the Open Air Theatre where Shakespeare plays are put on in summer. The boating lake is a tranquil spot, and Regent's Canal runs through the north of the park (*see page 242*).

Winfield House in the Outer Circle of Regent's Park – the US ambassador's residence – was built in the 1930s by Cary Grant and Barbara Hutton.

The main attraction of the park is **London Zoo** 40 (10 minutes' walk from Camden Town station, or 274 bus from Camden Town or Baker Street; 9am–5.30pm, last ticket 4.30pm). It has more than 8,000 animals, and the Penguin Pool by the Russian architect, Berthold Lubetkin, and Aviary by Lord Snowdon are of architectural interest. The animals can be handled in the children's enclosure. The Web of Life Exhibition, a glass pavilion, celebrates the variety of biological diversity.

On the north west side of the park is **Lord's Cricket Ground** 41, belonging to the Marylebone Cricket Club whose privileged members wear a garish scarlet and gold striped tie. This is the headquarters of the English game and its Long Room is a hall of fame. (St John's Wood Underground, guided tour twice daily,

BELOW: Lord's Cricket Ground, headquarters of English cricket.

phone first: 0171 432 1033). St John's Wood is also the home of the **Saatchi Collection**, at 98A Boundary Road. (St John's Wood Underground, 12–6pm Thur–Sun, free Thur). Charles Saatchi, of advertising agency fame, has amassed around 800 contemporary works of British and American painters, including Andy Warhol and Lucien Freud.

Television history was made in Portland Place.

Along Marylebone Road to the BBC

On Marylebone Road, a busy highway, is the grand neo-classical **Holy Trinity Church** ㊷, designed by Sir John Soane, architect of the Bank of England, and completed in 1828. The queues on Marylebone Road, however, are for a more contemporary attraction: the phenomenally popular **Madame Tussaud's** ㊸ waxworks (*see page 168*) and the adjacent **Planetarium** near Baker Street (daily 9am–5.30pm; Oct–June 10am–5.30pm, 9.30–5.30 weekends; entrance fee, combined tickets available). The Planetarium puts on excellent laser light shows. Just beyond it, to the east, is Park Crescent and **Portland Place**, conceived by the Adam brothers as a home for the rich. John Nash included it in his grand design to connect Regent's Park with St James's but the plan was never realised.

The Adam houses in Portland Place are now gradually giving way to more modern structures. Several embassies and a number of institutes and learned societies, such as the Royal Institute of British Architects (RIBA) are found here. At its southern end rises the imposing but nondescript mass of **Broadcasting House** ㊹**,** headquarters of the British Broadcasting Corporation, where the first public television transmission was made in 1932. The corporation's radio studios are here and the **BBC Experience** allows visitors to direct TV and radio soaps (open daily from 9.30am; 90-minute tours every 15 minutes, last tour at

BELOW: classical lines of the British Museum.

4.30pm, closed Mon morning; entrance fee). The sculpture of Prospero and Ariel on the Art Deco building is by Eric Gill. In **Langham Place**, which curves round to connect Portland Place with Regent Street, the circular **All Souls' Church** was built by Nash in 1822–24 to round off the northern end of Regent Street.

Map, page 136

To the east stands the distinctive **Telecom Tower ㊺**, which rises more than 600 ft (180 metres) above Charlotte Street, traditional home of Greek restaurants. In the 1930s this area was the drinking ground of creative people such as the Welsh poet Dylan Thomas and the painter Augustus John. They are rememberd in the bar of the Fitzroy Tavern in Charlotte Street. Fitzroy Square, where George Bernard Shaw and Virginia Woolf were sometime residents, gave its name to this artistic colony of **Fitzrovia**.

At 1 Scala Street, off Goodge Street, is **Pollock's Toy Museum**, based on the toys and theatres made by Benjamin Pollock at the turn of the century (10am–5pm Mon–Sat, entrance fee). Just beyond it is **Tottenham Court Road**, which has an intense concentration of hi-fi and computer stores, while the capital's best-known furniture maker, Heal's, lies at the northern end.

The British Museum and Bloomsbury

The eastern side of Tottenham Court Road marks the beginning of Bloomsbury, London's literary heart. The **British Museum ㊻** on Great Russell Street is the nation's greatest treasure house, with more than 6½ million items ranging from the oldest neolithic antiquities to 20th-century manuscripts (10am–5pm, Sun 2.30–6pm, free). It opened in 1759. Behind the famous Athenian frontage are the 5th-century BC Elgin Marbles "rescued" by Lord Elgin from the Parthenon in Athens in 1801, and the linguist's codebook, the Rosetta Stone, the key which

ABOVE: Greek horse from the Parthenon. **BELOW LEFT:** from the Middle East collection. **BELOW:** Pollock's Toy Museum.

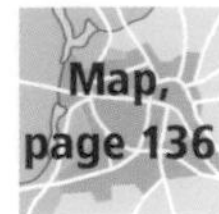

A curiosity of London University is the fully dressed skeleton of the philosopher and social reformer Jeremy Bentham (1748–1832). He sits in a cubicle with his head at his feet.

unlocked the mysteries of ancient Egyptian hieroglyphics. There are excellent Assyrian, Egyptian and Greek artefacts in the main museum. Though a world museum, it is guardian of the great British treasures, too, including the Sutton Hoo trove from a burial ship of an Anglo-Saxon king, the 7th-century illuminated Lindisfarne Gospels and Lindow man, a Briton killed 2,000 years ago and preserved in a peat bog.

Sir Anthony Panizzi, the chief librarian, designed the circular Reading Room in the British Library in 1857. Karl Marx did much of his research here for *Das Kapital*. But the entire Library of more than 9 million books – including a Gutenberg Bible, the Magna Carta and original texts by Shakespeare, Dickens and da Vinci – has been moved to new premises on the Euston Road. The Reading Room has become an education and information centre, with access via the museum's Great Court, newly roofed with a giant steel and glass canopy.

The museum's collection had an effect on the area, notably in Nicholas Hawksmoor's **church of St George** 47 in Bloomsbury Way, which was modelled on the tomb of King Mausolus and topped by a statue of George I in a toga.

Publishing heartland

Bloomsbury is blue plaque territory *par excellence*. In the early part of the 20th century it nurtured the Bloomsbury set. Virginia Woolf, Vanessa Bell, Duncan Grant, Dora Carrington, Roger Fry, Maynard Keynes and Queen Victoria's biographer, Lytton Strachey, all lived at various addresses around these streets. Although their inclinations spread across painting, philosophy and writing, their common connection was to challenge the accepted conventions of the day. They probably had more influence as a body than as individuals, and were bookish men and women in a bookish world. The area's industry is publishing, and publishing houses flourished around Bloomsbury and Bedford Squares, including the Bloomsbury set's own Hogarth Press. At the bottom of Gower Street are the art publishers Thames and Hudson, with steps decorated in Vanessa Bell tiles.

Many publishers, however, have since moved to less expensive premises, but the bookishness of the area remains in the shops around Museum Street and Great Russell Street, and in Gower Street where a large Dillon's bookshop serves students of the University of London. The university is identified by the grey turret of **Senate House** 48, built in 1936, on the western side of Russell Square. Among the university buildings in Gordon Square is the **Percival David Foundation of Chinese Art** 49, one of the finest Chinese ceramic collections in the west, with works from the 10th to the 18th centuries (10.30am–5pm, closed weekends, free).

Children rule the roost at **Coram Fields**, just beyond the children's hospital in Great Ormond Street. A sign on the gate enclosing the sheep-grazed field says that adults will be admitted only if accompanied by children. Thomas Coram was a sea captain who started a hospital and school for foundling children and encouraged artists to donate works to raise funds. William Hogarth was among them, and the collection can be seen at the **Thomas Coram Foundation for Children** 50 at 40 Brunswick Square (1.30–4.30pm, closed weekends). ❑

BELOW: adults are not allowed in Coram Fields unless accompanied by children.

Blue plaques

One of many pointers to London's varied past are the blue plaques slapped on sundry sites to commemorate famous people, events and buildings. There are plenty in Bloomsbury and Fitzrovia, but they are strewn all across London. More than 600 have appeared, like some sort of historic mould, on the sites of the dwelling places of the famous and the long dead. The first plaque was erected by the Royal Society of Arts in memory of the poet Lord Byron in 1867. In 1901 the London County Council took over the service, which is today administered by English Heritage.

Bona fide plaques are ceramic with white lettering on a circular blue background. They are bald statements of fact, giving little information about the person – simply their name, dates, profession and usually the year or years he or she lived in the building.

The awarding of a plaque is almost haphazard: there is no overall register of famous people who have lived in London. Many plaques are put up because descendants or adherents of the deceased put forward the suggestion to English Heritage. Thus plaques function as a barometer of public taste, as notions change about what constitutes fame. The range has been dominated by 19th-century politicians and artists, but in 1997 the first plaque to commemorate a rock star – Jimi Hendrix – went up in Brook Street.

There is a plaque at the site of the building of the *Great Eastern*, the largest 19th-century steamship. Mahatma Gandhi has one as a result of a quick stopover, and Mozart has one because he composed his first symphony in a house in Ebury Street.

Isaac Newton is remembered by a plaque on his house in Jermyn Street, although he had made his major discoveries about gravity before he came to live in the city. There are two plaques to the memory of the poet Samuel Taylor Coleridge, despite the fact that his private life was not one of unblemished rectitude.

A plaque-spotting tour would certainly not lack variety. Captain William Bligh of *Bounty* fame lived at 100 Lambeth Road, SE1; Charlie Chaplin lived at 287 Kennington Road, SE1; Sir Winston Churchill lived at 34 Eccleston Square, SW1; Benjamin Franklin lived at 36 Craven Street, WC2; Charles Dickens lived at 48 Doughty Street, WC1; Henry James lived at 34 De Vere Gardens, W8; Karl Marx lived at 28 Dean Street, W1; Florence Nightingale lived and died on the site of 10 South Street, W1; George Bernard Shaw lived at 29 Fitzroy Square, W1; and Mark Twain lived at 23 Tedworth Square, SW3.

Most candidates for plaques are submitted to lengthy scrutiny before their sojourn on earth is immortalised on a London wall. They must have been dead for at least 20 years; they must be regarded as eminent by luminaries in their profession; they should have made an important contribution to human welfare; the well-informed passer-by should readily recognise their name; and they should, by the kind of infuriatingly nebulous "general agreement" that has characterised British decision-making, deserve recognition. ❑

RIGHT: a blue plaque for Dickens put up by the London County Council.

31

KENSINGTON AND CHELSEA

The Royal Borough of Kensington and Chelsea is a sought-after residential area with up-market shops such as Harrods. It also has a Royal Palace, a fine park and a collection of top museums

Map, page 178

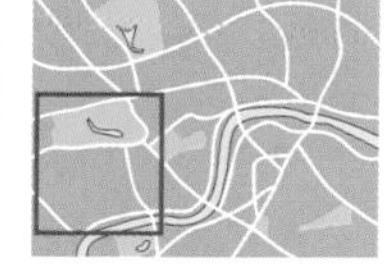

Much of the Royal Borough of Kensington and Chelsea is given over to the houses and apartments of the well-to-do. Their pleasant squares and cobbled mews have an elegant air reminiscent of the sedate family life lived by the likes of the Victorian Darling family whose children one night escaped through the bedroom window with Peter Pan. Chelsea, in the southern half of the borough, bordering the river, has a much more arty past, but apart from the Arts Club in Redcliffe Gardens, little remains of its bohemian roots.

The elegant mansions, terraces and squares have attracted embassies, smart hotels and sky-high prices. **Hyde Park Corner**, at the junction of Piccadilly, Park Lane and Knightsbridge, used to stand at the fringe of London. Apsley House, built in 1770 by Robert Adam, has the address "No. 1, London". It was bought by Arthur Wellesley, the first Duke of Wellington, in 1816, just after he had vanquished Napoleon at Waterloo. It is still inhabited by the family, and it also contains the **Wellington Museum** ❶, which has an impressive picture collection in six rooms overlooking Hyde Park. Among its fine furniture is a larger than life-size nude statue of Napoleon Bonaparte by Canova (11am–5pm Tues–Sun, entrance fee).

The arch in the middle of Hyde Park Corner was designed by Decimus Burton in 1828, and until 1992 housed a tiny police station. It is popularly known as the **Wellington Arch** ❷, because of the statue of the Duke which used to stand on top of it. However, Burton disliked both the statue and its positioning and left money in his will to have it removed. The present statue of a charioteer replaced it in 1912.

PREVIOUS PAGES: a modern Jeeves with duster, Chelsea.
LEFT: elegant Belgravia.
BELOW: Cubitt's terracing in Wilton Crescent.

Belgravia to Sloane Square

When most of the squares and terraces of **Belgravia** were built around 1824, these streets west of Hyde Park Corner were intended to rival Mayfair. They were so exclusive that the residents employed watchmen to operate gates to keep out the mob. From Knightsbridge the best entrance to Belgravia is via **Wilton Place** ❸. The stucco terraces were developed by architect Thomas Cubitt, who gave his name to the modern construction company known for its motorway bridges. **Belgrave Square** has suffered the same fate as much of Mayfair. Most residences are occupied by embassies and various societies and associations. The square usually has a heavy police presence. **Eaton Square**, to the south, is more residential. However, many of its supposed residents live in other parts of the world and the houses are dark and obviously under-used. Chopin gave his first London recital here at No. 88.

In 1895 the playwright Oscar Wilde was arrested in the Cadogan Hotel in Sloane Street, tried and sent to

Meter maid on the prowl. If your car is towed away, call 020-7747 4747 and prepare to hand over about £100.

prison for his homosexual conduct. Sloane Street leads from Knightsbridge to **Sloane Square** ❹, where **Chelsea** proper begins. On the east side of the square is the **Royal Court Theatre**, which dates from 1870. This atmospheric 395-seater, opening after refurbishment in autumn 1998, is where John Osborne's mould-breaking *Look Back in Anger* was first staged in 1956, and it still has a reputation for good new material.

Sloane Square, with a flower stall and a shady fountain of Venus, was named after a physician, Sir Hans Sloane (1660–1753), whose personal collection formed the basis of what is now the British Museum. Sir Hans laid out much of this area and his name crops up often on street plans. He also unwittingly gave his name to a typical young upper-class urbanite living in Chelsea: the Sloane Ranger, who wears flat-heeled shoes, pearls, a navy blue sweater, baggy skirt and a quilted jacket, and has a slight slouch.

Until 1829 **King's Road,** leading west from Sloane Square, was a private royal road leading from Hampton Court to the Court of King James. It rose to its pinnacle of fame in the Swinging '60s, and was the mecca for the 1970s punk

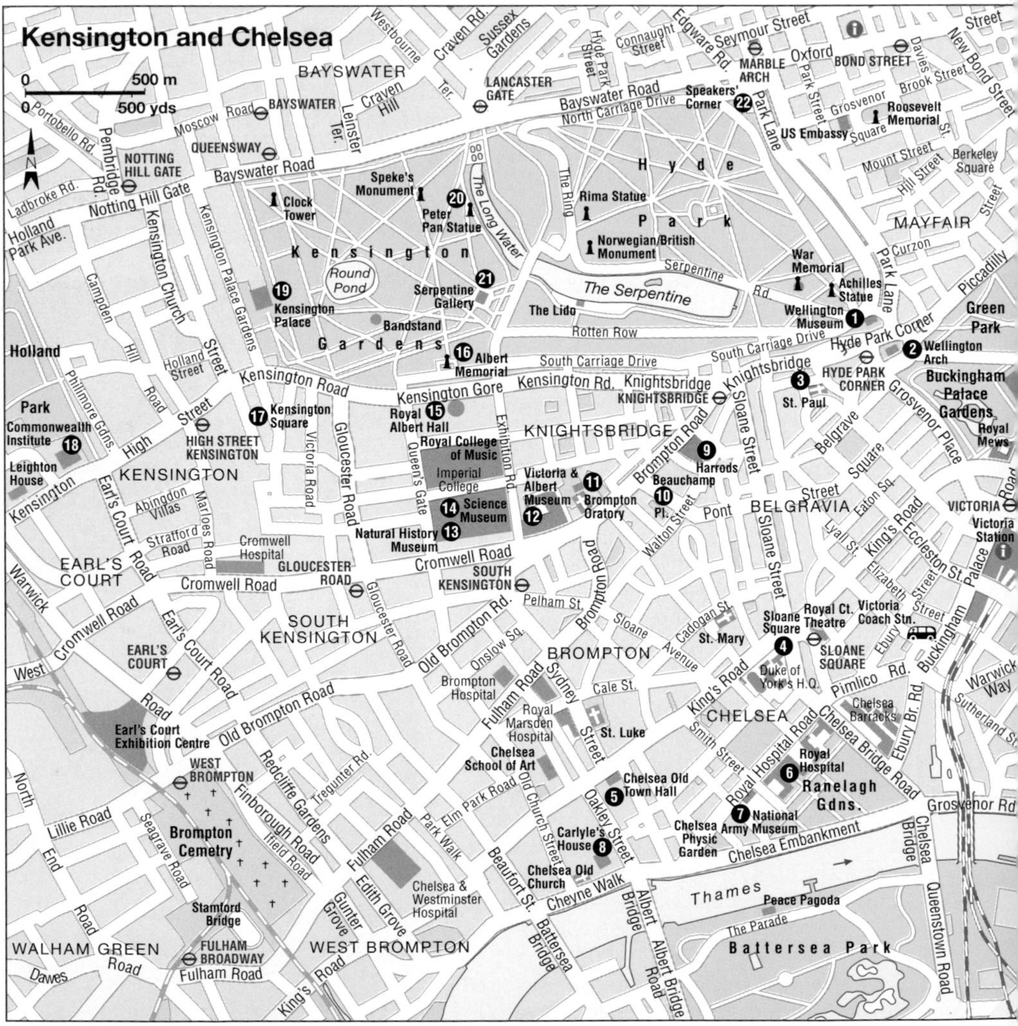

Kensington and Chelsea

fashions after Vivienne Westwood and Malcolm McLaren opened their designer shop, Sex, at No. 430. Westwood still sells her designs from this premises, renamed World's End which is what this part of Chelsea is called. Other shops have mirrored the changing fashions and some stalwarts remain, such as **Peter Jones**, the smart department store beside Sloane Square.

Map, page 178

Where the fashionable get married

Prettily painted 18th- and 19th-century terraces leading off King's Road have a tradition of housing artists and intellectuals. On the left-hand side of the road opposite Sydney Street stands the **Old Chelsea Town Hall** ❺. The old borough of Royal Kensington, given was given its royal appellation in 1901 by Queen Victoria, was merged much against its wishes with Chelsea in 1965, and took over the administration of both. The Old Chelsea Town Hall continues to provide a cultural and social focus for residents. The Register Office next door is well-known for society and celebrity weddings. In 1836, Charles Dickens was married more conventionally – in **St Luke's**, a stunning Gothic church half way up Sydney Street.

On either side of the Town Hall are two antique markets which are barely visible from the outside. Inside they are warrens of narrow passageways and tiny stalls. Chenil Galleries and Antiquarius contain hoards of English antiques and many stallholders come from the best English gentility. It's hard to believe that the whole world could house so many antique silver picture frames. Having walked all this way down the King's Road, there is one last haven before the return slog back to the Underground: the Man in the Moon pub at No.392 has a spacious wood-panelled interior and beautifully engraved windows.

Vivienne Westwood, fashion doyenne of Chelsea.

BELOW: Fresh bread today, King's Road.

Down Hospital Road

Among the leggy would-be models gliding along the King's Road are uniformed old gents with the initials RH on their caps. These are Chelsea Pensioners, retired war veterans who have found a home in the **Royal Hospital** ❻ (Mon–Sat 10am–noon, 2–4pm, in summer Sun 2–4pm). It is a magnificent building, inspired by the Hôtel des Invalides in Paris and built by Christopher Wren in 1692 on Royal Hospital Road, which runs parallel with King's Road. Here pensioners are boarded, lodged, clothed, nursed and given a small allowance, including a pint of beer a day. The **Chelsea Flower Show**, one of the largest of its kind in the world, is a great social event held in the Royal Hospital's spacious gardens in May.

ABOVE AND BELOW: Chelsea Pensioners, yesterday and today. **BELOW RIGHT:** Chelsea Flower Show.

On either side of the hospital are Ranelagh Gardens – the daily strolling ground for nannies of the well-to-do and their charges – and the **National Army Museum** ❼ (daily 10am–5.30pm, free). The Museum follows the history of the British Army from the defeat of the French at Agincourt in 1485 to the present day. Massive flamboyant paintings, some as long as 20ft (6 metres), celebrate soldiers' greatest and worst moments. There is the skeleton of Napoleon's favourite horse, Marengo, and displays relating to the Indian Army and the colonial land forces, some of whom still have close links with the British Army. Many of the museum staff are former soldiers. A piece of the Berlin Wall can be seen outside the National Army Museum.

Behind a high wall further down the road is the **Chelsea Physic Garden**, founded in 1676 for the study of medicinal plants (2–5pm, Wed and Sun, entrance fee). The garden contains an eccentric variety of rare trees and herbs, including poisonous specimens such as Mandrake and Deadly Nightshade. An olive tree in the garden occasionally bears fruit.

Map, page 178

At the foot of **Royal Hospital Road**, a statue of the Scottish essayist Thomas Carlyle (1795–1881) watches the traffic grind by on the Embankment. Behind him a fine row of Queen Anne houses make up **Cheyne Walk**, still one of London's most exclusive streets. A host of famous people have lived here, including the writers George Eliot and Hilaire Belloc, the artist J. M. W. Turner, and the millionaires Paul Getty and Mick Jagger. The pre-Raphaelite artist Dante Gabriel Rossetti lived with the poet Swinburne in No. 16, and they kept peacocks in their back garden. The birds so disturbed the neighbours that nowadays every lease on the row prohibits tenants from keeping them.

Woe in Cheyne Walk

Behind Cheyne Walk is a network of small, extremely pretty streets which are worth wandering around even if you don't visit **Carlyle's House** ❽ at No. 24 Cheyne Row (Mar–Oct, 11am–5pm Wed–Sun). The author lived here between 1834–81. The house is preserved exactly as it was – even to the point of not having electricity – and it is easy to imagine Mr and Mrs Carlyle sitting in their kitchen, although it may not have been a cosy scene. It was fortunate the Carlyles married each other, it was said; otherwise there would have been four miserable people in the world instead of two. Yet leading intellectuals of the time, including Charles Dickens, John Ruskin and Alfred, Lord Tennyson, used to come and visit Carlyle here.

Sir Hans Sloane's tomb is in **Chelsea Old Church** on Cheyne Walk, which has several fine Tudor monuments and was painstakingly rebuilt after being destroyed by a landmine in 1941. The site was formerly occupied by a 12th-century Norman church. Henry VIII, who had a large house on the river where

BELOW: beer stop at The Man in the Moon, King's Road.

Cheyne Walk now is, supposedly married Jane Seymour in secrecy here, several days before the official ceremony. Thomas More (1478–1535), author of *Utopia,* which sketched out an ideal commonwealth, had a farm here. His stormy relationship with Henry VIII, which resulted in his execution, was the subject of Robert Bolt's 1960 play *A Man For All Seasons.*

Knightsbridge for the select shopper

From the top of Sloane Street, just beyond Hyde Park Corner, Knightsbridge heads west, dividing into three arteries which lead to Kensington High Street, Cromwell Road (and on to Hammersmith and Heathrow Airport) and Fulham Road. Tidal waves of traffic sweep in or out according to the time of day, repeatedly snagging on the chauffeur-driven Rolls-Royces that bunch up outside the front doors of **Harrods** ❾ department store.

TIP

You might not get in to Harrods if you are not dressed "properly". One woman was ejected for wearing leggings she had bought in the store.

The Harrods shopping bag is the bag to be seen with anywhere in the world. The store's motto – *Omnia, Omnibus, Ubique*, "all things, for all people, everywhere" – means what it says. Its food hall is spectacular and an endless list of peculiar and exotic requests includes sending a pound of sausages to a customer in the Mediterranean and a sauna to someone in the Middle East. Harrods sales are spectacular events. The store can take up to £3 million and the lifts travel approximately 100 miles (160km) a day during sales. The most dignified of the English lose their dignity in the scramble to save hundreds of pounds. The more dedicated camp out for days on the street to be the first ones through the door. The store was started by Henry Charles Harrod when his grocery business opened in 1849, although the present building was opened in 1905. The Egyptian Al-Fayed brothers, hitherto little known, bought the store and other House of Fraser outlets for £615 million in 1983, and Mohamed Al-Fayed has a flair for publicity.

BELOW: Harrods in Knightsbridge – more an institution than a store.

If Harrods is daunting, there is no shortage of more modest shops in the area. **Knight's Arcade** and the **Brompton Arcade** are sumptuous but discreet. **Beauchamp Place** ❿ (pronounced *Beecham*), a villagey street west of Harrods, is the stamping ground of the well-heeled, including sundry royals.

Beyond Harrods, where Brompton Road begins, is the **Brompton Oratory** ⓫, a flamboyant Italian baroque building designed by a 29-year-old country-dwelling architect, Herbert Gribble, whose career took a sudden step forward as a result. It has a nave wider than St Paul's and was opened in 1884. The church, which is officially called the London Oratory, used to host the city's main Roman Catholic congregation, but this role has been supplanted by Westminster Cathedral in Victoria Street.

Kensington has a rich cosmopolitan life. The Lycée Français is at 35 Cromwell Road, teaching sons and daughters of diplomats, and the German Goethe Institute in Princes Gate looks after the cultural interests of German speakers. By South Kensington's fine Art Deco station is Ismaili Centre, built by the Agha Khan in 1979 as a cultural centre for Shia Ismailis, for whose sect the Agha Khan is the greatest living prophet. The money of this area is also reflected in the fact that Christie's and Phillips have auction houses in South Kensington.

Three Victorian museums

The Great Exhibition of 1851, held in Hyde Park, was an astonishing success. For the first time elements of the far-flung Victorian Empire were brought under the curious gaze of the public whose interest in the sciences and the arts had never been greater. The idea for the exhibition had come from Henry Cole (1808-82), chairman of the Society of Arts, and it had been taken up enthusiastically by Prince Albert, who chaired the committee to see it through. The resultant Crystal Palace built in the park was a great success, with more than 6 million visitors, and after it moved to Sydenham, south London, the following year, the profits were used to purchase 87 acres of land in adjoining South Kensington to build a more permanent home for the arts and sciences.

Greatest of them all is undoubtedly the **Victoria and Albert Museum** ⓬ (10am–5.50pm; Mon 12am–5.50pm, donation encouraged), which Henry Cole began assembling the year after the Great Exhibition, though Queen Victoria did not lay the foundation stone of the current building until 1899, 38 years after Albert was dead. Its 1909 facade is by Aston Webb, who put the front on Buckingham Palace. Inside is the richest and most diverse collection of decorative arts in the world and it is impossible to see everything in one visit. Plans issued at the entrance should be used to select an itinerary among the vast halls and galleries that cover six floors.

There are extraordinary collections of sculpture, pottery, china, engravings, illustrations, metalwork, paintings, textiles, period costumes and furniture, and it is hard to imagine anything has been left out. All are genuine, even colossal plaster-cast copies and the admitted forgeries and fakes. The Chinese, Japanese and Islamic rooms are splendid. An imperative visit is to the Morris, Gamble and Poynter rooms, leading from the Italian renaissance rooms on the ground floor. These spectacular Arts and Crafts designed rooms, with stained glass, Minton tiles and flourish of appropriate quotations, were the museum's original refreshment rooms. Today the restaurant is situated in the Henry Cole Wing, entered through Exhibition Road, where there also is a Frank Lloyd Wright room, a print collection, a selection of European paintings (including a John Constable collection) and shop.

On the other side of Exhibition Road is the neo-Gothic pile of the **Natural History Museum** ⓭, built between 1873 and 1880 and a fine space with a grand central hall, which can be hired for private parties (10am–5.50pm, Sun 1–5.50pm, entrance fee). The Life Galleries have exhibits on early man, Darwin's theory of evolution, human biology, birth and whales (including a life-size model of a blue whale), but undoubtedly the biggest draw is to the Dinosaur Gallery: the museum's showpiece is an 85-ft (26-metre) diplodocus skeleton. The Creepie-Crawlies section is bound to attract children. In the New Earth Galleries, you can experience a stimulated earthquake in a Japanese supermarket, complete with sound effects. An escalator rises up through a slowly rotating model of the globe, giving the eerie sensation that you are turning, not the globe.

The **Science Museum** ⓮, on the other side of it in Exhibition Road, completes this trio of instructive

Map, page 178

The V&A's Victorian copies of great works of art are often appreciated by art historians: Italians have come to study the museum's version of Trajan's Column, which is in much better repair than the original in Rome, the victim of traffic pollution.

BELOW: the Natural History Museum in Cromwell Road.

TIP

One of the best Indian restaurants in London is the Bombay Brasserie in Bailey's Hotel, by Gloucester Road Underground station. Try for a table in the conservatory (tel: 020-7370 4040).

museums (daily 10am–6pm, free after 4.30pm). It traces the history of inventions from the first steam train – Stevenson's Rocket – to the battered command module from the Apollo 10 space mission. There are a number of working models on the seven floors of exhibition space which encompass computing, medicine, photography, chemistry and physics. The vast Wellcome Wing, also stretching over several floors, has lots of hands-on displays plus (for an extra charge) an IMAX cinema and flight simulators. There are imaginative exhibits on genes and the future of digital communications.

Dwarfed by all these towering museums is a small, green-painted wooden building sitting on piles of bricks in the middle of the road. This is an exclusive restaurant, reserved for cab drivers, and one of a few dotted around London.

On the corner of Queen's Gate Terrace, opposite the Natural History Museum, stands **Baden-Powell House**, with a statue of the Boy Scouts' founder standing on watch outside. Inside, there is a small exhibition area dedicated to Lord Baden-Powell (1857–1941), a singular man who was by turns actor, secret agent, horseman, artist, writer, sportsman, public speaker and film maker.

Further memories of Prince Albert

Behind the Science Museum is the **Royal College of Music**, which has a collection of musical instruments, open on Wednesday afternoons in term time. Nearby is the 1875 **Royal College of Organists**, with elaborate, cream-cake fresco exterior. Next door, in a rather grim 1960s building, is the **Royal College of Art**, where occasional graduation exhibitions allow the public to buy the works of future greats for a mere few pounds. David Hockney, Henry Moore and the fashion designer Zandra Rhodes studied here.

BELOW: the Royal Albert Hall.

PRINCE ALBERT

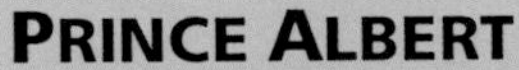

Albert of Saxe-Coburg-Gotha, who was born in Schloss Rosenau in Coburg, Germany, in 1819, was Queen Victoria's first cousin. Their marriage was arranged by her uncle Leopold, King of the Belgians, and when they married in 1839, both aged 20, his English was limited, but he was studious and he worked to improve it. He enjoyed hunting and winter sports, and was a family man, siring nine children and setting up royal homes at Balmoral in Scotland and Osborne on the Isle of Wight. He brought to England the custom of putting up a decorated tree at Christmas. His great interest in the sciences and the natural world made him a typical Victorian and he was largely responsible for establishing the museums in South Kensington. Victoria was shattered when he died in 1861, and she spent the next 40 years in mourning for him, wearing nothing but black clothes with jet-black jewellery and carrying a black parasol. She spent a lot of her time near Albert's mausoleum at Frogmore in Windsor. In particular, she recalled the moments when, on their honeymoon, he removed her stockings: that was, she said, the happiest time of her life.

But most impressive of all is the circular building they surround: the **Royal Albert Hall ⓯**, a huge, ornate building with a capacity of 8,000 designed by Francis Fowkes. It measures 272ft by 238ft (83 by 73 metres), the glass and iron dome is 135ft (41 metres) high internally and the 150-ton organ has 10,000 pipes. The frieze around the outside illustrates "The Triumph of Arts and Sciences". It was built in 1870 and much of the necessary money was raised by selling off in perpetuity 1,300 of its seats, many of which are still owned privately. Events at the hall range from tennis and boxing to classical and rock concerts. Every July the **Henry Wood Promenade Concerts**, a series of classical concerts where the promenading audience have the option of standing or sitting on the floor, provide a rich diet of music to those who usually wouldn't be able to afford a seat. These Proms, especially the televised Last Night, have something of the atmosphere of a football match, and the crowd's shouts make use of the hall's famous echo. The echo prompted a traditional joke that the hall is the only place where a British composer can be sure to hear his work twice.

The main road outside, running along Hyde Park and Kensington Gardens, is here called Kensington Gore. On the east side of the Albert Hall is the **Royal Geographical Society** which occupies buildings reminiscent of a gentleman's club. There is usually a small if ill-advertised exhibition in the hall inside. It is worth going in to spin the leather globe and to peer at the portraits of Britain's famous explorers. Its extensive library can be visited only by appointment (tel: 020-7589 5466).

The Royal Albert Hall sits in a road called Albert Court, with Prince Consort Road behind, but the apogee of the Albert cult is the **Albert Memorial ⓰** designed by Sir George Gilbert Scott in Kensington Gardens opposite the Albert

Map, page 178

On the Last Night of the Proms, Edward Elgar's "Land of Hope and Glory" is always played as the audience, on their feet, wave Union flags and sing uproariously to the tune many believe should be the British national anthem.

BELOW: the Albert Memorial.

ABOVE: antiques are big business.

Hall. Badly eroded by pollution, it was expensively restored to its former gilded glory – or gaudy vulgarity, depending on taste – in good time for the millennium. It depicts the prince as a great god or philosopher, clutching in his right hand the catalogue of the Great Exhibition which he masterminded. Marking the corners of the monument are symbols for the spread of the British Empire: a camel for Africa, a bull bison for America, an elephant for Asia and a cow for Europe (Australia, then the Empire's dumping ground for convicts, failed to merit a mention).

Kensington High Street

Kensington Gore runs into Kensington High Street, which is a major shopping area, a mixture of the trendy and the traditional. **Kensington Church Street**, branching off to the right towards Notting Hill Gate, is the place for genuine antiques. Almost opposite, in Derry Street, is the **Roof Garden** restaurant, six storeys above street level. The gardens are open every day if there is not a function on, but the restaurant is open to the public only on Thursday and Saturday evenings. An acre and a half of ornamental gardens, laid out in the 1930s, surrounds the exclusive restaurant owned by the creator of the Virgin empire, Richard Branson. Rolling Stones guitarist Bill Wyman owns the Sticky Fingers burger restaurant at the corner of Phillimore Gardens.

On the south side of the High Street is **Kensington Square** ⓱, one of the oldest in London, and an elegant mixture of architectural styles dating from the late 17th century. The Pre-Raphaelite painter Edward Burne-Jones lived at No. 41, and the philosopher John Stuart Mill, another eminent Victorian, at No. 18. There are elegant houses all around Kensington High Street. One that can be visited is **Leighton House** at 12 Holland Park Road (11am–5.30pm Mon–Sat, dona-

BELOW: Kensington Palace.

tions appreciated). This was the house designed by George Aitchison for the painter and Arabist Lord Leighton (1830–96), who was president of the Royal Academy and the only painter ever to have been made a peer. It contains his highly romanticised works, as well as many by fellow Pre-Raphaelites, and has a grand Arab Hall.

The **Commonwealth Institute** ⓲ is situated at the far end of Kensington High Street next to Holland Park (10am–5pm, Sun 2–5pm, entrance fee). A registered charity and a tireless educator, it took over from the Imperial Institute in 1958 and arrived in this 1962 purpose-built centre which has a roof of Zambian copper. It has an open gallery rising through three floors to show the culture and customs of each of the 53 member states. As the sun continues to set on the empire, funding has been withdrawn, and a hands-on "Commonwealth Experience" is just one item designed to increase interest – though around 250,000 still visit it each year.

Holland Park is a pleasant retreat, offering shady walks and attractive gardens. These are the grounds of the Jacobean Holland House, most of which was destroyed in the war. Peacocks screech and preen among the formal walled gardens. There is a restaurant in the Orangery and the ruins of the brick mansion provide one of the most appealing sets for open-air concerts, theatre and dance in the city. Its northern exits are near trendy Notting Hill Gate.

Kensington Gardens and Hyde Park

London's great green lung is **Hyde Park** and **Kensington Gardens** which cover one square mile (2.5sq km) – the same area as the City of London. Although they are a single open space, they are two distinct parks, divided by The Ring or

Map, page 178

The best located youth hostel in London is attached to the Jacobean Holland House in Holland Park (tel: 020-7937 0748).

BELOW: the Sunken Garden in Kensington Palace.

Peter Pan, the best known Kensington Gardens resident.

West Carriage Drive which goes from Alexandra Gate at the top of Exhibition Road to Victoria Gate in Bayswater Road. Kensington Gardens is a sedate place, where uniformed nannies traditionally push rich babies in the latest model prams, and boys push their sailing boats out on the Round Pond. This was once the private garden of **Kensington Palace** ⓳ and its presence still gives this part of the park airs and graces. The official London residence of Princess Margaret and the late Princess of Wales, it is referred to in royal circles as "KP". The Palace, which was given its present appearance by Sir Christopher Wren and Nicholas Hawksmoor, was the centre of the Court after William III bought the Jacobean mansion from the Earl of Nottingham in 1689, a year after his coronation, as the riverside Palace of Whitehall irritated his asthma. A number of monarchs were subsequently born here, the last of them Victoria in 1819, who 18 years later was called from her bed to be told she had become Queen.

Many of the first-floor State Apartments, decorated in early Georgian and Victorian styles, are open for viewing (9am–5pm, Sun 11am–5pm, admission fee, tel: 020-7937 9561), and there is an exhibition of art treasures and royal costumes. Around the grounds of the palace are an attractive sunken garden and an **Orangery**, designed by Hawksmoor with wood carvings by Grinling Gibbons, which is a suitable place to exchange gossip about the royals over a pot of tea.

An opening to the left of the park beside the gilded main gates on the south side of the palace leads to **Kensington Palace Gardens**. This is a far less daunting approach to "Millionaire's Row" than through the security barrier that blocks the road from High Street Kensington. It is impossible now to imagine that a single one of these mansions might have had a sole occupant: but they did. Now they are mostly ambassadors' residences. The lake in the middle of the park,

BELOW: The Long Water in winter.

Map, page 178

generally referred to as the Serpentine, is in fact called The Long Water in **Kensington Gardens**. Beside it, on the south bank, is an enchanting statue of J.M. Barrie's **Peter Pan** 20 by George Frampton. In 1912, with the connivance of the local authorities, the statue was erected secretly one night so it might seem as if it had appeared by magic. The **Serpentine Art Gallery** 21 by the road bridge stages adventurous exhibitions and there are a number of sculptures in the gardens, including Henry Moore's *Arch*.

Hyde Park

Across the road is **Hyde Park** which, the Domesday Book of 1086 records, was inhabited by wild bulls and boars. It was first owned by the monks of Westminster Abbey, and after ecclesiastic property had been confiscated in the Reformation, Henry VIII turned it into a royal hunting ground. It was opened to the public in the 17th century and then sold off in chunks by Oliver Cromwell, the Lord Protector, who accidentally shot himself in the leg while there. The **Serpentine**, which attracts hardy swimmers all year round at the lido, was created in the 1730s as a royal boating pond, and boats can still be hired from the north bank. Harriet Westbrook, the first wife of the poet Shelley, drowned herself here in 1816. Two years earlier it was the site of a spectacular re-enactment of Nelson's victory at the Battle of Trafalgar. Generally, the park is known for quieter pursuits. William III's Route du Roi (**Rotten Row**) is where the well-heeled canter their horses.

At the northeast corner, near Marble Arch, is **Speaker's Corner** 22, where anyone can pull up a soap box and sound off – a tradition going back to the days of the Tyburn gallows, when condemned men were allowed to have a last word. ❑

ABOVE: riding in Rotton Row.
BELOW: the parks offer relaxation.

PARK LIFE

London has more green spaces than any other city of its size in the world. Each has something different to offer and each has its own special flavour

London's eight major parks – Hyde Park, Kensington Gardens, Regent's Park, St James's Park, Green Park, Greenwich Park, Richmond Park and Bushy Park – are all owned and run by the Crown. Many of them once served as royal hunting grounds, and now, attractively landscaped and tended, they retain an elegant air. But they are useful, too. The former haunts of prize-fighters and duellists provide diversions with sports pitches, tennis courts and riding tracks, though most soccer and soft-ball players only need a patch of grass. The largest is Hyde Park (350 acres/140 hectares), a vast natural open space only a few paces away from bustling Oxford Street. The park adjoins Kensington Gardens, which have the air of a Victorian children's playground with model boats on the Round Pond, puppet shows, kites, flower walks and Peter Pan. The oldest of the royal parks is St James's, where jousts were once held. It is beautifully landscaped with fountains and views of Buckingham Palace and Whitehall. It keeps an impressive colony of ducks and its resident pelicans are fed at 3pm daily. Regent's Park is the home of London Zoo. It has more than 6,000 trees set among lawns, and an immaculate Rose Garden.

△ NANNY KNOWS BEST
Perambulators may have given way to buggies but in Kensington Gardens a spin round the park with nanny is still a traditional feature of the day.

BOATING WEATHER ▷
The Serpentine Lake in Hyde Park is the largest boating lake in London, but rowing boats can also be hired in Regent's and Battersea parks. The tidal Thames is too perilous for leisure activity.

◁ WHEEL EXCITEMENT
Roller blading is banned in some of London's parks, but in Hyde Park wide tracks are given over to this exhilarating high-speed activity.

△ SPEAKERS' CORNER
At the Marble Arch end of Hyde Park is Speakers' Corner, where freedom of speech is guaranteed. Anyone with a soapbox can get up and say what's on their minds.

CHRISTMAS CRACKERS ▷
Swimming at the Lido on the Serpentine is a fun summertime activity. Members of the Serpentine Swimming Club, however, swim every day come rain or shine – even on a freezing Christmas Day.

CONCERT VENUES

The sight of people sitting in striped deckchairs in a park on a warm summer's day listening to a brass band is reassuringly English. Five of the royal parks have their own bandstands and hold regular, free afternoon concerts at weekends. Musical entertainment is laid on throughout the summer. Jazz and woodwind recitals are given at Kensington Gardens and Regent's Park holds the three-day Sufi Music Village, Britain's longest running celebration of popular music and traditional dance from around the world. Sometimes the Proms in the Albert Hall spill over into Hyde Park. Concerts in Greenwich Park are held in a special park arena by the Royal Observatory. The evening concerts are held in mid-July and feature well known musicians.

Great houses provide other venues: classical concerts are held at Kenwood House, north London. Most people make it a special occasion by bringing a bottle of wine and a picnic. Concerts are also held in the grounds of Holland House in Holland Park, west London, and make a delightful evening. But the best place to be on a dry summer evening is watching an open-air Shakespeare production in Regent's Park.

△ **RICHMOND DEER**
Richmond Park was a royal hunting ground, but today red and fallow deer graze in peace. The park is also popular for horse riding.

◁ **KEW GARDENS**
The Royal Botanic Gardens at Kew are among the finest in the world. The grounds are extensive. Two magnificent Victorian greenhouses and a modern conservatory house rare and wonderful plants.

AQUARIUM
CANARY WHARF II

THE SOUTH BANK AND SOUTHWARK

Map on page 194–5

Highlights include the Imperial War Museum, the South Bank Centre's theatres and concert halls, the London Eye, Tate Modern, Shakespeare's Globe, Southwark Cathedral and HMS Belfast

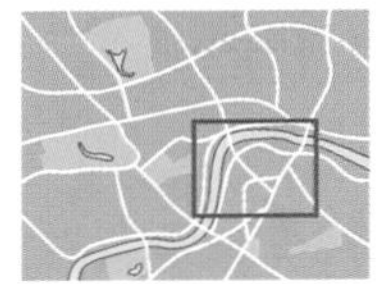

Historically, Southwark is an intrinsic part of the capital. The first bridge across the Thames was built by the Romans near London Bridge, and the community around it developed as an alternative to the City, as it lay in the county of Surrey, beyond the City's jurisdiction. In Shakespeare's day it was the place for putting on unlicensed plays and for setting up brothels, and it retained its reputation as an area of vice and squalor well into the 19th century. The Underground's Jubilee Line extension has transformed access to the area.

The Archbishop's London palace

Opposite the Houses of Parliament beside Lambeth Bridge, is **Lambeth Palace ❶**, which has been the London residence of the Archbishops of Canterbury since the 12th century. The fine Tudor brickwork of the entrance tower dates from 1485 but much of the rest is Victorian. The palace is rarely open to the public.

The garden and deconsecrated church of **St Mary**, by Lambeth Bridge, contains the **Museum of Garden History**, based on the work of two 17th-century royal gardeners, John Tradescant, father and son, who introduced exotic fruits such as pineapples to Britain (Mon–Fri 10.30am–4pm, Sun 10.30am–5pm). The **St Thomas's Hospital** complex by the river includes the **Florence Nightingale Museum ❷**, with memorabilia and an idea of her contribution to nursing (2 Lambeth Palace Road, 10am–5pm, closed Mon, admission fee).

Lambeth Road leads to the impressive **Imperial War Museum ❸** (daily 10am–6pm, entrance fee), housed in the 1811 Bethlehem hospital for the insane. The museum has a social conscience, and there is much civilian material from the two world wars as well as the latest in weaponry. An audio-visual recreates a wartime air raid on a London street, and visitors can effectively experience conditions in the trenches during World War I. The museum's **Holocaust Exhibition** is built around the testimonies of a selection of survivors who tell of their experiences chronologically from the origins of anti-Semitism through to its horrific conclusion. Larger items include a section of a deportation railcar, the entrance to a gas chamber, a dissection table, shoes collected from victims of the gas chambers and a large model of part of Auschwitz.

County Hall's attractions

Back by the river, downstream from Westminster Bridge and facing the Houses of Parliament, is the majestic **County Hall ❹**, built between 1909 and 1922 and seat of the Greater London Council, which

LEFT: the London Eye, beside County Hall. **BELOW:** the Imperial War Museum.

"Space Elephant" by the river outside the Dalí Universe.

ran London until an unsympathetic Thatcher government abolished it in 1986. Now owned by Japan's Shirayama Shokusan Corporation, it incorporates an upmarket hotel (Marriott), a utilitarian hotel (Travel Inn), an aquarium, an Dalí art gallery and attractions such as a games arcade and a branch of McDonald's.

The **London Aquarium** (daily 10am–6pm, last admission 5pm, admission charge, tel: 7967 8000) contains thousands of specimens representing 350 species of fish. Atmospheric sounds, smells and lighting have been employed to great effect. It's worth catching the shark and rainforest talks (tel: 7967 8029 for schedule) and feed times (shark feeding Tues, Thurs, Sat 2.30pm; piranha feeding Mon, Wed, Fri and Sun 1pm), when divers deliver a mix of mackerel and squid.

To the right of the Aquarium entrance as you face Country Hall, **Namco Station** (daily 10am–midnight) is a neon-lit entertainment centre with the latest Playstation and video games, bumper cars, fruit machines, and a bowling alley.

The **Dalí Universe** (daily 10am–5.30pm) puts more than 500 of Salvador Dalí's works on show. The three themed areas are: 'Sensuality and Femininity' (which includes the well-known Mae West Lips Sofa and the sculpture *Buste de Femme Retrospectif*), 'Religion and Mythology' (which includes St George and the Dragon and the epic illustration of Dante's *Divine Comedy*), and 'Dreams and Fantasy' (which includes *Persistence of Memory* and *Profile of Time*).

The London Eye

Towering over County Hall is the British Airways-sponsored **London Eye ❺**, the world's largest observation wheel, supported on one side only, like a giant desktop fan, and built to mark the turn of the millennium. At 450 ft (135 metres), it is the fourth highest structure in London. The 32 enclosed capsules, each hold-

BELOW: tanks for the memory at the London Aquarium.

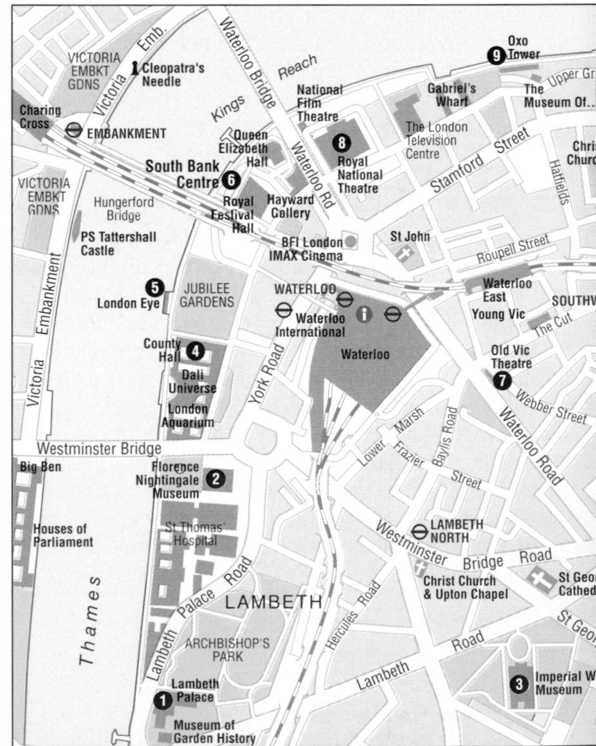

Map on pages 194–5

ing 25 people, take 30 minutes to make a full rotation – a speed slow enough to allow passengers to step in and out of the capsules while the wheel keeps moving. On a clear day, you can see for 25 miles (40 km). Plan ahead if you hope to ride the Eye at busy periods (automated telephone booking: 0870 5000 600).

The South Bank: premier arts venue

The **South Bank Centre** ❻ is Europe's largest arts complex. The **Royal Festival Hall**, the only permanent building designed for the 1951 Festival of Britain, is a major music venue. In 1967 the 2,900-seat RFH gained two smaller neighbours, the 917-seater **Queen Elizabeth Hall**, designed for chamber concerts, music theatre and opera, and the 372-seater **Purcell Room**, intended for solo recitals and chamber music. For bookings, ring 020-7960 4242 for all the halls.

On the upper level of the South Bank Centre complex is the **Hayward Gallery** (tel: 020-7960 4242), which has changing contemporary art exhibitions. The Hayward's cutting-edge programme focuses on four areas: single artists, historical themes and artistic movements, other cultures, and contemporary themes (notably shows on art and film and on sound).

Emblem of the 1951 Festival of Britain.

Next door is the **National Film Theatre**, Britain's leading arthouse cinema since 1952 (box office: 020-7928 3232). With three auditoria, it holds more than 2,400 screenings and events each year, from lovingly restored silent movies (to a live piano accompaniment) to pioneering world cinema productions. It also runs the **BFI London IMAX Cinema** (tel: 020-7902 1234), which rises like a behemoth from the roundabout at the south end of Waterloo Bridge. Large-format film – 10 times the size of standard 35mm stock – is projected onto a screen 66 ft high by 85 ft wide (20 by 26 metres).

The South Bank and Southwark

0 — 300 m
0 — 300 yds

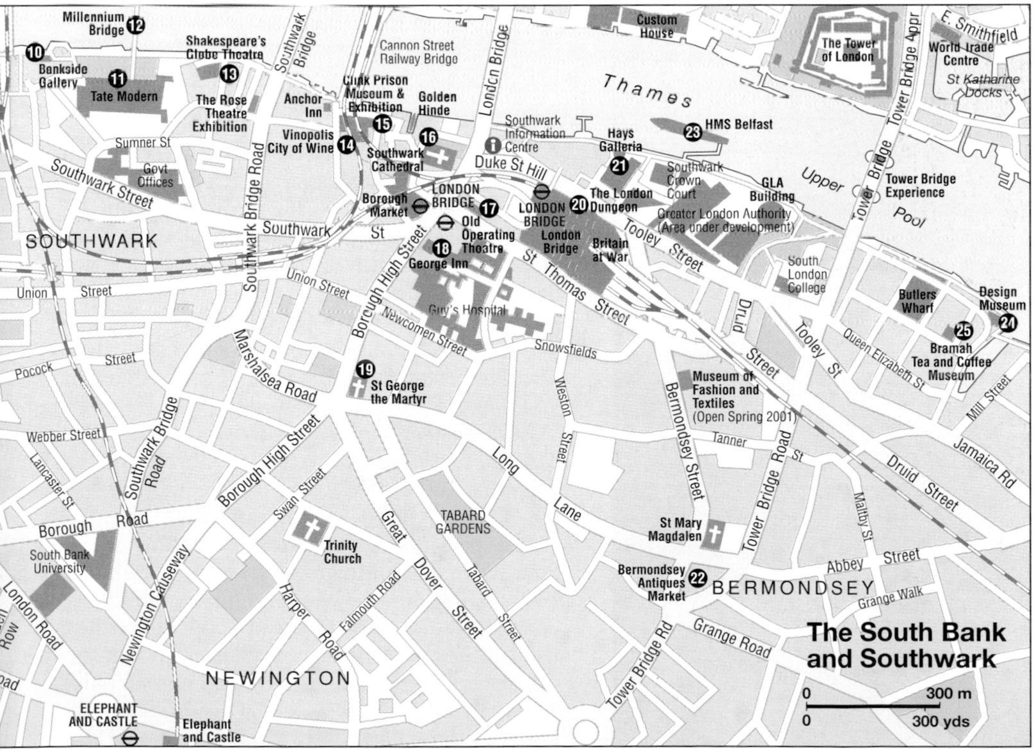

The Oxo Tower, with viewing platform overlooking the river.

Waterloo Road leads down to the **Old Vic** ❼ theatre (1811) in The Cut. This landmark has had a chequered history, from its early days as a music hall to its status as the first home of the National Theatre, and its present incarnation as a repertory theatre. Further along The Cut, the **Young Vic** mounts an adventurous programme, including many experimental plays.

The Royal National Theatre

Back by the river, on the other side of **Waterloo Bridge**, built largely by women during World War II, is the concrete bulk of the **Royal National Theatre** ❽ *(see page 81)*. Opened in 1976, it houses three theatres under one roof: the 1,200-seater **Olivier**, the 900-seater **Lyttelton**, a two-tier proscenium theatre, and the **Cottesloe**, an intimate space with galleries on three sides. For a peek behind the scenes, book a one-hour backstage tour (Mon–Sat at 10.15am, 12.30pm – or 12.15pm on Olivier matinee days – and 5.15pm; tel: 7452 3400).

To the east of the National Theatre, past an 18-storey tower housing London Weekend Television, is **Gabriel's Wharf**, a small group of speciality shops and restaurants backed by a striking set of *trompe l'œil* paintings. Set back from the river, the distinctive Art Deco **Oxo Tower** ❾ has pinprick windows outlining the words "Oxo", a gimmick the makers of the beef extract of the same name designed to get round a ban on advertising on the riverfront. A smart (meaning expensive) restaurant, bar and brasserie is situated on the top floor, run by the fashionable Knightsbridge store, Harvey Nichols. Immediately to the south of the Oxo Tower, located in an unconverted warehouse is **The Museum Of...** Its incomplete name indicates that it constantly changes its focus, holding temporary exhibitions (on subjects such as 'Me' and 'The Unknown').

BELOW:
Tate Modern.

Beyond Blackfriars Bridge, the riverside walk leads past the **Bankside Gallery** ❿, the home of both the Royal Watercolour Society and the Royal Society of Painter-Printmakers. It has changing exhibitions.

Tate Modern

Easily identifiable by its tall brick chimney, **Tate Modern** ⓫ (Sun–Thurs 10am–6pm, Fri–Sat 10am–10pm; admission free) occupies the former Bankside Power Station and houses the Tate's entire international modern collection and part of its contemporary collection. The contents of its 88 galleries range from Picasso's *Weeping Woman* and Dalí's *Lobster Telephone* to the very latest works of international artists. The main entrance, to the west of the building, takes you into the ground floor through a broad sweep of glass doors and then down a massive concrete ramp. The impressive space rising six storeys in front of you is the Turbine Hall, the old boiler room now capable of housing massive sculptural works.

The permanent collection, including work by Picasso, Matisse, Mondrian, Duchamp, Dalí, Bacon, Pollock, Rothko and Warhol, plus sculpture by Giacometti, Hepworth and Epstein, is housed on the third and fifth levels. Works are organised in four themes – the nude, landscape, still life and history painting. Although the thematic system of display has been criticised by those who prefer a more traditional chronological system of hanging, Tate Modern's curators argue that juxtaposing work produced before the 1970s with the work of contemporary artists shows how artists have learnt from one another since 1900.

Giving easy pedestrian access to Tate Modern from St Paul's Cathedral, across the river, the innovative **Millennium Bridge** ⓬ became in 2000 the first new river crossing in central London since Tower Bridge opened in 1894. A sort of stainless-steel scalpel, it uses horizontal suspension cables to enhance the thinness. However, opening-day crowds caused the bridge to sway excessively, and it had to be closed for several months of engineering adjustments.

Shakespeare's Globe

Bankside and Southwark are the South Bank's most historic areas. They grew up in competition with the City opposite, but by the 16th century had become dens of vice. Bankside was famous for brothels, bear and bull-baiting pits, prize fights and the first playhouses, including **Shakespeare's Globe** ⓭. The replica of the 1599 building opened in 1996 and is worth a visit even if you're not seeing a play (guided tours every half-hour 9.15am–12.15pm). The Globe has been painstakingly re-created using the original methods of construction. The season of the open-air galleried theatre runs from May to September (box office tel: 020-7401 9919). The theatre, which is particularly suited to Shakespeare's comedies, can accommodate 1,500 people – 600 standing (and liable to get wet if it rains) and the rest seated. The wooden benches can feel distinctly hard by Act III, but you can rent cushions. The fascinating Shakespeare's Globe Exhibition, to the right of the theatre, is well worth a visit.

Shakespeare also acted at the **Rose Theatre**, whose foundations were dis-

The original Globe burned down when a stage cannon fired during a performance of "Henry VIII" set fire to the thatched roof. The roof of the modern building – the only thatch permitted in London – is fire-proofed.

BELOW: Shakespeare's Globe on Bankside.

A warm welcome for visitors to the "Golden Hinde".

covered close by in 1989. Turn down New Globe Walk (by the Globe's box office) and then left into Park Street. At Number 56, the **Rose Exhibition** (daily 10am–5pm), a sound-and-light presentation narrated by Sir Ian McKellan, tells the story of the Rose, Bankside's first theatre, built in 1587.

Back on the riverside walk, by Southwark Bridge, is the **Anchor Inn** (tel: 020-7407 1577). The present building, dating to 1770–75, is the sole survivor of the 22 busy inns that once lined Bankside. A maze of passageways, the Anchor combines a minstrels' gallery, ancient oak beams, dark staircases and creaking floorboards. Dr Samuel Johnson, of dictionary fame, drank here.

Across the road from this boldly traditional pub is the main entrance to **Vinopolis, City of Wine ⓮**. Occupying 2½ acres (1 hectare) of cathedral-like spaces under railway arches, this sprawling attraction offers a visual wine tour through exhibits of the world's major wine regions. Individual audio units and earphones give access to four hours of recorded commentary in six languages, and the admission fee to the wine tour includes tickets for five wine tastings.

The Clink Exhibition

Like most country bishops, the bishops of the powerful see of Winchester had a London base. A single gable wall remains of **Winchester Palace**, their former London residence. They had their own laws, regulated the many local brothels and were the first authority in England to think of locking up miscreants. The prison they founded, in Clink Street, remained a lock-up until the 18th century, and the word Clink became a euphemism for jail. **Clink Exhibition ⓯** recalls the area's prostitution and displays working armoury (10am–6pm daily). Beside each exhibit, plaques give information on aspects of prison life and history.

BELOW: Southwark Cathedral, by Borough Market.

Clink Street leads on to Pickfords Wharf, built in 1864 for storing hops, flour and seeds, and now an apartment block. At the end of the street, in the **St Mary Overie Dock**, is a full-size replica of Sir Francis Drake's galleon, the ***Golden Hinde*** (open daily 9am–sunset). The Devon-built ship, launched in 1973, is the only replica to have completed a circumnavigation of the globe. It has thus clocked up more nautical miles than the original, in which Drake set sail in 1577 on the greatest piratical voyage in English history.

Southwark Cathedral

Southwark Cathedral ⓰, hemmed in by the railway, has a lovely interior and is one of London's great historic churches. In the 12th century it was a priory church, and it has a Norman north door, early Gothic work and a number of medieval ornaments. The cathedral is a rich fund of local history. A number of its memorials and chantries reflect Southwark's importance in Elizabethan and Jacobean London. A memorial to Shakespeare in the south aisle, paid for by public subscription in 1912, shows the bard reclining in front of a frieze of 16th-century Bankside. Above it is a modern (1954) stained-glass window depicting characters from his plays. Shakespeare was a parishioner for several years. John Harvard, who gave his name to the American university, was baptised here, and is commemorated in the Harvard

Chapel. Near the Shakespeare memorial is a plaque to Sam Wanamaker, the energetic actor who championed the Globe's re-creation.

Borough Market, outside the cathedral, is a wholesale fruit and vegetable market dating from the 13th century, and supplies restaurants and hotels in the centre of town. Trade begins in earnest at around 2am.

At 9A St Thomas Street, across Borough High Street from the cathedral, the **Old Operating Theatre & Herb Garret** ⓱ (daily 10.30am–5pm, tel: 020-8806 4325) is the only surviving 19th-century operating theatre in Britain. It offers a gruesome but fascinating insight into both the social history of Southwark and the sometimes fearsome medical techniques of the day. The Herb Garret displays herbs and equipment used in the preparation of 19th-century medicines.

Back on Borough High Street, at number 77, is the 17th-century **George Inn** ⓲, the only remaining galleried coaching inn in London. It was mentioned by Dickens in *Little Dorrit* and is now run by the National Trust. Further down Borough High Street is the **Church of St George the Martyr** ⓳, sometimes known as "Little Dorrit's Church" because Dickens's heroine was baptised and married there. There are recitals at 1pm on Thursdays (free but donations welcome), when you are invited to bring a packed lunch.

The 1940s look at the Britain at War Museum.

Around London Bridge

The present three span **London Bridge**, dating from 1967–72, is the latest of many on this site *(see page 114)*. The first bridge, probably made of wood, was built by the Romans around AD50. In Tooley Street, which runs beside London Bridge Station, the **London Dungeon** ⓴ includes ghoulish exhibits of the Black Death, the Great Fire of 1666 and Jack the Ripper's exploits. A few doors away, **Winston Churchill's Britain at War Museum** recreates the sounds and smells of the blitz through special effects. School parties have great fun trying on helmets and gas masks and has a lot of 1940s memorabilia. Opposite is **Hay's Galleria** ㉑, a small leisure mall carved out of a former tea wharf.

BELOW: a warm welcome at the London Dungeon.

To the southeast are several antiques shops, and **Bermondsey Antiques Market** ㉒, best visited early on Friday. Downstream from Hay's Galleria is **HMS *Belfast*** ㉓ *(pictured on page 115)*, a gun-bristling cruiser, and last of the warships to have seen action in World War II (daily 10am–6pm, Oct–Apr 10am–5pm). Its tour ranges from the bridge to the engine rooms.

The oval-shaped office building under construction by the river here is designated as the **headquarters of the Greater London Authority**, the body responsible for much of the city's administration.

The old warehouses east of Tower Bridge contain a gourmet's delight. The gourmet in question is Habitat founder Sir Terence Conran, who has opened up five restaurants in the biscuit-coloured **Butler's Wharf**. The **Design Museum** ㉔, also inspired by Conran, has an exhibition of influential design and artefacts, mainly 20th-century, as well as hands-on displays.

At the rear of the plain white building, at 1 Maguire Street, is the small and charming **Bramah Tea and Coffee Museum** ㉕, which gives a history of the long-established trade in London (10am–6pm). ❑

DICKENS
HOUSE

HOLBORN AND FLEET STREET

Between the West End and the City lies legal London and the ancient Inns of Court. National newspapers used to be based here, which accounts for the large number of congenial pubs

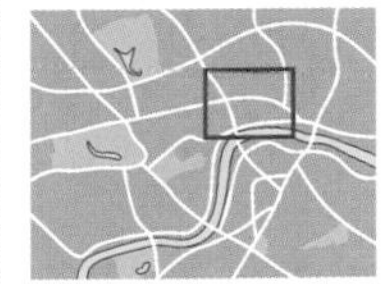

Kingsway marks the western boundary of legal London. It was named for George V, and its tunnel was a miracle of urban engineering in its day. It was built for trams to dive beneath the building on the half-moon shaped Aldwych, and emerge at Waterloo Bridge. In the middle of this island is the British Broadcasting Corporation's **Bush House** ❶, headquarters of the national broadcasting station's overseas service, floodlit by night. Its optimistic frontage with the motto, "Nation shall speak unto nation", is echoed by the soaring arch with its twin figures. From this building, the World Service broadcasts in most major languages to most corners of the world.

Opposite Bush House on the Strand, extending down to the Embankment by Waterloo Bridge, is **Somerset House** ❷, one of England's finest 18th-century buildings. It seems much too grand to have been built as an office block, but that's just what it was – the city's first when it was put up in 1770, and for many years it housed the official registry of births, marriages and deaths. It now accommodates the **Courtauld Institute**, a small but highly representative collection of 20th-century European art with major Impressionist paintings. Most of the works are so famous they will be familiar: the Institute is London University's art history studies centre (10am–6pm, Sun 2–6pm, admission fee). The **Gilbert Collection** of European silver, snuff boxes, Italians mosaics, clocks, and many other magnificent treasures is housed in the Embankment section of the building. This gives access to the splendid River Terrace, which in summer has a café with great views.

PRECEDING PAGES: griffins, guardians of the City, perched on Holborn Viaduct.
LEFT: Dickens House Museum.
BELOW: bewigged barristers outside the Law Courts.

Two churches sit on traffic islands in the Strand: by Bush House is the Baroque **St Mary le Strand**, built by James Gibbs in 1714; a short distance further east is **St Clement Danes** ❸, begun by Wren in 1769 and later given a "bonnet" by Gibbs. The church has an association with the Royal Air Force.

At the end of the Strand on the left are the **Royal Courts of Justice** ❹, which deal with libels, divorces and all civil cases. The courts moved to these new premises from Westminster Hall in 1884. The neo-Gothic confection of towers and spires has around 1,000 rooms, and newspaper and television journalists often hang around its entrance awaiting verdicts and reporting scandals. Visitors are free to sit in the public galleries of the 58 courts when trials are in session.

The lawyers' lodgings

All around this area are the **Inns of Court**, home of London's legal profession. The "Inns" were once, much as they sound, places of rest and comfort for trainee lawyers. From the 19th century onward, law was taught at King's College, next to Somerset House in the Strand, and at University College in Gower Street. Before then,

Manet's "Bar at Folies Bergères" is one of the many familiar paintings at the Courtauld Institute.

the only way to obtain legal training was to serve an apprenticeship in one of the Inns. Four still remain: **Middle Temple ❺** and **Inner Temple ❻** on the Embankment. and **Gray's Inn** and **Lincoln's Inn** on the north side of the High Court. With cobbled lanes, cramped chambers and brass plaques bearing Dickensian names, they are atmospheric places to stroll around, particularly the Temple Inns. These Inns take their name from the crusading Knights Templar who built the **Temple Church** here in the 12th century, inspired by the Church of the Holy Sepulchre in Jerusalem. The knights were based here until 1312; there are a number of the knights' tombs inside, and a tiny punishment cell by the altar.

Conservative though they might seem today, these Inns used to be far from respectable. A 17th-century Act of Parliament restrained the young lawyers; "they were not to wear beards of more than three weeks' growth upon pain of a fine of forty shillings". In 1601 the first performance of Shakespeare's *Twelfth Night* was given in the Inner Temple and other entertainment included dice, dancing, archery, football and wrestling. All were practised in the now-quiet quadrangles. Many traditions remain: a horn still summons members to dinner and would-be lawyers must to dine here a certain number of times each year.

North of the High Court, between Kingsway and Chancery Lane, is **Lincoln's Inn ❼**, alma mater of Oliver Cromwell, and the two great 19th-century prime ministers and rivals for Queen Victoria's favour, William Gladstone and Benjamin Disraeli. The Elizabethan writer Ben Jonson designed the gate house (9am–6pm, closed weekends). **Lincoln's Inn Fields** were created for students' recreation but the best sport of all was watching the early city planners try to outmanoeuvre each other: Inigo Jones sat on a 17th-century Royal Commission

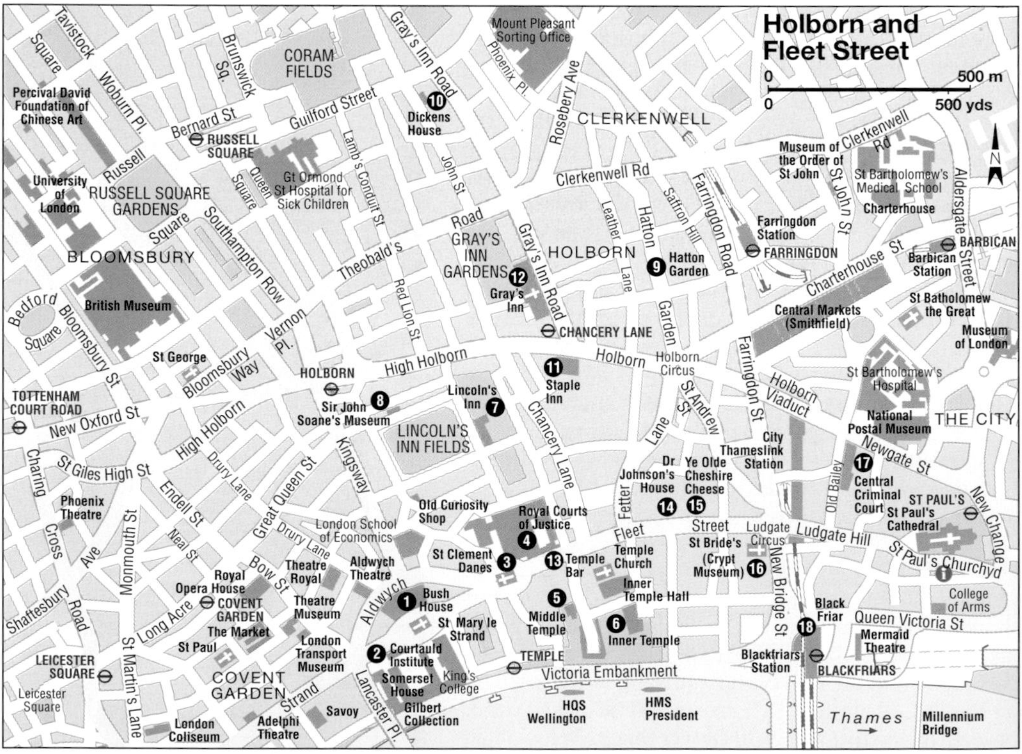

Walk around the Temple Inns at night: their courtyards and alleys are gas-lit, evoking a Dickensian world of quill pens.

Holborn and Fleet Street

to decide the area's fate. Today, visitors can puzzle out the significance of Barry Flanagan's large sheet-steel sculpture *Camdonian* in the northeast corner, watch the lunchtime netball games or pass on to one of London's gems, **Sir John Soane's Museum.** ❽ (10am–5pm, closed Sun, Mon; 6–9pm first Tue of each month, donations appreciated). This is a self-endowed monument to one of London's most important architects and collectors who died in 1837, the year of Queen Victoria's accession. He left his house and collection, including an Egyptian sarcophagus and Hogarth's *Rake's Progress*, much as they had been during his lifetime. Soane was also responsible for Britain's first public art gallery, the Dulwich Picture Gallery in south London *(see page 238)*. He built his private home on three sites along the north edge of Lincoln's Inn Fields (No.13) and it is a delight to visit – like being in a miniature British Museum.

Map, page 204

Dickens's world

The ghost of the great Victorian writer Charles Dickens (1812–1870) haunts the streets of Holborn. His most famous settings are here: **Bleeding Heart Yard**, scene of much of the domestic action in *Little Dorrit*, is only a quiet step or two away from the bustle of **Hatton Garden** ❾, the centre of London's diamond trade, and **Leather Lane**, a crowded street where market stalls sell fresh food and household goods. The museum of **Dickens House** ❿ is at 47 Doughty Street (10am–5pm, closed Sun, admission fee). Dickens was brought to London at an early age, and started work in a boot-blacking factory off the Strand. He became a reporter in the House of Commons, and began to write books which reflected areas and themes of London he knew well. His first marital home was on the site of the fine neo-Gothic Prudential Assurance building in Holborn, opposite

"Mr Weller's knowledge of London was extensive and peculiar"

— CHARLES DICKENS

BELOW LEFT: Royal Courts of Justice.
BELOW: Sir John Soane's Museum

"A tavern chair is the throne of human felicity".

— DR SAMUEL JOHNSON

the half-timbered row of shops at the bottom of Gray's Inn Road. This is **Staple Inn** ⓫, one of the former Inns of Chancery that dealt with commercial law. A survivor of the Great Fire of London, it shows how much of the city must have looked before 1666. Dickens suffered his legal apprenticeship at **Gray's Inn** ⓬ (10am–4pm weekdays). Dating from the 14th century, its grounds lie just to the west of Gray's Inn Road. The magnificent garden was laid out by Francis Bacon, the Elizabethan essayist. Among the host of other famous people to serve here were Bacon's contemporary, the poet Sir Philip Sydney, Hilaire Belloc (1870–1953) and the 20th-century socialist Sidney Webb. With an irony that must have tickled Dickens's sense of the law's ridiculousness, Gray's Inn Hall saw the first production of Shakespeare's *Comedy of Errors*.

East of Gray's Inn road is **Clerkenwell**, a district of immigrant and revolutionary traditions. In the 19th century, Chartists and Home Rule agitators collected around Clerkenwell Green. Lenin edited a newspaper in what is now the **Marx Memorial Library**, at 37a Clerkenwell Green, and Giuseppe Mazzini, the Italian revolutionary, lived at 10 Laystall Street.

The Street of Shame

Just beyond the Temple Inn and the Royal Courts of Justice is **Temple Bar** ⓭, marked by a menacing griffin on a plinth. This is the boundary between Westminster and the City of London, beyond which, theoretically, the monarch cannot pass without the permission of the Lord Mayor. It also marks the start of **Fleet Street**, which was the home of Britain's press after the first daily newspaper, the *Courant*, was published here in 1702. But the new technology introduced by William Caxton's printing press in the late 15th century was forced to give way to even newer technology in the 1980s.

BELOW: Fleet Street's most famous pub.

The Street of Ink and Adventure (or, to the more cynical, the Street of Shame) was abandoned by the owners for cheaper sites and left to the lawyers who spilled out of their cramped, ancient offices in the Inns of Court, and to financial institutions. But there is still evidence of the street's illustrious past. Dr Samuel Johnson, who famously quipped "A man who is tired of London is tired of life", lived in the back-courts at 17 Gough Square from 1748 to 1759 where, with the help of six assistants, he compiled the first English dictionary. **Dr Johnson's House** ⓮ is an evocative museum of this great man of letters (11am–5.30pm, closed Sun; Oct–Apr 11am–5pm, closed Sun, admission fee).

Drinkers in the nearby **Ye Old Cheshire Cheese** ⓯ pub in Wine Office Court will still raise a glass in his memory. The pub has small rooms with wooden seats, a reminder of the time when there were no bars and people sat at tables where they were waited on by the publican. Other popular literary figures are remembered here, including the crime writer Edgar Wallace (1875–1932) who is also immortalised on a plaque on the northwest corner of Ludgate Circus, at the far end of Fleet Street near St Paul's. He had his first newspaper job in the building that stands on this site. The other famous journalists' watering hole, **El Vino** wine bar, at No. 47, was notoriously reactionary, maintaining, even in the face of court action, its policy of not serving unaccompanied females at the bar. Not so long ago, it was packed daily with lawyers and with hard-drinking and hard-gossiping national newspaper journalists.

Two magnificent Art Deco buildings were designed, interestingly, for the most reactionary papers: the *Daily Telegraph*'s Elcock and Sutcliffe building at No. 135, now occupied by a bank, and the *Daily Express*'s black-and-silver flagship at No. 121. Opposite is the Reuters building, designed by Sir Edwin Lutyens in 1935, behind which is "the journalists' and printers' church", **St Bride's** ⓰, where the ghosts of Fleet Street's past live on. It was near here that the aptly named Wynkyn de Worde, an associate of William Caxton from Alsace, set up the street's first press. Now there is a small museum of Fleet Street in the Crypt, where a magpie collection of Roman mosaics from a villa on this site, Saxon church walls, William Caxton's *Ovid* and a large number of coffins are stored – much was revealed when the building was badly bomb-damaged in World War II. Samuel Pepys, the celebrated diarist, was baptised at St Bride's (he was born in 1633 in Salisbury Court, off Fleet Street) and he records in his diary how he had to bribe the sexton to find room for his brother's corpse here. The church's elegant spire makes it Sir Christopher Wren's tallest church and it is said to have inspired the first tiered wedding-cake. Lunchtime concerts are often held here during the week.

ABOVE: the Black Friar Art Deco pub. **BELOW:** Staple Inn, lone remnant of London before the 1666 Great Fire.

Monks' and miscreants' cells

Ludgate Circus, at the end of Fleet Street, leads up to St Paul's. The River Fleet used to be a "disembouging stream", according to the 18th-century poet Alexander Pope, which "rolls the large tribute of dead dogs to Thames". The river, which acted as a sluice for Smithfield meat market, was finally buried underground in the 18th century. It marked the western edge of the Roman city of London, which was pierced by six gates. Ludgate was named after a mythical 4th-century BC King Lud.

The Fleet Prison for debtors was on the right bank of the river, Newgate prison on the left. Executions took place here after 1868, when a law brought an end to the rowdy public spectacles they had become. It was latterly an open-air construction to lessen the risk of judges and jurors catching "gaol fever".

On the site of the former prison, just beyond Ludgate Circus is the **Central Criminal Court** ⓱, universally known by the name of the street in which it is located, **Old Bailey**. Some of the country's most unpleasant criminals have been brought to account here, and in the forbidding No. 1 Court, until the abolition of the death penalty in 1965, convicted murderers were sentenced to be hanged, the judges placing black caps on their heads as they passed sentence. On top of the Old Bailey, a golden figure of justice by F.W. Pomeroy stands with a sword in her right hand and scales to weigh the evidence in her left.

The underground River Fleet enters the Thames at Blackfriars Bridge, named after a monastery that was here from 1278 to 1530. A fine monument to this monastic order is the 1905 **Black Friar** ⓲, on the corner of Queen Victoria Street, the most spectacular Arts and Crafts pub in London. ❑

Mirth

ST PAUL'S AND THE CITY

The City, covering just one square mile, is Britain's main financial centre. This was the original London, contained by Roman walls, and it retains its own government and police force

Map, page 212

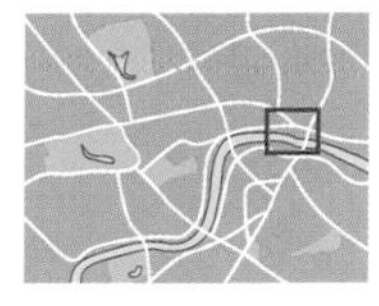

The City, London's ancient financial quarter, is a world apart from the rest of the capital. It runs its own affairs and is quite separate from London's local government organisation. It has its own police force and a very distinct set of hierarchies. Here, even the Queen treads carefully: on her coronation drive in 1953, she was obliged – by tradition rather than force – to stop at Temple Bar and declare, before continuing into the City, that she came in peace. The name "Square Mile" is given to this financial district that was until relatively recently regarded as "the clearing-house of the world", but it signifies far more than a limited geographical area. For most of its 2,000-year history, the City *was* London. Today the area is humming with late 20th-century technology, but is still heavy with archaic traditions which have helped a potentially faceless financial world retain a certain degree of character.

Like any closed world, the City doesn't open up easily to the outsider. Peering out of a tourist bus at acres of glass and concrete is far too superficial an examination; time and legwork in the network of alleys and backstreets which thread through the office blocks will reveal much more.

The City's past isn't readily accessible through its buildings. It has been devastated twice. In 1666 the Great Fire devoured four-fifths of the City, and in the winter of 1940–41 Germany's Luftwaffe pounded it night after night during the Blitz, leaving one-third in smoking ruins.

● *An interior plan of St Paul's can be found on the last page of this book.*

PRECEDING PAGE: dolphin fountain by Tower Bridge.
LEFT: St Paul's with fairground organ.
BELOW: the Lord Mayor in his coach.

The miraculous St Paul's

Rising majestically above the wartime smoke, miraculously unharmed, was the magnificent dome of **St Paul's Cathedral** ❶ (Mon–Sat 9.30am-4pm, entrance fee, tours at 11am, 11.30am, 1.30pm, 2pm). The first purpose-built Protestant cathedral is Sir Christopher Wren's greatest work. A tablet above Wren's plain marble tomb reads: *Lector, si monumentum requiris, circumspice*, "Reader, if you wish to see his memorial, look around you."

Historians believe that the first church on the St Paul's site was built in the 7th century, although it only really came into its own as Old St Paul's in the 14th century, and by the 16th century it was the tallest cathedral in England. Much of the building was destroyed in the Great Fire of 1666. Construction on the new St Paul's Cathedral began in 1675, when Wren was 43 years old.

The architect was an old man of 78 when his son Christopher finally laid the highest stone of the lantern on the central cupola in 1710. In total, the cathedral cost £747,954 to build, and most of the money was raised through taxing coal arriving in the port of London. The building is massive and the Portland stone dome alone weighs more than 50,000 tons. Generations of schoolchildren have giggled secret messages in St Paul's

The City Information Centre on the south side of St Paul's has details of walks, talks and events (tel: 0171 332 1456).

Whispering Gallery, more than 100 ft (30 metres) of perfect acoustic, as the most musical of royal weddings bore witness when Prince Charles married Lady Diana Spencer in 1981.

Associated with the church were the great metaphysical poet John Donne (1572–1631), who was Dean, and the victor of the Battle of Trafalgar: Admiral Lord Nelson, whose body lies in the crypt. The magnificent, much copied Holman Hunt painting *The Light of the World*, hangs in the south aisle. There are fine statues by Flaxman and Bacon of the painter Sir Joshua Reynolds (1723–92) and of the great wit and lexicographer Samuel Johnson (1709–84). Much of the wood carving in the church is by the master sculptor Grinling Gibbons (1648–1720).

The area around St Paul's, and in particular the ancient market site known as **Paternoster Square**, has been developed. The only contemporary echo of the shepherding and marketing that used to be done here is Elizabeth Frink's sculpture of a flock of sheep, a sight that has sobered up many a drinker on a foggy night. The mediocrity of most of the buildings hemming in St Paul's has long been criticised and Prince Charles joined in the chorus of disapproval. New plans are being studied to reconcile God and Mammon by replacing the box-like offices with new buildings and giving the cathedral room to breathe.

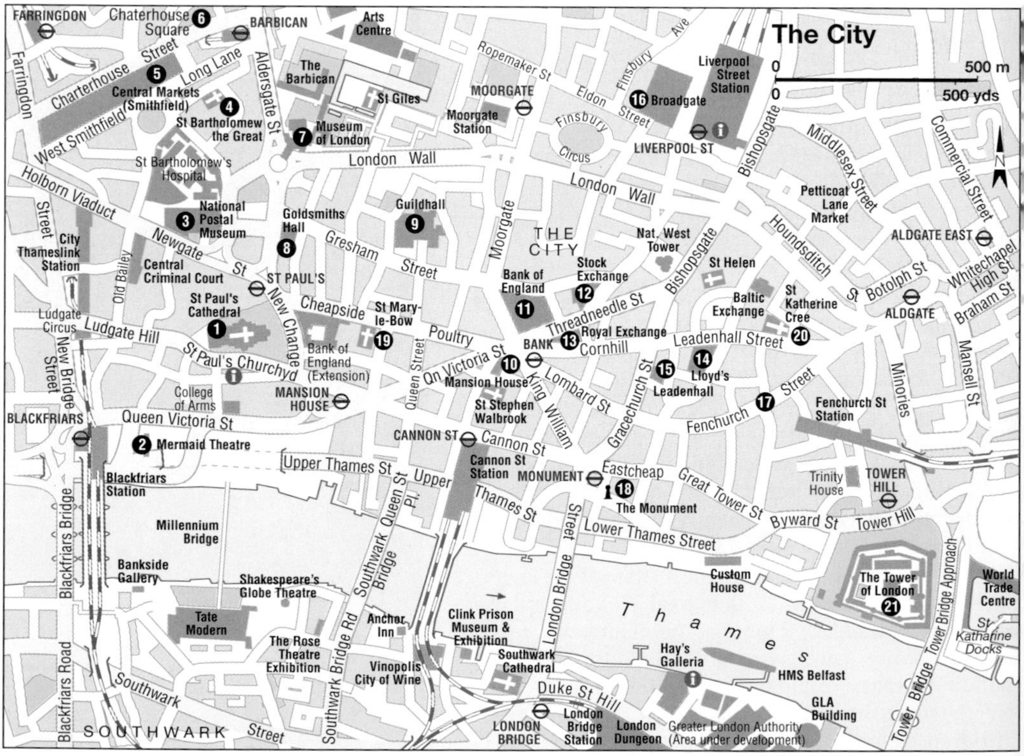

Down the hill from St Paul's and closer to the river is the quaintly named **Puddle Dock**, which today looks not so quaintly like a motorway. There was once, apparently, a Mr Puddle. In 1616, the year Shakespeare died, a movement to open a theatre here was thwarted by the monks at the nearby monastery of Black Friars (who gave this area its modern name). It wasn't until 1956 that the lively **Mermaid Theatre** ❷ was founded; currently it is given over to corporate events rather than drama. There are several Wren churches in the warren of roads that lead from St Paul's to the river. **St Andrew-by-the Wardrobe** in St Andrew's Hill, was named because it stood near a royal furniture store. **St Nicholas Cole Abbey** is followed by **St Benet's** which serves as the Metropolitan Welsh Church. On the other side of Queen Victoria Street is the **College of Arms** with a fine 17th-century interior by William Emmett and a library of heraldry and genealogy which, for a fee, deals with genealogy enquiries (10am–4pm week-days). Other Wren churches here include **St James Garlickhythe** on busy Upper Thames Street, which was disastrously struck by a crane which demolished its rose window in 1991, and **St Michael Paternoster**, the burial place of Dick Whittington (1423), a Lord Mayor of London, who has gone into British mythology as a pantomime figure, with his cat, Puss-in-Boots. This rags-to-riches story sets out to prove that even country bumpkins could be elected Lord Mayor of the City, though the real Whittington came from a wealthy county family and amassed a fortune as a merchant.

Map, page 212

Market at work

North of St Paul's, on Newgate Street is the **National Postal Museum** ❸ (10am–4pm, closed weekends) which claims to have the most extensive collection of postage stamps in the world, as well as other memorabilia of the Royal Mail. Behind is the great block of **St Bartholomew's Hospital**, founded in 1122 and the oldest in London; its venerability, however, didn't shield it from savage government cutbacks in the 1990s. Opposite it, high on the wall at the corner of **Giltspur Street** and **Cock Lane**, is a naked golden figure of a urinating boy, symbolising the eventual extinguishing of the Great Fire at this point. Just

Below: St Paul's majestic nave and choir stalls carved by Grinling Gibbons.

beyond, in **West Smithfield**, are memorials to the Scottish hero William Wallace, victim of a spot of judicial butchery here in 1305, and to the 270 "Marian martyrs", Protestants burned at the stake for religious heresy by Queen Mary before her own unhappy end. The church of **St Bartholomew the Great ❹**, one of the oldest in the city, hides in a corner of the square, perhaps a trifle shocked or shamed by what has passed before, for this was also the site of the Bartholomew Fair, immortalised in Ben Jonson's noisy play.

The unlikely adjacent confection of iron and plaster is **Smithfield meat market ❺**, which should be visited (by non-vegetarians) early on a winter's morning. Here the porters and workers known as "bummarees" thunder about with their barrowloads of carcasses, the refrigerated lorries roar and rumble, and the knife-grinders shower sparks out of the backs of their vans. Through all the commotion, it's still possible to hear "backchat", Smithfield's equivalent of Billingsgate profanity, designed to fool unwanted listeners. The Smithfield day ends as most people's day is beginning. The area has long been a haunt for late-night and early-morning revellers who like to rub shoulders in the pubs and cafés with market workers, while pursuing the high-cholesterol "breakfasts" which are the porters' dinners.

ABOVE: St John's Gate.
BELOW: Roman fragment in the Museum of London.

Smithfield is the last of the great markets still on its original site. It originally traded in live animals which were herded in from the country, but the gore of slaughter proved too much for the Victorians, who made some changes: Stinking Lane became Newgate Street, Blow Bladder Lane became King Edward Street, and the Smithfield meat was slaughtered outside the capital.

Smithfield has resisted becoming a shopping *piazza* like Covent Garden, but the area has already gone "up-market". Just north of Smithfield are the remains

ROMAN LONDON

London's 2,000 years of history are still accessible through a section of Roman Wall in Moorgate, through a Tudor oriel window in Cloth Fair, through the street names and through the people. The Romans established the City in AD 45, but there are few remains. The **Roman Wall** which was 2 miles (3 km) long, 20 ft high and 9 ft wide (6 by 3 metres) and had six magnificent gates (Ludgate, Aldersgate, Cripplegate, Newgate, Bishopsgate and Aldgate) is now found only in fragments. Good sections can still be seen at London Wall, Noble Street, Cooper's Row and the Museum of London. There are also remains on the approach to the Tower of London from Tower Hill Underground station.The wall's course can be traced with the help of maps which have been set up on the City's pavements. Constant building is always unearthing new finds. The mosaic above was found under Leadenhall Street.

In 1869 the **Bucklersbury Mosaic** was discovered in Cannon Street and in 1954 the **Temple of Mithras** was found under the Bucklersbury building. The reconstructed temple can now be seen on the Bucklersbury site and the mosaic and sculptures found at the original site are in the **Museum of London**.

of two religious houses. The quiet of the Georgian **Charterhouse Square** ❻, with gas lamps and cobbles, is a favourite location for "period" film-makers. The carthusian **Charterhouse** still has around 40 residents**.** To the left of it, approached through the medieval **St John's Gate** off Clerkenwell Road, is St John's priory, founded by the crusading Order of the Knights of St John. Little remains of the buildings dissolved by Henry VIII, but there is a small museum in the Gate House (Mon–Fri 10am–5pm, Sat 10am–4pm; admission fee), and there are guided tours of the Grand Hall and remains of the Priory Chapel which, like the Temple Church off Fleet Street, was round.

Museum of London and the Barbican

A flavour of the the City's trading past remains today in the main shopping thoroughfare, **Cheapside**, behind St Paul's. In medieval times Cheapside (from the old English word *ceap* – to barter) was the City's mercantile heart. The names of the side-streets, Bread Street, Milk Street and Wood Street, give an idea of the merchandise. Just beyond Cheapside was the poulterers' area, now known simply as **Poultry**. **Cannon Street** (a corruption of candlewick), which runs parallel, was the candlemakers' area. **Garlick Hill** could be smelt from Cheapside.

For a feeling of how the City used to be, the **Museum of London** ❼ is an essential stop (Mon–Sat 10am–5.50pm, Sun 12–5.50pm, entrance fee). The galleries run in chronological order from prehistoric London to the present day and feature lovingly reconstructed rooms ranging from an Elizabethan parlour to a 1930s barber shop. A highlight of the visit is the audio-visual recreation of the Great Fire. The museum is on the site of a Roman fort and lies beside The **Barbican Centre**, based around three 42-storey towers, the only residential

"I am still unable to decide whether the City is a person, or a place, or a thing... You read in the morning paper that the City is "deeply depressed"... at noon it is "buoyant", and by four o'clock it is "wildly excited".

— Stephen Leacock, *My Discovery of England*

Below: St Bartholomew the Great.

The Barbican Centre is home to the London Symphony Orchestra and is the London base of the Royal Shakespeare Company.
For information, tel: 020-7638 4141.

block in the City. With an arts centre and business space, it was devised by the Corporation after World War II to attract residents and boost a falling City population. It took more than 20 years to build and has been attacked since its opening for its inaccessibility and maze-like interior. The community ideal was never realised as the flats were sold at exorbitant prices. However, anyone who braves the ubiquitous orange carpet will find a cultural cornucopia including an art gallery, a cinema, the Royal Shakespeare Company and the London Symphony Orchestra within the centre. During the day there are foyer performances and live music on the terrace of the Waterside café which overlooks the fountains.

Guildhall and the livery companies

Craftsmen with the same trade tended to congregate in small areas, and clubbed together to form medieval guilds. Like trade unions, the guilds operated to ward off foreign competition and established an apprenticeship system. They set standards for their goods and ran mutual aid schemes which helped members in difficulty. The more prosperous guilds built halls to meet and dine in and wore lavish uniforms or "liveries", in due course becoming **livery companies**.

For years there was considerable inter-guild rivalry and in 1515 the Lord Mayor interceded and named a top 12 based on wealth: Mercers (dealers in fine cloth), Grocers, Drapers, Fishmongers, Goldsmiths, Skinners, Merchant Taylors, Haberdashers, Slaters, Ironmongers, Vintners and Clothworkers. Competition between the Skinners and Merchant Taylors, who both claimed the number six slot, was particularly vicious. The Lord Mayor, with Solomon-like decisiveness, decreed they should alternate positions six and seven every year. His action originated the expression "at sixes and sevens" meaning "uncertain".

BELOW: a guild member in regalia. **BELOW RIGHT:** a memorial to Horatio Nelson in Guildhall.

Down the centuries the livery companies shed their Mafia image and became part of the establishment, promoting charities and founding some of England's better educational institutes, including Haberdashers' College and Goldsmiths' College.

Today some of the most impressive portals in the City belong to livery halls. Behind their gleaming paintwork and elaborate carvings members dine as lavishly as ever. Most spectacularly pompous is **Goldsmiths** ❽ in Foster Lane, between the Museum of London and St Paul's, where the integrity of gold and silver issued the previous year is checked in an annual ceremony. The use of the word "hallmark" as a seal of value originated here. Unfortunately visitors are not usually allowed inside the livery halls, except in special circumstances.

While the 96 livery companies today have little connection with their original crafts, they still exert influence in their home territory. The City is governed by the City Corporation, chaired by the **Lord Mayor**. The office of Lord Mayor dates from 1189 and since then a number of colourful and sometimes bizarre ceremonies have become attached to the job. The new Mayor is elected each year on Michaelmas Day, 29 September, when the reigning Lord Mayor and his aldermen parade through the streets carrying small posies of flowers to ward off the stench which filled the City when the ceremony began.

In November the mayor is sworn in at the **Guildhall** ❾, taking up his symbols of office in a ceremony known as the Silent Change, so called because no words are spoken. The Guildhall is open every day and is the best place to glimpse the guilds' past (daily 9am–5pm, free). Dating from the 15th century and several times restored, it is decorated with the liveries' banners and shields. The Clockmakers' Company displays timepieces in an adjacent room (9.30am–4.45pm

Map, page 212

BELOW LEFT: the Royal Exchange.
BELOW: St Stephen Walbrook, "Wren's best" church.

weekdays, free). The Lord Mayor's Show is held a day after his swearing-in. This colourful parade through the streets starts at the Guildhall and passes through the City, culminating at **Mansion House** ⑩, opposite the Bank of England. This is the Lord Mayor's official residence, designed by George Dance the Elder in 1785, but its magnificent rooms are not open to the public.

Behind Mansion House is **St Stephen Walbrook**, dating from 1096, and the Lord Mayor's church, considered Wren's best. Its dome is believed to be a dry run for St Paul's, and its controversial "cheeseboard" altar is by Henry Moore.

The mythical griffin decorates much of the City's street

Monuments to the money men

The triangular inter-section known as **Bank** can intimidate. Civic architecture abounds, with Sir Edwin Lutyens' Midland Bank building on the north-west, the Mansion House on the western corner, the Royal Exchange building to the east and Sir John Soane's implacable facade of the Bank of England to the north. All the City's great institutions grew from the fulfilment of the most basic needs and have only subsequently acquired their superior air. Banking first came to the City in the 17th century when Italian refugees set up lending benches (*banca* in Italian) in **Lombard Street**, running eastwards from the Bank of England. Today the businesses seem far from temporary, and range from merchant banks in quaint 18th-century houses to major clearing banks such as the National Westminster in its 600-ft (180-metre) tower in Old Broad Street, 200 yards east of the Bank of England.

The **Bank of England** ⑪ dominates the Bank square as it does the British financial scene. Popularly known as the Old Lady of Threadneedle Street, a name which probably originates from a late 18th-century cartoon depicting an

BELOW: Commodity Exchange dealers.

old lady (the bank) trying to prevent the then Prime Minister, Pitt the Younger, from securing her gold. The name stuck because it aptly describes the conservative, maternalistic role the Bank played in stabilising the country's economy – a role strengthened in 1997 when the new Labour government freed it from direct government control. The Bank of England was set up in 1694 to finance a war against the Dutch. In return for a £1.2 million loan, it was granted a charter and became a bank of issue (with the right to print notes and take deposits). Today it prints and destroys 5 million notes daily and stores the nation's gold reserves. Its present home was largely rebuilt between 1925 and 1939. It covers 3 acres (1.2 hectares) and contains the **Bank of England Museum** with items of interest from the banking world (10am–5pm weekdays, free).

Map, page 212

Stocks and shares

The **Stock Exchange ⓬**, just along Threadneedle Street, was formed in a similar fashion, by merchants who were trying to raise money for a Far Eastern trip in 1553. It has changed enormously since 1986. Before that time it was an exclusive club with cosy, restrictive practices which benefited members and excluded competition. Members divided into jobbers and brokers. Brokers traded in the market for their clients while jobbers acted as wholesalers. A minimum commission was charged for transactions.

In October 1986, threatened with legal action from the Government, the Stock Exchange agreed reluctantly to radical changes in its practices. The "Big Bang" abolished the fixed commission system, merged jobber and broker functions, and transferred dealing to SEAQ, a computerised quotation system. Not only individuals, but also institutions were allowed to become members, which meant

BELOW: the London Stock Exchange.

that foreign securities houses could buy in. As a result, the market is now a much fairer place, but a duller one and there is no longer a visitors' gallery from which to watch the activity. The trading floor, which was once crowded with frantic, pin-striped figures, now echoes like a vast swimming bath – empty apart from a handful of options traders. A leisurely game of cricket is even rumoured to have been played on this floor, the holy turf of the financial world. However, some 7,000 listed securities change hands here and 60,000 bargains are still struck every day, in business amounting to several billion pounds.

Trading has certainly not diminished in the City. Today's traders are not dealing in beef or boxes of carnations, but commodities measured in thousands of tons. The commodity markets, the **London Commercial Sale Rooms** and **Plantation House** in Fenchurch Street, fix prices and place orders for commodities as diverse as coffee and rubber. Impersonal deals are struck by phone and on screen except for "futures" (promises to take deliveries in the future) where dealing is done in person on the trading floor.

The real cut and thrust of buying and selling takes place in the ring of the **London Metal Exchange** in Fenchurch Street and on the dealing floor of **Liffe** (London International Financial Futures Exchange) in the **Royal Exchange** ⓭ at Cornhill by the Bank of England. Each metal is traded for five minutes only and up to 45,000 bargains may be struck in a single day as animated young men in traditional garish blazers shout and wave for their professional lives.

Lloyd's of London

The Big Bang brought immediate demands for new office buildings which would be purpose-built for modern communications and, by 1991, 1.7 sq. miles

BELOW: Leadenhall Market, a popular lunchtime place.

(4.4 sq. km) of office space had been built in the City. One of the first, and the most dramatic, is Sir Richard Rogers's 1986 **Lloyd's of London** ⓮ building in Lime Street. For so long the biggest insurance group in the world, Lloyd's began life operating out of a coffee house. The business started in the 17th-century coffee house of Edward Lloyd, where underwriters, shippers and bankers gathered. Its practices remained largely unchanged for 300 years, but in the late 1980s sundry international disasters led to some huge payouts and millions of pounds were lost. Many "names" – investors who shouldered the insurance risks, often through syndicates, and who had always thought their investment as safe as the Bank of England – lost life savings and owed more than they could ever possibly pay; a few killed themselves.

The building is no longer open to visitors, but a walk around the outside, where glass elevators whisk employees to their offices is a highlight of the modern City. Hidden from site on a magnificent marble floor is a wooden rostrum housing the **Lutine Bell**, which was rung once for bad news and twice for good. The huge **Casualty Book** contains a record of all ships lost at sea.

Beside this modern building is the more accessible **Leadenhall** ⓯, once the wholesale market for poultry and game, and now a handsome commercial centre. It has been prettified and its magnificent airy Victorian cream and maroon structure has a collection of sandwich bars, stylish restaurants, food and book shops, which attract city workers at breakfast and lunchtime.

London's other steel-and-glass Victorian constructions – the railway stations – were also given facelifts during the 1980s building boom. **Liverpool Street** was overhauled along with the adjacent **Broadgate** ⓰, one of the most ambitious developments in the City, with 13 office-block buildings around three

Map, page 212

Above: voluptuous "Broadgate Venus".
Below: Sir Richard Rogers's 1986 Lloyd's building.

squares including an ice rink at Broadgate Square. Fernando Botero's hugely voluptuous *Broadgate Venus* is a high point. **Fenchurch Street** ⓱ acquired the 1930s Manhattan-style **1 America Square** over its railway lines.

Above: Wren's Monument marks the spot where the Great Fire began. **Below:** a panorama of the City from the Lloyd's building.

Monument to Sir Christopher Wren

The best view of Lloyd's is from the top of the **Monument** ⓲, in Monument Yard (9am–5.40pm; 2–5.40pm weekends; Oct–Mar 9am–3.40 closed Sun; admission fee). After the destruction caused by the Great Fire in 1666, Sir Christopher Wren was asked to redesign large parts of the City, including numerous churches. The Monument, a Roman Doric column erected according to Wren's designs to commemorate the fire, stands 202 ft (61 metres) high. The height is exactly the same as the distance between the monument's base and the king's baker's house in Pudding Lane where the fire began.

The Great Fire lasted five days and spread through 460 streets, destroying 89 churches and more than 13,000 houses. At the base of the column is a relief depicting the king and his citizens fighting the blaze. Inside, 311 steps wind giddily up to a small platform, from which the view is spectacular. Ron Koster of the Netherlands holds the record for ascending and descending the column in a speedy 2 minutes and 40 seconds, though such activity is not encouraged.

Appropriately enough, the Monument gallery affords a chance to appreciate the remarkable vision Wren imposed on the City through his spires. There are 56 Wren spires, and you risk severe Wren-fatigue if you attempt to see them all. Selected visits reveal the work of the artist at the height of his powers.

St Mary-le-Bow ⓳ is the home of the famous Bow bells, which give their own kind of baptism – that of being a true Londoner, or cockney – to anyone born within earshot. The original bells were destroyed in the war, but new ones were recast from the fragments. The church interior after restoration is rather vulgar, but the Norman crypt, now a restaurant called The Place Below, is worth a look. Wren left his mark on London because so much of it had been destroyed in the Great Fire, but several churches survived the conflagration, including **St Katherine Cree** ⓴, a mix of Classical and Gothic, in Leadenhall Street. Henry Purcell played on its fine 17th-century organ, and the painter Hans Holbein, a plague victim, was buried here in 1543.

East of the Monument is the **Tower of London** ㉑, the City's oldest building. At first sight it can look like a cardboard model, but closer inspection reveals an awesome solidity which encompasses much of Britain's history (Mon–Sat 9am–5pm, 10am–5pm Sun, closes at 4pm Nov–Feb; admission fee. *See pages 224–5*). **The Tower Hill Pageant** on Tower Hill Terrace offers a whistle-stop tour of the City's history, with tableaux, models and documents presented by the Museum of London (9.30am–5.30pm daily, entrance fee).

Visits to the Tower are exhausting, but refreshment is within easy walking distance. The **Ship** pub off Eastcheap and the **Samuel Pepys** on the river have real character and real ale. For a taste of City fare, visit **Sweetings** in Queen Victoria Street, the City's oldest fish restaurant. This is an institution, and it behaves like one. You can't book and you have to fight for a drink in the bar. The menu ranges from excellent fresh fish to stodgy nursery-school puddings, catering to the public-school clientele. Around the corner in Cannon Street is the less genteel **Corney and Barrow**, an exclusive wine bar. Here you can sip pink champagne, and listen to the under-30s crowd swap details of their deals and salaries. ❑

Map, page 212

Queen Victoria Street was built in 1867–71, and the District Line was constructed beneath it at the same time.

THE TOWER OF LONDON

One of the city's great attractions is its medieval palace and fort. Guardian of the crown jewels and steeped in the blood of martyrs, it brings history to life

Encircled by a moat (now dry), with 22 towers and standing at the edge of the medieval City walls by Tower Bridge, the Tower of London is Britain's finest medieval military monument. Uniquely, it served as a fort, arsenal, palace and prison. It was also the treasury, record office, observatory, royal mint and zoo, as animals given to monarchs were, until 1834, kept in the Lion Tower by the present entrance.

At its centre is the White Tower built by William I after his conquest of England in 1066 and containing the fine Norman Chapel of St John on the first floor. Henry VIII added the domestic architecture of the Queen's House behind the Tower on the left, which is where the Tower's governor lives. The most recent buildings are the 19th-century Museum and Waterloo Barracks, to the right of the Tower, which contains the Jewel House where the Crown Jewels are a major attraction. There are a dozen crowns and a glittering array of swords, sceptres and orbs used on royal occasions. Many date from Charles II's reign (1660–85), when the monarchy was restored.

THE CROWN JEWELS ▷ The Imperial State Crown was made in 1937 for the coronation of George VI. The largest of its 2,800 diamonds is the Star of Africa and it is topped with a sapphire dating from Edward the Confessor, last of the Saxon kings.

◁ RAVEN'S NEST The raven is the symbol of the Tower. Nine live here, looked after by The Ravenmaster, a Yeoman Warder. It is said that the day the ravens leave the Tower, England will fall. As a precaution, their wings have been clipped.

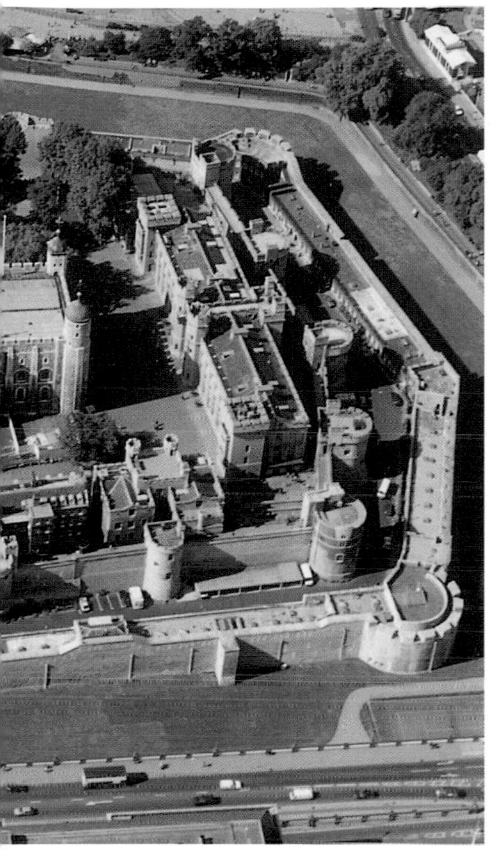

△ THE NEW ARMORIES
The Royal Armouries collection was started by Henry VIII. His own suits of armour have been moved, along with a large part of the collection, to a site in Leeds in the north of England. A small collection remains.

◁ THE WHITE TOWER
At the centre of the fortress, the White Tower has walls 15ft (5m) thick. Designed by a Norman monk, Gandulf, it is 90ft (27m) high with an entrance 15ft (5m) above ground level. It is not square and each tower is different.

EMINENT PRISONERS

These carvings in Beauchamp Tower may be the last written words of prisoners awaiting their fate. The prestigious jail was reserved for eminent enemies of the state. Henry VI and Richard II were among royal prisoners, while Edward IV's heirs, Prince Edward, aged 12, and Prince Richard, 10, were murdered in the Bloody Tower in 1483.

The executioner's axe came down on Tower Hill, but the privileged lost their lives on the block inside the Tower's grounds, among them two wives of Henry VIII: Anne Boleyn and Catherine Howard. In World War II German spies were shot here. The Duke or Orleans, captured at the Battle of Agincourt in 1485, composed verse and contemplated his fate here for 25 years. One of Shakespeare's patrons, the Earl of Southampton, was painted with his cat, said to have climbed down the chimney to find him. The most eloquent prisoners were Sir Thomas More and Sir Walter Raleigh. More, author of *Utopia*, refused to recognise Henry VIII as head of the church, and before his execution he wrote *Dialogue of Comfort against Tribulation*. Raleigh, the Elizabethan buccaneer, wrote *The History of the World* during his 12-year incarceration here with his family.

◁ THE BEEFEATERS
Forty Yeomen Warders live in the Tower. Attired in Tudor uniforms, they first took up their posts under Edward VI (1547–53). Their nickname, Beefeaters, may come from the French *buffetier*, a servant, though an "eater" was also used to describe a servant in English.

△ A ROYAL PALACE
The Tower of London was a royal palace until the mid-16th century. The main palace buildings were above Traitors Gate, the river entrance through which prisoners were brought. The Wakefield Tower, part of the complex, housed the state archives from 1360 to 1856.

NS

SANPELLEGRINO

DOCKLANDS AND THE EAST END

Map, page 230

Once, this was the warehouse of the world and the working-class heartland of London. Now the cargo ships have gone and an astonishing new city of high-tech offices and printworks has arisen

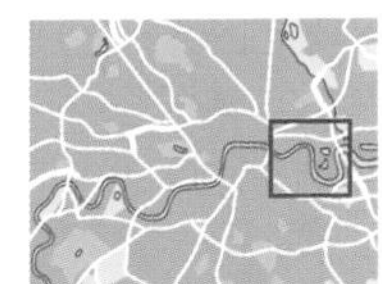

The East End was the workhouse as well as the entry point to London. Where the City ended, the poorer districts of Spitalfields, Whitechapel, Wapping, Stepney, Bow and Hackney began, growing with the trade coming in through the massive dock system which, in the second half of the 19th century, had 55 miles (88 km) of wharves and quays. This was the seedy end of town, where pirates, prize-fighters and sundry villains were to be considered, though it was also a haunt of Pepys and Dickens. The East End is a broad term and it covers everything east of the City, including Docklands, and stretches down the widening Thames towards Essex The stiletto spires of Wren churches in the City give way to the solid white square towers of his successor, Nicholas Hawksmoor (1661–1736), which suffered along with everything else during the 1940 Blitz, and hurried post-war housing left much to be desired.

PRECEDING PAGES: Mudchute Farm on the Isle of Dogs.
LEFT: dining out in Docklands.
RIGHT: passing yachts in St Katharine's Dock.

From the 1960s, when container ports were built at the Thames estuary, the docks slid into a swift and inexorable decline. In 1981 Billingsgate Market, the home of fresh fish and foul language, moved from the City to the Isle of Dogs, at the start of a massive redevelopment of the 25 sq. miles (65 sq. km) of docklands. The government earmarked £350 million for the regeneration of the area, and set up the London Docklands Development Corporation (LDDC) to oversee it. Land values rocketed. A prime site that was valued at £70,000 an acre in 1981 increased to £3 million by 1987, when the Docklands Light Railway was opened.

But the recession took a savage toll. Olympia and York, who had set the tone with the massive buildings of Canary Wharf, had to be bailed out in 1991 and building did not get underway again until 1996. By this time there was an 80 percent occupancy of the Wharf, with such prestigious tenants as Citibank and Reader's Digest joining the Fleet Street newspapers which had been in the vanguard of the move east. Local authorities began to take over responsibility for Docklands in 1997, and by 2000 the builders were at work on the next phase.

Getting there

Docklands begins on the downstream side of Tower Bridge, principally on the north bank which can be divided into three distinct areas: Wapping and Limehouse in the west; the Isle of Dogs in the centre; and the Royal Docks around the mouth of the River Lea, in the east. Docklands is essentially a business area, and there is little community life to be found, but its architecture is breathtaking, and a ride through it on the **Docklands Light Railway** (DLR) is an adventure: there is often a running commentary from a guide on the train. The

Ostrich feathers in St Katharine's Dock. At the end of the 19th century, fashion houses imported 400 tons a year.

opening of the Jubilee Line extension in 1998, linking up the south bank, is bound to make the whole area more accessible.

Notable in **Wapping**, a former seafarers' area by Tower Bridge where Dr Samuel Johnson said you could see "such modes of life as very few could even imagine", is **St Katharine's Dock** ❶, built by Thomas Telford in 1828 and the first to be refurbished as a tourist attraction. Captain Scott and his ship the *Discovery* set sail from here on their disastrous voyage to the South Pole in 1910. Today the Dickens Inn, built around an 18th-century brewery, provides a pleasant place to sit and watch the yachts in the basins, including a number of historic vessels such as the handsome Thames Barges.

Wapping and Canary Wharf

To the east is Rupert Murdoch's printing and publishing plant, the subject of vicious labour clashes when his papers were brought here from Fleet Street in 1988. Until he arrived, most Londoners associated Wapping with riverside pubs such as the **Prospect of Whitby** ❷ in Wapping High Street, long a tourist haunt. It dates from 1520, and Gustave Doré drew its intimate interior while J.M.W. Turner and James Whistler sketched the river from its terrace. It is probably London's oldest pub still in use, though the Town of Ramsgate, next to **Wapping Old Stairs** where condemned pirates were chained to be drowned, is nearly as ancient. Wapping is headquarters of the River Police.

Beyond Wapping is **Limehouse**, the Chinese quarter of Victorian London, where Sherlock Holmes went for his fixes in the opium dens. It is hard to imagine them here now, but a little atmosphere remains, again around the traditional pubs such as the Grapes, which has a wooden verandah over the river. The Black

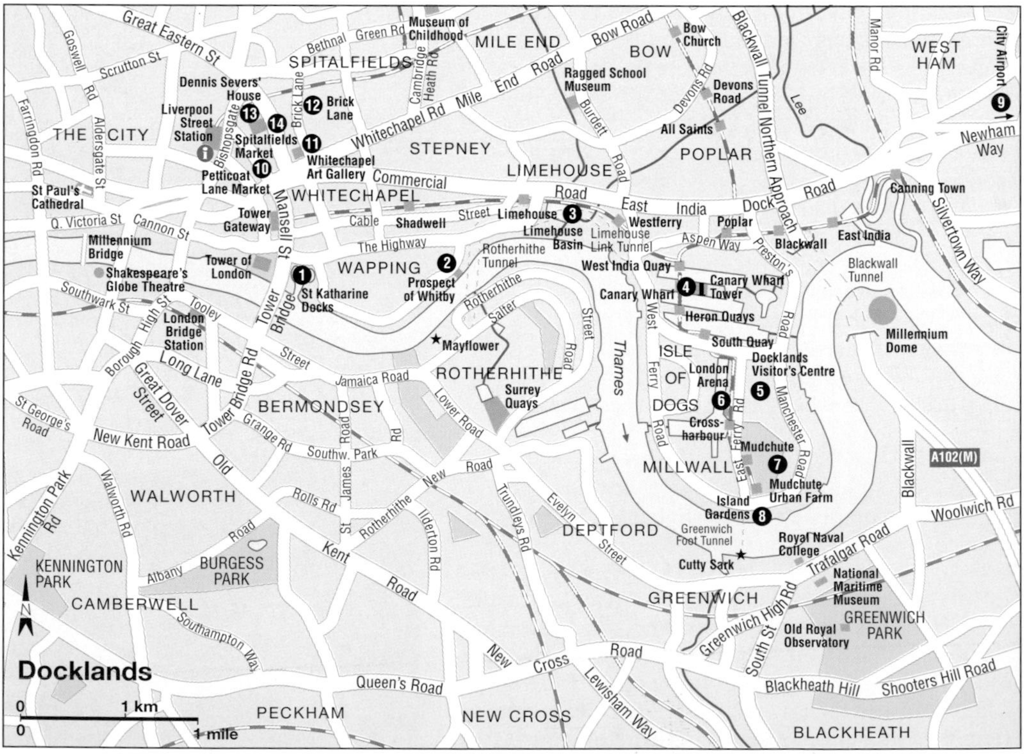

Docklands

Horse on the opposite side of the street has been renamed The House They Left Behind, after recent redevelopment. Hops growing outside are a reminder that Limehouse brewery stood nearby. The colourful, pencil-thin canal barges in the **Limehouse Basin** ❸ are evidence that this is where the **Regent's Canal** slips almost unnoticed into the Thames (*see page 242*). **Narrow Street**, which has become rather a smart address, was a bottleneck into the Isle of Dogs, and traffic on the Highway from Wapping now disappears beneath Limehouse Link, near the entry point to the Rotherhithe cross-Thames tunnel, and re-emerges on the edge of the Canary Wharf developments.

A canal cut from Limehouse through to the River Lea isolates the land to the south, but long before it was cut, the marshy area of the Isle of Dogs was used by Henry VIII for hunting, and his hounds may have given the Isle of Dogs its name. Alternatively, the name may be a corruption of "ducks", which once flocked to this marshy region, where, in the 18th century, the largest dock system in the world was created in the West India and Millwall Docks.

The **Canary Wharf** ❹ complex dominates this area today, centred on Cesar Pelli's 800-ft (244-metre) tower, the largest in London, set down on a massive man-made island in the middle of the West India docks. Arriving by Docklands railway, it seems like a bustling modern terminal, with shops and offices leading immediately from the station, and a sudden business-like air. Canary Wharf lies between the West India and South Docks, the Surrey Quays, where the newspaper industry has spread comprehensively enough to attract an IRA bomb in 1996. The incident led to the closure of the tower to the public.

Alight at Crossharbour by Millwall Docks for the **London Docklands Visitors Centre** ❺ (8.30am–6.30pm weekdays, 9.30am–5.30pm weekends), which

Map, page 230

Offices were lured to Canary Wharf with 100 percent capital allowances against tax and zero business rates for 10 years.

BELOW: Docklands Light Railway.

gives a good account of the area, and the **London Arena** ❻, which stages occasional big concerts.

The next stop, Mudchute, is beside **Mudchute Urban Farm** ❼, built out of mud excavated from Millwall docks and moved by a chute to this site. It covers 35 acres (14 hectares) and is home to a variety of farm animals (9.30am–4,30pm, phone to find out events: 0171 515 5901). The farm is in **Millwall** on the southern edge of the Isle of Dogs, with tidy terraces and some heart. **Cubitt Town** on the southeast corner was built in the 1840s by the future Lord Mayor of London, William Cubitt.

Millwall docks were a favourite spot for villains to dispose of bodies, putting them inside stolen cars and pushing them off the quays. The LDDC maintains that when developers started work in the 1980s, the dock was so full of old cars they let them rest in peace.

The last stop on this branch of the DLR is **Island Gardens** ❽, and from here there is a magnificent view of Wren's beautiful Royal Naval College (*see page 240*) at Greenwich, with the Observatory behind and the masts of the *Cutty Sark* pricking the skyline. It has been described as the best view of London, and it was famously painted by Antonio Canaletto. A foot tunnel, built in 1902 for local workers to cross to the West India Docks, goes under the river from here.

On the east side of the Isle of Dogs are the Royal Docks and the **City Airport** ❾, with scheduled flights to UK and northwest Europe. The airport, aimed at businessmen, is served by small aircraft only, with strict noise limits.

Troubled East End streets

The large Jewish community in East London was centred along Commercial Road and Cable Street, where in the 1930s Oswald Mosley, leader of the British Union of Fascists, provocatively led a march and was soundly beaten off by the local residents. Bloom's, the great East End Jewish restaurant in **Whitechapel**, closed in 1996, reflecting the demographic change in the area, which is now

BELOW: old barge, new docks.

predominantly Asian and its business almost entirely in inexpensive and ethnic clothes. The area, however, has a gruesome past. From 30 August to 9 November 1888, Jack the Ripper terrorised the streets, murdering five prostitutes, identified by his trademark – a double slash of the throat. His victims were destitute women who pawned their petticoats in **Middlesex Street** ❿, better known as **Petticoat Lane**, and sold their bodies.

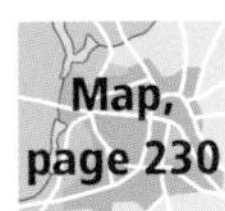

Whitechapel Art Gallery ⓫, near Aldgate Underground station, is a fine Art Nouveau building by Charles Harrison Townsend (1901). Its exhibitions of contemporary painters are often free and there is a good restaurant and café.

Nearby **Brick Lane** ⓬ is the centre of the Bengali community, and street signs are in Bengali. This is a great place for Indian food, particularly *balti*, and the prices are extremely cheap.

The streets of **Spitalfields** leading off the west side of Brick Lane contain several streets of architectural interest. These 18th-century houses were the homes of Huguenot silk weavers. With intricate porticos, large doors and shutters, many have been restored, and walking down **Fournier Street** at night you can see chandeliers lit in authentic, small, panelled rooms, with paintings on the walls and pewter plates on shelves. Most original is **Dennis Severs' House** ⓭ at 18 Folgate Street, a four-storey town house still lit only by gaslight. It is a private home but it can be visited on the first Sunday afternoon of each month, or on the first Monday evening by prior arrangement (tel: 0171 247 4013).On the edge of these streets is **Christ Church**, completed in 1729 and considered the greatest of Hawksmoor's churches, but its fortunes declined as the 19th-century Industrial Revolution made silk weavers obsolete.

ABOVE: Jack the Ripper, scourge of Whitechapel.

BELOW: Laser show from the tower at Canary Wharf.

To the west lies **Spitalfields Market** ⓮. This is a good evening haunt, with traditional pubs in the narrow lanes surrounding the former market place where there is a clutch of intriguing restaurants, such as the Salvo Jure and the Victorian Oven. A **Tourist Information Office** is in the market.

Further afield

Beyond Whitechapel, in Cambridge Heath Road, is the **Bethnal Green Museum of Childhood**, one of the largest of its kind in the world. It is run by the Victoria and Albert Museum and contains toys from all over Europe and North America, as well as some from other parts of the world. It also shows the social history of children over the past 300 years (Bethnal Green Underground, 10am–5.50pm, weekends 2.30–5.30pm, closed Fri, free). One aspect of childhood is also covered in the **Ragged School Museum** at 46 Copperfield Road, E3. This shows how the orphans of a Dr Barnardo's School lived at the end of the 19th century (Mile End Underground, 10am–5pm, Wed–Thur, 2–5pm first Sun in month, free).

Hackney, north of Spitalfields, is known for its popular concert venue, the Hackney Empire. It also has the **Geffrye Museum**, an 18th-century almshouse in Kingsland Road, the gift of Sir Robert Geffrye, a Lord Mayor of London, in 1715. Its 10 main rooms have been decorated to represent interiors from different ages of history from Tudor times to the 1950s (Old Street Underground, 10am–5pm, Sun 2–5pm, closed Mon, free). ❑

ALES
THE CAMDEN

AD
SA N BAR

VILLAGE LONDON

London grew by swallowing up villages. But they're still there in spirit, each with its own distinctive character

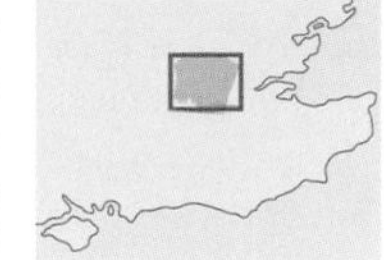

At its widest point, from South Croydon to Potter's Bar, the metropolis is nearly 60 miles (100 km) across and, though the overall population has been in decline since World War II, London remains one of the world's most populous cities. Perhaps because it is so big, many of those who live within its confines hardly think of it as a unified city at all, but as a collection of largely independent villages or communities. While Londoners may commute many miles to work, they are likely to do their shopping in their local High Streets and build their social lives on their home patch.

The River Thames cuts through London, forming an effective physical and psychological block to free movement. While south Londoners stream across London Bridge to work in the City every day, they are more likely to go shopping in Croydon or Bromley than in the West End, and north Londoners will head further north to such shopping citadels as Brent Cross. Many people born within the metropolis do not move more than a few miles from their home, and would not dream of "transponting" to the other side of the river.

Many of London's "villages" were once true villages surrounded by open fields. Others are more accurately described as "communities", where concentrations of different ethnic groups have created their own environments over years of immigration. Central London has lost many of its most historic buildings to such natural disasters as the Great Fire, and to unnatural disasters such as World War II bombing and the onward march of voracious developers. However, some have been able to preserve their historic hearts.

Many villages have been swamped by development. Croydon, once a village to the south, now has pretensions to city status. If it were recognised as a separate entity, it would rank as one of the 15 largest cities in the United Kingdom. Already it has a Manhattan-style high-rise town centre, which houses the head offices of major national and multi-national corporations, superlative shopping facilities and good night life, including theatres and one of London's best concert halls.

While most visitors are busy with the tourist haunts of the City and West End, those who go further afield are rewarded with a glimpse of what the locals call "real London": the London where Londoners live. All but Dulwich, Blackheath and Greenwich, which are served by overground railways, are on the Underground network. All are served by London Transport buses. ❑

PRECEDING PAGES: a pub in Camden, north London – pubs are at the centre of local life.
LEFT: Brixton market, south London: minorities give communities their style

DULWICH

Gypsy Hill in Dulwich was a meeting place of the nation's gypsy community until the end of the 19th century. The gypsies used to come down to the village to tell fortunes. One old fortune-teller sat cross-legged on Dulwich green for so long that when she died they buried her sitting up.

One of the finest views of London's sprawl is from the clubhouse at Dulwich Golf Club. Yet the foreground is green and wooded, like the heart of the English countryside. With leafy streets and Georgian, Victorian and Edwardian houses, with a village school and a spacious park which inspired the poet Robert Browning, Dulwich is an oasis of rural calm. It is largely the creation of one man, Edward Alleyn, an Elizabethan actor-manager who bought land in the area in 1605 and established the Estates Governors of God's Gift to administer a chapel, almshouses and a schoolroom for the poor.

Today, the estate has more than 15,000 homes, Dulwich College, Alleyn's School and James Allen Girl's School. The land has not changed hands for more than 300 years, and the last village farm disappeared only in 1954. The Dulwich college silver was pawned during the Civil War to provide funds for the Royalist cause, but recovered its fortunes, and a bequest of valuable paintings (originally intended for the Polish National Gallery) to the college led to the opening of **Dulwich Picture Gallery**. The magnificent building was designed by Sir John Soane and opened in 1814. Included in the gallery are important works by Rembrandt, Rubens, Van Dyck, Gainsborough, Murillo and others and, although it's a little off the beaten track, art connoisseurs will be well rewarded by a visit.

At one end of Dulwich village the **Old Grammar School** was built to the plans of Charles Barry, who later designed the Houses of Parliament. His son, Charles Barry the Younger, was responsible for the superb Italianate edifice, reminiscent of Venice, which now houses Dulwich College. ❑

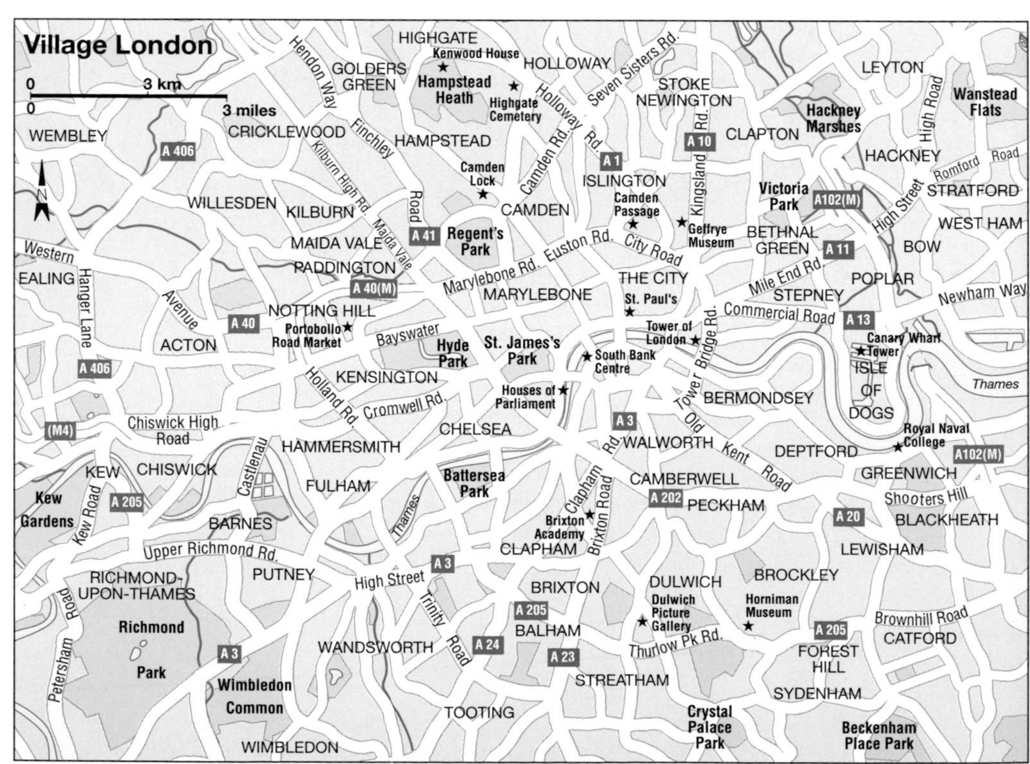

Blackheath

Map, page 238

Blackheath is a desirable community of Georgian and Victorian houses in east London en route to Kent. It lies alongside Greenwich Park and is traversed by Shooters Hill, on the road from London to the channel port of Dover, where the first motor vehicle in Britain took to the highway. Blackheath Village is a dip around the station at the back of the heath with small shops, wine bars and restaurants. It was built in the 1820s to service the smart houses going up in the area. Today the **Reminiscence Centre** – a re-created shop in the middle of the village, where visitors can poke their noses into cupboards and drawers – offers an opportunity to step back in time .

St Michael's, on the edge of the village and heath, was built in 1829, and has a fine neo-gothic interior, appreciated in concert recitals. Its roof beams were inspired by Venice's Bridge of Sighs and its tapering spire is known as "the needle of Kent". The crop-haired **heath,** danced on by ravens and brightened by kite flyers, gained its name from the colour of its soil. It was a favourite place for highwaymen, but it has more momentous associations. Henry V was welcomed here after his victorious battle against the French at Agincourt in 1415, and this is where James I introduced golf to England, in 1608.

The heath was the also the gathering place for the Peasants' Revolt of 1381, encouraged by the "mad priest of Kent", John Ball, who preached from the text "When Adam delved and Eve span/ Who was then the gentleman?"A popular fair on the heath was banned in the 19th century because of fairgoers' behaviour. A donkey ride path is still visible by the gates into Greenwich Park. ❑

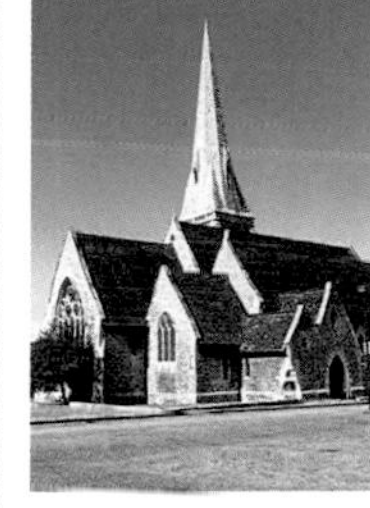

Above: St Michael's, the Needle of Kent. **Below:** kite flying on the Heath.

The 24-hour clock at Greenwich Observatory, and the Millennium Dome.

GREENWICH

One of the best ways to get to Greenwich is the time-honoured tradition of arriving at this maritime centre by water. Boats leave the Westminster Pier daily from 10am (10.40am in winter) and take about 50 minutes, taking in some of London's best-known sights along the way. Alternatives are the train to Greenwich or Maze Hill station, or the Docklands Light Railway, the latter providing a more interesting, above-the-streets journey right into the centre of Maritime Greenwich. Parking is difficult, especially on busy Sundays.

A peninsula polluted by a disused gasworks was reclaimed as the site of the **Millennium Dome**, a huge structure covering 20 acres (8 hectares) and housing 14 themed zones celebrating British ideas and technology. The one-year exhibition, open during 2000, was a commercial disaster *(see page 44)* but the dome itself is an impressive artefact.

This purposeful theme park was sited here because of its proximity to Sir Christopher Wren's **Old Royal Observatory**, where Greenwich Mean Time was established in 1884 (10am–5pm, admission fee). It houses Britain's largest refracting telescope, and has a fine display of time-keeping ephemera, including John Harrison's famous clocks whose story was told in Dava Sobel's 1995 book *Longitude*. A brass rule on the ground marks the dividing line between the Eastern and Western hemispheres, making it possible to have a foot in both worlds. It's a steep climb to the observatory, but the views are great.

The **National Maritime Museum** (daily 9am–5pm) has been redeveloped to create 16 new galleries around a spectacular courtyard spanned by the largest glazed roof in Europe. It traces the history both of the Royal Navy and the Merchant Navy, as well as the colonisers and discoverers. There are primitive coracles and glittering royal barges and memorabilia include the tunic worn by Lord Nelson at the Battle of Trafalgar in 1805, with the hole made by the bullet which killed him; the battle itself is replayed with computer-generated realism. Craft on display include Robin Knox-Johnson's round-the-world yacht..

BELOW: the *Cutty Sark*.

The *Cutty Sark*

In dry dock on the waterfront is the record-breaking ***Cutty Sark***, a sailing ship from the great days of the tea-clippers which used to race to be the first to bring the new season's tea from China. The figurehead shows it takes its name from the Scottish dialect for a torn petticoat, used by Robert Burns in *Tam O'Shanter,* and there is a collection of other figureheads below deck (10am–6pm, Sun 12–6pm; 5pm in winter; admission fee).

Dwarfed by it is the tiny ***Gypsy Moth IV***, in which Sir Francis Chichester sailed single-handed around the world in 1966–67. The *Cutty Sark* set a record by sailing 363 miles (581 km) in 24 hours; Chichester sailed 29,630 miles (47,408 km) in 226 days.

The superbly proportioned **Royal Naval College** was built in two halves to leave the view from Queen's House to the river (2.30–4.45pm, free). **Queen's House**, further back in the park, was a gift to Anne of Denmark from her husband, James I, designed by Inigo Jones, though not completed until 1637, in Charles I's reign. This was the first building in England to be designed entirely in the Classical style. It has a well restored 17th-century interior (10am–5pm, Oct–Apr 10.30am– 3.30pm. A single admission passport covers all the sites).

The Royal Naval College is one of the most majestic sights of London. Designed by Wren, Hawksmoor and Vanbrugh, with gardens laid out by Le Nôtre, it was built as a hospital for naval pensioners to match Wren's Royal Hospital in Chelsea. The highly decorated chapel is open to the public, as is the Painted Hall, an astonishing piece of work which took the artist, Sir James Thornhill, 18 years to paint. The highly decorated chapel, restored in Rococo style after a fire in 1779, hosts concerts and recitals as well as services. On display in Queen Mary's Court are the Crown Jewels of the Millennium, a splendid collection of authentically recreated crown and state jewels from around the world. The copies were commissioned for posterity at the end of the 19th century by the historian P. J. McCullagh when he realised that monarchies were collapsing all over Europe and their crown jewels being broken up and lost.

The heart of Greenwich lies just to the west of the park, where a covered market and neighbouring Greenwich Church Street are especially lively on a Sunday. There is also a thriving community centre in the **Greenwich Theatre**, with a restaurant, art gallery and jazz club. In one of Greenwich's elegant period houses in Croom's Hill is the **Fan Museum** with an unusual collection from fashion and the stage (11am–4.30pm, Sun 12–4.30pm, closed Mon). Hawksmoor's **St Alfege** church, which gives its name to Church Street, is built on the site of an earlier church dedicated to an 11th-century Archbishop of Canterbury who was taken hostage and slain by the Vikings. Its wood carvings are by Grinling Gibbons. ❑

The best view of Greenwich is from Island Gardens on the opposite side of the river. Use the 1,217-ft (365-metre) pedestrian tunnel by the *Cutty Sark* to reach it. The tunnel was built in 1897–1902 to enable workers to reach the West India Docks on the north bank.

BELOW: figurehead collection on board the *Cutty Sark*.

Camden Lock and Regent's Canal

Camden Lock, with busy market stalls brightening its refurbished warehouses, is one of the most attractve stretches of the Regent's Canal. This 8½-mile (14-km) stretch of water running from Paddington in west London to Limehouse in Docklands drops 86ft (25 metres) through 12 locks beneath 57 bridges. It is only about 4 ft (1.2 metres) deep, and in most places it is wide enough for two narrowboats to pass. The whole length of the canal can be walked using the paths on which barge horses once strained, except for two long tunnels where barge hands had to "leg it", lying on boards on their backs and pushing the boats through by "walking" on the tunnels' dank brick ceilings. The one at Islington is 970 yards (878 metres) long.

There are some delighful rural stretches along the canal, overhung with willows, bobbing with ducks and swans, and in spring nightingales arrive with the cherry blossom.

The canal was dug between 1812 and 1820 to link London's docks directly with the Grand Junction Canal at Paddington, which served the industrial Midlands. A leading enthusiast for the waterway was the great Regency architect and town planner John Nash (1752–1835) who wanted the canal to enhance his new development at Regent's Park. In the end, however, it was decided that the innate foulness of such a highway – the aroma of some boats' coal-fired stoves, the muck of the horses and the language of the bargemen – was not something the residents of this smart new area of town would expect. So the canal skirted the north side of the park, which was fortunate, for in 1874 a barge carrying gunpowder exploded, demolishing the North Gate Bridge at the park's entrance. In 1929 the Regent's and Grand Junction canals became part of the Grand Union Canal, but they were already declining in importance.

From Camden Lock it is only a 15-minute walk along the towpath to London Zoo, passing the MTV studios, the backs of the attractive houses in St Marks Crescent, and Feng Shang, a floating Chinese restaurant.

To get a flavour of life on the narrowboats, trips are offered on several boats, such as the *Jenny Wren* at Walker's Quay Waterside Restaurant. A 90-minute round trip goes up past the zoo to Little Venice, where strikingly painted narrowboats and houseboats line the banks. These are sought-after residences, and permanent moorings are highly prized (Virgin boss Richard Branson has one). A three-day canalway cavalcade attracts nearly 150 boats every May.

Most of today's watermen are itinerant, enjoying the freedom of the canals. Generally moorings are free, even around busy Camden Lock, but stays are limited to 14 days.

East from Camden Lock, the warehouses lining the canal show what an industrious waterway it must have been. One of them belonged to Carlo Gatti, a popular Victorian ice-cream maker, and his premises at Battlebridge Basin, complete with ice wells 42 ft (13 metres) deep, are now occupied by the London Canal Museum, which gives a history of life on the waterway. ❑

LEFT: Regent's Canal.

ISLINGTON

Although once dubbed "the Red Republic of Islington" because of its rabidly left-wing local council, Islington symbolises more than any other district the new-style gentrification of London's inner city. This is where Tony and Cherie Blair lived before selling up when they moved to 10 Downing Street. House prices have escalated in a dizzying fashion as whole areas of the borough have been restored to their original Georgian and Victorian graciousness.

At the southern end of Islington, on Rosebery Avenue, which leads down to Holborn, stands **Sadler's Wells**, a 1,500-seat theatre and the city's main dance venue. It was built in 1683 by Thomas Sadler and the well which he discovered is under the floor backstage. Islington Spa, which stood opposite, was known as New Tunbridge Wells because its medicinal waters rivalled those of the fashionable spa town of Tunbridge Wells in Kent. The qualities of the local water led to the development of the huge Whitbread Brewery in Chiswell Street and the Gordon's Dry Gin distillery.

In late Anglo-Saxon times, Islington was called Gislandune, meaning Gisla's Hill.

The crossroads at the heart of Islington's shopping district is known as the **Angel**, and is a familiar destination sign on London buses: it is also the name of the nearest Underground station, on the Northern Line. The name refers to an old coaching inn, a stop-over for travellers in and out of London; it fell derelict and was rebuilt as a bank in 1982. Close by, in the direction of Upper Street, is **Chapel Market**, a busy street market.

Restorers have also been at work on the old **Royal Agricultural Hall**, on Liverpool Road. Established originally in 1798 as home for the Smithfield Club's annual agricultural and livestock shows, the Hall is known locally as the "Aggie". An impressive edifice, the main hall contains 1,000 tons of cast iron and has a 130-ft (40 metre) roof span. Within, the hall space of nearly 5 acres (2 hectares) was the venue for the 1873 World Fair. As the London Business Design Centre, it now hosts conferences and exhibitions.

One of Islington's prettiest assets is **Camden Passage**. The elegant buildings and arcades have been turned into a treasure trove of antique shops, ranging from simple stalls to grand shops. Prices reflect the popularity of the place and it's hard to find great bargains.

Islington has had a number of distinguished artistic and literary residents, including the essayist Charles Lamb (1775–1834) who had a cottage with a spacious garden of vines, pears, strawberries and vegetables. An artistic air remains, with several fringe theatres.

The borough has a history of entertainment, as it was regarded as a safe haven from the muggings and plague in the City. The gentry also liked to travel "out of town". In the 17th century there were five theatres, and the first-ever actress (as opposed to men dressed as women) appeared on stage here. Today there are seven regular venues, of which the better known are the **Almeida** (with a good lunchtime food bar) in Almeida Street, the **King's Head** in Upper Street and the **Old Red Lion** in St John Street. The **Little Angel** in Dagmar Passage, off Upper Street, is a marionette theatre. ❑

BELOW: Islington Georgian terrace.

HAMPSTEAD AND HIGHGATE

Hampstead has long been regarded as one of the most desirable addresses in the city. Today's media, literary, film and music luminaries live in the same houses as the famous of previous centuries. Bishop's Avenue between Highgate and Hampstead has earned the sobriquet of Millionaire's Row. Open spaces predominate. The 3 sq. mile (8 sq. km) **Heath** is the main open space, leading down to **Parliament Hill** which provides splendid views across London, as does the 112-acre (45-hectare) **Primrose Hill** which overlooks Regent's Park to the south. These are all welcome acres over which locals stride, walk dogs, fly kites, skate and swim in the segregated ponds. **Whitestone Pond**, at the top of the hill on the main road, is the highest point in London, 440ft (134 metres) above sea level, and the Underground system tunnels 200ft (60 metres) beneath it.

ABOVE: Highgate, London's most famous cemetery. **BELOW:** suburban, smart Hampstead.

In 1880 Hampstead village was 4 miles (7 km) from the edge of London; now it is all part of the city. Its streets are full of chic shops, restaurants and pubs and its population is young and rich. On the north of the Heath, the **Jack Straw's Castle** pub is named after one of the ringleaders of the Peasants' Revolt. The **Spaniards Inn** figures in an 18th-century insurrection when angry Gordon rioters rampaged up Hampstead Hill. The landlord of the Spaniards plied the rioters with free drink until the military arrived to restore order. The **Old Bull and Bush**, another popular pub, was immortalised in a music hall song.

Kenwood House, Lord Mansfield's stately Robert Adam house, looted in the Gordon riots, contains the **Iveagh Bequest**, a major art gallery with works by Rembrandt, Vermeer, Reynolds, Gainsborough and Turner given by the Guinness family (10am–6pm, Oct–Mar 10am–4pm, donations appreciated). Poetry readings and chamber music recitals are held in the Orangery, and lakeside cocerts are held here in summer.

Sigmund Freud, fleeing the Nazis in Vienna, came to live at 20 Maresfield Gardens in 1938, and his daughter Anna looked after it after his death a year later. The **Freud Museum** preserves the house as they left it (12–5pm Wed–Sun, admission fee).

Much of the greatest work by the poet John Keats (1795–1821), including *Ode to a Nightingale*, was composed in the two years he lived at Wentworth Place. The building, **Keats' House**, is open to the public (closed 1–2pm and Sun mornings) and contains memorabilia such as his letters and a lock of his hair. Keats fell in love with the daughter of his neighbour.

Neighbouring **Highgate,** a pleasant hill-top suburb built round a pretty central square, could well claim to be the dead centre of London. Ironically, the gate from which the district takes its name was removed in 1769 because it was too low. Highgate contains London's grandest cemetery, where 300 famous people are buried. Consecrated in 1839, **Highgate Cemetery** was the fashionable resting place for Victorian Londoners (open 10am–5pm, 4pm in winter). Besides its catacombs and impressive memorials, the main attraction remains the rather grim bust of Karl Marx, who was buried here in 1883. ❑

NOTTING HILL

Map, page 238

The 1999 romantic comedy *Notting Hill* was set in the area principally because the film's writer, Richard Curtis, happened – like many media people – to live there. What the film didn't convey is the fact that Notting Hill is a melting pot in which several races and just about every social class rub shoulders. Grand, expensive Georgian townhouses at the Holland Park end contrast with their run-down counterparts a short distance northwards, where they are divided into bed-sits.

A focal point is **Notting Hill Gate**, on the main west-east road, the A40. Taking its name from a turnpike gate installed here in the 18th century, it's a lively centre, with many trendy pubs and restaurants, late-opening shops, and two cinemas (one, the Coronet, is a splendid former theatre which still permits smoking).

The main north-south artery, **Ladbroke Grove**, is the parade route for the **Notting Hill Carnival**, a massive three-day Caribbean festival which takes over the area in the last weekend of August, with children's parades on the Sunday and adults' parades on Monday. It was started in 1966 in an attempt to unite the local communities after appalling race riots in the streets the previous year. Months of work go into the elaborate costumes worn by the dancers in the procession, which features Trinidadian steel bands and attracts 750,000 onlookers and 10,000 police officers. It's usually a joyous occasion, but many feel it has outgrown the area.

ABOVE: antiques in Portobello Road.
BELOW: reveller at Europe's largest street carnival.

The Ladbroke Estate was an early attempt at town planning by James Weller Ladbroke in the 1830s and 1840s. A map of the area reveals a geometric pattern of circles, crescents and gardens – Ladbroke's attempt to marry town and country living. He even opened a racecourse, the Hippodrome, in 1837, but it failed.

Where the crowds head for now is **Portobello Road**. Built on the site of a pig farm named after an English victory over Spain at Porto Bello in the Gulf of Mexico in 1739, it has developed over the past 50 years into a major antiques market. By far the busiest time is on Saturday mornings, when the street fills with stalls, attracting a steady stream of tourists who emerge from Notting Hill Gate tube station and head northwest in search of elusive bargains. Traders pretend to be local characters but are much sharper than they may seem, and the only certain bargain is the lively atmosphere. Genuine antique dealers occupy the south end of the street, food stalls the middle portion and junk beneath the Westway flyover.

In Portobello Road, the **Electric Cinema**, London's oldest movie house, dates from 1905. It has opened and shut regularly under various recent owners.

From here, **Westbourne Grove** runs east to intersect with **Queensway**. Both have a continental flavour, with immigrants from Germany, Italy, Greece and the Middle East, and are packed with eating places, especially Chinese and Indian. Shops are open late, and evening strollers encompass an amazing range of nationalities.

Westbourne Grove was planned as a shopping street to rival Kensington High Street and at one time Whiteley's department store, at the bottom of Queensway, was the largest in the world. But development elsewhere drew away customers, and Whiteley's is now a multi-shop complex, with restaurants and a multi-screen cinema. ❑

BRIXTON

In Brixton, a once elegant and classy 19th-century suburb, Edwardian and Victorian terraces stand comfortably side by side with sprawling housing estates. The fringes of town, notably towards Stockwell, attract young professionals keen to own their own homes.

It is not the architecture but the people who give Brixton its character, colour and energy: on a good day this is a lively and fun place to be. The local population is around 60 percent white, and the balance includes a high proportion of Cypriots, Vietnamese, Chinese, African and Caribbean people. Some of the first non-white settlers arrived from Jamaica on the *Empire Windrush* in 1948. Resident communities have lived in relative harmony ever since, though the area became the *enfant terrible* of London during civil unrest in 1981.

VOICE

MONTSERRATIANS HEAD FOR UK

8 £1,450

London's black newspaper is based in Brixton and has a distinctive outlook.

There is a rich cultural and architectural history and noteworthy sights do exist. The **Brixton Windmill** was built in 1816 and still stands, although vandalism has destroyed its mechanism.

On the street corner heading south along Brixton Hill is the imposing **Lambeth Town Hall**. Further up the hill, **Brixton Prison** is the main centre for prisoners on remand awaiting trial. The authorities were embarrassed several years ago when it was revealed that an inmate used to escape every evening to the local pub, returning to his cell at closing time.

Brixton is home to *The Voice* newspaper, a black weekly journal, and to some of the city's liveliest nightlife, including a cinema complex, restaurants, clubs and bars. There's also a gallery and the **Black Cultural Archives Museum** (Mon–Sat 10.30am–6pm, archive searches by appointment only, tel: 0171 738 4591).

BELOW: Brixton's eclectic food market.

The Academy is an award-winning music venue in Stockwell Road. Bought for just £1 in 1984, the multi-million-pound refurbishment that followed drew the likes of Bob Dylan, the Rolling Stones and Bruce Springsteen to south London.

A thriving club scene offers everything from rock to reggae, soul to salsa. The **Fridge** is one of London's trendiest clubs. Across the road is **St Matthew's**: the front of the building is still a functioning church, while the remainder has been converted into **The Brix** theatre and bar. The **Bah Humbug** vegetarian and fish restaurant and bar are also on the site (tel: 0171 738 3184).

Behind a restored 1912 facade, the original single-screen **Ritzy Cinema** is now a five-screen art-house complex, with bars and eateries.

The crescent of **Electric Avenue**, one of London's first streets to be lit by electricity, in 1888, is also the heart of the **outdoor market** (8am–5.30pm, closed Wed afternoons and Sun). This vibrant area is a key part of the neighbourhood spread beneath a number of covered Victorian arcades – Market Row, Granville Arcade and Reliance Arcade – and it sells an impressive variety of Caribbean, African, Asian and European food. Here one can find things that supermarkets don't regularly stock: salted pig's tails, snapper, jackfish, yam, green bananas, ackee and callaloo. ❑

RICHMOND AND KEW

Map, page 238

Richmond Park and Kew Gardens, both in the Borough of Richmond through which the Thames delightfully glides, are classic days out for Londoners, reached easily by District Line underground or by British Rail from Waterloo. The main attraction of Richmond is **Richmond Park**, at 2,350 acres (950 hectares) the largest of the royal parks, grazed by herds of red and fallow deer who enjoy the bracken thickets and gather beneath the dappled canopies of huge oaks. The park is also popular with horse riders. A traditional verse exhorts visitors to come in lilac time, but rhododendrons and azaleas in May make the Isabella Plantation a particular high spot. The original royal residence in the park is the Palladian White Lodge (1727), now used by the Royal Ballet School.

Richmond Green is the handsome centre to the town, lined with 17th- and 18th-century buildings, and the remains of the 12th-century royal palace. Richmond Bridge is the oldest on the river, and the waterfront here is always lively: rowing boats can be hired. From **Richmond Hill** there is a grand view of the river. Below, reached along the towpath, is **Ham House**, a 17th-century Palladian building with a richly furnished interior and paintings by Peter Lely and Joshua Reynolds (open afternoons only; closed Thur–Fri and weekdays in winter, National Trust, entrance fee). On the opposite side of the river, reached by ferry in summer, is the less grand but perfectly pleasant **Marble Hill House**, a 1729 Palladian Villa (10am–6pm, 10am–4pm in winter, free).

The largest and smelliest flower in Kew Gardens is the Rafflesia Arnoldi, *named after Sir Stamford Raffles, founder of Singapore. It flowers every five years.*

Kew lies on the north side of Richmond and is synonymous with the **Royal Botanic Gardens** (9.30am–dusk, entrance fee). The 300-acre (120-hectare) gardens were established in 1759 with the help of Joseph Banks, the botanist who named Botany Bay on Captain James Cook's first voyage to Australia. Other explorers and amateur enthusiasts added their specimens over the centuries, making this a formidable repository and research centre. The gardens are also very beautiful, with grand glasshouses, including the Palm House and Waterlily House, Orangery, mock Chinese pagoda, and the Dutch House, a former royal palace. George III was locked up here when it was thought that he had gone mad. His wife Charlotte had a thatched summerhouse built in the grounds as a picnic spot. There are also two small art galleries of horticultural subjects.

BELOW: the waterlily house, Kew Gardens.

Kew has a village green comparable to Richmond's, and cricket games give both a rural atmosphere. Beside the green is St Anne's church where the painter Thomas Gainsborough is buried.

On the other side of the river is **Syon House**, home of the Dukes of Northumberland (11am–4pm Wed–Sun Apr–Sep, Sun only Oct–14 Dec, entrance fee). Its 18th-century interior by Robert Adam is unsurpassed. The grounds were laid out by Capability Brown and the Great Conservatory provided inspiration for the gardener Joseph Paxton when he designed the Crystal Palace in 1851. Today Syon Park attracts paying customers with a Butterfly House and, at weekends, a miniature steam train. ❑

THE SEASON

The Season is when London society is on display. The events are mostly sporting, but a sense of style is far more important than a sense of fair play

The English Season was an invention of upper-crust Londoners as a series of mid-summer amusements. This was the time when young girls "came out" at society balls, at which eligible young men would be waiting. Thus matched, the families would repair to their country homes. Royalty is an important ingredient, and the royal family have long had a keen interest in the sports highlighted by the Season.

The events are completely insignificant compared to their importance as social gatherings. People who care nothing for rowing attend Henley Regatta; philistine amateurs flock to the Royal Academy's Summer Exhibition; the musically challenged die for a ticket to Glyndebourne; and people queueing for tickets to Wimbledon seem to believe it's the only tennis tournament in the world.

Eliza Dolittle, played by Audrey Hepburn in *My Fair Lady* (right), summed it up when, beautifuly dressed by Cecil Beaton for the Royal Enclosure at Ascot, she forgot who she was supposed to be and urged a horse to "move yer bloomin' arse!". Such working-class passion is not required at an event where decorum, good breeding and a fancy hat take precedence over any sporting enthusiasms.

HENLEY REGATTA ▷ Striped blazers and boaters are *de rigueur* at this Edwardian, public-school outing among the beer and Pimm's tents on the banks of the Thames.

▽ ROYAL ASCOT Hats are the main talking point of Royal Ascot in June, and the Royal Enclosure is the only place to be on this fine flat race course near Windsor.

△ POLO IN THE PARK International Polo Day at the Guards Polo Club, Windsor Great Park, is the height of this sport of kings (Prince Charles is a keen player) and rich South Americans. The pitch here – and the one in Richmond Park – is usally lined by Range Rovers and Rolls-Royces.

△ **GLYNDEBOURNE**
Charmingly set on the South Downs near Brighton, this summer opera location is renowned as much for its lavish picnic hampers as it is for its performances, now staged in a new, enlarged building.

▽ **CROQUET**
The Hurlingham Club, by the river in Fulham, is host to the national championships of England's eccentric and surprisingly vicious game of croquet, otherwise played on country-house lawns.

▽ **CHELSEA FLOWERS**
The Chelsea Flower Show in the grounds of the Royal Hospital Chelsea in May is an early taste of the Season. It can be a terrible crush but thousands find it rewarding.

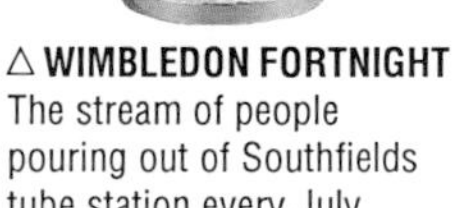

△ **WIMBLEDON FORTNIGHT**
The stream of people pouring out of Southfields tube station every July contains a large number of young girls, who act like pop fans, coming to root for this season's favourite player.

THE ALTERNATIVE SEASON

Muddy fields and dripping camp sites fail to dampen the spirits of those attending the "alternative" season – the round of music festivals supported by thousands of Londoners every year. The larger festivals attract the best bands from around the world and you don't have to be a hippy, crustie or a member of a youth tribe to attend. Many people take a tent to the large weekend events, some come only for one day.

The largest rock event, the Glastonbury Festival in Somerset, takes place at the end of June. More than 1,000 performances are given on 17 stages by more than 500 bands. It is fast becoming *the* place to be seen and tickets sell out quickly. If you can't get to Glastonbury, try the four-day Phoenix festival which takes place in mid-July at Stratford-upon-Avon. This is a family-oriented event, with a crèche and seven music stages vying with comedy, circus and funfair entertainment. The best world music festival is Womad, held in Reading in mid-July. There are workshops and arts and crafts, with good facilities for families. The Reading Festival in late August is well established and attracts some of the best rock groups from America. Among smaller, though no less enthusiastically supported events are the July Cambridge Folk Festival and the Irish Fleadh, in Finsbury Park, north London, in June.

DAY TRIPS

Within striking distance of the capital is a vast range places to visit, from castles to country houses, theme parks to seaside resorts. Oxford, Cambridge and Canterbury are within reach, too

The roads around the capital are as busy as any European city's and unless following a complex itinerary, it is usually best to reach the points of interest by train. Often tickets can be bought which combine the train ticket with a visitor's ticket to the site (Hampton Court, Leeds Castle). The cities and towns are all easy to walk around. Check opening times before setting out.

Hampton Court ❶ is a favourite day out (by train from Waterloo; open daily to 4.30pm Nov–Mar and to 6pm at other times, last ticket 45 minutes before closing; tel: 020-8781 9500), and there is a lot to see. This vast building which Henry VIII took over from a disfavoured courtier, Cardinal Wolsey, in 1529 intended to rival Versailles in France. Henry added the Chapel Royal, three kitchens and a wine cellar, but most of the palace is the creation of architect Sir Christopher Wren, working in the 17th century on behalf of William III and Queen Mary. The imposing state rooms are full of interest, and the mature 370-acre (150-hectare) gardens on the banks of the Thames have an extensive 18th-century maze. The palace has not been used by a reigning monarch since George II's death in 1760 but it remains a symbol of regal splendour.

PRECEDING PAGES: Hampton Court Palace gardens. **LEFT:** the palace entrance. **BELOW:** carriage at Windsor Castle.

Classic castles

Another great royal institution is **Windsor Castle** ❷ (accessible by coach excursions and rail; open daily to 4pm Nov-end–Feb and to 5.30pm at other times; last admission 1 hour before closing; tel: 01753-868286), still a favourite residence of the Royal Family. William the Conqueror began fortification here in 1066, immediately after defeating King Harold at the Battle of Hastings. The present stone castle was started 100 years later by Henry II. It was here that Edward III founded the prestigious Order of the Garter in 1348, giving special status to the castle in which he had been born, and this order of knights still congregates in an annual ceremony. Queen Victoria had a special love for Windsor and she is buried, along with her beloved Albert, at the **Frogmore Mausoleum** about a mile away.

Though overshadowed by its vast castle, **Windsor** is a vibrant town in its own right. It has a waxworks and a restored Victorian railway station as well as pleasant riverside walks. Take the bridge across the Thames to **Eton**, famed for its exclusive fee-paying school that nurtures the nation's future leaders – hence the old saying that Britain's wars were won on the playing-fields of Eton. Spreading to the south and west of Windsor, the **Great Park** has unspoilt woodland and parkland.

A great draw for children is **Legoland Windsor** (2 miles/ 3 km from town centre on the B3022 Bracknell/Ascot road; open daily Mar–mid-Oct; tel: 0990 040404). This theme park is based on the children's building blocks –

ABOVE: Sir Winston Churchill, born in the family home at Blenheim.

in this case, millions of them. Its 150 acres (60 hectares) of wooded landscape has rides, shows and workshops. Lego is a contraction of two Danish words, *Leg Godt*, meaning "Play well", and the park puts a worthy emphasis on learning.

Leeds Castle ❸ (open daily, tel: 01622-765400; near Maidstone in Kent, served by mainline trains – buy a combined entrance/train ticket at either Charing Cross or Victoria stations) has been described as "the most perfect castle in the world". Still occupied, and set like a jewel in a placid moat, Leeds was transformed by Henry VIII from a Norman fortress into a magnificent royal palace. The hot-air balloons which take off from the grounds add to the landscape.

Hever Castle ❹ near **Edenbridge** in Kent was the family home of Anne Boleyn who lost her head, figuratively and literally, to Henry VIII.

Great houses and gardens

Blenheim Palace ❺, just outside the Oxfordshire village of Woodstock, claims to be the largest private house in England (8 miles /13km north of Oxford, open-mid Mar–Oct, daily to 4.45pm; tel 01993-811091). It cover 3 acres (1.5 hectares) and was built by John Vanbrugh for the first Duke of Marlborough as a reward for his victory over the French at the Battle of Blenheim in 1704. Winston Churchill was born here. The house stands in a 2,500-acre (1,000-hectare) park designed by Capability Brown.

Knole ❻, another of the great stately homes of England, built by Thomas Bourchier, the Archbishop of Canterbury, between 1456 and 1486, also claims to be the largest private house in England today (British Rail from Charing Cross to Sevenoaks, then 1½ miles/2km; National Trust; open Apr–Nov Wed–Sun, tours Thur am; tel: 01732-462100). Its sumptuous interior includes a wealth of

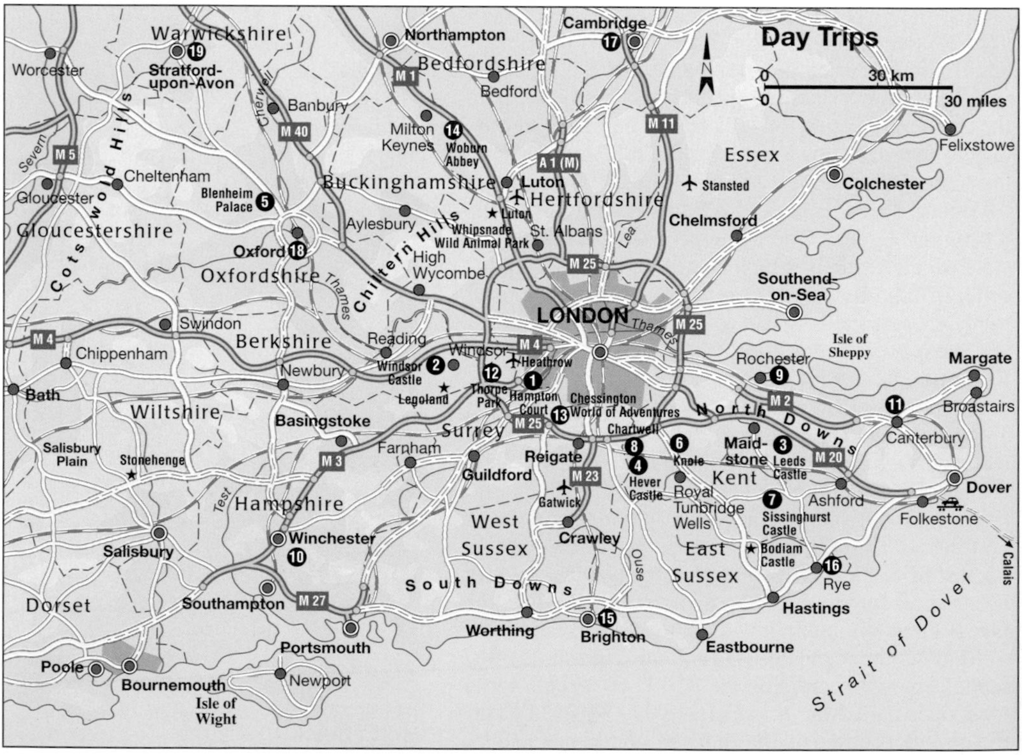

Map, page 254

fine furniture and one of the largest extant collections of period tapestries, rugs and bed hangings. A room is devoted to works by Joshua Reynolds. Knole belongs to the Sackville family and Vita Sackville-West was born here in 1892. She later transformed the garden in the ruins of the Elizabethan **Sissinghurst Castle** ❼ (5½ miles from Staplehurst station, on Charing Cross-Ashford International line; closed Mon and Oct–Mar; National Trust; tel: 01580-715330).

Also in Kent, the picturesque small town of **Westerham** is full of historical interest. It was here that General Wolfe stayed before embarking on his conquest of Quebec. Sir Winston Churchill's country home at **Chartwell** ❽ (open end-Mar–end-Oct, Wed–Sun and Bank Hol Mon; National Trust; tel: 01732-866368) is just down the road.

Cathedral towns

Rochester ❾ has a lovely Norman cathedral, and its huge castle, a gaunt ruin, stands brooding over the River Medway, 30 miles (48 km) east of London from London Bridge station. Home to Charles Dickens for many years and featured in some of his novels, the town still has a Dickensian atmosphere. Here there is a fine **Dickens museum** (open Easter–mid-Oct 2–5pm daily; tel: 01843-861232). In the winter, when the Medway is covered with snow, the quaint High Street can look like the archetypal Dickens Christmas card.

Winchester ❿, a refined country town, was the capital of England in Saxon times and it was from here that King Alfred unified the Anglo-Saxon nation for the first time in the face of Danish invasions. The town is compact and has enticing alleyways and shopping streets around its impressive cathedral, which has a beautiful English Perpendicular interior and impressive treasures.

BELOW: Blenheim Palace.

Canterbury ⓫, like Winchester, has an importance in English history which far exceeds its size. The premier cathedral, where Thomas à Becket was martyred in 1170, is one of the finest religious buildings in Europe. It is surrounded by interesting buildings from every period of English history, including some with Roman mosaics. The city's ancient walls are largely intact.

Map, page 254

Worlds of adventure

Children enjoy the attractions of **Thorpe Park ⓬** (open daily Feb–Nov; tel: 01932-569393), a lively theme park situated just where the M25 orbital motorway crosses the Wessex-bound M3. There are dozens of different rides (all included in the admission price), but there can be long waits for the more popular ones.

On the fringe of the Surrey countryside near Kingston, **Chessington World of Adventure ⓭** (open daily Mar–Nov; tel: 01372-727227) is a zoo and funfair, with features such as a runaway goldrush mine train and the Safari Skyrail monorail, and themed areas such as Transylvania.

Run by the London Zoological Society, **Whipsnade Wild Animal Park** (open Feb–Nov daily; tel: 0990-200123), covers 500 acres (200 hectares) of chalk downs at the eastern end of the Chiltern Hills near Dunstable. It has more than 3,000 species,in relatively unconstricted environments. Steam trains run through the "plains of Asia" and there are dolphin and bird of prey shows.

A similar wildlife park with additional funfair is the **Safari Park** at **Woburn Abbey ⓮**, home of the Dukes of Bedford for more than 350 years (just off the M1, 45 miles north of London; open Mar–Nov daily; tel: 01525-290407).

Left: Hever Castle, Kent.
Above: the Prince Regent who made Brighton famous.
Below: the resort's Palace Pier.

By the seaside

An old-fashioned seaside resort has long been a place to escape for a breath of bracing air. The seafronts of some of London's favourites (all best reached by rail) are now somewhat run-down, though efforts are being made to smarten them up.

Brighton ⓯ is a perennially bright spot. The old-fashioned pedestrianised streets known as The Lanes are a maze of antique shops, booksellers and souvenir stores. The exotic Indian-style **Royal Pavilion** (open daily; tel: 01273-290900) was built between 1787 and 1822. It was intended as a summer home for the Prince Regent who, more than anyone else, made Brighton a fashionable resort. The interior has more of a Chinese feel with its luxurious furnishings, and an extraordinary kitchen adds to its splendour. There is also a fine museum nearby, with an excellent costume and Art Deco collection.

The Theatre Royal, established in 1806, is one of Britain's most lovely provincial theatres, and Brighton's arts festival is the largest in England. Brighton's other attractions include an aquarium, a fine racecourse high on the South Downs and a large modern marina, with moorings for 1,800 yachts.

Rye ⓰ is a delightful cobbled old town once an important port but now set back from the sea. It was one of the ancient Cinque Ports, given privileges in return for defending the coast. It is full of antique shops which are open on Sunday.

University towns

Within a two-hour train ride from the capital are the country's finest university towns, Cambridge (served by Liverpool Street station) and Oxford (served by Paddington).

Cambridge ⓱ takes its name from the River Cam, where students punt on lazy summer days, drifting down the "Backs" – the narrow riverways behind the colleges. The first college, Peterhouse, was founded in 1281, but undoubtedly the finest of all the college buildings is King's College Chapel, which boasts magnificent fan vaulting, 16th-century stained glass windows and Rubens' *Adoration of the Magi*. The college also has the most famous choristers in England. Cambridge town is pleasant and compact, and is best explored on foot.

Henry James referred to **Oxford** ⓲ as "the finest thing in England" and John Keats was even more smitten, declaring it "the finest city in the world". Coach-loads of tourists seem to agree as they troop respectfully round the University's three dozen colleges, a few of which have been centres of learning for up to seven centuries. There's something about the light in Oxford, reflecting off the ancient stones, that gives the town a unique allure.

The town's setting is equally magical. Oxford is not a large place and you don't need to climb far up one of its dreaming spires to spy the lush green countryside encircling it. The **Cotswolds** to the west of Oxford beckon, their quaint showpiece villages seeming to grow out of the earth, so perfect is their relationship with the landscape. Tourism is intensive, though.

Stratford-upon-Avon ⓳, birthplace of Shakespeare, is 40 miles (64 km) further north, on the far side of the Cotswolds. His birthplace is the start of a town tour that takes in all the houses that had an association with England's greatest literary figure, and includes Anne Hathaway's Cottage and Mary Arden's House. ❑

RIGHT: the "dreaming spires" of Oxford.
OVERLEAF: the "old crocks" race to Brighton.

V.C.C.
1904
RAC
404
SE-22

INSIGHT GUIDES

TRAVEL TIPS

TIMBUKTU KALAMAZOO

Global connection with the AT&T Network | AT&T direct service

www.att.com/traveler

AT&T Direct® Service

The easy way to call home from anywhere.

AT&T Access Numbers

Argentina .0800-555-4288	Czech Rep.▲.00-42-000-101
Australia...1-800-881-011	Denmark........8001-0010
Austria●....0800-200-288	Egypt●(Cairo) ...510-0200
Bahamas..1-800-USA-ATT1	France.....0800-99-00-11
Belgium● ..0-800-100-10	Germany..0800-2255-288
Bermuda✚ 1-800-USA-ATT1	Greece● 00-800-1311
Brazil 000-8010	Guam 1-800-2255-288
Canada...1 800 CALL ATT	Guyana○ 165
Chile 800-225-288	Hong Kong ..800-96-1111
China, PRC▲ 10811	India▲ 000-117
Costa Rica .0-800-0-114-114	Ireland 1-800-550-000

AT&T Direct® Service

The easy way to call home from anywhere.

AT&T Access Numbers

Argentina .0800-555-4288	Czech Rep.▲.00-42-000-101
Australia...1-800-881-011	Denmark........8001-0010
Austria●....0800-200-288	Egypt●(Cairo) ...510-0200
Bahamas..1-800-USA-ATT1	France.....0800-99-00-11
Belgium● ..0-800-100-10	Germany..0800-2255-288
Bermuda✚ 1-800-USA-ATT1	Greece● 00-800-1311
Brazil 000-8010	Guam 1-800-2255-288
Canada...1 800 CALL ATT	Guyana○ 165
Chile 800-225-288	Hong Kong ..800-96-1111
China, PRC▲ 10811	India▲ 000-117
Costa Rica .0-800-0-114-114	Ireland 1-800-550-000

Global connection with the AT&T Network | **AT&T direct service**

The best way to keep in touch when you're traveling overseas is with **AT&T Direct**® **Service**. It's the easy way to call your loved ones back home from just about anywhere in the world. Just cut out the wallet card below and use it wherever your travels take you.

For a list of AT&T Access Numbers, cut out the attached wallet guide.

Israel	**1-800-94-94-949**	**Portugal▲**	**800-800-128**
Italy●	**172-1011**	**Saudi Arabia▲**	**1-800-10**
Jamaica●	1-800-USA-ATT1	Singapore	800-0111-111
Japan●▲	**005-39-111**	**South Africa**	**0800-99-0123**
Korea, Republic●	**0072-911**	**Spain**	**900-99-00-11**
Mexico▽●	**01-800-288-2872**	**Sweden**	**020-799-111**
Netherlands●	**0800-022-9111**	**Switzerland●**	**0800-89-0011**
Neth. Ant.▲❂	**001-800-USA-ATT1**	**Taiwan**	**0080-10288-0**
New Zealand●	**000-911**	Thailand❮	001-999-111-11
Norway	**800-190-11**	**Turkey●**	**00-800-12277**
Panama	00-800-001-0109	U.A. Emirates●	800-121
Philippines●	**105-11**	**U.K.**	**0800-89-0011**
Poland●▲	**00-800-111-1111**	**Venezuela**	**800-11-120**

FOR EASY CALLING WORLDWIDE

1. Just dial the AT&T Access Number for the country you are calling from. *2.* Dial the phone number you're calling. *3.* Dial your card number*

For access numbers not listed ask any operator for **AT&T Direct**® Service.
In the U.S. call 1-800-222-0300 for **AT&T Direct** Service information.
Visit our Web site at: **www.att.com/traveler**
Bold-faced countries permit country-to-country calling outside the U.S.

- ● Public phones require coin or card deposit to place call.
- ✚ Public phones and select hotels.
- ▲ May not be available from every phone/payphone.
- ○ Collect calling only.
- ▽ Includes "Ladatel" public phones; if call does not complete, use 001-800-462-4240.
- ❂ From St. Maarten or phones at Bobby's Marina, use 1-800-USA-ATT1.
- ❮ When calling from public phones, use phones marked Lenso.
- * AT&T Calling Card, AT&T Corporate, AT&T Universal, MasterCard®, Diners Club®, American Express®, or Discover® cards accepted.

When placing an international call *from* the U.S., dial 1-800-CALL ATT.

WW ©6/00 AT&T

Israel	**1-800-94-94-949**	**Portugal▲**	**800-800-128**
Italy●	**172-1011**	**Saudi Arabia▲**	**1-800-10**
Jamaica●	1-800-USA-ATT1	Singapore	800-0111-111
Japan●▲	**005-39-111**	**South Africa**	**0800-99-0123**
Korea, Republic●	**0072-911**	**Spain**	**900-99-00-11**
Mexico▽●	**01-800-288-2872**	**Sweden**	**020-799-111**
Netherlands●	**0800-022-9111**	**Switzerland●**	**0800-89-0011**
Neth. Ant.▲❂	**001-800-USA-ATT1**	**Taiwan**	**0080-10288-0**
New Zealand●	**000-911**	Thailand❮	001-999-111-11
Norway	**800-190-11**	**Turkey●**	**00-800-12277**
Panama	00-800-001-0109	U.A. Emirates●	800-121
Philippines●	**105-11**	**U.K.**	**0800-89-0011**
Poland●▲	**00-800-111-1111**	**Venezuela**	**800-11-120**

FOR EASY CALLING WORLDWIDE

1. Just dial the AT&T Access Number for the country you are calling from. *2.* Dial the phone number you're calling. *3.* Dial your card number*

For access numbers not listed ask any operator for **AT&T Direct**® Service.
In the U.S. call 1-800-222-0300 for **AT&T Direct** Service information.
Visit our Web site at: **www.att.com/traveler**
Bold-faced countries permit country-to-country calling outside the U.S.

- ● Public phones require coin or card deposit to place call.
- ✚ Public phones and select hotels.
- ▲ May not be available from every phone/payphone.
- ○ Collect calling only.
- ▽ Includes "Ladatel" public phones; if call does not complete, use 001-800-462-4240.
- ❂ From St. Maarten or phones at Bobby's Marina, use 1-800-USA-ATT1.
- ❮ When calling from public phones, use phones marked Lenso.
- * AT&T Calling Card, AT&T Corporate, AT&T Universal, MasterCard®, Diners Club®, American Express®, or Discover® cards accepted.

When placing an international call *from* the U.S., dial 1-800-CALL ATT.

WW ©6/00 AT&T

CONTENTS

Getting Acquainted

Planning the Trip

Practical Tips

Getting Around

Where to Stay

Eating Out

Culture

Nightlife

Shopping

Sports

Further Reading

Getting Acquainted

The Place

Situation 51.30°N 0.10°W, on the same latitude as the Kamchatka peninsula in Pacific Russia and the north tip of Newfoundland, Canada. The capital of the United Kingdom is on the River Thames 40 miles (64km) from the North Sea.
Population 6.4 million, 9 million in the larger metropolitan area.
Area 610 sq miles (1,580 sq km).
Language English.
Religion Protestant (Church of England): the monarch is the titular head of the church; the primate is the Archbishop of Canterbury whose London address is Lambeth Palace.
Currency pounds divided into 100 pence (£1 is approximately US$1.50).
Weights & Measures officially metric, though imperial is still used, notably for distances (miles) and beer (pints).
Electricity 220 volts. Square, three-pin plugs; two-pin shaver plugs.
Time Zone Greenwich Mean Time (GMT), 1 hour behind Continental European Time and 5 hours ahead of Eastern Seaboard Time.
Summer time (+ 1 hour) from March to September.
Direct dialling from abroad:
London numbers changed in 2000. From abroad, dial 44 + 20, then an 8-digit number. Internally, codes are not needed: an old central London number such as 0171-234 5678 will now be 7234 5678, and an old outer London number such as 0181-234 5678 will now be 8234 5678.

Climate

The English are justly famous for their preoccupation with the weather, a fascination which is largely due to its unpredictable nature. The climate in London is mild, with the warming effects of the city itself keeping off the worst of the cold in winter.

Snow and temperatures below freezing are unusual, with January temperatures averaging 43°F/6°C. Temperatures in the summer months average 64°F/18°C, but they can soar, causing the city to become airlessly hot (air-conditioning is not universal).

However, temperatures can fluctuate considerably from day to day and surprise showers catch people unawares all year round. Therefore visitors should come prepared with wet weather clothes whatever the season. Generally speaking, short sleeves and a jacket are fine for summer, but a warm coat and woollens are recommended for the winter.

For recorded weather information, tel: 0891-500 401.

Government

When people refer to London, they mean the county of Greater London. When they speak of the City of London, they generally mean the financial district, the historic square mile between St Paul's Cathedral and the Tower of London, governed by the Corporation of London and headed by the Lord Mayor, which even has its own police force. The rest of the metropolis is run by 12 inner boroughs and 20 outer boroughs, each of which is responsible for local services.

After Margaret Thatcher abolished the Labour-leaning Greater London Council (GLC) in the 1980s, London was the only major European city without its own government for fifteen years – and this showed, for example, in poorly coordinated public transport. In May 1998 a referendum was held, and Londoners voted in favour of a new governing body and an elected mayor of the city. The Labour government, though it supported such devolution in principle, was keen that its power should not be overshadowed by a high-profile mayor. They were therefore disappointed by the election of Ken Llvingstone. This former leader of the GLC was rejected by the Labour Party as candidate for the post, and chose to end a lifetime of Labour membership and stood as an independent. It is too early to evaluate the impact of his mayorship on London, but improving public transport is likely to be his main priority.

Public Holidays

- **January** New Year's Day (1)
- **March/April** Good Friday, Easter Monday
- **May** May Day (first Monday), Spring Bank Holiday (last Monday)
- **August** Summer Bank Holiday (last Monday)
- **December** Christmas Day (25), Boxing Day (26)

Economy

In the 19th century it was the largest city in the world. Now its economy is almost entirely financial and service-based, with tourism playing a huge part. Its manufacturing industries and shipping have moved out, accounting for the 20 percent drop in population. The financial sector is still based mainly in the City of London.

Business Hours

Shop and office hours are usually 9 or 10am–5.30pm or 7pm, Monday–Saturday. Shops in the centre of town rarely close for lunch and may stay open later, particularly around Covent Garden and Piccadilly Circus. Increasing numbers of shops are open on Sunday, particularly supermarkets and large warehouse stores away from the centre. Late-night shopping until 8pm is on Thursday in Oxford and Regent streets and on Wednesday in Knightsbridge and Kensington. Some West End shops stay open until 8pm anyway, a few until midnight.

Planning the Trip

Visas and Passports

To enter the United Kingdom, you need a valid passport (or any form of official identification if a citizen of the EU) to enter the UK. Commonwealth citizens, Americans, EU nationals or citizens of most other European and South American countries do not need visas.

Health certificates

Health certificates are not required unless you have arrived from Asia, Africa or South America.

If you wish to stay for a protracted period or apply to work in the UK, contact:
Immigration and Nationality Directorate
Whitgift Centre, Block C
Wellsey Road
Croydon, Surrey CR9 1AT
tel : 0870 606 7766.
Open: Mon–Fri 9am–4.30pm
www.homeoffice.gov.uk/ind

Money Matters

Most banks are open between 9.30am and 4.30pm Monday–Friday, with Saturday morning banking common in shopping areas. Major English banks tend to offer similar exchange rates; it's only worth shopping around if you have large amounts of money to change. Banks charge no commission on sterling traveller's cheques. If a London bank is affiliated to your own bank, it will make no charge for cheques in other currencies either. However, there will be a charge for changing cash into another currency.

Some High Street travel agents, such as Thomas Cook, operate *bureaux de change* at comparable rates. There are also private *bureaux de change* (some are open 24 hours) where rates can be very low and commissions high. If you do have to use one, ensure it's carrying a London Tourist Board code of conduct sticker. Chequepoint is a reputable chain with branches at Piccadilly Circus, Leicester Square, Marble Arch, Bayswater Underground and Victoria mainline station.

Credit cards

International credit cards are widely accepted. However, there are notable exceptions, and many a visitor has been embarrassed at the check-out of John Lewis and Peter Jones.

Eurocheques

Eurocheques are widely accepted by hotels; look out for the EC sticker in shop and restaurant windows.

Health

If you fall ill and are a national of the EU, you are entitled to free medical treatment for illnesses arising while in the UK. Many other countries also have reciprocal arrangements for free treatment. However, most visitors will be liable for medical and dental treatment and should ensure they have adequate health insurance.

In the case of minor accidents, your hotel will know the location of the nearest hospital with a casualty department. If you sprain your wrist, hail a cab. Cab drivers seem to know everything.

Chemists (pharmacists)

Boots is a large chain of pharmacies with numerous branches throughout London that will make up prescriptions. The branch at 75 Queensway, W2 is open until 10pm daily, whilst Bliss Chemist at Marble Arch is open until midnight daily.

Accidents

In the case of a serious accident or emergency, dial **999**.

Customs Regulations

There are no official restrictions on the movement of goods within the European Union, provided those goods were purchased within the EU, and EU nationals no longer need to exit through a red or green channel. However, British Customs have set the following personal-use "guide levels".

Tobacco 800 cigarettes, 400 cigarillos, 200 cigars, 1kg tobacco.
Alcohol 10 litres spirits, 20 litres fortified wines, 90 litres wine, 110 litres beer.

Travellers from further afield are subject to the following allowances:
Tobacco 200 cigarettes or 100 cigarillos or 30 cigars or 250g of tobacco.
Alcohol 1 litre of spirits, or 2 litres of fortified or sparkling wine, or 2 litres of table wine (an additional 2 litres of still wine if no spirits are bought).
Perfume 60cc perfume, 250cc toilet water.

The following are prohibited entry into the United Kingdom:
Animals Under the PETS scheme, cats and dogs may now enter Britain from EU countries providing they have the appropriate documentation. All other pets are still placed in quarantine for six months at the owner's expense. For further details, log on to www.maff.gov.uk.
Plants and **perishable foods** such as meats and meat products, eggs, fruit; some drugs (check with your doctor if you need to bring strong medication on your trip).
Firearms and ammunition brought without special arrangement.
Obscene film or written material.
There are no restrictions on the amount of currency you can bring into the country.

Getting There

BY AIR

London is served by two major international airports: Heathrow, 15 miles (24 km) to the west (mainly scheduled flights); and Gatwick, 24 miles (40 km) to the south (scheduled and charter flights), with the smaller airports of Stansted and Luton to the north of London. There is also the tiny London City Airport in Docklands, a few miles from the City, used by small aircraft connecting London with European cities.

Heathrow Airport

Heathrow airport can be a daunting place to arrive (the walk to the central building from an international gate can seem like miles). It's important to plan how you'll get into central London in advance. The fastest connection is the Heathrow Express to Paddington Station, which runs every 15 minutes and takes 15 minutes. Paddington is on the District, Circle, Bakerloo and Hammersmith and City Underground (Tube) lines *(see map inside back cover)*. The fare is £10 single, £20 return (tickets are valid for three months).

There is also a direct *Underground* route (£3.50 single), on the Piccadilly Line, which reaches the West End in around 40 minutes. It goes directly to Kensington, Knightsbridge, Park Lane (Hyde Park Corner) Piccadilly, Covent Garden and Bloomsbury (Russell Square) and operates from 5am (6am on Sunday) until 11.40pm daily. Keep your ticket: you'll need it to exit the system.

For Underground enquiries Tel: 020-7222 1234.

London Regional Transport (LRT) runs an Airbus service with red double-decker and single-decker buses picking up from terminals 1 to 4. The A2 goes to Euston and Kings Cross via Marble Arch and Baker Street. Buses leave at half-hour intervals from 6.30am to 10.15pm daily, take about an hour and stop at major hotels on the way. A single fare of around £7 can be bought from the driver. For 24-hour Airbus travel information, tel: 020-7222 1234. For information regarding bus and coach services tel: 0990-747 777. Heathrow is also well-served for taxis. A ride into town in a familiar London "black cab" will cost from £25, depending on destination.

Car Hire If you want to hire a car, the following are the Heathrow offices of major car rental firms:
Avis, tel: 020-8899 1000
Budget, tel: 0800-181 181
Europcar, tel: 020-8897 0811
Hertz, tel: 020-8897 2072
National Car Rental, tel: 020-8750 2800.

Gatwick Airport

Gatwick airport isn't on the Underground network, but it has sophisticated train and coach services into London running to and from Victoria Station. The *Gatwick Express* leaves every 15 minutes from 5am to midnight then hourly through the night. It takes 30 minutes and costs around £10 one-way. Children under four years old travel free; children aged between five and 15 travel for half of the adult fare. **Gatwick Express Information Line**, tel: 0990-301 530.

Connex SouthCentral runs rail services direct from Gatwick to Victoria station. Journey time is 30 to 35 minutes. Thameslink runs trains from four London stations: Kings Cross, Farringdon, London Blackfriars and London Bridge. Journey time to London Bridge from Gatwick is 30 minutes.

Flight Information

- Heathrow Airport, tel: 0870-0000123
- Gatwick Airport, tel: 01293-535353
- Luton Airport, tel: 01528-405100
- Stansted Airport, tel: 01279-680500
- London City Airport, tel: 020-7646 0000

Coach Connections

National Express run a coach service connecting Heathrow, Gatwick, Stansted and Luton airports with one another and the first three airports with Victoria coach station. Enquiries and credit card bookings, tel: 0990 808 080.

Flightline 777 coaches leave from both the North and South terminals and take about 70 minutes to reach Victoria (traffic is heavy). A single fare is £7.50.

Speedlink Heathrow also operates *Jetlink* (£12 single, £18 return) between Heathrow and Gatwick. Tel: 0990-747 777.

Car Hire from Gatwick:
Avis, tel: 01293-529 721
Budget, tel: 0800 181 181
Europcar, tel: 01293-531 062
Hertz, tel: 01293-530 555
National Car Rental, tel: 01293-567 790.

Luton Airport

Luton Airport is connected by Thameslink rail services via King's Cross and Blackfriars. There is a shuttle bus between the station and the airport. The journey to King's Cross takes about 40 minutes and runs every 20 minutes. Green Line coach services also run via Victoria station (tel: 0345-788 788) and take about 1 hour and 30 minutes.

Stansted Airport

From Stansted Airport a direct rail link goes to Liverpool Street Station every half-hour; journey time of 45 minutes. Flightline coaches run every hour between Victoria and Stansted.

London City Airport

London City Airport connects to destinations in Europe and is mainly used by business commuters. A dozen carriers have frequent services to and from 18 European cities. The airport is badly served by public transport despite its close proximity to the City (6 miles/10 km). There are two frequent

"Shuttlebus" services connecting the airport with central London: to Liverpool Street Station via Canary Wharf Underground station, taking around 25 minutes; and to the Canning Town interchange station. Alternatively, take bus 473 from the airport to reach the District Line at Plaistow; West Ham for the connecting Silverlink Metro rail service; or Prince Regent Station to connect with the Docklands Light Railway service For airport and flight enquiries, tel: 020-7646 0000; www.londoncityairport.com.

Tourist information at airports

The London Tourist Board produces a pack, free to visitors, full of interesting and useful information. It's worth stopping off at the Tourist Information Centres (TICs) at the following points of arrival:

Heathrow Terminals 1, 2, 3 Underground Station Concourse (open 8am–6pm daily) or at Terminal 3 Arrivals Concourse (open 6am–11pm daily).

CHANNEL TUNNEL

The Channel Tunnel provides Eurostar passenger services by rail from Paris Nord (3 hours, Eurostar Paris, tel: 33 1-49 70 01 75) and Brussels Midi (2 hours 40 minutes, Eurostar Brussels, tel 32 2-322 5259) to London's Waterloo. UK Eurostar bookings, tel: 0990 186 186, for bookings in the UK from abroad, tel: (44) 1233-617 775. In the US call 1-800-EUROSTAR or 1-800 356 66711.

Vehicles are carried by train through the tunnel to Folkestone in Kent from Nord-Pas de Calais in France by Le Shuttle. Bookings are not essential, but advisable at peak times. Fares vary according to the time of travel: late at night or in the early morning is much cheaper. Enquiries in France: 33 1-49 70 01 75 and in the UK: 0990 353 535.

BY FERRY

Sea services operate between 12 British and over 20 Continental ports. The major ferries have full facilities and for people arriving by boat there is a sense of occasion that can never be matched by an underground train. The shortest ferry crossing time from the Continent is about one hour 30 minutes, from Calais to Dover.

Brittany Ferries (UK tel: 0990 360 360) sails to Portsmouth from St Malo (33-2 99 82 80 80) and Caen (33-2 31 36 36 36), to Poole in Dorset from Cherbourg (33-2 33 88 44 44), and to Plymouth from Roscoff (33 2 98 29 28 00) and St Malo depending on season. They also sail from Santander in Spain (34-4 222 0000).

Hoverspeed (www.hoverspeed.co.uk; general enquiries in the UK tel: 0990 240 241) runs a service to Dover from Calais (tel 33-3 21 46 14 14) and to Folkestone from Boulogne (tel: 33-321 302 726). There is also a Hoverspeed service between Ostend and Dover. To contact Hoverspeed in Ostend tel: 32-5 955 9911.

P&O Stena Line (www.posl.com; UK tel: 0990 980980) sails to Dover from Calais (33-3 21 46 04 40); Portsmouth from Cherbourg and Le Havre (33-2 35 19 78 50); Newhaven from and to Dieppe. Services also run from Bilbao in Spain to Portsmouth.

Seafrance (UK tel: 0870 571 1711) operates a ferry service from Calais to Dover; P&O North Sea Ferries (www.ponsf.com; UK tel: 01482 311 177) runs from Zeebrugge to Hull

The Channel Tunnel

The Channel Tunnel, opened in 1994, finally linked Britain to the Continent. It was not a new idea: a start had been made in the 19th century. Nor was it universally popular. Used to their insularity, some Britons felt shocked that they should be so closely linked to France. There was also concern that foxes and other mammals might enter Britain, which has for so long been free of rabies. Fears dissolved as people realised that this was by far the quickest and most comfortable way to reach Paris and Brussels. For Londoners, lunch in a left-bank café suddenly became a real option for a day out.

However, the worst fears about the tunnel were confirmed in November 1996, when a fire broke out on a lorry embarked at Calais. It was almost six months before Le Shuttle could operate again, and passenger sales dropped off. That did not prevent the company reporting its first operating profit the following year, boosted by a £52 million insurance payout for the fire, but there was a small matter of some outstanding debts and a £4.4 billion refinancing package. The £5 million profit turned into a £215 million loss.

Since then the picture seems to have altered for the Tunnel. In 1998, the first full year of unhindered service, saw over 13 million passengers use the Tunnel. Operating profit increased three-fold and a net profit of £64 million was reported. Indeed, the Tunnel carried 52 percent of all Dover/Calais car traffic in 1998 and recent figures show steady growth in all these areas.

There are now more than 1,500 Eurostar passenger train services passing through the Tunnel every month, providing serious competition for the airlines as well as the ferry companies.

The one remaining problem is the absence of a direct rail link from Folkestone into London. However, financially troubled plans for this have been rescued and the link is scheduled to become a reality in 2007.

Practical Tips

Lost Property

If you can't find a policeman, dial 192 and ask for the number of the nearest police station. Don't call the emergency number 999 unless there has been a serious crime or accident. If your passport has been lost, let your embassy know as well. For possessions lost on public transport, contact London Transport Lost Property, 200 Baker Street, NW1 5RZ (tel: 020-7486 2496) Monday–Friday 9.30am–2pm, or fill in an enquiry form, available from any London Underground station or bus garage. Allow three working days to elapse after the loss before making a visit. If you left something in a taxi, the Taxi Lost Property office is at 15 Penton Street, N1 9PU, tel: 020-7833 0996. Open Monday–Friday 9am–4pm.

Left Luggage

Most of the main railway stations have left luggage departments where you can leave your suitcases on a short-term basis, although all are very sensitive to potential terrorist bombs. Left luggage offices close at 10.30pm with the exception of Euston (open 24 hours, last deposit at 11pm) and Paddington (open until midnight).

Tipping

Most hotels and many restaurants automatically add 10–15 percent service charge to your bill. It's your right to deduct it if you're not happy with the service. Sometimes when service has been added, the final total on a credit card slip will still be left blank, the implication being that a further tip is expected; don't pay it. In London, you don't tip in pubs, cinemas, theatres or elevators. You do tip hairdressers, sightseeing guides, railway porters and cab drivers. They get around 10 percent.

Radio Stations

Commercial stations

- Capital Radio – 95.8fm, 24-hour pop.
- Capital Gold – 1548am, 24-hour golden oldies.
- Classic FM – 100.9fm, 24-hour classical music.
- LBC Newstalk – 97.3fm, news, talk shows.
- Jazz FM – 102.2fm, jazz alone didn't provide big enough audiences, so it broadened to include soul and blues.
- Kiss FM – 100fm, 24-hour dance.

BBC (advertisement-free)

- Radio 1 – 98.8fm, mainstream pop.
- Radio 2 – 89.2fm, easy-listening music, chat shows.
- Radio 3 – 91.3fm, 24-hour classical music, plus drama.
- Radio 4 – 93.5fm, news, current affairs, plays.
- Radio Five Live – 909mw, rolling news, sport.
- GLR (Greater London Radio) – 94.9fm, London-oriented music and chat station.
- BBC World Service – 648 kHz, international news.

Media

NEWSPAPERS

Politically speaking, the *Daily Telegraph* and *The Times* are on the right, *The Independent* is in the middle, and *The Guardian* is on the left. On Sunday *The Observer* is more liberal than the *Sunday Times*, *Independent on Sunday* and *Sunday Telegraph*. The *Financial Times* is renowned for the clearest, most unslanted headlines in its general news pages (plus, of course, its exhaustive financial coverage).

The tabloids are the smaller ones. *The Sun* and *The Star* are traditionally on the right (and obsessed with royalty, soap operas and sex), ditto the Sunday *News of the World*. *The Mirror* and *Sunday Mirror* are slightly left-ish, as is the *Sunday People*. *The Daily Mail* and *Mail on Sunday* are slightly more upmarket equivalents of the politically eclectic *Express*.

Editions of the London-only *Evening Standard* come out Monday–Friday from late morning and are good for cinema and theatre listings.

Listings magazines

Supreme in this field is the long-established weekly *Time Out*, but the *Evening Standard* includes a good (and free) listings magazine, *Hot Tickets*, on Thursdays.

Foreign newspapers and magazines

Foreign newspapers and magazines can be found at many street newsstands, at mainline stations, and at these outlets:
Capital Newsagents: 48 Old Compton Street, W1.
A Moroni & Son: 68 Old Compton Street, W1.
Selfridges: Oxford Street, W1.
Eman's: 123 Queensway, W2.

TELEVISION

Britain has a reputation for fine broadcasting. There are five national terrestrial channels: BBC1, BBC2, ITV, Channel 4 (C4), and Channel 5 (C5). Both the BBC (British Broadcasting Corporation) and ITV (Independent Television) have regional stations which occasionally opt out of the national schedule to broadcast local programmes. The BBC is financed by compulsory annual television licences and therefore doesn't rely on advertising for funding. The independent channels (ITV, C4 and C5) are funded entirely by commercials.

BBC1, ITV and C5 broadcast programmes aimed at mainstream audiences; BBC2 and C4 cater slightly more for arts, cultural and minority interests. However, the advent of a host of cable and satellite channels has forced terrestrial stations to fight for audiences with a higher incidence of programmes such as soap operas, game shows and situation comedies.

There are more than 60 cable and satellite channels, ranging from sport and movies to cartoons and golden oldies. A major provider is the BSkyB network, controlled by Rupert Murdoch.

Pricier hotels will often have a choice of cable stations such as CNN or NBC's Super Channel.

Teletext

A vast range of information (covering news, business, sport and entertainment) is available on the teletext services transmitted by all the terrestrial channels.

Postal Services

Post offices are open 9am–5pm Monday–Friday, 9am–noon Saturday. Stamps are available from post offices and selected shops, usually newsagents, and from machines outside most post offices. There is a two-tier service within the UK: first-class should reach a UK destination the next day, second-class will take at least a day longer. The rate to Europe for letters weighing less than 20gm is the same as first-class letter post.

London's main post office is at Trafalgar Square, behind the church of St Martin-in-the-Fields. It stays open until 8pm Monday–Saturday. Queues tend to be long over the lunch period.

Useful Numbers

- Emergency – police, fire, ambulance: 999
- Operator (for difficulties in getting through): 100
- Directory Enquiries: 192
- Directory Enquiries (for international telephone numbers): 153
- London Regional Transport 24-hr information: 020-7222 1234
- Rail information for all London stations: 0345-48 49 50.
- Accommodation bookings: 020-7604 2890.

Telephones

It is cheaper to use a public phone than one in your hotel as some hotels make high profits out of this service.

British Telecom (BT) is the main telephone operating company. Most kiosks will accept both coins and plastic phone cards, which are widely available from post offices and newsagents in varying amounts between £1 and £20. Credit card phones can be found at major transport terminals.

London numbers changed in spring 2000. The dialling code for the whole of London is now 020 followed by an 8 digit local number. For example: 0171 123 4567 has become 020 7123 4567, 0181 123 4567 has become 020 8123 4567. If you're in London and want another London number you only need to dial the 8-digit local number. If you want to dial central London from outer London or vice versa you no longer need to dial the national code.

PHONING ABROAD

You can telephone abroad directly from any phone. Dial 00 followed by the international code for the country you want, and then the number. Some country codes:
Australia (61)
Ireland (353)
New Zealand (64)
South Africa (27)
US and **Canada** (1).
If using a **US credit phone card**, first dial the company's access number as follows:
Sprint, tel: 0800-890 877
MCI, tel: 0800-890 222
AT&T, tel: 0800-890 011.
(For Mercury phones, replace 0800 with 0500.)
The International Operator is on 155. Operator-assisted calls are more expensive. International directory enquiries is 153.
To send telegrams (now called telemessages), dial 0800 190 190.

Tourist Offices

To contact the London Tourist Board for information before your visit, write to them at: Glen House, Stag Place, London SW1E 5LT, tel: 020-7932 2000; www.londontown.com. The main centre for information about Britain is Britain Visitor Centre, 1 Regent Street, SW1Y 4NX. South of Piccadilly Circus, it's open to personal callers only, Monday 9.30am–6.30pm; Tuesday–Friday 9am–6.30pm; weekends (Jun–Oct) 9am–5pm; weekends (Nov–May) 10am–4pm.

Tourist information centres (TICs) can book hotels and tours for people who come to their office. The Victoria Station office makes theatre bookings and hotel reservations within England.

Tourist Board News

Visitorcall is a recorded information service provided by the London Tourist Board. Calls are charged at a higher rate than regular calls and the numbers cannot be obtained from outside the UK. Phone or fax 0839 123, followed by one of the following numbers:

- Attractions: 480
- Current exhibitions: 403
- Guided tours and walks: 431
- Museums: 429
- Palaces: 481
- Pubs, restaurants, teas: 485
- River trips/boat hire: 432
- Rock and pop concerts 422
- Shopping in London: 486
- West End shows: 416
- What's on this week: 400
- What's on for children: 404

Heathrow TIC: In the Tube foyer for terminals 1–3, daily 8am–6pm. Terminal 3 Arrivals concourse, daily 6am–11pm.
Selfridges TIC: Selfridges, Oxford Street, W1. Open during store hours.
Liverpool Street Station TIC: In the Underground station, EC2. Open Mon–Fri 8am–6pm, Sat–Sun 8.45am–5.30pm.
Victoria Station TIC: Victoria Station forecourt, SW1. Open Mon–Sat 8am–6pm, Sun 8.30am–4pm.
Waterloo International Terminal: Arrivals Hall, London SE1. Open daily 8.30am–10.30pm.

Embassies

Australia Australia House, Strand, WC2 4LA. Tel: 020-7379 4334
Canada Macdonald House, 1 Grosvenor Square, W1X 0AB. Tel: 020 7258 6600
India India House, Aldwych, WC2B 4NA. Tel: 020-7836 8484
Ireland 17 Grosvenor Place SW1X 7HR. Tel: 020-7235 2171
Jamaica 2 Prince Consort Road, SW7 2BZ. Tel: 020-7823 9911
New Zealand 80 Haymarket, SW1Y 4TQ. Tel: 020-7930 8422
South Africa South Africa House, Trafalgar Square, WC2N 5DP. Tel: 020-7451 7299
United States 24 Grosvenor Square, W1A 1AF. Tel: 020-7499 9000.

Getting Around

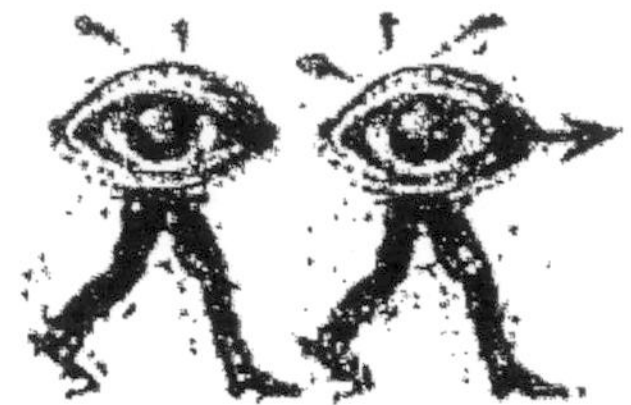

Driving

If you're only staying a short while in the Greater London area, and are unfamiliar with the geography of the capital, don't hire a car. Central London is a nightmare to drive in, with its web of one-way streets, bad signposting, and impatient drivers (taxi drivers are particularly intolerant of hesitation).

Parking is a major problem in congested central London. Meters are slightly cheaper than NCP car parks, but only allow parking for a maximum of two or four hours. If parking at a meter, keep your wits about you. Do not leave your car parked a moment longer than your time allows and do not return and insert more money once your time has run out. These are considered offences for which you can face a fine in the region of £40 and there are plenty of traffic wardens ready to give you a ticket; many are employed through private contractors and are expected to get results. Most meter parking is free after 6.30pm each evening, after 1.30pm in most areas on Saturday afternoons and all day Sunday. However, always check the details given on the meter.

When driving in England you should drive on the left and observe the speed limits. It is strictly illegal to drink and drive and penalties are severe. The law also states that drivers and passengers (front-seat and back-seat) must wear seat belts. Failure to do so can result in a fine. For further information on driving in Britain consult a copy of the *Highway Code*, widely available in bookshops.

Clampdown

Don't ever leave your car on a double yellow line. Clamping, whereby your vehicle is rendered completely immobile until you pay to have it released some hours later, is a common result. If your car disappears, consult a policeman as it will most likely have been towed away to a car pound. To retrieve it will cost you more than £100 plus the £40 parking fine.

- If you want to find out if your car has been towed away, phone 020-7747 4747.

Speed Limits

- 30 mph (50 kph) in urban areas (unless otherwise indicated)
- 60 mph (100 kph) on normal roads away from built-up areas
- 70 mph (112 kph) on motorways and dual carriageways (divided highways).

Car rental

To rent a car you must be over 21 years old and have held a valid full driving licence for more than a year. The cost of hiring a car usually includes insurance and unlimited free mileage. It does not include insurance cover for accidental damage to interior trim, wheels and tyres or insurance for other drivers without prior approval. Some companies offer special weekend and holiday rates, so shop around.

Car rental companies

All major car rental firms have representation in London. The following selection are all members of the London Tourist Board:
Europcar, tel: 0870 607 5000
Alamo Car Rentals, tel: 0990 99 3000
Hertz Rentacar, tel: 0990-996 699
Avis, tel: 0990 90 0500
Weekly hire rates start at around £200.

Travel Passes

The One Day Travelcard is a day pass that allows you unlimited travel on the Tube, buses, Docklands Light Railway and most overground rail services in the London area for a fixed fee. You can choose to buy Travelcards to cover two, three, four or all six zones. The card can be used after 9.30am on weekdays and all day at weekends and on public holidays. Available from Underground stations and newsagents.

Travelcards that are valid for a week or a month can be used at any time. To buy these Travelcards you need a passport-sized photograph.

Car breakdown

The following organisations operate 24-hour breakdown assistance. Phone calls to these numbers are free, but the service is only free to members:
AA, tel: 0800-887 766
RAC, tel: 0800-828 282
Green Flag, tel: 0800-400 600

Public Transport

THE TUBE

The Underground (colloquially known as the Tube, see map on the inside back flap) is the quickest way to get across town and most Londoners use it. But it badly needs investment and there has been talk of partial privatisation. In the rush hours (8am–9.30am and 5–6.30pm) every station is packed with commuters travelling to and from work; they cram into carriages like sardines in a tin. Services run from 5.30am to around midnight. If you're heading for the end of a line, your last train may leave closer to 11pm.

Make sure you have a valid ticket and keep hold of it after you have passed it through the electronic barrier – you will need it to exit at your destination. There is no flat-fare system throughout London, stations are divided into one of six zones depending on their location (travel between two stations in Zone One, for example, costs £1.50). A carnet of 10 one-way Zone 1 tickets costs £11.

It is illegal to smoke within the Underground system or on the buses.

The Docklands Light Railway

This is one of the best (and cheapest) ways to see the old but revived docks area. The fully automated service runs from Bank and Tower Hill Tube stations to Beckton, east London. A branch line goes to Island Gardens, on the Isle of Dogs, close to the Greenwich foot tunnel, and to Stratford for tube connections. An extension from Island Gardens via Greenwich to Lewisham has now been completed. The railway is part of London Regional Transport and operates like the Tube, with similar fares. Some of the views along the routes are superb.
For further information, tel: 020-7363 9700.

Penalty Fares

Ensure you have a ticket for your whole journey before starting your journey: all the transport systems operate heavy on-the-spot fines.

BUSES

London buses follow the same working pattern as the Underground although their routes are intended to supplement the Tube lines. Night Buses take over the most popular routes, running hourly through the night until dawn. Trafalgar Square is their starting point; a full bus route map and Night Buses leaflet are available at Travel Information Centres.

SIGHTSEEING TOURS

One of the best ways for first-time visitors to orient themselves is to take a special one-hour or two-hour ride on a double-decker tour bus. Some are open-topped so that, weather permitting, you can enjoy

Station Terminals

Britain's rail services are run by a variety of private companies. These are the principal mainline stations, with the areas they serve:
Charing Cross Station. Services to south London and southeast England: Canterbury, Folkestone, Hastings, Dover Priory.
Euston Station. Services to northwest London and beyond to Birmingham and the northwest: Liverpool, Manchester, Glasgow.
King's Cross Station. Services to north London and beyond to the northeast: Leeds, York, Newcastle, Edinburgh and Aberdeen.
St Pancras Station. For points not quite so far north, such as Nottingham, Derby and Sheffield.
Liverpool Street Station & **Fenchurch Street.** Services to east and northeast London, Cambridge and East Anglia.
Paddington Station. Services to west London and beyond to Oxford, Bath, Bristol, the west, and Wales.
Victoria Station. Services to south London and southeast England, including Gatwick airport, Brighton, Newhaven and Dover.
Waterloo Station. Mainly commuter services to southwest London, Southampton, and southern England as far as Exeter, including Richmond, Windsor and Ascot. The international Eurostar service also operates from here with regular services to Brussels and Paris; both can be visited as day trips.

Other termini, such as **Marylebone**, **Cannon Street** and **Blackfriars**, are principally commuter stations.

For information on **train times**, tel: 0345 48 49 50.

fresh air and uninterrupted camera angles. Others allow you to jump off at various stops and catch a later bus without buying an additional ticket.

Tours begin at many points around London, such as Marble Arch, Trafalgar Square or Piccadilly Circus.

TAXIS

Taxis in London are licensed and display the regulated charges on the meter *(see "Cabbies" chapter, page 69)*. If you should have a complaint, make a note of the driver's licence number and contact the Carriage Office, tel: 020-7230 1631.

Remember if you telephone for a taxi you will be charged for the time and miles it takes to pick you up as well. Minicabs are unlicensed, and can only be hired by telephoning for one; they're not allowed to pick up passengers on the street. Late at night, when black cabs are scarce, they are often to be found touting for business in central London. Use these minicabs with caution, particularly if travelling alone, as the drivers are not always trustworthy.

COACH

Coach travel is generally cheaper than travelling by train. National Express runs a comprehensive service throughout the country leaving from Victoria Coach Station, Buckingham Palace Road, SW1. Tel: 0990-808 080.

For day trips to Oxford, the Cotswolds, Stratford-upon-Avon, Canterbury, Windsor and Hampton Court, try Green Line Coaches (tel: 0870 08721).

Guided Tours

A guided tour of London by bus or coach is the best way for new visitors to familiarise themselves with the City. All tours that are registered with the London Tourist Board use their famous Blue Badge Guides, whose ranks now number around 1,000.

The Big Bus Company, tel: 0800-1691365. Open-top bus tours over a choice of two routes lasting either an hour or two hours. Passengers are free to hop on or hop off at any of the 80 stops. Buses run every 5–15 minutes. All tours have live commentary in English. Tickets are valid for 24 hours; buses operate 8.30am–6pm in the summer and to 4.30pm in the winter. Cost: £15 for adults and £6 for children.

Evan Evans, tel: 020-7950 1777. An all-day comprehensive introduction to the City with emphasis on historic sites. Admittance to St. Paul's, Royal Albert Hall and the Tower of London are part of the tour. Picks up from many hotels. Cost: £51.50 (£46.50 for children under 16 years). Thames cruises also available.

Frames Rickards, tel: 020-7837 3111. Various tours of the city in air-conditioned coaches accompanied by guides who hold the coveted "Blue Badge". The London Experience full-day tour takes in major sights such as the Tower with optional stops at Westminster Abbey and Kensington Palace and costs £54, £46 for under 16s; £51 for adults and £43 for children on Sunday. Cost includes admission charges a river cruise and lunch in a riverside tavern. Other trips include the Elizabethan Banquet tour where you can enjoy an evening of feasting and entertainment in a 15th-century palace in the grounds of Hatfield House. Cost: £48 Tuesday, Friday and Saturday. Certain tours are provided with French, German, Spanish and Italian translations.

The Original London Sightseeing Tour, tel: 020-8877 1722. A choice of four different tours in traditional red double-decker buses, some of which are open-top in fine weather. The Original tour features live commentary in English; the other three have recorded commentary in a choice of seven languages. A unique feature is the recorded children's commentary – by kids for kids. Tours run from 8.30am approximately every 12 minutes and passengers can hop on and off at any of the 90 stops. Tickets cost £12.50 for adults and £7.50 for children under 16 and are valid for 24 hours. Departure points throughout central London; Marble Arch, Baker Street, Strand, Haymarket, Victoria, amongst others.

Jack the Ripper & Haunted London, tel: 020-7233 7030. As the title suggests, an after-dark tour which explores London's more murky past and shady courtyards. Includes pub visits along the way. Evenings (from 7 to 11pm) on Monday, Wednesday, Thursday, Saturday and Sunday only. Departure points are from major central hotels. Cost: £15.50.

River Tours

Thames Passenger Services Federation, tel: 020-7345 5122. Many of the passenger vessel owners on the Thames belong to this association which promotes tourism and provides information about services.

Bateaux London, tel: 020-7925 2215, offer romantic dinner cruises along the Thames with cabaret and dancing.

Thames Cruises, tel: 020-7930 3373, offer 3-hour round trip cruises from Westminster Pier to the Thames Barrier and back. During the cruise passengers can disembark at Canary Wharf for sightseeing in London's Docklands and in Greenwich via the foot tunnel under the river. Passengers can also catch the DLR back to the Tower of London. The cruise also stops at the Thames Barrier where you can disembark and take a later vessel back.

Circular Cruises, tel: 020-7936 2033. One-hour circular cruises from Westminster Pier with stops at London Bridge City Pier and St Katherine's Pier. Full live commentary, private charter available.

Westminster Thames Passenger Services, tel: 020- 7930 4721. Offers trips between Westminster and Greenwich Piers every 30 minutes. There is also a boat service from Westminster to Hampton Court and Kew starting at

10.15am and taking around 3 hours. The fare to Hampton Court is £8 one-way; £12 return; to Kew it is £6 single, £10 return. Children can travel for just over half price. The association also has evening cruises which depart from Westminster at 7.30pm and 8.30pm for a fare of £5. Private charters are also available.
Catamaran Cruisers, tel: 020-7987 1185, operate a regular service downstream to the Tower of London and Greenwich with live multi-lingual commentary starting from 10.30am. Departures are from Embankment Pier, tickets range from £2.50 to £10.

Canal Trips

Jason's Trip, Little Venice, Bloomfield Road, W9.
Tel: 020-7286 3428. Traditional painted narrow boat making 90-minute trips along the Regent's Canal between Little Venice and Camden Lock, taking in Regent's Park and the zoo. April–October. Cost: £5.95 return, £4.95 single (£4.50 return, £3.75 single for under-14s). Family tickets are also available.
Adelaide Marine Ltd, tel: 020-8571 5678. Self-drive 2–10 berth boats from £20 per night available for weekly hire or for short breaks.
London Waterbus Company, Camden Lock Place, NW1.
Tel: 020-7482 2550. From Camden Lock to Little Venice with discounted tickets to the zoo at Regent's Park. £4 single, £2.60 under-14s. (Cockney Cruises to the Thames are available in the summer).

A booklet entitled *Explore London's Canals* is available from the tourist information centre at Victoria Station.

Walking Tours

Some walking tour operators use London Tourist Board trained Blue Badge Guides – a guarantee of quality. Walks generally last about two hours. *Time Out* magazine lists a selection of weekly walks in its Visitors section.

Original Guided Walks, tel: 020-8530 8443. Offers London's only ghost walk and the Jack the Ripper Walk featuring the Alam Tavern and the Jack the Ripper Exhibition.
Historical Tours, tel: 020-8668 4019. Programme of walks includes "The London of Dickens and Shakespeare" every Sunday at 11am, starting from exit 1, Blackfriars tube station. Cost: £5.
The Original London Walks, tel: 020-7624 3978. Programme includes Jack the Ripper, Shakespeare, Dickens, and other historical walks. Cost: £5.
Tours of London theatres and Wembley Stadium are available:
Royal National Theatre, tel: 020-7452 3400. Daily conducted tours of the building including workshops and backstage area. Tours start at 10.15am, 12.30pm and 5.15pm, every day except Sunday, and should be booked in advance.
Theatre Royal Drury Lane, tel: 020-7494 5091. Daily tours lasting about 1 hour.

Graveyards

London's graveyards, dating back to the 1800s, are some of the most historical and interesting places to visit.
Brompton Cemetery, Old Brompton Road, SW10. Many soldiers are buried here because of the proximity of Chelsea Hospital. Also Sir Henry Cole, organiser of the Great Exhibition (1882), Emmeline Pankhurst, fighter for women's rights (1928) and Frederick Leyland, patron of the Pre-Raphaelites (1892).
City of London Cemetery, Alderbrook Road, Manor Park, E12. This is the largest municipal cemetery in Europe and is the resting place for more than a million people.
Hampstead Cemetery, Fortune Green Road, NW6. Buried among its 26 acres are Kate Greenaway (1901), the Grand Duke Michael of Russia (1929) and the actress Gladys Cooper (1971).
Highgate Cemetery, Swain's Lane, Highgate, N6. The most famous of London's cemeteries, occupied by the German philosopher Karl Marx (1883), the female novelist George Eliot (1880) and actor Sir Ralph Richardson (1983). Some parts may only be visited with a guide.
Jews' Cemetery, Pound Lane, Willesden, NW10. Members of the de Rothschild family are buried here.
Kensal Green Cemetery, Harrow Road, W10. One of the first commercial burial grounds built to relieve the overcrowding in churchyards. Three gravel tracks wind among grand tombs. Buried here are the engineer, Sir Isambard Kingdom Brunel (1859), and novelists William Makepeace Thackeray (1863), Anthony Trollope (1882) and Wilkie Collins (1889).

Day Trips

For day trips out of town to places such as Oxford, the Cotswolds, Stratford-upon-Avon, Canterbury, Windsor and Hampton Court, try Green Line Coaches (tel: 0870 6087261) which also leave from Victoria.

For guided tours to these destinations, try London Coaches (operated by London Regional Transport, tel: 020-7222 1234), Golden Tours (tel: 020-7233 7030) or Frames Rickards (tel: 020-7837 3111). These operators also provide guided tours of London.

Fast trains operate to the West Country, so it's possible (though not cheap) to take a day trip to Bath. Trains leave from Paddington station (for times, tel: 0345 48 49 50).

Where to Stay

Choosing a Hotel

London has a range of hotels to match any major city in the world. There is everything from grand hotels of international renown to family-run hotels, guest houses, self-catering flats and youth hostels. The choice of accommodation can make or break a visit to the capital; this is especially true from a budget point of view. The flip-side of the massive choice is the equally massive prices charged in too many cases. This is particularly prevalent at the top end of the range where prices appear to be aimed exclusively at multi-millionaires.

However, there are bargains to be had. As with most things, you need to shop around. If a clean room and a hot breakfast are all you ask, a small hotel offer them for about a sixth of the price of a top hotel. The smaller hotels are often more friendly, making up in the welcome what they may lack in facilities.

HOTEL AREAS

There are hotels everywhere in London, but some areas have more than others. And don't necessarily expect to find a bargain two minutes walk from Piccadilly Circus. The main concentrations tend to be around Victoria, Earls Court/ Kensington, the West End and Bayswater. SW1 is London's traditional hotel district. There are some delightfully old-fashioned hotels in Victoria, in most price brackets, and the streets close to Victoria Station are full of terraced bed-and-breakfast accommodation. There are also streets full of terraced (or rather town-houses, for this is Kensington) hotels in the second big hotel area of SW5 and SW7. This zone, around Kensington High Street, Earl's Court and the Gloucester Road, is another major centre for medium range hotels of dependable comfort and, at least, some style.

The West End is the third area and the best-known zone. You'll pay more for budget or moderate accommodation here than you will in SW1 or SW5. W1 hotels at the bottom end of the price range can be very humble. WC1 is a clever choice: it's central and has reasonable prices, and there is still some dignity, even romance, in Bloomsbury (don't expect to find either of these qualities in Oxford Street).

Bayswater, or at least the area roughly between Edgware Road, Bayswater Road, Paddington and Queensway, is full of hotels. It does have a few large expensive hotels on its fringes but has a greater concentration of moderate and budget accommodation. Quality and prices vary enormously but the area is convenient for the West End and there is plenty of bustle around Queensway.

PRICES & BOOKING

The following listings are arranged into price brackets. The categories are based on one night's accommodation for one person, exclusive of breakfast. Generally you can get whatever your heart desires in expensive hotels. In budget accommodation, you're not buying a view; if you get one it's a bonus. Almost all hotels offer special deals that are cheaper than the published "rack rate", particularly at weekends and outside peak season, so it is always worth checking.

Book ahead. London fills up in the summer months (May and September are particularly crowded because of conference traffic), but if you arrive without a reservation, head straight for a Tourist Information Centre *(see page 267)*. The London Tourist Board operates an efficient bed-booking service.

Hotel bills usually include service and no extra tip is needed, but if you wish to repay good service, 10 percent split between the deserving is the custom. Equally, you can insist that service be deducted if you feel you've been treated less than impressively.

Ensure when booking that the price quoted is inclusive, and isn't going to be bumped up by a mysterious "travellers' charge" or other extras on the final bill. If you reserve in advance, you may be asked for a deposit. Reservations made, whether in writing or by phone, can be regarded as binding contracts, and you could be prosecuted for failing to honour that contract by not turning up on the day. Rooms must usually be vacated by midday on the day of departure.

Finally, make the most of your hotel. Many offer a wide range of services – free information, theatre ticket booking, etc, all of which are much harder to obtain on the street.

Hotel Listings

Top class

Berkeley Hotel
Wilton Place, SW1X 7RL.
Tel: 020-7235 6000
Fax: 020-7235 4330.
Many rate the Berkeley as the best in London. It's low-key, seldom advertised, with a country-house atmosphere. Swimming pool. A lot of English customers. **££££**

Claridge's
Brook Street, W1A 2JQ.
Tel: 020-7629 8860
Fax: 020-7499 2210.
Has long had a reputation for dignity and graciousness. **££££**

The Dorchester
Park Lane, W1A 2HJ.
Tel: 020-7629 8888
Fax: 020-7495 7342.
One of the most expensive. Lovely views over Hyde Park. **££££**

The Four Seasons Hotel
Hamilton Place,
Park Lane, W1A 1AZ.
Tel: 020-7499 0888
Fax: 020-7493 1895.
A temple of modern opulence. Friendly staff. **££££**

Lanesborough Hotel
1 Lanesborough Place, SW1X 7TA.
Tel: 020 7259 5599
Fax: 020 7259 5606.
Deluxe hotel overlooking Hyde Park Corner. The stately Neo-classical facade of the former St George's hospital complements the opulent Regency-style interior. Despite being a relative new-comer this is now one of London's finest hotels. **££££**

London Intercontinental Hotel
1 Hamilton Place,
Hyde Park Corner, W1V 0QY.
Tel: 020-7409 3131
Fax: 020-7493 3476.
One of the hotel group, and the most opulent of the Park Lane "millionaire's row". Modern and well equipped. Superb views over the park. **££££**

The Savoy
Strand, WC2R 0EU.
Tel: 020-7836 4343
Fax: 020-7240 6040.
Another of London's greats, with a solid reputation for comfort (its 207 rooms are excellent) and personal service (if a little formal). Central, but set back from the road and close to theatreland and Covent Garden. **££££**

Luxury

Athenaeum Hotel
116 Piccadilly, W1V 0BJ.
Tel: 020-7499 3464
Fax: 020-7493 1860.
Small hotel (157 rooms and apartments) in the heart of smart London, close by shops and with views over Green Park. A very English hotel, full of character of the "gentlemen's club" kind. Excellent service. **££££**

Blakes Hotel
33 Roland Gardens, SW7 3PF.
Tel: 020-7370 6701
Fax: 020-7373 0442.
Very trendy and up-to-the-minute hotel popular with theatrical and media folk. Cosmopolitan, tolerant, laid-back in style. 51 rooms. **£££–££££**

Brown's Hotel
30 Albemarle Street, W1A 4BP.
Tel: 020-7493 6020
Fax: 020-7493 9381.
A distinguished, very British, Victorian-style hotel. Smart Mayfair location. 118 rooms. **££££**

Capital Hotel
22 Basil Street, SW3 1AT.
Tel: 020-7589 5171
Fax: 020-7225 0011.
Luxurious little hotel (48 rooms) in the heart of Knightsbridge. Restrained in style, with tasteful decor, and rooms in the Laura Ashley style. Friendly service. Restaurant has Michelin star. **££££**

The Connaught
16 Carlos Place, W1Y 6AL.
Tel: 020-7499 7070
Fax: 020-7495 3262.
One of the best hotels in London, and very popular with British visitors. Discreet but immaculate service, superb decor (if a little gentlemen's club-ish) and a restaurant with a Michelin star. Only 90 rooms. **££££**

Price Categories

Price categories are for a double room without breakfast:
£ = under £100
££ = £100–£150
£££ = £150–£200
££££ = more than £200

Conrad International
Chelsea Harbour,
Off Lots Road, SW10 0XG.
Tel: 020-7823 3000
Fax: 020-7351 6525.
Luxury hotel (160 rooms) within the exclusive Chelsea Harbour complex by the Thames. **££££**

Duke's Hotel
35 St James's Place,
SW1A 1NY.
Tel: 020-7491 4840
Fax: 020-7493 1264.
Small (81 rooms) traditional hotel in smart St James's. The courtyard is lit by gas-lamps, and every suite is named after a duke. **££££**

Grosvenor House Hotel
86–90 Park Lane, W1A 3AA.
Tel: 020-7499 6363
Fax: 020-7493 3341.
Least showy of the Park Lane set (440 rooms). Large banqueting room a popular choice for smart London parties. Also has apartments for rent. **££££**

The Halcyon
81 Holland Park, W11 3RZ.
Tel: 020-7727 7288
Fax: 020-7229 8516.
Former townhouse in west London turned into small hotel with a country-house ambience. **££££**

Landmark London
222 Marylebone Road, NW1 6JQ.
Tel: 020-7631 8000
Fax: 020-7631 8080.
Opened in 1993, the modern eight-storey building with a glass domed atrium has good-sized rooms and all facilities. **££££**

Langham Hilton
1 Portland Place, Regent Street,
W1N 4JA.
Tel: 020-7636 1000
Fax: 020-7323 2340.
Elegant hotel renovated to a high standard. Two bars and a good restaurant. The attractive fountain room is a good place for taking afternoon tea. 379 rooms. **££££**

Le Meridien Waldorf Hotel
Aldwych, WC2B 4DD.
Tel: 020-7836 2400
Fax: 020-7437 3574.
Renowned Edwardian hotel (292 rooms). Modernised with a superb location, close to Covent Garden and theatreland. **£££–££££**

London Hilton on Park Lane,
22 Park Lane, W1Y 4BE.
Tel: 020-7493 8000
Fax: 020-7208 4142.
Has its devotees. Of its 446 rooms, double rooms are classed as "executive", "deluxe" or plain "superior". **££££**

Mandarin Oriental Hyde Park
66 Knightsbridge, SW1Y 7LA.
Tel: 020-7235 2000
Fax: 020 7201 3633.
A hotel of character (185 rooms), right on Knightsbridge, close to Harrods. Sumptuous in a Victorian marble-and-chandeliers style. **££££**

Metropolitan
19 Old Park Lane, W1Y 4LB.
Tel: 020-7447 1000
Fax: 020-7447 1100.
Christina Ong's attempt to create a New York ambience. In the exclusive and achingly trendy bar the staff are known as "mixologists". **££££**

Montcalm Hotel
34–40 Great Cumberland Place, W1A 2LF.
Tel: 020-7402 4288
Fax: 020-7724 9180.
It's part of an elegant Georgian crescent. 120 rooms. Rather plush. **£££–££££**

One Aldwych
1 Aldwych, WC2B 4BZ.
Tel: 020-7300 1000
Fax: 020-7300 1001.
Currently the place to be seen as well as to stay. Smart and stylish, it has an excellent location a stone's throw from theatreland and Covent Garden. This brand new hotel is a showcase of modernity throughout with high-profile guests to match. 105 rooms, each with a minimum 6-ft (2-metre) wide bed and television in the bathroom. **££££**

The Ritz
150 Piccadilly, W1V 9DG.
Tel: 020-7493 8181
Fax: 020-7493 2687.
One of the most famous hotel names in the world. 130 rooms. Not quite what it was, despite refurbishment. Jackets and ties must be worn. Tea at the Ritz available *(see page 287)*. **££££**

Royal Garden Hotel
2–24 Kensington High Street.
Tel: 020-7937 8000
Fax: 020-7361 1991.
Recently refurbished from top to bottom, this is now Kensington's only 5-star hotel. Decorated throughout in a luxurious contemporary style, it has a health club and one of London's finest views over Kensington Gardens from the top-floor Tenth Restaurant. 400 rooms. **££££**

St Martin's Lane
45 St Martin's Lane, WC2.
Tel: 020-7300 5500
Fax: 020-7300 5501.
Designed by Phillipe Starck, and currently the most fashionable hotel in London. Outlandish lighting, good expensive food and 204 blindingly white bedrooms. **££££**

Sheraton Park Tower
101 Knightsbridge, SW1X 7RN.
Tel: 020-7235 8050
Fax: 020-7235 8231.
The modern circular tower of this popular hotel (289 rooms) is five minutes' walk from Harrods, and close to Hyde Park. Attracts a lot of business visitors. Casino next door. Friendly service. **££££**

Stafford Hotel
16 St James's Place, SW1A 1NJ.
Tel: 020-7493 0111
Fax: 020-7493 7121.
Beautifully located just minutes away from Piccadilly. Good choice for those who like small hotels (80 rooms); old-fashioned service. **££££**

Price Categories

Price categories are for a double room without breakfast:
£ = under £100
££ = £100–£150
£££ = £150–£200
££££ = more than £200

Moderate

Adelphi Hotel
127–129 Cromwell Road, SW7 4DT.
Tel: 020-7373 7177
Fax: 020-7373 7720.
On a busy street just a short ride from Harrods – or you can even walk there. 68 rooms. **£££**

Basil Street Hotel
8 Basil Street, SW3 1AH.
Tel: 020-7581 3311
Fax: 020-7581 3693.
Hotel with a tremendous reputation, and certainly lots of old-fashioned charm. For those who like a country house atmosphere. Rooms and service can vary with rates. Close to Harrods. 90 rooms. **£££**

Cadogan Hotel
75 Sloane Street, SW1X 9SG.
Tel: 020-7235 7141
Fax: 020-7245 0994.
Another 19th-century style hotel, owned by Historic House Hotels. 65 rooms. Interesting position between Knightsbridge and Chelsea. Lily Langtry once lived in what's now the bar. **£££**

Charing Cross Hotel Strand
The Strand, WC2N 5HX.
Tel: 020-7839 7282
Fax: 020-7839 6685.
Located right next door to Charing Cross station and Underground. Comfortable and reliable, in a busy, central location close to Covent Garden. **£££**

The Gore
189 Queen's Gate, SW7.
Tel: 020-7584 6601
Fax: 020-7589 8127.
www.gorehotel.co.uk
Idyosyncratic Kensington hotel close to the Royal Albert Hall. Every inch of the walls is covered in paintngs and prints, and it attracts a lively, fashionable crowd. 54 individually themed rooms. **£££**

Goring Hotel
15 Beeston Place, Grosvenor Gardens, SW1W 0JW.
Tel: 020-7396 9000
Fax: 020-7834 4393.
Family-owned (the present manager, George Goring, is last in a long line of Goring managers), delightfully traditional hotel not far from Buckingham Palace. Relaxed atmosphere. Homemade food, including the bread. **£££–££££**

Hazlitt's
6 Frith Street, W1V 5TZ.
Tel: 020-7434 1771
Fax: 020-7439 1524.
One of London's oldest houses, dating from 1718, in the heart of Soho. 23 rooms, all with bath and all furnished with antiques – even the baths. **£££**

Holiday Inn
57–59 Welbeck Street, W1M 8HS.
Tel: 020-7935 4442
Fax: 020-7487 3782.
Very central but also a quiet hotel, modern behind its Edwardian facade. 137 rooms. **£££–££££**

Hotel Russell
Russell Square, WC1B 5BE.
Tel: 020-7837 6470
Fax: 020-7837 2857.
Spacious Forte hotel in the heart of Bloomsbury. Close to the British Museum and the Underground. 328 rooms, all with bath. Meals. **£££**

Mayfair Intercontinental
Stratton Street, W1A 2AN.
Tel: 020-7629 7777
Fax: 020-7629 1459.
Traditional hotel with 290 rooms (25 of which have Jacuzzis) with modern international restaurant. **£££**

Mount Royal Hotel
Bryanston Street, W1A 4UR.
Tel: 020-7629 8040
Fax: 020-7499 7792.
A truly central hotel, overlooking Oxford Street. Very large, with 700 rooms. **£££**

Park Lane Hotel
Piccadilly, W1Y 8BX.
Tel: 020-7499 6321
Fax: 020-7499 1965.
Established grand hotel (300 rooms) in a grand position. The 17th floor has spectacular views over Buckingham Palace gardens. **£££**

Post House Bloomsbury
Coram Street, WC1N 1HT.
Tel: 0870 4009222
Fax: 020-7837 5374.
Modern, pleasant hotel in a central quiet area. Close to the British Museum. 284 rooms, all with private bath. **£££**

Post House Regent's Park
Carburton Street, W1P 8EE.
Tel: 0870 4009222
Fax: 020-7383 2806.
Comfortable hotel close to Regent's Park and London Zoo. 326 rooms. Special weekend break rates available. **£££**

Royal Horseguards Thistle Hotel
2 Whitehall Court, SW1A 2EJ.
Tel: 020-7839 3400
Fax: 020-7925 2263.
Unusual location, overlooking the Thames and the Royal Festival Hall. 280 rooms. **£££–££££**

Royal Westminster Thistle Hotel
49 Buckingham Palace Road, SW1W 0QT.
Tel: 020-7834 1821
Fax: 020-7931 7542.
Close to Buckingham Palace and St James's Park. Half the size of its sister above, with 134 rooms. **£££**

The Rubens
39-41 Buckingham Palace Road, SW1W OPS.
Tel: 020-7834 6600
Fax: 020-7233 6037.
Traditional style hotel with a newly fitted Regency Floor of 45 rooms. Smart location opposite the Royal Mews, and close to Victoria station. 175 rooms. B

St George's Hotel
Langham Place, Regent Street, W1N 8QS.
Tel: 020-7580 0111
Fax: 020-7436 7997.
Close to the BBC and Oxford Street. Impressive views from its public rooms. Only 86 rooms. **£££**

Sloane Square Moat House
Sloane Square, SW1W 8EG.
Tel: 020-7896 9988
Fax: 020-7824 8381.
A stone's throw from the King's Road, and within walking distance from Harrods. A variety of eating and drinking places: the No. 12 Sloane Square restaurant, the Courts Café Wine Bar, and a "traditional English tavern". 104 rooms. **£££**

Strand Palace Hotel
The Strand, WC2R 0JJ.
Tel: 0870 400 8702
Fax: 020-7836 2077.
Massive, long-established, London hotel. Terrific location, refurbished in 1992. 783 rooms. **£££**

Tower Thistle Hotel
St Katherine's Way, E1 9LD.
Tel: 020-481 2575
Fax: 020-823 5966.
A big modern hotel situated on the banks of the Thames, close to the Tower of London, Tower Bridge and hany for the City. 801 rooms. **£££**

Inexpensive

Abbey Court
20 Pembridge Gardens, W2 4DU.
Tel: 020-7221 7518
Fax: 020-7792 0858.
Beautifully restored Notting Hill town house, with the atmosphere of a private home. 22 rooms, with Italian marble bathrooms with whirlpool baths. **££**

Academy Hotel
21 Gower Street, WC1A 6HG.
Tel: 020-7631 4115
Fax: 020-7636 3442.
A small and welcoming Bloomsbury hotel. Licensed bar; evening meal available. 48 rooms, 5 with private bath. **££**

Barkston Hotel
34–48 Barkston Gardens, SW5 OEW.
Tel: 020-7373 7851
Fax: 020-7370 6570.
Set in a quiet tree-lined street, but close to the bustle of Earls Court. Meals available. 92 rooms, all with private bath. **££**

Kennedy Hotel
43 Cardington Street, NW1 2LP.
Tel: 020-7387 4400
Fax: 020-7387 5122.
Modern air-conditioned hotel located next to Euston station. 360 rooms with private bath. **££**

Knightsbridge Green Hotel
159 Knightsbridge, SW1X 7PD.
Tel: 020-7584 6274
Fax: 020-7225 1635.
Astonishingly good value for its area, a family-run hotel. Unusual in that it consists mostly of suites, double and family-sized rooms. 23 rooms, all non smoking. **££**

Mercure London City Bankside
75–79 Southwark Street, SE1 0JA.
Tel: 020-7902 0800
Fax: 020-7902 0810.
New French chain hotel close to Tate Modern and the Globe Theatre. **££**

Norfolk Towers Hotel
34 Norfolk Place, W2 1QW.
Tel: 020-7262 3123
Fax: 020 7224 8687.
Elegant hotel with cocktail bar and restaurant, convenient for the West End attractions. 85 rooms. **££**

Sherlock Holmes Hotel
108 Baker Street, W1M 2LJ.
Tel: 020-7486 6161
Fax: 020-7486 0884.
Handy for Oxford and Regent street shopping. 125 rooms. **££**

Tophams
28 Ebury Street, SW1W OLU.
Tel: 020-7730 8147
Fax: 020- 7823 5966.
Old-style hotel with faded charm. Very popular and certainly one of the best value places to stay in London. Homely atmosphere. **££**

The Willett
32 Sloane Gardens, SW1.
Tel: 020-7824 8415
Fax: 020-7730 4830.
willett@eeh.co.uk
Excellent small hotel with 19 rooms in a fashionable neighbourhood – it's on a quiet street just yards from Sloane Square. Very good value for money. **££**

Least expensive

(Prices usually include breakfast)

Abbey House
11 Vicarage Gate, W8 4AG.
Tel: 020-7727 2594.

Grand Victorian house overlooking a pleasant garden square in Kensington. Basic furnishing, but well maintained, and often cited as the "Best B&B in London" in surveys. 15 rooms, none en suite. **£**

Abcone Hotel
10 Ashburn Gardens, SW7 4DG.
Tel: 020-7370 3383
Fax: 020-7460 3444.
Not far from Kensington High Street in a pleasant, rather old-fashioned hotel district. 35 rooms, 26 with bath. **£**

Airways Hotel
29–31 St George's Drive, SW1V 4DG.
Tel: 020-7834 0205
Fax: 020-7932 0007.
Pleasant hotel close to Buckingham Place, Westminster Abbey, and Harrods. Friendly service. 40 en-suite rooms. **£**

Andrews House Hotel
12 Westbourne Street, W2 2TZ.
Tel: 020-7723 5365
Fax: 020-7706 4143.
Family-run, in a busy area close to Lancaster Gate, Paddington and Marble Arch. 17 rooms, 10 with bath. **£**

Bayswater Inn
8–16 Princes Square, W2 4NT.
Tel: 020-7727 8621
Fax: 020-7727 3346.
Situated in a quiet residential square, close to Portobello Road Market, and handy for the Underground. 127 rooms, all with private bath. **£**

Beverley House Hotel
142 Sussex Gardens, W2 1UB.
Tel: 020-7723 3380
Fax: 020-7262 0324.
Well-equipped hotel between Oxford Street and Hyde Park. 23 rooms. **£**

Chester House
134 Ebury Street, SW1 9QQ.
Tel: 020-7730 3632
Fax: 020-7824 8446.
Bed and breakfast accommodation in a good location close to Sloane Square. 12 rooms including 2 family-sized. 4 with private bath. **£**

Clearlake Hotel
19 Prince of Wales Terrace, W8 5PQ.
Tel: 020-7937 3274
Fax: 020-7376 0604.

Price Categories

Price categories are for a double room without breakfast:
£ = under £100
££ = £100–£150
£££ = £150–£200
££££ = more than £200

Comfortable bed and breakfast in a quiet location with views of Hyde Park. 17 rooms. Good value. **£**

Crescent Hotel
49-50 Cartwright Gardens, WC1H 9EL.
Tel: 020-7387 1515
Fax: 020-7383 2054.
Pleasantly situated in a quiet Bloomsbury crescent, with private gardens and tennis courts. 27 rooms. **£**

Curzon House Hotel
58 Courtfield Gardens, SW5 ONF.
Tel: 020-7373 6745
Fax: 020-7835 1319.
Economical but comfortable small hotel which is close to Gloucester Road tube. 18 rooms including dormitories at £16 per person. **£**

Elizabeth Hotel
37 Eccleston Square, SW1 VPB.
Tel: 020-7828 6812
Fax: 020-7828 6814.
Friendly hotel set in an elegant period square, only two minutes' walk from Victoria Station. 40 rooms, 22 with bath. **£**

Enterprise Hotel
15–25 Hogarth Road, SW5 0QJ.
Tel: 020-7373 4974
Fax: 020-7373 5115.
Good location close to Kensington High Street and the Underground in a popular hotel area. 95 en-suite rooms. **£**

Garden Court Hotel
30–31 Kensington Gardens Square, W2 4BG.
Tel: 020-7229 2553
Fax: 020-7727 2749.
Friendly bed and breakfast hotel set in a traditional English garden square. 34 rooms, 12 with bath. **£**

Georgian House Hotel
35 St George's Drive, SW1V 4DG.
Tel: 020-7834 1438
Fax: 020-7976 6085.
Bed and breakfast hotel close to Victoria station. Friendly family atmosphere. 34 rooms, 21 of them en suite. **£**

Grapevine Hotel
117 Warwick Way, SWIV 4HT.
Tel: 020-7834 0134
Fax: 020-7834 7878.
Friendly, privately-owned hotel in Victoria. Good English breakfast (no other meals). 27 rooms. **££**

Kenwood House Hotel
114 Gloucester Place, W1H 3DB.
Tel: 020-7935 3473
Fax: 020-7224 0582.
Friendly family-run hotel with bed and breakfast accommodation in a central location. 16 rooms, 2 family rooms. **£**

Lonsdale Hotel
9-10 Bedford Place, WC1B 5JA.
Tel: 020-7636 1812
Fax: 020-7580 9902.
Old-established bed and breakfast hotel with real character in the heart of Bloomsbury. 39 rooms, 1 with private bath. **£**

Montagu House Hotel
3 Montagu Place, W1H 1RG.
Tel: 020-7935 4632
Fax: 020-7486 1443.
Well-equipped bed and breakfast hotel. All rooms have TV, phones and tea-making facilities. 18 rooms (3 with bath). **£**

Oliver Plaza Hotel
33 Trebovir Road, SW5 9NF.
Tel: 020-7373 7183
Fax: 020-7244 6021.
Bed-and-breakfast hotel with good service and comfortable rooms, all 32 of which have private baths. Good value. **£**

The Regency Hotel
19 Nottingham Place, W1M 3FF.
Tel: 020-7486 5347
Fax: 020-7224 6057.
An elegantly converted mansion in the heart of the West End close to Regent, Oxford and Harley streets. Comfortable and well-furnished. 20 rooms. **£**

Royal Adelphi Hotel
21 Villiers Street, WC2N 6ND.
Tel: 020-7930 8764
Fax: 020-7930 8735.
Behind Charing Cross station, and close to the Embankment Tube station and the river, in a busy little street. A short walking distance

from Covent Garden and theatreland. 47 rooms, 37 with bath. **£**

Stanley House Hotel
19-21 Belgrave Road,
SW1V 1RB.
Tel: 020-7834 5042
Fax: 020-7834 8439.
Modern family-style bed and breakfast hotel. 45 spacious rooms, 13 of them with bath. **£**

Strand Continental
143 Strand, WC2R 1JA.
Tel: 020-7836 4880
Fax: 020-7379 6105.
Despite the fancy name, one of the cheapest hotels in London, and one of the most central. Superb location. 23 rooms, none with private bath. No credit cards. **£**

Outer London Hotels

North London

Buckland Hotel
6 Buckland Crescent
Swiss Cottage, NW3 5DX.
Tel: 020-7722 5574
Fax: 020-7722 5594.
Victorian bed and breakfast hotel in a smart, bustling area. 15 rooms, 12 of them with private baths. **£**

The Clive Hotel
Primrose Hill Road, Hampstead,
NW3 3NA.
Tel: 020-7586 2233
Fax: 020-7586 1659.
Near affluent and fashionable Primrose Hill. Relaxed atmosphere. Restaurant and bar. 100 rooms. **££**

Dillons Hotel
21 Belsize Park,
Hampstead, NW3 4DU.
Tel: 020-7794 3360
Fax: 020-7431 7900.
Small family-style guesthouse in affluent Hampstead. Charming area close to public transport. 13 rooms, 9 with private bathrooms. No credit cards. **£**

Forte Post House Hotel,
215 Haverstock Hill, NW3 4RB.
Tel: 0870-400 9037
Fax: 020-7435 5586.
Forte hotel close to Hampstead Heath. 140 rooms. **££**

Hendon Hall Hotel
Ashley Lane, Hendon, NW4 1HF.
Tel: 020-8203 3341
Fax: 020-8203 9709.
A converted 18th-century Georgian mansion with its own grounds, giving a country atmosphere in the middle of suburban north London. Fully modernised. Meals available. 52 rooms. **£££**

Swiss Cottage Hotel
4 Adamson Road, NW3 3HP.
Tel: 020-7722 2281
Fax: 020-7483 4558.
Furnished in a superb Victorian house-style. 60 en-suite rooms. **££**

South London

Bardon Lodge Hotel
15 Stratheden Road, Blackheath,
SE3 7TH.
Tel: 020-8853 4051
Fax: 020-8858 7387.
Elegant Victorian house close to Greenwich and its magnificent park. 37 rooms. **££**

Selsdon Park Hotel
Addington Road,South Croydon,
CR2 8YA.
Tel: 020-8657 8811
Fax: 020-8651 6171.
Between London and Gatwick, and the country's biggest owner-managed hotel. Set in over 200 acres of parkland, with 205 bedrooms. Swimming pool. **££**

Southwest London

Kingston Lodge Hotel,
Kingston Hill, Kingston upon
Thames, KT2 7NP.
Tel: 020-841 4481
Fax: 020-8547 1013.
Country house hotel in a pretty location to the west of London. 64 rooms. **££**

The Petersham Hotel
Nightingale Lane, Richmond, Surrey,
TW10 6UZ.
Tel: 020-8940 7471
Fax: 020-8939 1098.
Great views over parkland and the river. Richmond BR or Tube for easy transport into London (40 minutes). 57 rooms. **££**

Richmond Hill Hotel
146-150 Richmond Hill, Richmond,
Surrey, TW10 6RW.
Tel: 020-8940 2247
Fax: 020-8940 5424.
Traditional English hotel with a friendly atmosphere, and views over parkland. Close to Richmond village, Kew Gardens and Richmond station. 137 rooms. Meals available. **£££**

West London

Foubert's Hotel
162-168 High Road
Chiswick, London W4 1PR.
Tel: 020-8995 6743 (no fax).
Small family-run hotel with its own restaurant and wine cellar-bar. Live music on weekends. 31 en-suite rooms. **£**

Bed & Breakfast

Staying in a private home ensures that you meet at least one London family. **The London Bed & Breakfast Agency** specialises in such accommodation, with prices from around £20–£40 a person per night, depending on area.
Tel: 020-7586 2768
Fax: 020 7586 6567
www.londonbb.com

Near Heathrow Airport

Forte Post House
118 Bath Road, Hayes, Middlesex
UB3 5AJ.
Tel: 020-8759 2552
Fax: 020-8564 9265.
186 rooms, all with private bathroom. **£–££**

Jarvis International
Bath Road, Cranford, Middlesex,
TW5 9QE.
Tel: 020-8897 2121
Fax: 020-8897 7014.
About 10 minutes from the airport, smaller and less international in style than other airport hotels. Lovely English garden. 73 rooms. **££**

Edwardian International
Bath Road, Hayes, Middlesex,
UB3 5AW.
Tel: 020-8759 6311
Fax: 020-8759 4559.
459 rooms. Swimming pool. **£££**

The Excelsior
Bath Road, West Drayton,
Middlesex, UB7 ODU.
Tel: 020-8759 6611
Fax: 020-8759 3421.
Near airport entrance, terminals 1, 2 and 3. 828 rooms. **£–££**

Heathrow Park
Bath Road, Longford, Middlesex UB7 0EQ.
Tel: 020-8759 2400
Fax: 020-8759 5278.
306 rooms. **£**

Hotel Ibis
112-114 Bath Road, Hayes, Middlesex UB3 5AL.
Tel: 020-8759 4888
Fax: 020-8564 7894.
354 rooms. Coach service is available to Heathrow. **£**

Osterley Four Pillars Hotel
764 Great West Road, Isleworth, Middlesex TW7 5NA.
Tel: 020-7568 9981
Fax: 020-7569 7819.
Small hotel with its own pub. 61 en-suite rooms. Meals. Special weekend discounts. **£**

Quality Hotel
London Road, Colnbrook, Slough SL3 8QB.
Tel: 01753 684001
Fax: 01753 685767.
112 rooms. **££**

Sheraton Skyline
Bath Road, Hayes, Middlesex, UB3 5BP.
Tel: 020-8759 2535
Fax: 020-8750 9150.
Rather showy hotel, with tropical garden and pool. 351 rooms. **£££**

Near Gatwick Airport

Gatwick Hilton International, Gatwick Airport, West Sussex RH6 0LL.
Tel: 01293 518080
Fax: 01293 528980.
Just a covered walkway away from airport terminals. 550 rooms.
££–£££

Holiday Inn Gatwick
Langley Drive, Crawley, West Sussex, RH11 7SX.
Tel: 01293 529991
Fax: 01293 515913.
Located in a pleasant area with courtesy bus to the airport. 223 rooms. **££**

Price Categories

Price categories are for a double room without breakfast:
£ = under £100;
££ = £100–£150;
£££ = £150–£200;
££££ = over £200.

Youth Hostels

The English describe Youth Hostel accommodation as spartan. Visitors might regard it as extremely basic. You get a single bed in a dormitory with basic washing and cooking facilities. Most hostels also have restaurants. The price is low: around £22 for bed and breakfast in any of the seven London hostels. You must be a member to stay in a hostel. To join, write to the YHA:
Trevelyan House
8 St Stephen's Hill, St. Albans, Herts, AL1 2DY
www.yha.org.uk.
Or fill in a form at one of the hostels located at:
36 Carter Lane, EC4 5AB (City Hostel). Tel: 020-7236 4965. 193 beds.
4 Wellgarth Road, NW11 7HR (Hampstead). Tel: 020-8458 9054. 200 beds.
King George VI Memorial Hostel, Holland House, Holland Walk, W8 7QU (Kensington). Tel: 020-7937 0748. 201 beds. Set in charming Holland Park, it is the best of the London youth hostels. Book well ahead.
Details of other student and budget accommodation are free from the London Tourist Board at one of their Tourist Information Centres *(see pages 267–8)*.

A Place of Your Own

There's no shortage of agents and private companies offering London apartments, many of them luxurious, others basic and frankly overpriced. Be wary – not all people are reputable. Decide what you want to pay, and stick to it, and don't book an apartment without seeing it first

If you're planning to stay in London for a while, it's better to look at flats from a temporary base when you arrive. The variety of properties

Flats & Apartment Rentals

Rental in the following apartments includes all bills excluding the telephone.

Allen House, Allen Street, W8. Tel: 020-7938 1346. 42 Kensington flats, 1–3 beds. From £980–£1,700 a week.

Apartment Services, 2 Sandwich Street, WC1H 9PL. Tel: 020-7388 3558. 60 flats in central London, particularly Bloomsbury and Covent Garden. From £350–£1,700 a week.

Aston's, 31 Rosary Gardens, South Kensington, SW7 4NQ. Tel: 020-7370 0737. 12 designer studios and 1–4 bed studio flats in South Kensington. From £400–£1065 per week.

Dolphin Square, Chichester Street, SW1V 3LX. Tel: 020-7798 8890. 154 suites near the river and the Tate Gallery. £100– £300 a night including use of pool, sauna and steam room.

Holiday Flats, 1 Princess Mews, Belsize Crescent, NW3 5AP. Tel: 020-7794 1186. Studio flats to 3 bed flats in Hampstead, St John's Wood and Swiss Cottage. £380–£900 a week (inclusive of utility bills).

Holiday Serviced Flats Ltd, 273 Old Brompton Road, SW5 9JA. Tel: 020-7373 4477. Have a large number of serviced flats throughout Greater London from £350 weekly for a studio to several thousand pounds for five-star luxury apartment. Brochure available.

Kensbridge Apartments, Kensgate House, 38 Emperor's Gate, SW7 4HJ. Tel: 020-7589 2923. Three Victorian houses split into studio to 1-bed apartments in Kensington and Victoria. Prices from £164–£450 a week.

can be bewildering, and going through a reputable agent is often the answer. Estate agents also act as letting and management agents for their clients – there is a comprehensive list in the Yellow Pages telephone directory. Agents and apartment owners also advertise in the *Evening Standard* newspaper, but these are usually the more expensive properties. The London Tourist Board is another good source of reputable agents.

The payment of a deposit is standard practice when renting and it can be as much as four weeks' rent (a returnable insurance against breakages, etc). But many holiday letting agencies ask for a deposit which is also to cover against cancellation. Avoid agents who charge a fee for finding you accommodation (such a fee is chargeable only when you have agreed to take a property).

Historic Lodgings

If you fancy staying in one of Britain's historic buildings, contact the Landmark Trust, who rent 160 properties in the UK for stays of one night or longer. In London their star attraction is an apartment in Hampton Court, but you'll need to book well in advance:
The Landmark Trust, Shottesbrooke, Maidenhead, Berkshire SL6 3SW, tel/fax: 01628 825417, e-mail: bookings@landmarktrust.co.uk, www.landmarktrust.co.uk.
The Landmark USA Inc, 707 Kipling Road, Dummerston, Vermont 05301, tel: 802-254 6868, fax: 802-257 7783

Where to Eat

How to Choose

London is one of the great culinary cities of the world. This is partly due to the breadth of cosmopolitan cuisines available and also the fact that the past decade has seen the re-evaluation of the indigenous cuisine of the British. Its once scorned reputation of badly cooked, unimaginative, stodgy meals has been overturned by the new generation of innovative modern-minded British chefs. They have injected new life into traditional English recipes, indeed re-discovering many, by combining them with French and ethnic influences. They now take pride in making the best of top quality and seasonal ingredients whilst also making meals lighter – for example, dishes such as "roast best end of lamb with two sauces of lime and coriander, yogurt and mint" (Wilson's) or "courgette flowers with lobster mousseline and a caviar butter sauce" (Sutherlands).

The traditional English practices of Sunday lunch, roast carveries, and fish and chips are still very much part of the scene and sampling them provides an insight into everyday life in England. However, choose carefully, as there is a huge difference between good and bad versions of these meals. Even the 1996 "mad cow disease" scare didn't entirely kill demand for roast beef – although some chefs tactfully found other European sources for their meat.

The main concentration of London's restaurants are to be found in the West End, with Soho providing the most interesting and widest choice, whilst Covent Garden offers good value pre-theatre suppers. The City, meanwhile, with its oyster bars and restaurants traditionally catering for the business luncher, becomes a ghost town in the evenings.

Although London's restaurants are expensive, reflecting the high cost of living, eating out in this capital has arguably never been so good. Ethnic restaurants provide some of the best value, whereas pubs and wine bars often provide good inexpensive snacks in surroundings that are preferable to a fast food hamburger joint. For a really cheap meal you can't go far wrong with a take-away of good old English fish and chips.

RESTAURANT PRICES

Prices quoted are indicators of the cost of a three-course evening meal for two not including drinks or service charge. Restaurant opening times do vary, so it is advisable to check beforehand and if required, book a table. Most Londoners would consider restaurants which charge over £60 for two as expensive, but the £100-plus meal is becoming increasingly common at fashionable restaurants.

It is worth noting that the best value at quality restaurants is often provided by a set lunch.

Price Guide

For two (without wine):
Inexpensive = less than £25
Moderate = £25–£50
Expensive = £50 plus

Restaurant Listings

Traditional English

The House
3 Milner Street, SW3.
Tel: 020-7584 3002.
Quaint chintzy English dining room within a pretty Chelsea town house. The surroundings may be a touch frilly, but the food has flair and historical associations. The puddings are particularly good. **Expensive.**

Fortnum and Mason, St James's Restaurant
4th floor, 181 Piccadilly, W1A 1ER.
Tel: 020-7734 8040.
Good English food, as you would expect from a restaurant located within this famous food emporium. Surprisingly not overpriced, it serves traditional cooked breakfasts and excellent roast lunches, as well as afternoon and high teas. **Moderate.**

Fox & Anchor
115 Charterhouse Street, EC1.
Tel: 020-7253 5075.
City pub close to Smithfield meat market that is famous for its huge English breakfasts. Very popular with meat porters and the local workforce. **Inexpensive.**

Greens Restaurant & Oyster Bar
36 Duke Street, SW1.
Tel: 020-7930 4566.
There is a clubby, English atmosphere served up with solid British food in the heart of St James. **Expensive.**

The Guinea
30 Bruton Place, SW1.
Tel: 020-7499 1210.
Excellent English food in a pub setting. The menu changes monthly but is strong on traditional grills such as beef and lamb. The signature dish is the multi-award winning steak and kidney pie. **Moderate.**

Jack's Place
12 York Road, SW11.
Tel: 020-7228 8519.
For a restaurant with real London character serving good homely food, this is difficult to beat. The proprietor, Jack, can tell a good tale or two and he's not mean with the portions. **Moderate.**

The Lindsay House
21 Romilly Street, W1.
Tel: 020-7439 0450.
Sister restaurant to The House in Chelsea, this also plays on the theme of the very English dining room, serving classy food within a traditional town house. **Expensive.**

Porters
17 Henrietta Street, WC2.
Tel: 020-7836 6466.
Large and noisy English pie theme restaurant with a range of savoury pies and good stodgy puddings. Also English wine and real ale. **Moderate.**

Restaurant Call

A useful number is that of Restaurant Services, who can supply up-to-date impartial information on London's restaurants and a free booking service.

- Tel: 020-8888 8080

The Quality Chop House
94 Farringdon Road, EC1.
Tel: 020-7837 5093.
A 19th-century city clerks' dining room with its original interior of fixed wooden seating still intact. The food, however, is up-market with the likes of blue fish with fennel sauce on the menu beside plain lamb chops. **Moderate.**

The Ritz, Louis XVI Restaurant
Piccadilly, W1.
Tel: 020-7493 8181.
Elegant Edwardian restaurant decorated in Louis XVI style. The dining room is sumptuous but some say that the food could do with improvement considering the price. Jacket and tie dress code. **Very expensive.**

RK Stanleys
6 Little Portland Street, W1.
Tel: 020-7462 0099.
Very British cuisine with a menu based on sausages in a multitude of varieties. The atmosphere is very relaxed and the portions are colossal. A really nice place to eat; the staff are excellent and kids eat for free on Saturdays. **Moderate.**

Rules
35 Maiden Lane, WC2.
Tel: 020-7836 5314/379 0258.
Old-established dining room that is exceptionally good for English game such as grouse, wild salmon, Highland roe deer and wild boar, when in season. Does a good roast beef, traditional puddings and real ale. **Expensive.**

Simpsons-in-the-Strand
100 Strand, WC2.
Tel: 020-7836 9112.
The Grand Divan Tavern is an Edwardian dining room renowned for serving the best roast beef in London. Staunchly traditional and formal, Simpsons is as popular as ever with the English establishment. **Expensive.**

Tate Gallery Restaurant
The Tate Gallery, Millbank, SW1.
Tel: 020-7887 8825.
Beautifully decorated with Rex Whistler's mural, this fine lunch restaurant has a excellent wine list. **Moderate.**

Wilson's
236 Blythe Road, W14.
Tel: 020-7603 7267.
Has justly earned a reputation for serving one of the best Sunday lunches in town. **Moderate.**

Modern European

Alastair Little
49 Frith Street, W1.
Tel: 020-7734 5183.
The chef-owner is something of a celebrity for his inventive approach to food in a basic French mode. Delicious, fresh, nouvelle-style cooking. Trendy, stark retro-Eighties decor. Booking essential. **Expensive.**

Bank
1 Kingsway, WC2.
Tel: 020-7379 9797.
Big, bustling and brave. The decor is modern and colourful with grand gestures. The food is an innovative mixture of flavours and ingredients and the menu is comprehensive. An experience – especially in the evening. **Expensive.**

Bibendum
Michelin House, 81 Fulham Road, SW3.
Tel: 020-7581 5817.
Set in this beautifully modernised Art Nouveau building, this is a landmark restaurant in more ways than one. The cuisine is a modern fusion of styles and flavours and the service is impressive. Unfortunately, so are the prices. **Expensive.**

Bluebird
350 King's Road, SW3.
Tel: 020-7559 1000.
Conran's European/Pacific Rim fusion restaurant in Chelsea. The place is noisy and glamorous and the food innovative. **Expensive.**

Coast
26b Albemarle Street, W1.
Tel: 020-7495 5999.

Huge restaurant serving interesting modern cuisine. The cooking is adventurous and exemplary with harmonious combination dishes. The service is friendly and the decor is futuristic. **Expensive.**

L'Escargot
48 Greek Street, W1.
Tel: 020-7437 2679.
Ever fashionable landmark in Soho popular with the theatrical and media crowd. Restaurant upstairs and a brasserie on the ground floor. Modern English and French cuisine. First-class wine list. **Moderately expensive.**

Hilaire
68 Old Brompton Road, SW7.
Tel: 020-7584 8993.
Classy South Kensington establishment with a continuing reputation for delicious unpretentious British cooking with modern European influence. **Expensive.**

The Ivy
1 West Street, WC2.
Tel. 020-7836 4751.
High-quality decor, gallery-worthy art, and well thought-out food have made for the successful regeneration of the Ivy which re-opened its doors in 1990. Like its relative, Le Caprice, this is a fashionable place to be seen, and booking ahead is essential. **Expensive.**

Kensington Place
201 Kensington Church Street, W8.
Tel: 020-7727 3184.
Fashionable and informal, this New York style restaurant is always bustling. The decor is modernist, while the food is fairly conservative in style. **Moderately expensive.**

Mash
19–21 Great Portland Street, W1.
Tel: 020-7637 5555.
Decorated in airport lounge chic with formica, steel and concrete, this restaurant serves good, innovative food. The menu has an astonishing range – breakfast, brunch, pizzas, pasta and options from the wood-burning oven. Own brewery on the premises. **Moderate.**

Mezzo
100 Wardour Street, W1.
Tel: 020-7314 4000.
Three different Conran restaurants and café under one roof. Bright, modern and trendy. **Expensive.**

Oxo Tower
Wharf, Barge House Street, SE1.
Tel: 020-7803 3888.
Brasserie and restaurant run by Harvey Nichols. Main attraction is the stunning river view. **Expensive.**

Pharmacy
150 Notting Hill Gate, W11.
Tel: 020-7221 2442.
Originally a collaboration between Marco Pierre White and the artist Damien Hirst, this restaurant is decorated with surgical instruments, pills in cabinets and glass tanks of surgical waste. Cuisine is modern European with a French influence. **Expensive.**

Le Pont de la Tour
Butlers Wharf Building,
36D Shad Thames, SE1.
Tel: 020-7403 8403.
Chic Conran restaurant with superb Thames views. The fixed price menus are a bargain for this level of cuisine; otherwise it's quality at a price. **Expensive.**

Price Guide

For two (without wine):
Inexpensive = less than £25
Moderate = £25–£50
Expensive = £50 plus

Quaglino's
16 Bury Street, SW1.
Tel: 020-7930 6767.
Reproduces the buzz of Thirties London, with a wide menu. **Expensive.**

French

Belvedere Restaurant
Holland House, Holland Park, off Abbotsbury Road, W8.
Tel: 020-7602 1238.
One of the most romantic places to dine in London, located within a converted stable block in the grounds of Holland Park. Menu has an international flavour and is particularly good for fish. **Expensive.**

Le Café Des Amis Du Vin
11–14 Hanover Place, WC2.
Tel: 020-7379 3444.
Always crowded, largely due to its Covent Garden position and reliable French food with an international flavour. Typical French brasserie menu and efficient service. Bar downstairs and Salon upstairs. No obligation to eat a full meal. **Moderate.**

Le Caprice
Arlington House, Arlington Street, SW1.
Tel: 020-7629 2239.
Black and white café-style restaurant that is a fashionable place to graze and be seen. Pianist in the evenings. Excellent New York style Sunday brunch. **Expensive.**

Chez Gérard
8 Charlotte Street, W1.
Tel: 020-7636 4975.
Especially good for meat, this French bistro serves excellent steak and chips. Also good traditional cooking such as *soupe de poisson* and Chateaubriand. Pleasant simple French decor. **Moderate.**

Criterion
224 Piccadilly, W1.
Tel: 020 7930 0488.
Quite possibly the most beautiful restaurant in London. The high-ceilinged hall in covered in mosaics, mirrors and drapes. The food is modern French and the service rather too rushed. An experience nonetheless. **Expensive.**

Le Gavroche
43 Upper Brook Street, W1.
Tel: 020-7408 0881.
Having confidently been one of England's top restaurants for many years, its standards do not waver. The excellence of Albert Roux made this the first British restaurant to earn three Michelin stars. Set lunch is best value. **Very expensive.**

Gordon Ramsay
68–69 Royal Hospital Road, SW3.
Tel: 020-7352 4441.
A luxurious setting for the Michelin-starred chef's interpretation of classic French cuisine. Genuine haute cuisine and a true gastronomic experience. The set lunch is good value; à la carte is pricey. **Expensive.**

Langan's Brasserie
Stratton Street, W1.
Tel: 020-7491 8822.
Langan's reputation for attracting

celebrities often overshadows the notable food. British actor Michael Caine is part-owner of this continually fashionable brasserie. **Expensive.**

Nico Central
35 Great Portland Street, W1.
Tel: 020-7436 8846.
A passionate perfectionist, Nico Ladenis serves classic French cuisine and has two Michelin stars, among other awards. **Moderately expensive.**

L'Odeon
65 Regent Street, W1.
Tel: 020-7287 1400.
A long sweeping dining room with a fine view out over Regent Street. Decorative modern French cuisine done well. The set meals are good value. **Expensive.**

Odins
27 Devonshire Street, W1.
Tel: 020-7935 7296.
Glamorous and richly adorned with paintings by the likes of David Hockney. Delicate food with traditional English and French influences. **Expensive.**

Quo Vadis
29 Dean Street, W1.
Tel: 020-7437 9585.
One of the oldest and most reputed restaurants in Soho in a building once inhabited by Karl Marx. French cuisine by Marco Pierre White, who has now ended his collaboration with the artist Damien Hirst. **Expensive.**

Simply Nico
48A Rochester Row, SW1.
Tel: 020-7630 8061.
Following Nico Ladenis's opening of Chez Nico, this restaurant adopted the prefix "Simply", a new chef and a bright and airy brasserie feel. But the food is still to be taken seriously. **Expensive.**
There is another branch in the London Bridge Hotel close to the railway station (tel: 020-7407 4536).

Thierry's
342 King's Road, SW3.
Tel: 020-7352 3365.
Good, unfussy traditional French food, along with vegetarian options. The set lunch is a bargain. **Moderate.**

Italian

Assaggi
The Chepstow, 39 Chepstow Place, W2.
Tel: 020-7792 5501.
For a small restaurant above a pub with questionable decor, this place is incredibly popular. The ambience is good, the service impeccable and the food superb. The only drawback is the price. **Expensive.**

Bertorelli's
44a Floral Street, WC2.
Tel: 020-7836 3969.
Black and white Art Deco style restaurant that has become something of an institution in Covent Garden. Serves cheap and reliable modern Italian food. **Moderate.**

Café Venezia
15–16 New Burlington Street, W1.
Tel: 020-7439 2378.
Informal restaurant serving home-made pasta. **Moderate.**

Price Guide

For two (without wine):
Inexpensive = less than £25
Moderate = £25–£50
Expensive = £50 plus

Chapter House Pizza Express
Southwark Cathedral
Montague Close, SE1.
Tel: 020-7378 6446.
In the unusual setting of the Chapter House of Southwark Cathedral, this lunch restaurant is a branch of the popular Pizza Express chain. **Inexpensive.**

Cibo
3 Russell Gardens, W14.
Tel: 020-7371 6271.
Comfortable and airy with intriguing art on the walls, modern northern Italian cooking. **Moderate.**

La Famiglia
7 Langton Street, SW10.
Tel: 020-7351 0761.
Successful restaurant with pleasant food and decor done the southern Italian way. Has one of the largest outdoor eating areas in London. **Moderate.**

Orso
27 Wellington Street, WC2.
Tel: 020-7240 5269.
More up-market than its brother restaurant, Joe Allen *(see Late Eating)*. Set in a basement with simple decor, authentic north Italian food and good service. Fashionable with actors and theatregoers alike. **Expensive.**

Pizzeria Castello
20 Walworth Road, SE1.
Tel: 020-7703 2556.
Always packed, Castello's has a long standing reputation for serving the cheapest and the best pizzas in town. Well worth a detour to the Elephant and Castle. **Inexpensive.**

Pizza lovers please note: Pizza Express is a very civilised chain, with live jazz at the Dean Street branch. The classiest is the Pizza on the Park branch at 13 Knightsbridge, whereas Kettners at 29 Romilly Street, W1 is the most fashionable. The Chicago Pizza Pie Factory has various branches and is best for deep-pan pizzas. Pizza Hut, all over town, is reasonable, predictable and very cheap.

San Lorenzo
22 Beauchamp Place, SW3.
Tel: 020-7584 1074.
Fashionable and busy posh Knightsbridge restaurant. The menu is a mixture of the exciting and the mundane. Extraordinary decor incorporates a sliding roof for summer. **Expensive.**

The River Café
Thames Wharf, Rainville Road, W6.
Tel: 020-7381 8824.
By the Thames near Hammersmith, designed by the controversial architect Richard Rogers and run by his wife. Delightful northern Italian food and riverside tables. **Expensive.**

Chinese

China City
White Bear Yard, 25A Lisle Street, WC2.
Tel: 020-7734 3388.
Traditional Chinese food served in a beautiful, tranquil setting. Two spacious, airy rooms overlook a courtyard with a fountain. An oasis of calm amid the central London bustle. **Moderate.**

Chuen Cheng Ku
17 Wardour Street, W1.
Tel: 020-7437 1398.

Huge, functional place that has a reputation for serving some of the best dim sum in town (until 6pm). Popular with locals at lunch time. **Moderate**.

Fung Shing
15 Lisle Street, WC2.
Tel: 020-7437 1539.
Has long been one of the best Chinatown restaurants and consequently is always packed. Some original dishes with particularly good fish. **Moderate**.

Harbour City
46 Gerrard Street, W1.
Tel: 020 7439 7859.
A great place to have dim sum with a wide selection of tasty dishes being served. Translated menu in English helps along the selection process. **Moderate**.

Magic Wok
100 Queensway, W2.
Tel: 020 7792 9767.
One of the best Chinese restaurants in the area. Specials board is worth a look for some interesting dishes. **Moderate**.

Memories of China
67 Ebury Street, SW1.
Tel: 020-7730 7734.
The late Ken Lo, renowned Chinese cookery writer, started up this classy restaurant where dishes originate from the many regions of China and standards are high. Second branch within the Chelsea Harbour complex, SW10. **Expensive**.

Poon's
4 Leicester Street, W1.
Tel: 020-7437 1528.
The best of several branches of Poon in Central London. Wind-dried meats are a distinctive feature on the long menu of more than 200 dishes. Good value. **Moderate**.

Vong
Berkeley Hotel, Wilton Place, SW1.
Tel: 020-7235 1010.
Inspirational take on Oriental cuisine. The dishes are both classic and modern using the freshest ingredients. **Expensive**.

Wong Kei
41–43 Wardour Street, W1.
Tel: 020-7437 6833.
Regulars aren't deterred by the rude service for which this place is famed. Huge, on three floors, serving good value Cantonese food. Cash only. **Inexpensive**.

Zen Garden
15-16 Berkeley Street, W1.
Tel: 020-7493 1381.
Luxury surroundings with equally showy food. **Expensive**.

1997
19 Wardour Street, W1.
Tel: 020-7734 2868.
Popular with young Chinese Londoners, this is a good place for a casual quick meal. The decor is funky and eccentric, and the food is simple and reasonably priced. **Inexpensive**.

Chinatown

Many of London's best Chinese restaurants are to be found in Chinatown which centres around Gerrard Street. Paved over and made into something of a theme park with pagoda phone boxes and oriental style arches, this lively area is crammed with restaurants serving mainly Cantonese cuisine. If you are baffled by the choice, those well patronised by the Chinese themselves are often a good bet. (Tubes: Piccadilly, Leicester Square)

Indian

Bombay Brasserie
Bailey's Hotel, Courtfield Close, SW7.
Tel: 020-7370 4040.
The stylish decor harks back to the days of the Raj. The menu is well thought-out, with dishes from many regions. Lunch-time buffet is good value. **Expensive**.

Chutney Mary
535 King's Road, SW10.
Tel: 020 7351 3113.
Booking is essential for this popular restaurant which serves a variety of dishes from all over India. **Expensive**.

Veeraswamy
Victory House, 101 Regent St, W1.
Tel: 020-7734 1401.
London's oldest Indian restaurant. Elegant, colonial style. **Expensive**.

Great Nepalese
48 Eversholt Street, NW1.
Tel: 020-7388 6737.
Specialises in the milder and less oily cuisine of Nepal, incorporating a lot of chicken and lamb. Authentic and always popular. **Moderate.**

Khan's
13 Westbourne Grove, W2.
Tel: 020-7727 5420.
This huge Indian dining room is famous for being great value. Crowded in the evenings, the atmosphere is that of constant hustle and bustle. **Moderate**.

Kundan
3 Horseferry Road, SW1.
Tel: 020-7834 3434.
Handy for Houses of Parliament and popular with MPs. First-class Punjabi cuisine. **Moderate**.

Last Days of the Raj
22 Drury Lane, WC2.
Tel: 020-7836 1628.
One of London's most respected Indian restaurants, good for Bengali dishes. **Moderate**.

Ragam
57 Cleveland Street, W1.
Tel: 020-7636 9098.
One of the few restaurants in London offering unusual specialities from the Indian coastal state of Kerala. Good, healthy food. **Moderate**.

The Red Fort
77 Dean Street, W1.
Tel: 020-7437 2115.
Renowned Soho restaurant which offers good Mogul cooking in comfortably luxurious surroundings. Its creator, Amin Ali, has produced a stylish setting and the restaurant is noted for its interesting menu. **Expensive**.

Salloos
62 Kinnerton Street, SW1.
Tel: 020-7235 4444.
Hidden away in a Knightsbridge mews, this high-class family run restaurant specialises in well prepared Pakistani cuisine with lamb and chicken dishes a speciality. **Expensive**.

Suruchi
82 Mildmay Park, N1.
Tel: 020-7241 5213.
Lovely restaurant where you can eat outside in the summer. Mostly

Indian Restaurants

London has many Indian restaurants, a pleasant legacy of its colonial past, with the most distinctive being those that specialise in the cuisine of a particular region. Concentrated areas of cheap Indian restaurants can be found in Brick Lane and Southall which have large Asian communities. Drummond Street, close to Euston Station, is good for vegetarian Indian restaurants such as Ravi Shankar and Diwana Bhel Poori House, which are also notably cheap.

South Indian cooking with a good selection of vegetarian dishes. **Moderate.**

Taste of India
25 Catherine Street, WC2.
Tel: 020-7836 2538.
Good value pre-theatre menus and reduced price lunches. **Moderate.**

Japanese

Ikeda
30 Brook Street, W1.
Tel: 020-7629 2730.
Sit at the Yakitori and Sushi bars to get the best Japanese experience at this fashionable Mayfair restaurant. **Expensive.**

Ikkyu
67 Tottenham Court Road, W1.
Tel: 020-7636 9280.
Relaxed basement restaurant with good value, quality food and less of the usual Japanese emphasis on decor and service. Has a large Japanese following. **Moderate.**

Miyama
38 Clarges Street, W1.
Tel: 020-7499 2443.
Sophisticated restaurant with good personal service. Two teppan-yaki counter where a chef cooks sizzling dishes on a hot plate. **Expensive.**

Suntory
72 St James's Street, SW1.
Tel: 020-7409 0201.
London's most expensive Japanese restaurant. Excellent food is served with traditional style. Michelin star. **Expensive.**

Yoshino
3 Piccadilly Place, W1.
Tel: 020-7287 6622.
Sit at this bar below the Japan Centre and try some of the cheapest Japanese food in town. **Inexpensive.**

Yo Sushi
52 Poland Street W1.
Tel: 020-7287 0443.
Fun eating, with robot service and what's claimed to be the longest conveyor belt service in the world. **Inexpensive.**

Wagamama
101A Wigmore Street, W1.
Tel: 020-7409 0111.
Minimalist fast food noodle restaurant. Good fresh interesting Japanese food at reasonable prices. Branches also inJamestown Road NW1 and Lexington Street W1. **Inexpensive.**

Other Ethnic Eateries

Belgo Centraal
50 Earlham Street, WC2.
Tel: 020-7813 2233.
Great fun Belgian theme restaurant. Food revolves around the traditional mussels and chips but there is plenty more besides. The many set meal deals are very reasonable and ensure the place is consistently packed. The list of Belgian beers has to be seen to be believed. **Moderate.**

Beotys
79 St Martin's Lane, WC2.
Tel: 020-7836 8768.
One of London's oldest Greek/ Cypriot restaurants, luxurious Beotys is set in the heart of theatreland. Go for the Greek specialities rather than the international menu. **Moderate.**

Blue Elephant
4–6 Fulham Broadway, SW6.
Tel: 020-7385 6595.
A tropical jungle in the middle of Fulham. Excellent Thai food and charming service from waitresses in traditional costume. Carefully explained menu. **Expensive.**

Calabash
38 King Street, WC2.
Tel: 020-7836 1976.
Situated below the Africa Centre close to Covent Garden Piazza with dishes from many regions of the African continent. Coffee is particularly good. Also African wine and beer. **Moderate.**

Chiang Mai
48 Frith Street, W1.
Tel: 020-7437 7444.
Thai restaurant modelled on the traditional stilt house. Friendly staff will help you to decipher the menu which is primarily based on the cuisine of northern Thailand and lists over 100 dishes. A set menu for beginners, otherwise experiment with the rarer dishes. **Moderate.**

Daquise
20 Thurloe Street, SW7.
Tel: 020-7589 6117.
Central to London's Polish community since World War II. East European food is served in a rather basic environment with a nice relaxed café atmosphere. **Inexpensive.**

Fakhreldine
85 Piccadilly, W1.
Tel: 020-7493 3424.
Overlooking Green Park, this is one of London's smartest and most established Middle Eastern restaurants. Fine Lebanese cuisine. **Expensive.**

Gay Hussar
2 Greek Street, W1.
Tel: 020-7437 0973.
A long menu of mouth-watering dishes, such as wild cherry soup, keep this fine established Hungarian restaurant very popular. It endeavours to provide value for money. **Expensive.**

Nikita's
65 Ifield Road, SW10.
Tel: 020-7352 6326.
Sophisticated Russian restaurant located in an intimate basement with a good range of vodka, caviar and well prepared traditional dishes. **Moderate.**

Rebato's
169 South Lambeth Road, SW8.
Tel: 020-7735 6388.
Spanish restaurant worth a detour.

Price Guide

For two (without wine):
Inexpensive = less than £25
Moderate = £25–£50
Expensive = £50 plus

The atmosphere and decor provide a perfect setting in which to enjoy the authentic food, especially the range of tapas. Musicians add to the experience in the evenings.
Moderate.
Solly's
146 Golder's Green Road, NW11.
Tel: 020 7455 0004.
Multi-floored Jewish restaurant with takeaway service available. Open on Sunday. **Moderate.**

Fish

Geales
2-4 Farmer Street, W8.
Tel: 020-7727 7528.
Busy traditional fish restaurant at Notting Hill Gate. Good fish and chips cooked in beef dripping. Just a trifle pretentious. **Moderate.**
Live Bait
43 The Cut, SE1.
Tel: 020-7928 7211.
also at 21 Wellington Street, WC2.
Tel: 020 7836 7161.
Handy for the Young Vic theatre but relatively small so booking is advisable. Good shellfish and imaginatively presented fish dishes.
Expensive.
Fish!
Cathedral Street, close to Borough Market SE1.
Tel: 020-7836 3236.
Lively restaurant in the shadow of Southwark Cathedral, serving fresh fish in simple dishes. Best atmosphere at lunch time.
Moderate.
Manzi's
1–2 Leicester Street, WC2.
Tel: 020 7734 0224
Timeless Italian-run fish restaurant close to Leicester Square. Good traditional fish dishes. **Expensive.**
Rudland & Stubbs
35–37 Greenhill Rents, Cowcross Street, EC1.
Tel: 020-7253 0148.
English and French-style fish dishes in a characterful setting with tiled walls and raw floor boards, around the corner from Smithfield Meat Market. **Moderate.**
Sea Shell Fish Bar
49–51 Lisson Grove, NW1.
Tel: 020-7723 8703.
Renowned fish and chip restaurant and take-away. Although, as this English delicacy goes, it is not cheap, its wide choice of fish is consistently very fresh and well cooked. **Moderate.**
Sheekey's
28-32 St Martin's Court, WC2.
Tel: 020-7240 2565.
Edwardian fish restaurant which reflects its theatrical surroundings. The menu includes traditional potted shrimps, fish pies and eels and mash at somewhat high prices.
Expensive.
Le Suquet
104 Draycott Avenue, SW3.
Tel: 020-7581 1785.
Popular first-class chi-chi French fish restaurant with fresh Mediterranean style decor. **Expensive.**
Sweetings
39 Queen Victoria Street, EC4.
Tel: 020 7248 3062.
Beautiful interior of tiles and mosaics add to the atmosphere of this busy, traditonal City hang out. Varied menu which includes potted shrimps and stodgy English puddings. **Expensive.**

Vegetarian

The Gate
51 Queen Caroline Street, W6.
Tel: 020-8748 6932.
This restaurant is housed in a grand artist's studio in fashionable Hammersmith. The food is accomplished and ambitious.
Moderate.
Food For Thought
31 Neal Street, WC2.
Tel: 0171-836 0239.
Small and crowded at lunch times, with queues for take-aways. The food is never dull. Bring your own wine. Dinner served until 8.30pm.
Inexpensive.
Manna
4 Erskine Road, NW3.
Tel: 020-7722 8028.
One of the best vegetarian restaurants in London. In wealthy Primrose Hill, but with a relaxed atmosphere and reasonable prices.
Moderate.
Mildred's
58 Greek Street, W1.
Tel: 020-7494 1638.
Imaginative cooking put together in cafe-style surroundigns. Vegan options. **Inexpensive.**

Late-night eating

Borshtch 'n' Tears
46 Beauchamp Place, SW3.
Tel: 020-7584 9911.
Last orders 2am.
Zany Russian restaurant with a sense of humour that attracts a mostly young clientele who are prepared to participate in the music and gaiety. The inexpensive menu includes Russian delicacies such as blinis and caviar, chicken kiev, golubtsy and Siberian Pilmenni.
Moderate.
Costa Dorada
47–55 Hanway St, W1.
Tel: 020-7636 7139.
Last orders 2.30am.
One of London's best known late-night spots, this lively restaurant/ tapas bar with a strong Spanish following fills up in the late evening when diners flock in for the colourful flamenco dancing and live Spanish music. **Expensive.**
Joe Allen
13 Exeter Street, WC2.
Tel: 020 7836 0651.
Last orders 12.45am.
Continually fashionable American restaurant hidden down an alley in Covent Garden. Largely patronised by those involved with the media and showbiz. Booking essential.
Moderate.

Fish & Chips

Britain's culinary gift to the world provides an inexpensive meal, and there are "chippies" all over town, from Old Compton Street in Soho to the Taxi drivers' favourite on Waterloo Road. Cod and plaice are the principal fish, soaked in batter and fried. Malt vinegar is a must for the chips (often bought separately and eaten from the paper bag). Saveloys – sausages made of little more than breadcrumbs – are also a feature of fish and chip shops. Indulgence rules: nothing green or healthy should be eaten with fish and chips.

Maroush II
38 Beauchamp Place, SW3.
Tel: 020-7581 5434.
Last orders 2am.
Largely patronised by nocturnal Middle Eastern high rollers who congregate here after a night out at London's smarter clubs. The food, which includes Lebanese delicacies such as *sujuk* (spicy sausages) and *shish taouk* (cubes of chicken charcoal grilled), is well presented. **Expensive.**

Mr Kong
21 Lisle St WC2.
Tel: 020-7437 7341.
Last orders 2am.
Renowned for seafood, Mr Kong's food is amongst the best in Chinatown. However, the decor falls a long way short of the quality of the fare, so to get the maximum enjoyment from your meal aim to sit on the ground floor and leave the top floor to the regular Chinese patrons and the basement to someone else. **Moderate.**

Theme restaurants

Beefeater by the Tower
Ivory House, St Katharine's Dock, E1.
Tel: 020-7480 7017.
The court of Henry VIII is recreated with a touch of kitsch in basement vaults close to the Tower of London. Diners eat a five-course meal with an unlimited supply of wine and ale from serving wenches whilst being entertained by court jesters, minstrels, magicians, and fire eaters. Merriment continues after the meal with a disco. Reserve. **Expensive.**

Price Guide

For two (without wine):
Inexpensive = less than £25
Moderate = £25–£50
Expensive = £50 plus

Café Pacifico
5 Langley Street, WC2.
Tel: 020-7379 7728.
Young, loud Tex Mex joint with typical repertoire of enchiladas, fajitas and tacos and, of course, those essential margueritas. Located in a converted Covent Garden warehouse. **Moderate.**

Canal Café Theatre
Bridge House, Delamere Terrace, W2.
Tel: 020-7289 6054.
Pub with a small theatre next to the Regent's Canal in Little Venice. Dine on simple food to fringe theatre and cabaret shows. **Moderate.**

Hard Rock Café
150 Old Park Lane, W1.
Tel: 020-7629 0382.
A shrine to rock music that is not only a good restaurant, serving some of the best burgers in London, but has also become a sight on most young tourists' itineraries. Houses an exceptional collection of rock memorabilia that continues to grow. **Moderate.**

Improv Comedy Club Restaurant
6161 Tottenham Court Road, W1.
Tel: 020-7387 4173.
British and international comedians provide improvised entertainment. Food is international modern. **Moderate.**

Planet Hollywood
Trocadero, 13 Coventry Street, W1.
Tel: 020-7287 1000.
Ubiquitous celeb-owned movie-theme eatery. Always buzzing and packed with memorabilia it's a good place to take kids. The menu is strong on burgers, pizzas, pasta and grills. Not haute cuisine but a fun experience. **Moderate.**

Players Theatre
The Arches, Villiers Street, WC2.
Tel: 020-7839 1134.
Victorian-style music hall within a new purpose-built theatre. Join in with lively fun of cockney sing-alongs, comedians and musicians. Acts change regularly every two weeks. Separate supper room offers set or à la carte menu. **Moderate.** Theatre meal inexpensive (booking advisable).

Rainforest Café
20 Shaftesbury Avenue, W1.
Tel: 020-7434 3111.
A tropical rainforest in the Trocadero Centre has such main course dishes as *rasta pasta* and *rumble in the jungle*. Should keep the children amused. **Moderate.**

Smollensky's on the Strand
105 Strand, WC2.
Tel: 020-7497 2101.
Friendly American style restaurant that caters well for children with Punch and Judy shows and circus entertainments at weekeneds. **Moderate.**

Cyber Cafés

Cyber cafes provide snacks and basic food to nibble on while surfing the Web, collecting e-mail or playing the latest computer games. The following cafés all have disabled access.

Cyberia Cyber Cafe, 39 Whitfield Street, W1. Tel: 020-7209 0982. The first Internet café to be set up in London provides a wide range of games to play and snacks to eat.

Cafe Internet, 22–24 Buckingham Palace Road, SW1. Tel: 020-7233 5786. Apart from using the Web and playing games you can hire a colour scanner or word processor by the hour.

EasyEverything, 9–13 Wilton Road, SW1. Tel: 020-7233 8456. One of many branches throughout central London, with all the usual facilities.

Café Life

Fashionable places to linger a while with a drink, meet your friends, be seen, and maybe eat.

Bar Italia
22 Frith Street, W1.
Tel: 020-7437 4520.
Retaining its genuine 1950s feel, this is London's most famous Italian bar. No hype, just excellent coffee, a characterful atmosphere and an interesting crowd.

Cheers London Bar & Restaurant
72 Regent Street W1.
Tel: 020-7494 3322.
A replica of the Boston bar from the TV series is situated on the ground floor of the Cafe Royal. American beers.

Denim
4A Upper Saint Martin's Lane, WC2.
Tel: 020-7497 0376.
Plush and flamboyant basement bar close to Covent Garden. A good place to hang out with a drink or have a meal in the upstairs restaurant.

Dome 354 King's Road, SW3.
Tel: 020-7352 2828.
Popular place to drink, read a newspaper and watch the wildlife of the King's Road go by. Many branches around London.

Freud's
198 Shaftesbury Avenue, WC2.
Tel: 020-7240 9933.
Basement bunker bar that attracts the trendy. It hosts art exhibitions, live music and on busy evenings you could be excused for thinking that a "street fashion" show is taking place. Inexpensive.

Joe's Café
126 Draycott Avenue, SW3.
Tel: 020-7225 2217.
Sleek and chic bar which attracts the well-heeled for coffee, or maybe a spot of champagne and a bite to eat, after the tiring business of shopping across the road at Joseph.

Konditor & Cook
Young Vic, 66 The Cut, SE1.
Tel: 020-7620 2700.
Great cakes, croissants and Danish pastries supervised by a German pastrycook. Small but imaginative menu.

Lisboa Patisserie
57 Golborne Road, W10.
Tel: 020-8968 5242.
Fabulous and unusual Portuguese pastries draw trendy browsers from the Portobello Road and Notting Hill into this café which is a part of the local Portuguese community.

The Lobby Bar
One Aldwych, WC2.
Tel: 020-7300 1000.
A place to see and be seen. The last word in modern chic, this former newspaper office is patronised by the likes of Robbie Williams and Roger Moore.

Maison Bertaux
28 Greek Street, W1.
Tel: 020-7437 6007.
This rival to Patisserie Valerie, with its own set of regulars, certainly merits queuing for a table. Upstairs you can tranquilly enjoy delicious pastries with tea or coffee.

Market Bar
240a Portobello Road, W11.
Tel: 020-7229 6472.
Inside the shell of an old pub is this triumph of the art of the distressed interior. Decadent candelabras covered in dripping wax abound in this fashionable retreat from the market.

Patisserie Valerie
44 Old Compton Street, W1.
Tel: 020-7437 3466.
Central to Soho life, this ever popular meeting place is worshipped by its arty and intellectual regulars who crowd the place. Who could pass by the best gâteaux and croissants in town?

Drinking Notes

Wine & Cocktail Bars

Almeida Theatre Wine Bar
1 Almeida Street, N1.
Tel: 020-7226 0931.
Relaxed atmosphere at this earthy theatrical wine bar. Casual.

Alphabet
61 Beak Street, W1.
Tel: 020-7439 2190.
A very hip hang-out in the heart of Soho. The basement bar is sparsely furnished with car seats and the floor is covered by a London street-plan. The ground floor features benches and zinc-topped tables. There's a short, eclectic food menu and drinks range from wine to juices and cocktails. Can get seriously crowded.

American Bar
Savoy Hotel, Strand, WC2.
Tel: 020-7836 4343.
London's classic cocktail bar within the sophisticated Savoy Hotel. Jacket and tie.

Bar des Amis du Vin
11–13 Hanover Place, WC2.
Tel: 020-7379 3444.
Dark, atmospheric basement bar with a good solid wine list and decent French snacks reflecting the food in the restaurant above. Casual.

Boot and Flogger
10–20 Redcross Way, SE1.
Tel: 020-7407 1116.
Wine bar with an air of quiet comfort and exclusivity. Relax in leather

Afternoon Tea

Traditionally the English "take afternoon tea" at around 3.30pm, settling down to indulge themselves genteelly with thinly-cut sandwiches, a variety of cakes and, of course, a pot of tea. Choice of brew varies from the classic Indian teas such as Assam and Darjeeling, both rich in flavour, to the more flowery Earl Grey.

Brown's Hotel, 30 Albemarle Street, W1.
Tel: 020-7518 4108.
Tea is served formally in comfortable wood-panelled lounges with an air of civility. Expensive.

Maison Sagne
105 Marylebone High Street, W1.
Tel: 020-7935 6240.
This patisserie maintains an air of dignity harking back to the 1920s. Afternoon tea is served between 3–5pm. Old-fashioned service.

Palm Court, The Waldorf Meridien, Aldywch, WC2.
Tel: 020-7836 2400.
This hotel's magnificent Palm Court hosts traditional tea dances. As well as partaking of tea, you take to the floor with your partner for a waltz.

Park Room, Hyde Park Hotel, 66 Knightsbridge, SW1.
Tel: 020-7235 2000.
Tea is served to the accompaniment of a pianist while you gaze at the view of Hyde Park.

Ritz Hotel
Piccadilly W1
Tel: 020–7493 8181
Probably the quintessential afternoon tea experience, though some find it overrated. Opulent surroundings, elegant service and piano accompaniment. Very formal and very popular – the hotels advised booking a month ahead.

armchairs and enjoy the traditional food and their wide selection of ports and madeiras, wines and sherries. Open Monday–Friday 11am–8pm only. Casual.

Cork and Bottle
44-46 Cranbourne Street, WC2.
Tel: 020-7734 7807.
An excellent retreat from Leicester Square, this basement wine bar offers decent food and a notable selection of wines. Casual.

El Vino
47 Fleet Street, EC4.
Tel: 020-7353 6786.
Once famous as a Fleet Street haunt for journalists and lawyers, this good wine bar remains a bastion of tradition, insisting on jacket and tie for men and smart dress for women.

Green's
36 Duke Street, SW1.
Tel: 020-7930 4566.
Friendly smart Champagne bar in St James's with a gentleman's club atmosphere and traditionally courteous service, although rather expensive. Smart.

Julie's Bar
137 Portland Road, W11.
Tel: 020 7727 7985.
Comfortable Holland Park bar decorated with Gothic style which has attracted a notable crowd since the 1960s. Casual.

The King's Bar
Hotel Russell, Russell Square, WC1.
Tel: 020-7837 6470.
Cocktails taken traditionally, shaken or stirred, in an elegant wood-panelled Edwardian lounge. Smart.

Truckles of Pied Bull Yard
Bury Place, WC1.
Tel: 020-7404 5338.
Attractive wine bar with a peaceful open courtyard close to the British Museum. Casual.

Whisky Bar
Athenaeum Hotel, Piccadilly, W1.
Tel: 020-7499 3464.
Discreet and old-fashioned cocktail bar that offers an unrivalled selection of malt whiskies. Smart.

Pubs

The Albion
10 Thornhill Road, N1.
This attractive pub in a pretty area of Islington has the atmosphere, as well as the appearance, of a village pub. Cosy bars and a beer garden at the back.

Anchor Bankside
34 Park Street, SE1.
This 18th-century riverside pub has higgledy-piggledy rooms with oak beams and a minstrels' gallery. There has been a pub on this site for 1,000 years; Samuel Johnson was a regular and wrote part of his dictionary here. Near Shakespeare's Globe.

Angel
21 Rotherhithe Street, SE16.
Built on stilts over the Thames, this old pub dates back to the 15th century when monks from the Bermondsey Priory ran it as a tavern. The balcony and upstairs restaurant offer outstanding views of the Thames, including the Pool of London and Tower Bridge.

Black Friar
174 Queen Victoria Street, EC4.
Built in 1875 on the site of the Black Friars Monastery, this is London's only Art Nouveau pub. The spectacular marble interior carries bronze friezes depicting the activities of monks.

Bunch of Grapes
207 Brompton Road, SW3.
Fine example of a late Victorian pub which is protected by a preservation order. Complete with "snob" screens for privacy.

Old Cheshire Cheese
145 Fleet Street, EC4.
Famous olde-worlde pub, rebuilt after the Great Fire but which still has a medieval crypt beneath it. It has been frequented through the ages by many well-known literary figures including Charles Dickens, Dr Samuel Johnson and possibly William Shakespeare.

Cittie of Yorke
High Holborn, WC1.
The main room of the pub has the air of an old baronial hall. It has reputedly the longest bar counter in England, a high raftered ceiling, huge wine vats and intimate, ornately-carved cubicles. There has been a pub on this site since 1430.

Dickens Inn
St Katharine's Way, E1.
Successful conversion of an old warehouse into a spit-and-sawdust pub that has an authentic feel as well as a fabulous location, facing as it does St Katharine's Dock and Tower Bridge.

The Dove
19 Upper Mall, W6.
Quaint 18th-century riverside pub on a pleasant stretch of the Thames at which James Thomson is supposed to have written the words of *Rule Britannia*. It once housed the Doves Press, whilst William Morris set up the Kelmscott Press nearby.

Freemason's Arms
32 Downshire Hill, NW3.
The last court of the old English game of Pell-Mell was located in the large garden of this pub which is situated adjacent to Hampstead Heath. Old London skittles is still played in the basement.

The Bitter Truth about British Beer

The British are renowned for beer drinking and, with over 400 breweries in the country, each producing several beers (from bitter, stout and pale ale to lager and real ale), they certainly have more than enough to choose from.

Fans of real ale, led by the Campaign for Real Ale (CAMRA), have promoted a greater appreciation of this traditional brew, which undergoes a second natural fermentation in the cask and is served without gas pressure. Many local breweries now produce their own real ale, and quirky brews are not uncommon (from an ale flavoured with whisky to seasonal beers named after the 12 signs of the zodiac).

However, three-quarters of Britain's beer market is dominated by multi-national brewing companies, and weak, fizzy lagers have won a large share of the market.

George Inn
77 Borough High Street, SE1.
London's sole surviving galleried coaching inn. Dating from the 17th century, this lovely old building is now protected by the National Trust. At lunchtime it is awash with pin-striped suits, and the service can be a bit slow. The courtyard is a popular meeting place on summer evenings.

The Grenadier
Old Barrack Yard, 18 Wilton Row, SW1.
Hidden away in a quiet cobbled mews, this pub is a real gem. It used to be the mess of the Duke of Wellington's officers.

Lamb and Flag
33 Rose Street, WC2.
Originally known as the "Bucket of Blood", this timber building was once a venue for bare fist boxing. Its character is enhanced by its quaint skew-whiff walls and doorways.

Market Porter
9 Stoney Street, SE1.
This is the plce to come to sample real ales; they usually have up to 30 on tap. It is dark, low-ceilinged and atmospheric, with an extremely odd selection of stuffed animals as decoration.

The Mayflower
117 Rotherhithe Street, SE16.
Dark olde-worlde pub backing on to the Thames with seating outside on the jetty.

Ye Olde Mitre
1 Ely Court, Ely Place, EC1.
A quaint pub full character and history and a warren of small dark-panelled rooms. The original 1547 inn was built to service the needs of the nearby palace belonging to the Bishops of Ely.

Phoenix and Firkin
5 Windsor Walk, SE5.
Firkin pubs brew their own beer on the premises and are decorated in the spit-and-sawdust style. This particular one is situated in a large Victorian railway station which is on a bridge and has a small train running around the ceiling.

Princess Louise
208 High Holborn, WC1.
Relic from the High Victorian age with notable tiling and fittings. The gents' toilet is worth a visit. Real ales on sale.

Prospect of Whitby
Wapping Wall E1.
Great fun, Thames views and amazing history. Built in 1520 and once popular with river smugglers, its regulars have included Pepys, Turner and Dickens. Pewter counter, bare boards, panelling and flagstones plus a waterside courtyard.

Spaniards Inn
Spaniards Road, NW3.
This historic pub is situated at an old toll gate on the north side of Hampstead Heath. It dates back to the 16th century and is reputed to have been used by highwayman Dick Turpin.

Swan
66 Bayswater Road, W2.
The present building dates from the 19th century, but this is reputed to be the site of the last pub for 17th centuy criminals before heading for the gallows at Tyburn. Beer garden.

Culture

Ballet

Coliseum
St Martin's Lane, WC2N 4EF.
Tel: 020-7632 8300.
Hosts performances of ballet in the summer months by the Royal Festival Ballet and visiting companies. Is particularly popular with visiting Russian Ballets. Tube: Leicester Square.

Sadlers Wells Theatre
Rosebery Avenue EC1.
Tel: 020-7863 8000.
Re-opened after extensive renovation this is now a flexible, state-of-the-art performance space. Offers an exciting and innovative programme of dance and opera. Once again restored as London's leading venue for contemporary and classical dance. Tube: Angel.

Royal Opera House
48 Floral Street, WC2.
Tel: 020-7240 1066.
Home to the Royal Ballet and the Royal Opera. Re-opened after extensive refurbishment. Backstage tours are available (tel: 020-7304 4000). Tube: Covent Garden.

Opera

Coliseum
St Martin's Lane, WC2N 4EF.
Tel: 020-7632 8300.
This elegant Edwardian theatre is easily distinguished on London's skyline by the illuminated golden globe on its roof. Home to the English National Opera (ENO), this is where English language operas are performed. Productions tend to be more theatrical than those of the Royal Opera. Tube: Leicester Square.

Royal Opera House
48 Floral Street, WC2.
Tel: 020-7240 1066.
More traditional than the Coliseum, this theatre attracts the crème de la crème of the Opera world. Operas are performed in their original language and tickets are very expensive. Dressy affair. Now re-opened after extensive refurbishment. Tube: Covent Garden.

Theatre

The only way to get a ticket at face value is to buy it from the theatre box office. Most are open from 10am until mid-evening. You can pay by credit card over the phone for most theatres, or reserve seats three days in advance before paying. A ticket booth in Leicester Square offers unsold seats at half-price (plus booking fee) on the day of performance. There are booking agents throughout London, but beware: some charge high fees. Two reputable ones that are open 24 hours are:
First Call at 020-7420 0000
Ticketmaster at 020-7344 4444
You can also book many of the West End shows at the **Theatre Museum**. Tel: 020-7943 4700. Ignore ticket touts unless you're prepared to pay several times a ticket's face value for sell-outs.
For further details see Theatre chapter, page 77.
The Barbican Arts Centre
Silk Street, Barbican, EC2Y 8DS.
Tel: 020-7638 8891.
Home to the London Symphony Orchestra and to the Royal Shakespeare Company who sadly, due to financial difficulties, do not perform here all year round. Contains the Barbican Theatre, Concert Hall and The Pit which are well thought-out and comfortable with good acoustics, although they're somewhat sterile. Several different productions run concurrently. Tube: Barbican. 24-hour information, tel: 020-7382 7272.
Royal National Theatre
South Bank, SE1.
Tel: 020-7452 3000.
Three repertory theatres are housed within its concrete mass: the Olivier, the Lyttelton and the Cottesloe. They always provide a good and varied selection of plays. The current director is Trevor Nunn. Tube: Waterloo/Embankment.

Classical Music

Barbican Arts Centre
Silk Street, EC2Y 8DS.
Tel: 020-7638 8891.
Home to the London Symphony Orchestra and the English Chamber Orchestra. This huge concrete complex built for the arts is one of London's major classical concert venues. Tube: Barbican.
Holland Park Open Air Theatre
Holland Park, W14.
Box Office Tel: 020-7602 7856.
During the warm summer months opera, dance and theatre performances are staged here in the semi-open air. Tube: Holland Park/High Street Kensington.
Kenwood Lakeside Theatre
Hampstead Lane, NW3.
Tel: 020-8233 7435.
Quality open-air performances of classical music and opera in the beautiful grounds of Kenwood House. Usually includes a production by the Royal Opera. Tube: Golders Green/Archway.
The Royal Albert Hall
Kensington Gore, SW7 2AT.
Tel: 020-7589 8212.
Erected in the memory of Prince Albert, this circular hall comes alive every summer for the Henry Wood Promenade Concerts, simply known as The Proms. The acoustics have been improved over the past few years, making this a more enjoyable venue. Tube: Kensington High Street (10-minute walk)/South Kensington.
Royal Festival Hall
South Bank, Belvedere Road, SE1 8XX.
Tel: 020-7960 4242.
London's premier classical music venue. Built as part of the Festival of Britain of 1951, the exterior of this hall appears somewhat dated and arouses mixed public comment on its appearance. However, it is an excellent concert hall with space for large-scale performances. Next door is the Queen Elizabeth Hall where chamber concerts and solos are performed. Also the small Purcell Room. Tube: Waterloo/ Embankment.
Wigmore Hall
36 Wigmore Street, W1H OBP.
Tel: 020-7935 2141.
Delightful intimate hall with seating for 550. It has a pleasant atmosphere and excellent acoustics and is most renowned for chamber recitals. Also Sunday Morning Coffee Concerts. Tube: Bond Street.

Listings Sources

For entertainment listings consult:

- *What's On* (weekly events' magazine for tourists)
- *Time Out* (the weekly events' magazine Londoners read)
- *Hot Tickets*, free with the Evening Standard newspaper on Thursdays
- *The Guide*, with Saturday's Guardian newspaper.

CHURCHES

Many of London's churches also offer superb music. Three of the best are:
St John's, Smith Square
Westminster, SW1 3HA.
Tel: 020-7222 1061.
This church has been converted into a concert hall hosting chamber music and BBC lunchtime concerts. Tube: Westminster.
St Martin-in-the-Fields
Trafalgar Square, WC2.
Tel: 020-7839 8362.
Concerts are held at lunchtimes and evenings in this church designed by James Gibbs. Tube: Charing Cross.
St Mary-le-Bow
Cheapside, EC2 6AU.
Tel: 020-7248 5139.
Thursday lunchtime recitals. This church is home to the famous Bow bells. Tube: St Paul's/Mansion House/Bank.

Rock & Pop

Rock and pop music is one of Britain's greatest exports, so what better city in the world to hear it live?

Apollo Hammersmith
Queen Caroline Street, W6 9QH.
Tel: 020-7416 6080.
Famous long-standing music venue (formerly the Hammersmith Odeon) that is on the tour circuit for major bands. Sitting is compulsory so it is rather like being in a cinema, but despite this, good fun is usually had by all. Tube: Hammersmith.

Astoria
Charing Cross Road, WC2.
Tel: 020-7434 0403.
This former theatre has large dance floor and hosts a variety of music including rock, folk, reggae and R&B. Tube: Tottenham Court Road or Leicester Square.

Borderline
Orange Yard, Manette Street (off Charing Cross Road), W1V 5LB.
Tel: 020-7734 2095.
Known for featuring young and up-and-coming new bands, this small cellar-venue gets packed at the weekends. Tube: Tottenham Court Road.

Brixton Academy
211 Stockwell Road, SW9.
Tel: 020-7924 9999.
Large and lively venue with a buzzing atmosphere. Tends to attract both local and trendy bands and crowds. Good viewing, no seats. Tube: Brixton.

Mean Fiddler
22–28a Harlesden High Street, NW10 4AX.
Tel: 020-8963 0940.
This medium-sized venue features mainly lively rock bands and has an excellent reputation for roots music. Well worth the trek out of the centre of town. Tube: Willesden Junction.

Palladium
8 Argyll Street, W1V 1AD.
Tel: 020-7494 5020.
One of the most grand and famous theatres in London that occasionally hosts rather more subdued bands and singers. Tube: Oxford Circus.

Rock Garden
The Piazza, Covent Garden, WC2E 8HA.
Tel: 020-7240 3961.
Provides a stage for new unknown bands in central London. Small venue in a dark cavernous basement. Tube: Covent Garden.

Wembley Arena and Stadium
Empire Way, Wembley, Middlesex.
Tel: 020-8902 0902.
Acoustics and viewing can be a problem at the Arena, London's largest indoor venue. However, this is dwarfed by the huge football stadium next door which has a capacity of 70,000. The stadium is for mega-concerts and, unless you arrive early to get a good viewing position, expect to watch the action on the large video screens.
Tube: Wembley Park/Wembley Central.

Live Like a Lord

Here are a few extravagant things you might like to do in London:

★ Silver service breakfast at the Royal Garden Hotel, Kensington High Street, W8, with fabulous views over Hyde Park.
★ Pick up a picnic from Harrods and go boating on the Serpentine in Hyde Park.
★ Traditional roast lunch at Simpsons-in-the-Strand.
★ An ice cream soda at Fortnum & Mason, Piccadilly, W1 – the most upmarket fast food in town.
★ Tea dance in the elegant Palm Court of the Waldorf Hotel.
★ A cocktail at the American bar, Savoy Hotel, Strand WC2. Get there at 6pm for a table (dress code: jacket and tie).
★ Dine and dance at the Roof Restaurant on the 28th floor of the Hilton, Park Lane (tel: 020-7493 8000).

Jazz

100 Club
100 Oxford Street, W1.
Tel: 020-7636 0933.
Decked out in a basic manner with two bars at each end serving drinks at pub prices, this is a renowned venue for live jazz, rhythm-and-blues from established bands and young unheard-ofs alike. It tends to be packed out every night. Closes 2am. Tube: Tottenham Court Road.

606 Club
90 Lots Road, SW10.
Tel: 020-7352 5953.
Basement club hidden behind an elusive doorway on Lots Road which hosts live jazz every night. Up-and-coming musicians play alongside more established names. The food is good, the atmosphere relaxed; popular with musicians who come to eat, drink and join in with impromptu sessions. Closes 2am. Tube: Fulham Broadway.

Dover Street
8–10 Dover Street, W1.
Tel: 020-7629 9813.
London's largest jazz restaurant. Basement venue featuring modern European cuisine and a variety of live music from jazz to soul via blues. Smartish. Closes 3am. Tube: Green Park

Jazz Cafe
5 Parkway, NW10 7PG.
Tel: 020-7916 6060.
One of the liveliest places in town. Can get crowded. For the best seats, book a table for a meal on the balcony. Tube: Camden Town.

Ronnie Scott's
47 Frith Street, W1V 6HT.
Tel: 020-7439 0747.
In the heart of Soho is London's most famous jazz venue, attracting all the major names of the jazz world and a varied clientele. Food and service are less of an attraction than the music and atmosphere. Membership is not essential. Arrive early as it gets very crowded, especially at weekends. Closes 3am. Tube: Leicester Square.

Vortex
139–141 Stoke Newington Church Street, N16.
Tel: 020-7254 6516.
All types of jazz are played in this intimate venue. Very busy at weekends when booking is advisable. Stoke Newington overground station (on a line out of Liverpool Street station).

Diary of Events

January

New Year's Day Parade from Parliament Square to Berkeley Square.

London International Boat Show, Earl's Court: the world's largest exhibition of its kind.

Charles I Commemoration (last Sunday): English Civil War Society dress up as Royalists from the King's army and make their way from Charles I's statue in Whitehall to his place of execution outside Banqueting House.

February

Chinese New Year: colourful Chinese celebrations centring around Gerrard Street in Chinatown.

Valentine's Day (14th): the most romantic day of the year.

March

Ideal Home Exhibition, Earl's Court. Tel: 020-7385 1200: exhibition of new ideas and products for the home.

London Book Fair, Olympia.

Chelsea Antiques Fair, Old Town Hall, Kings Road, SW3: wide range of antiques on sale.

Easter Parade, Battersea Park. Carnival with floats and fancy dress costumes.

Camden Jazz Festival, Camden Town. Includes jazz, opera, dance, film and exhibitions.

April

Oxford and Cambridge Boat Race: annual race between university oarsmen held on the Thames between University Stone in Putney and Mortlake since 1856.

April Fool's Day (1st): throughout the morning Britons go out of their way to hoodwink one another.

London Marathon, Greenwich Park. One of the world's biggest, with a route from Greenwich Park to Westminster.

Queen's Birthday (21st): the Queen's real birthday (as opposed to her official one in June) is celebrated with a gun salute in Hyde Park and at the Tower of London.

May

Chelsea Flower Show, Royal Hospital, SW3. Tel: 020-7834 4333: major horticultural show, featuring spectular displays, and social event in the fine grounds of the Chelsea Royal Hospital.

FA Cup Final, Wembley. Final of the nation's main football competition.

Oak Apple Day, Chelsea Royal Hospital: parade of the Chelsea Pensioners in memory of their founder, Charles II.

June

Beating Retreat, Horse Guards Parade, Whitehall. Annual ceremonial display of military bands.

Derby Day, Epsom Racecourse. Tel: 01372-470047: famous flat race for 3-year-old colts and fillies.

Royal Academy Summer Exhibition, Burlington House, Piccadilly. Tel: 020-7300 5760: large exhibition of work by professional and amateur artists running until August. All works for sale.

Trooping the Colour, Horse Guards Parade. Tel: 020-7414 2357: the Queen's official birthday celebrations, with a royal procession along the Mall to Horse Guards Parade for the ceremonial parade of regimental colours. Followed by the presence of the royal family on the balcony of Buckingham Palace.

Royal Ascot, Ascot Racecourse. Tel: 01344-622211: elegant and dressy race meeting attended by royalty.

Grosvenor House Antiques Fair, Grosvenor House Hotel, Park Lane. Tel: 020-7499 6363: a large and prestigious event.

Wimbledon Lawn Tennis Championships, All England Club. Tel: 020-8946 2244: world-famous fortnight of tennis played on grass courts.

Cinemas

Most cinemas in central London (mainly close to Leicester Square) are part of the big companies and show the new releases; independent cinemas tend to be on the fringes of the central area or in the suburbs. There is a giant screen Imax cinema at the Bullring at Waterloo, in front of the mainline station. Advance bookings. Tel: 020-7902 1234. Monday night is reduced ticket price night in many West End cinemas. It's often also cheaper to see a film before 6pm.

Repertory Cinema

These venues show regularly changing programmes of new and old English and foreign-language films:

National Film Theatre, South Bank, SE1 8XT. Tel: 020-7928 3232. Hosts the London Film Festival. Presents short seasons of films dedicated to themes such as international regions, actors and film directors. Two cinemas, bookshop and a good café. Daily membership 40p (£15.95 per year). For information, tel: 020-7633 0274. Tube: Waterloo.

Riverside Studios Cinema, Crisp Road, W6 9RL. Tel: 020-7237 1000. Cosy cinema showing mostly arthouse films and classics. First-runs are usually played at the weekend. Tube: Hammersmith.

ICA Cinema & Cinemathèque, Nash House, The Mall, SW1 5AH. Tel: 020-7930 3647. Shows a selection of international avant-garde movies. Access to the Institute of Contemporary Art requires a £2.50 weekend membership. Tube: Charing Cross.

Everyman, Hollybush Vale, NW3. Tel: 020-7431 1818. The oldest repertory cinema in the country. A drill hall, then a theatre, it opened as a cinema in 1933. Shows a variety of films which change each night. Tube: Hampstead.

July

Henley Royal Regatta, Henley-on-Thames, Oxfordshire. Tel: 01491-572153: international rowing regatta that's also an important social event for the well-heeled. Worth a day-trip if you like drinking Pimm's.

Henry Wood Promenade Concerts, Royal Albert Hall. Series of classical concerts known as The Proms.

Royal Tournament, Earl's Court. Tel: 020-7385 1200: military displays from the Royal Army, Navy and Air Force.

Swan Upping on the Thames: all the swans on the Thames belong to the Queen, the Vintners and the Dyers and for five days every year officials can be seen rowing up and down the river registering them.

Doggett's Coat and Badge Race, London Bridge: race for single scull boats between London Bridge and Chelsea that has been a tradition since 1715.

August

Notting Hill Carnival, Ladbroke Grove (bank holiday weekend): colourful and lively West Indian street carnival (Europe's largest) with exciting and imaginative costumes, live steel bands and reggae music.

London Riding Horse Parade, Rotten Row, Hyde Park: elegant competition for best turned-out horse and rider.

International Street Performers' Festival, Covent Garden Piazza: free street entertainment.

September

Chelsea Antiques Fair, Old Town Hall, King's Road, SW3: contact Tel: 01444-482514.

Horseman's Sunday, Church of St John and St Michael, W2: morning service dedicated to the horse with mounted vicar and congregation. Followed by procession through Hyde Park.

October

Judges' Service marks the beginning of the legal year in Britain with a procession of judges in full attire from Westminster Abbey to the Houses of Parliament.

Horse of the Year Show, Wembley Arena. Tel: 020-8902 0902: major international equestrian competition attracting the world's top horses and riders.

Costermongers' Pearly Harvest Festival (1st Sunday), Church of St Martin-in-the-Fields, Trafalgar Square. Pearly Kings and Queens (street traders) attend this service in their traditional attire, which is elaborately adorned with pearl buttons.

Trafalgar Day Parade commemorates Nelson's victory over the French and Spanish at Trafalgar on 21 October.

Motor Show, Earl's Court: major international car show held every two years.

November

London to Brighton Veteran Car Run (1st Sunday): hundreds of immacuately preserved veteran cars and their proud owners start out from Hyde Park and make their way sedately to Brighton.

Lord Mayor's Show: grand procession, including the Lord Mayor's gilded coach, from the Guildhall in the City to the Royal Courts of Justice, celebrating the annual election of the Mayor who rides in the coach.

Remembrance Sunday (nearest the 11th): to commemorate those lost at war. Main wreath laying service at the Cenotaph, Whitehall.

State Opening of Parliament, House of Lords, Westminster. Official re-opening of Parliament (following the summer recess) by the Queen, who travels down the Mall in a state coach.

Guy Fawkes Day (5 November): traditional firework celebration of the failure to blow up the Houses of Parliament by Guy Fawkes in 1605. Bonfires and organised firework displays all over London.

Christmas Lights: switched on in Oxford and Regent streets.

December

Olympia International Horse Show, Olympia: major international show jumping championships.

Christmas Carol Services, Trafalgar Square: carols are sung here in the evenings beneath the giant tree which is presented each year by Norway, a tradition dating from the reign of Queen Victoria. Carol services are also held in many churches all over London.

"January" sales: excellent bargains can be found at these sales which seem to begin earlier and earlier every year as retailers try to take maximum advantage of consumers' extravagant pre-Christmas spending.

New Year's Eve, Trafalgar Square: thousands of people congregate around the fountains to drink, hold hands and sing Auld Lang Syne at midnight.

Nightlife

Late Spots

If you're under 30 years old and believe the hype, London is one of the best places to party in the world. But not all nightlife in the capital is dance-till-dawn. Older swingers in town can enjoy dinner dances, drinking bars, casinos and smart nightclubs.

Despite its reputation, however, the grooviest city in the world still has some of the toughest licensing laws and most restaurants have wound down by 1am, leaving just a few determined cafés and shops to stagger on until the city awakes.

Nevertheless, there is something magical about being out all night in London, buying the day's newspaper before the day breaks, swapping tales over breakfast in a café, detouring home through one of the markets or watching the sun rise over the Thames.

To experience late-night London at its best, it is advisable to plan in advance, so read on to find out where you can eat, drink, listen to jazz, or just buy a newspaper whilst the rest of the city sleeps.

Dinner Dance

Concordia Notte
29 Craven Rd, W2.
Tel: 020-7723 3725.
Last orders midnight. Set within a tastefully luxurious cavern is this sophisticated restaurant which courts the rich and famous. The superb classic Italian cuisine is accompanied by an impressive wine list, charming service and gentle dance music with which to while away the night.

Elephant on the River
129 Grosvenor Road, SW1.
Tel: 020-7834 1621.
Last orders 12.30am. Flamboyant riverbank neighbour of the Villa Restaurant, serving so-so Italian food in elegant surroundings and with a dance floor on which to float against a backdrop of moonlit views over the Thames.

The London Hilton Roof Restaurant
22 Park Lane W1.
Tel: 020-7493 8000.
Last orders midnight. Twenty-eight floors above London, the Roof Restaurant provides a sensational evening of dining and dancing with its combination of spectacular views and excellent French cuisine. The perfect setting for a memorable, but expensive, night out.

Villa Restaurant
135 Grosvenor Rd, SW1.
Tel: 020-7828 7453.
Last orders 12.30am. An evening at this plush riverside restaurant is like being in a glamorous scene from a James Bond movie. You may rub shoulders with the rich and famous as you dance to the resident five-piece band or just enjoy the haute cuisine Italian food.

Some of the best and most romantic dine and dance places are at the luxury hotels.

Drinking Bars

Atlantic Bar & Grill
20 Glasshouse Street, W1
Tel: 020-7734 4888
Open until 3am, food served until 2.30am. Lavish and ornate with wonderfully high ceiling. Drinks prices are also lavish.

Cantaloupe
35 Charlotte Road, EC2.
Tel: 020-7613 4411.
Situated in trendy Hoxton, this bar stays open until midnight. Food can be eaten in a small restaurant area.

Freedom
60-66 Wardour Street, W1.
Tel: 020-7734 0071.
If you're looking for somewhere loud and fashionable, where the gay arty crowd of Soho hang out, then this is the place. Also contained in the building is a theatre and gallery, open till late.

Blues Bistro and Bar
42–43 Dean Street, W1
Tel: 020-7494 1966
Open until 1am, restaurant last orders midnight. Art deco style bar in front of the restaurant. Upmarket and expensive, DJs on Fri/Sat.

Bar Soho
23-35 Old Compton Street, W1
Tel: 020-7439 0439
Open until 3am. Loud and busy, this is not the place for quiet drink. Smart crowd. Entrance fee after 11.30pm.

What to Wear

All discos and nightclubs have a door policy. There's always someone at the door, ensuring only the right sort of people get in. At many places, it's just a matter of weeding out the jeans and trainers. At some, though, it means your face has to fit.

These terms categorise the establishments and give you an idea of what to expect:

Smart means civilised, well-dressed, appealing to an older audience.

Hip means you've got to be cool and look the part; dress codes are pronounced.

Trendy means it is just a good disco where everyone is welcome (unless, perhaps, they're wearing jeans).

Casual means you can get away with jeans.

One-nighters are places where every evening has its own music and crowd, and you should check what it is before setting out. *Time Out* magazine gives a listing.

Nightclubs

Café de Paris
3 Coventry Street, W1.
Tel: 020-7734 7700.
Renovated posh old dance hall attracts an older sophisticated crowd. Trendy/smart.

Electric Ballroom
184 Camden High Street, NW1.
Tel: 020-7485 9006.
This old dance hall is rather frayed at the edges, but has a huge main dance floor and is popular on a

Saturday night. Has a jazz room upstairs and cheap bar prices. Casual.

Equinox
Leicester Square, WC2.
Tel: 020-7437 1446.
The Equinox is big in size, big in lighting and big in suburbia. Indeed, it is one of the biggest discos in Europe, attracting a young trendy crowd.

The Fridge
Town Hall Parade, Brixton Hill, SW2.
Tel: 020-7326 5100.
The coolest and hippest venue south of the river. Spectacular one-nighters. Worth seeking out.

Gossips
69 Dean Street, W1
tel: 020-7434 4480
Soho basement club with a variety of one nighters catering for all musical tastes, from reggae to heavy metal. Trendy.

Heaven
The Arches, Craven Street, WC2.
Tel: 020-7930 2020.
Submerged beneath the Charing Cross development is one of the best dance clubs in town. Gay nights are Tuesday, Wednesday, Friday and Saturday. Very casual dress code.

Hippodrome
Charing Cross Road, WC2.
Tel: 020-7437 4311.
One of the largest dance floors in London to shuffle around on. Popular with out-of-towners and the not so hip but still good fun if you want a bop in the centre of town. Casual.

Jongleurs
Venues at Camden Lock and in Battersea.
Tel: 020-7564 2500.
Started as a stand-up comedy club operating only at weekends, Jongleurs has now widened its net to include live music, particularly its jazz club on Sunday afternoons.

Legends
29 Old Burlington Street, W1.
Tel: 020-7494 2271.
Glossy Mayfair club which attracts a smart and trendy crowd who like to dress up and try out crazy dance moves. Hosts a variety of one-nighters. Smart.

Casinos

Casinos have suffered a decline in England over the past few years. The 1968 Gaming Act succeeded in subduing gambling, preventing casinos from advertising or lists of venues being published. By law, you must be a member to enter a casino, and membership must be applied for at least 48 hours in advance. However, Central London has a variety of casinos for all pockets, so if you wish to gamble during your stay, your hotel should be able to advise.

The British have always had an ambivalent approach to gambling. While recent governments encouraged everyone to participate in the stock market and the National Lottery, casino gambling has remained hemmed in by restrictions. The 1968 Act by implication even excluded the publication of a list of venues in a book such as this as being a potential "stimulation" to gamble.

Nevertheless, 75 percent of the nations's gambling "drop" is spent in London, and mostly by visitors. They need to be dedicated gamblers, too: the Gaming Act precludes live shows or bands, and no alcoholic drink is allowed on the gaming premises. No wonder James Bond preferred to gamble abroad.

Limelight
136 Shaftesbury Avenue, W1.
Tel: 020-7434 0572.
A converted church as a venue provides most of the atmosphere. Not as hip as it used to be in the mid-80s but still rated. Hip/smart.

Home
1 Leicester Square, WC2
Tel: 020-7909 000
Dance super-club in Leicester Square. Very popular, as the queue to get in will testify. Hip.

Ormonds
6 Ormands Yard, SW1.
Tel: 020-7930 2842.
Relaxed club which is aimed at an older clubbing crowd. Very chic. Smart.

Salsa
96 Charing Cross Road, WC2.
Tel: 020-7379 3277.
A good Latin venue in the heart of the West End. Lots of fun, very busy and a good place to practise your moves. Casual.

Samantha's
3 New Burlington Street, W1.
Tel: 020-7734 6249. Mainstream disco that has been around for a long time. Attracts well dressed and the more mature clubbers. Smart.

Stringfellows
16 Upper St Martin's Lane, WC2.
Tel: 020-7240 5534.
Reputed as a popular location for paparazzi photographers and the first club in London to feature tabledancing. This club is strong on glamour, so dress accordingly.

Subterania
36 Acklam Road, Ladbroke Grove W10.
Tel: 020-8960 4590.
West London's main club with its well designed modern interior hewn out of the concrete structure of the Westway. This refreshing addition to the club scene regularly features live bands. Trendy/Hip.

Wag Club
35 Wardour Street, W1.
Tel: 020-7437 5534.
This Soho club attracts a mixed crowd. Heavy duty dance music and fresh fruit bar to keep you going. Hip.

Cabaret

Madame Jo Jo's
8 Brewer St, W1.
Tel: 020-7734 2473.
Closes 3am. Lacking in the sleaze and daring associated with Soho's past, Madame Jo Jo's still offers one of the best late-night outings in London with captivating cabaret shows from Ruby Venezuela and her male leggy lovelies in their amazing costumes.

Comedy Store
1a, Oxenden Street, SW1.
Tel: 020-7739 5706

A night at this well established venue for stand-up comedians will remind you that comedy need not always be accompanied by canned laughter. On a good night, the comedians in the audience are as famous as those on stage. Avoid sitting in the front row unless you want to become part of the show.

Round the Clock

Takeaways

Bagel Bake
159 Brick Lane, E1.
Tel: 020-7729 0616.
Open 24 hours.
Join Londoners who ritually pile across to Brick Lane after a night out to tank up with freshly baked bagels filled with smoked salmon and cream cheese washed down with cups of hot coffee.

Burger King
17 Leicester Square, WC2.
Tel: 020-7930 0158.
Monday–Saturday to 4.30am, Sunday to 2am.
This branch of the fast food chain stays open through the night serving burgers to hungry clubbers.

Dionysius
325 Oxford Street, W1.
Tel: 020-7434 4204.
Sunday–Thursday to 3am, Friday/Saturday to 5am.
Popular fast food joint serving kebabs, humous, taramasalata and good old fish and chips to eat in or takeaway.

Ridley Road Hot Bagel Bakery
13 Ridley Road, E8.
Tel: 020-7923 0666.
Open 24 hours.
Grab a black cab and take a detour to Ridley Road on your way home for the fashionable late-night snack. This famous bagel hot spot in Dalston is as much of an institution as its Brick Lane rival.

Coffee/Breakfast

Bar Italia
22 Frith Street, W1.
Tel: 020-7437 4520.
Open 24 hours.
A piece of real Italy located in the centre of Soho. No matter what the hour this family-run bar is always buzzing. At weekends local trendies and genuine Italians alike queue for one of the best cappuccinos in town and a large screen at the end of the bar plays MTV when it's not showing live Italian football. On summer evenings it's fun to sit outside in true Italian style and watch a bewildering variety of people promenade through Soho.

Chelsea Bridge Snack Kiosk
Open all night.
Although some say that "it has been around so long that Dick Turpin used to stop there", a kiosk is reputed to have been doing hot food and teas at this location since the 1920s. This is a long-standing landmark on the late-night landscape of London and is ever popular with early-morning truck drivers, cabbies and their passengers.

Shopping

Themed Centres

Covent Garden did it first: many have tried to follow. "Themed" shopping malls have been a way of preserving or enhancing historic environments, often incorporating an added attraction such as a museum or cinema.

Chelsea Harbour
Lots Road, SW10.
Exclusive post-modernist development on the river with small sophisticated shops and service industries.

Hay's Galleria
Tooley Street, SE1.
Not many shops, but a pleasant riverside pub and restaurants.

Trocadero/London Pavilion
Piccadilly Circus, W1.
Two shopping malls next to each other, the principal interest of both being their attractions and eateries. The Pavilion is home to Rock Circus, Rock Island Diner and the Rainforest cafe. The Trocadero has Segaworld (with thousands of noisy electronic games – great for teenagers, hell for their parents), Planet Hollywood and the Pepsi IMAX Theatre. Both contain shops of course, but with the exception of Food Street and the themed Eastern supermarket they are at best utilitarian.

Whiteley's
Queensway, Bayswater, W2.
This shopping complex in a former department store contains leading chain stores, cafes and restaurants, whilst still retaining the grandeur of the original structure. It has the added attraction of a cinema complex with 8 screens.

Department Stores

Barkers of Kensington
63 Kensington High Street, W8.
Tel: 020-7937 5432.
A grand old store but newly redesigned and substantially upgraded. Now stocks an impressive range of designer clothing, fashion accessories and household goods.

Conran Shop
Michelin Building, 81 Fulham Road, SW3.
Tel: 020-7589 7401.
Sir Terence Conran's unique and stylish shop sells designer furniture and household accessories, having the tendency to resemble a design museum. Set within the beautiful art nouveau tiled Michelin Building, it is worth a visit just to browse.

Debenhams
334 Oxford Street, W1.
Tel: 020-7580 3000.
Re-vamped with a bright fresh image, this store seems to have lost much of its personality, tending to resemble a shopping mall. Sells the variety of goods you would expect from a large department store. Everything from perfumes to bed linen.

Fortnum and Mason
181 Piccadilly, W1A 1ER.
Tel: 020-7734 8040.
Fortnum and Mason opened their store in the 18th century with the grocery needs of the Palace in mind. They began importing exotic and unusual foodstuffs which have long been the basis of the shop's success. The Queen's grocer also stocks fine clothes and household goods. At Christmas the window displays are a joy to behold and many hanker after one of their famous hampers. Pop in for a browse and to see very proper English folk buying their expensive groceries. A fashionable place to have tea.

Harrods
Knightsbridge, SW1.
Tel: 020-7730 1234.
One of the world's largest and most famous department stores, now owned by Egypt's Al-Fayed family. Since the 19th century Harrods has maintained a reputation for quality and service, priding itself on stocking the best of everything. No one should miss the fabulous displays in the Edwardian tiled food halls. Harrods sales are major events with those hungry for bargains and prepared to queue a long time to be first through the door.

Liberty
Regent Street, W1.
Tel: 020-7734 1234.
The goods on sale in this distinctive and characterful store are still largely based along the same lines as the Oriental, Art Nouveau and Arts and Crafts furniture, wallpaper, silver, jewellery and fabrics Liberty began selling in the late 19th century. There are particularly fine furniture and fashion accessory departments and an exotic bazaar in the basement.

Marks & Spencer
458 Oxford Street, W1.
Tel: 020-7935 7954.
M & S stays clear of extremes of fashion, maintaining a good strong policy of quality merchandise that is safe, but well designed, and value for money. The whole nation seems to favour M&S underwear whilst the food department, with its gourmet ready-cooked meals, goes from strength to strength. This Marble Arch branch is used to test out new lines.

Peter Jones
Sloane Square, SW1.
Tel: 020-7730 3434.
This King's Road branch of John Lewis promises customers that its prices cannot be beaten and assures to refund the difference if you can prove otherwise. Stocks a variety of quality goods, most notably household furnishings and appliances.

Selfridges
Oxford Street, W1.
Tel: 020-7629 1234.
Enormous store dating back to 1909 that is to be rivalled only by Harrods in its size and variety of quality goods.

Shopping Zones

High-street shopping is dominated by the big stores (Regent Street is much classier than Oxford Street). Knightsbridge, the King's Road, and Kensington High Street, despite their reputations, are now equally overrun by national chains. **Designer shops** and mini-stores are found down the side roads of Chelsea, Kensington and the West End. Exclusive as ever are South Molton Street, Bond Street and Sloane Street. In St Christopher's Place, W1, an alleyway just off Oxford Street, a designer village has sprung up. SW1, centring around Jermyn Street, is full of solid, traditional shopping with the emphasis on aristocratic menswear and old world grocers. SW3, Chelsea, is a real melting pot of styles, where the chic and trendy mingle on the pavements on Saturday mornings.

Covent Garden, although touristy, is a mecca for clothes shopping. Neal Street and the Thomas Neal Centre cater for more avant-garde fashions. Long Acre is more high-street fashion and Floral Street is the place for designer gear. The Market itself and the area in general is good for books, arts and crafts and one-off's like Neal's Yard where organic food and herbs have taken a hold. The shops are open late seven days a week. **Bloomsbury** is still a rather sombre, bookish area, but has surprises if you delve a little deeper into its maze of backstreets around the British Museum and university. Soho, known for its European grocers, is a new centre for designer clothing. **London's villages** – Camden, Islington, and Portobello – are outstanding for antiques, bric-a-brac, period clothing, jewellery and crafts.

Haute Couture

In the search for Haute Couture, the best place to start is Knightsbridge, where you will be spoilt by the choice of designer names. In pretty Beauchamp Place several small chic boutiques are to be found, including Caroline Charles and Bruce Oldfield.

Around the corner in the Brompton Road is Emporio Armani with a more casual range than the other branch nearby in Sloane Street. Indeed, Sloane Street can be rivalled only by Bond Street for its endless list of world-class designers. Here you will find D.K.N.Y, Kenzo, Jaeger, Joseph, Max Mara and Valentino. If you cannot locate your favourite designer here you will probably discover them within Harvey Nichols or Harrods, close by.

For design-conscious children, Sloane Street can offer Oilily or La Cicogna.

Bond Street, however, has an older tradition of offering the best that money can buy. If any of London's streets are paved with gold surely it must be this one. Here, among the big international names such as Valentino, Chanel and Christian Lacroix, are London's major jewellery houses, auction houses and elite fine art galleries, while parallel Cork Street is the place to pick up a Picasso.

Close by in South Molton Street the tension on your wallet can be released very slightly. This street, with many upmarket fashion houses, caters to a younger fashion-conscious customer. Browns houses collections by Gaultier, Romeo Gigli, Alaia, Conran and Ozbek. Close by in Brook Street is G-Gigli, Roland Klein, Antony Price and Gianfranco Ferre.

Laura Ashley
256 Regent Street, W1.
Distinctive style of feminine clothes in pretty floral fabrics. Also home furnishings and fabrics.

Liberty
210-220 Regent Street, W1.
Well-known for scarves, ties and garments in art nouveau and floral prints. Excellent for more unusual fashion accessories and gifts.

Marks & Spencer
458 Oxford Street, W1.
The original English high street store, with clothes for all the family. Has extended its reputation beyond quality traditional garments to fashionable items with flair. Excellent for basics, particularly jumpers and underwear. Value for money.

Selfridges
400 Oxford Street, W1.
Wide selection of men's, women's and children's wear to rival Harrods. Everything from serious formal wear to the young and trendy "Miss Selfridge".

Clothing

London's finest

Aquascutum
100 Regent Street, W1.
Conservative classics and country separates aimed at the executive man and woman. Japanese-owned.

Austin Reed
103–113 Regent Street, W1.
Gentlemen's suits, casual menswear, women's separates. The place for horse-riding clothes and gear.

Burberry's
21–23 New Bond Street, W1
For classic mackintoshes, trenchcoats and accessories in the famous plaid.

Dickens & Jones
224–244 Regent Street, W1.
Smart store for those with a more mature and conservative taste. Many top designers are represented, though there's a better choice for women than for men. Fashion consultant service. Excellent accessories.

Fenwick
63 New Bond Street.
Classy store with an extensive range of clothes and accessories for all tastes and ages, ranging from the casual and trendy to smart and chic designer wear.

Fortnum and Mason
181 Piccadilly, W1.
Exclusive store with quality clothes; particularly good for formal suits and evening wear. Polite service from formally dressed assistants. Good range of accessories.

Harrods
Knightsbridge, SW1.
Extensive selection of quality clothes for all ages and tastes in the famous Knightsbridge store. Formal menswear on the ground floor, vast designer collection for women on the first and trendy women's fashion on the fourth.

Harvey Nichols
Brompton Road, next to Harrods.
London's leading fashion department store, with an excellent range of menswear in the basement. Women and children are also well catered for, with many top designers' goods under one roof.

Designer gear

Agent Provocateur
16 Pont Street, SW1.
Innovative, fashionable lingerie.

A la Mode
36 Hans Crescent, SW1.
Stocks a wide range of designer clothing including some very well-known labels.

Alexander McQueen
47 Conduit Street, W1
The bad boy of British fashion now has a London store. At first sight it looks more like an art gallery than a clothes shop, with glass display cabinets holding installations.

Ted Baker Ltd
1–4 Langley Court, WC2.
Trendy clothing for men at affordable prices at branches across London.

Browns
23 South Molton Street, W1.
With branches across town stocking a wide range of designer clothing for men and women, this one of the best places to shop for those essential items.

Dolce & Gabbana
6–8 Old Bond Street, W1.

Outrageous and beautiful clothing from the famous duo.

The Duffer of St George
29 Shorts Gardens, WC2.
The penultimate in casual street cred for men.

Jaeger
204 Regent Street, W1.
Tailored classic English clothes for men and women with formal, business and casual ranges.

Jones
13 Floral Street, WC2.
Hip men's outlet for avant-garde designers such as Nick Coleman and Gaultier. Also Jones's own label.

Koh Samui
65 Monmouth Street, WC2.
A cornucopia of the hottest British and European designers. Chic clothes in a wide variety of styles.

Ghost
36 Ledbury Road, W11
This Notting Hill designers sells pretty, feminine, and highly fashionable women's clothes.

Lulu Guinness
3 Ellis Street, SW1.
Simply the hottest bags around. Frothy, fun collectors items.

Manolo Blahnik
49-51 Old Church Street, SW3.
Whether you want towering stilettos or cool sandals, these are the ultimate in sharp shoes. Worn by the likes of Bianca Jagger and Naomi Campbell, they'll do wonders for your feet if not for your credit card bill.

Mulberry
41 New Bond Street
Modern clothes on a classic British Imperialist theme in fabrics such as Gaberdine, wool, linen and cotton. Accessories for the modern gentleman include Mulberry's famous leather luggage and briefcases.

Nicole Farhi
158 New Bond Street, W1.
Smart, yet comfortably casual, classic separates in soft fabrics.

Patrick Cox
129 Sloane Street, SW1.
Designer shoes with massive street cred. Traditional and modern designs worn by TV presenters and pop stars.

Paul Smith
41-44 Floral Street, W1.
Designer famous for his bright shirts and ties. Clothes combine classic tailoring with a modern twist. Men's and women's clothing.

Prada
15 Old Bond Street, W1.
Cutting-edge designer clothing which is currently greatly sought-after. They also do a range of designer sport/leisure wear. Miu Miu in New Bond Street is their younger sister label.

Sam De Teran
151 Fulham Road, SW3.
Fashionable sportswear for all seasons. Flattering swimwear, cool beachwear, ski-wear and knitwear.

Tommy Hilfiger
51 New Bond Street, W1.
Ubiquitous American leisurewear designer. Colourful, loud and sporty gear – not high fashion but promise your teenage kids a visit and they'll keep their room tidy for weeks!

Urban Outfitters
36-38 Kensington High Street, W8
A boutique featuring all the coolest young designers. Not only clothes, but all a stylish young person's lifestyle needs from jewellery to curtains.

Vivienne Westwood
6 Davies Street, W1.
This is formal compared to Westwood's wacky World's End boutique on the King's Road, and is the outlet for her more tailored collections. Her menswear collection is available at 44 Conduit Street, W1.

Whistles
20 The Market, Covent Garden.
One of the best places to shop for good in-house label clothing and a range of young designer-wear.

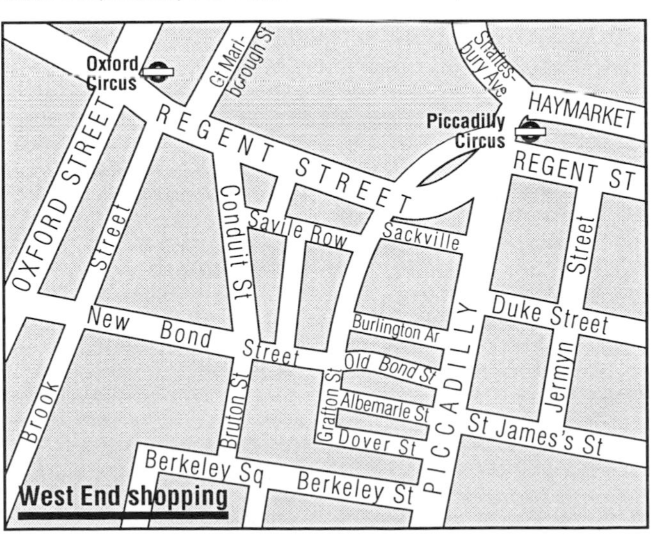

For Men

London is well served for men's clothes shops. Covent Garden is full of them: quality fashion shops such as Paul Smith in Floral Street and designers such as Michiko Koshino. What really distinguishes London's menswear from any other is its traditional gentlemen's outfitters. Savile Row is the best known street for tailor-made suits. Gieves & Hawkes at No. 1 is synonymous with hand-made and off-the-peg classic English tailoring and has a long and noble history. As does the prestigious Anderson and Sheppard at the other end of the street, who have discreetly tailored suits for Marlene Dietrich and Prince Charles, amongst other notables. Tommy Nutter, across the road, was the young upstart of the Row. Popular with pop and film stars, Nutter had a reputation for flamboyant and eccentric tailored suits. Huntsman & Sons, like many tailors in the Row, has been established since the 18th century.

The St James's area, which is littered with gentlemen's clubs, is full of shops selling expensive well-made clothes, toiletries and shoes. In St James's Street is John Lobb, considered to make some of the finest hand-made shoes in the world, and the fine hat maker James Lock. In Jermyn Street are Turnbull & Asser, famed for their made-to-measure and striped shirts. Bates hat shop and Geo Trumpers traditional toiletry shop are here too. Dover Street and Burlington Gardens are also worth a visit.

If you want the look without paying the price, second-hand and period clothes shops are one option. Try Hills Dresswear at 15 Henrietta Street, WC2, which is particularly good for fine dinner suits from the 1930–50 era. For new men's classics, at affordable prices, try Blazer at 117 Long Acre. For the fashion-conscious man, Covent Garden also has Emporio Armani and Jigsaw for Men.

Street Smart

For street fashion with style, King's Road is still popular, but Covent Garden is now at the forefront. Young chain-store fashion which echoes the new cuts and colours of the season are found on Oxford Street, in shops like Hennes, Top Shop and Miss Selfridge. Kensington High Street and Kensington Church Street (W8) are also worth a visit. Urban Outfitters, in Kensington High Street, has adventurous, upmarket collections from young designers.

Unusual Sizes

The Base, 55 Monmouth Street, WC2. Exclusive quality clothes for larger women.
High & Mighty, 81 Knightsbridge, SW1. Classic English clothes for the larger than average gentleman. Also sport and leisurewear.
Long Tall Sally, 21–25 Chiltern Street, W1. Elegant clothes for tall women. Reasonable prices. (Crispins on the opposite side of the road caters for those with big feet).
The Small and Tall Shoe Shop, 71 York Street, W1. For those customers with very short or long, narrow or wide feet.

Period Clothes

London's markets, and the area surrounding them, are often excellent for second-hand and period clothing, particularly Portobello, Camden, Islington and Covent Garden.

American Classics
400 King's Road, SW10.
Not original vintage clothing, but still the place for American retro style.

Cobwebs
60 Islington Park Street, N1.
Small, but well-maintained stock of fine men's and women's period clothing.

Cornucopia
12 Upper Tachbrook Street, SW1.
Overwhelming range of clothes and accessories with an emphasis on the eccentric.

Hacketts
65 New King's Road, SW6.
Old and new gentlemen's classics including dinner suits, plus-fours, brogues and braces.

Laurence Corner
62 Hampstead Road, NW1.
Weird and wonderful army surplus and theatrical costumes.

Sam Walker
41 Neal Street, WC2.
Quality classic clothes and accessories from the 1940s and '50s.

Steinberg & Tolkien
193 King's Road, SW3.
Tel: 0171-376 3660.
Top quality vintage clothing mostly with designer labels. Also has a good range of vintage costume jewellery.

The Country Look

Piccadilly and St James's are again the places to go for upmarket country clothes. In the West End, the department stores are usually well-stocked with country casuals and waterproofs; some of the sports/mountaineering suppliers around Covent Garden also have surprisingly high-quality outerwear. For the Great British Sweater, look no further than Marks & Spencer. Their lambswool is the cheapest in London, with quite a wide choice of colours and styles. Scottish Merchant at 16 New Row, WC2 has fascinating Scottish-made sweaters of supreme quality (and great price). The Scotch House in Knightsbridge is also very popular. The Irish Shop at 14 King Street WC2 also has good knitwear, as well as the traditional Irish linen.

Antiques

London has an enormous and widespread selection of antique shops and markets. Over 400 of the most elite dealers are in Mayfair, centering around Old Bond Street, with valuable collections of silver, fine art, jewellery, porcelain, carpets, furniture and antiquities.

Chelsea and Knightsbridge have a large share of fine dealers. The Fulham and the King's roads are excellent for period furniture and decorative items.

Westbourne Grove in W11 has many interesting dealers. The whole area comes to life on Friday and Saturday mornings when hordes of tourists descend on the antique arcades and stalls of the Portobello Road market.

Kensington Church Street in W8 is filled with a variety of expensive antique shops dealing in everything from fine art to porcelain.

Bermondsey's early-morning Friday antique market at Bermondsey Square, SE1, is a major trading event. The best items change hands by 10am.

Islington, N1, is also a popular but more expensive area with more then 100 dealers. Particularly interesting is the Mall Antiques Arcade at 359 Upper Street and the adjacent Camden Passage.

Further advice and information on buying antiques in Britain as a whole can be obtained from:
London and Provincial Antique Dealers' Association,
535 King's Road, SW10
Tel: 020-7823 3511.
They run an up-to-date computer information service on auctions, specific items and the antiques situation throughout the country and they also publish their own comprehensive booklet called *Buying Antiques in Britain*.

Auction Houses

London's leading auction houses for antiques and fine art are Christie's, 8 King Street, SW1 and Sotheby's, 34 New Bond Street, W1. There are also the smaller fine art auction houses of Phillip's at 101 New Bond Street, W1 and Bonham's in Montpelier Street, SW7. Bloomsbury Book Auctions, 3 Hardwick Street, EC1, is the only specialist book auction house in the country, with maps and manuscripts also going under the hammer.

Art

Cork Street is famous for its art galleries. Here in the Waddington, Redfern, Nicola Jacobs and Odette Gilbert galleries, you can view or purchase works by major modern masters. Nearby in Dering Street are three Anthony d'Offay galleries which feature the work of British Post-Impressionists and leading international modern artists. The work of established British artists can be found in the Bernard Jacobson Gallery in Clifford Street, W1, and the Marlborough Gallery in Albemarle Street, W1, which had Francis Bacon among its artists.

For those interested in old masters there are various galleries dotted around Mayfair.

For young British talent that won't set you back more than £2,000 visit the Albemarle Gallery in Albemarle Street, or the Austin/Desmond Gallery at 15a Bloomsbury Square. The Scottish Gallery in Cork Street promotes young Scottish talent.

Flowers East at 199–205 Richmond Road, E8, is worth the trek to see young British talent displayed in a vast white space.

A community of fresh and exciting galleries has sprung up around Portobello Road, including the Anderson O'Day, Creaser, Todd, and Vanessa Devereux galleries.

Photography

In Kensington Park Road is the Special Photographers Company which displays innovative fine art photography. The Photographer's Gallery in Great Newport Street, WC2 has exhibitions of major international photography and a fine collection of prints for sale in the Print Room. Hamiltons in Carlos Place, W1 is another major photography gallery. If you are interested in cartoons, check out the Cartoon Gallery at 83 Lamb's Conduit Street, WC1.

Books

Charing Cross Road is traditionally the home of bookselling. Cecil Court is its old fashioned heart, selling second-hand and rare books of all kinds. Foyles on Charing Cross Road is still among the largest, but it's eccentric style means it is not the place to go if you are in a hurry.

Waterstone's and Books Etc are two well-stocked chains with good travel sections. Borders (Oxford St) and Waterstone's (Piccadilly) are both superstores with the usual coffe bars, sofas and events. The W.H. Smith chain has a smaller, more general selection.

Bookshops in W1 project an up-market image: Hatchard's on Piccadilly, London's oldest book-shop, features a huge variety of biographies and fiction. Of the second-hand and rare booksellers in W1, Quaritch in Lower John Street is the best known.

Specialist bookshops abound. Zwemmer's on Charing Cross Road is known for fine art and photography. Bertram Rota at Langley Court WC2 is good for modern first editions. Edward Stanford on Long Acre is the best map and travel bookshop. Daunt Books, at 83 Marylebone High Street, has a great mix of travel-oriented books and guidebooks. Biografia at 49 Covent Garden market has the largest selection of biographies and memoirs. French's, the theatre bookshop, is at Fitzroy Street, W1. Grant & Cutler on Great Marlborough Street, W1 is the place to go for foreign language books. Close to Portobello market is The Travel Bookshop at 13 Blenheim Crescent, W11, made famous by Hugh Grant in the 1999 film *Notting Hill*.

VAT and the Export Scheme

England has 17.5 percent VAT (Value Added Tax) on most goods, including clothes. Anything you buy in a department store is likely to have had VAT built into the ticket price. Most big stores (and many smaller shops selling goods like Scottish woollens or English china) operate a VAT Refund Scheme or Export Scheme. Ask the salesperson. You can get your VAT back by filling in a form which is stamped by customs. Shops may require a minimum purchase (often £50) before the customer can participate in the scheme.

China and Glass

All of the big department stores have excellent china and glass departments, with a full range of styles and prices.

For more upmarket English goods, try Thomas Goode at 19 South Audley Street, W1. Wedgwood is at 266–270 Regent Street; not everything here is dazzlingly expensive. Their other shop, Waterford Wedgwood, is at 173 Piccadilly. Bargain prices are at the

Reject China Shop at 183 Brompton Road, for discount china and kitchenware with a few imperfections.

Food

The food halls at Harrods are justly famous, but don't neglect Fortnum's or Selfridges. SW1 and Soho are the places for old-fashioned grocers: Justin de Blank at 42 Elizabeth Street, and Paxton & Whitfield on Jermyn Street, the best cheese shop in London. Soho is the place for European delicatessens and Chinese grocers. Gerrard Street has authentic Chinese supermarkets. Neal's Yard in Covent Garden specialises in organic vegetables and wholefood.

Supermarkets

Several supermarkets are in the centre of town. Waitrose at 196 King's Road is the best. Hollywood, 75 Charing Cross Road, is more expensive than most but is open 24 hours a day. There's Safeway at 23 Brunswick Square, WC1, and Tesco at 18–24 Warwick Way, SW1. Tesco Metro in Bedford Road, Covent Garden, is open until 10pm. Sainsburys on Cromwell Road, SW7 is where Kensingtonians (or their nannies) go for their asparagus tips. It is one of the largest supermarkets, but customers are requested not to use roller skates or blades.

Jewellery

For innovative modern jewellery, head for Fulham Road and check out Theo Fennell at No. 169. For period or Art Deco jewellery try Cobra & Bellamy at 149 Sloane Street while at the other end is Boodle & Dunthorne for classic and modern designs at 1 Sloane Street. The finest costume jewellery can be found at Butler & Wilson, 20 South Molton Street or Agatha, 4 South Molton Street. At 25A Old Compton Street you'll find Janet Fitch, a range of innovative young designers under one roof.

If you want to spend serious money on serious rocks or simply gawp at the gems, then head for Bond Street where you'll find the likes of Asprey & Garrard, Cartier, Bulgari and Graff.

The other main centre is Hatton Garden EC1, a street of nothing but jewellery retailers and wholesalers. A lively area and home to the London Diamond Bourse.

Markets (Covered)

Alfies, 13–25 Church Street, NW8. London's largest covered antiques market with over 250 dealers providing an enormous selection of antiques and collectable items. Meanwhile, outside in Church Street, are several fine shops with a strong decorative arts bias.

Antiquarius
135–141 King's Road, SW3.
A whole range of antiques, decorative arts and period clothing. Can be expensive.

Chelsea Antique Market
245–253 King's Road, SW3.
Smaller and less expensive than the others with a good range of antiquarian books and men's period clothing.

Chenil Galleries
181–183 King's Road, SW3.
Classy antiques market with fine art, furniture and objets d'art.

The Furniture Cave
533 King's Road, SW10.
Has several floors of dealers selling fine period furniture and garden ornaments.

The Galleries
157 Tower Bridge Road, SE1.
Enormous warehouse with three floors predominantly filled with furniture, and interesting pieces of architectural salvage.

Gray's Antique Market
58 Davies Street, W1.
Has a good reputation for fair dealing. Over 200 stalls dealing in a variety of antiques from art deco furniture to Victorian toys.

London Silver Vaults
Chancery House, 53 Chancery Lane, WC2.
High-security vaults where stall holders trade in valuable gold and silverware.

Markets (Traditional)

Most open early in the morning and close at around 2pm.

Berwick Street Market
Berwick Street, W1.
Daily market that is famous for its fruit and veg at surprisingly good prices given its central location. Also sells clothes and fabrics. Monday to Saturday.

Borough Market
Borough High Street, SE1
Located on the same site since 1756, Borough Market is primarily a wholesale fruit and veg market which gets going around 2am and closes mid-morning. A twice-weekly retail market here sells an unusual range of organic and high-quality fish, meat, cheese, fruit and

Gifts from London

British Museum Shop British Museum, WC1. A variety of tasteful gifts, some very expensive, like the superb Egyptian cats.

The National Gallery and National Portrait Gallery at Trafalgar Square are good for posters, calendars and other arty gifts.

Alfred Dunhill 48 Jermyn Street, SW1. Famous for traditional accessories for gentlemen.

Asprey 165 New Bond Street, W1. If money is no object, here are the most decadent gifts in town – e.g. a leather Scrabble board.

Inderwicks 45 Carnaby Street, W1. Hand-made pipes.

Mansfield 30-35 Drury Lane, WC2. Antique personal accessories like pens and luggage.

Naturally British 13 New Row, WC2. A wide selection of British goods in natural materials, including lovely sweaters and inexpensive jewellery.

London Brass Rubbing Centre St James's Church, Piccadilly W1. In addition to brass rubbings, have your family coat-of-arms researched and painted.

vegetables, as well as tasty hot snacks. Friday noon–6pm and Saturday 9am–4pm.

Brick Lane Market
Brick Lane, E1.
Bustling East End market with a strong ethnic influence, selling cheap clothes, fruit, veg and bric-a-brac. There are also bicycles, electrical and other goods of dubious origin. Sunday.

Camden Lock Market
Camden Town, NW1.
This market centres around an attractive canal lock (within walking distance of London Zoo and Regent's Park) and is always packed, especially at weekends when there are lots of second-hand clothes, hand made jewellery and bric-a-brac (Saturday and Sunday). Antiques market on Thursday.

Camden Passage
Islington Green, N1.
Close to Islington's cluster of quaint antique shops. This is a pretty open-air market that is popular with tourists. Wednesday and Saturday.

Columbia Road Flower Market
Columbia Road, E2.
Even if you have no intention of buying, it is worth a visit on a Sunday morning just to take in the delightful colours, smells and East End bustle of this glorious flower market. Daily, but you have to get up early!

Covent Garden Market
The Piazza, WC2.
Attractive market with antiques on Monday and crafts from Tuesday to Saturday. But beware: although there are some beautifully hand-crafted items, bargains are thin on the ground.

Greenwich Market
Market Square, SE10.
Four good weekend markets close together where you will find second-hand books, clothes and bric-a-brac. Includes a crafts section with hand-made wares such as baskets, toys, jewellery, jumpers. Saturday and Sunday.

Leadenhall Market
Whittington Ave, EC3.
Quality meat, poultry and fish in a beautiful Victorian covered market. Weekdays.

Leather Lane Market
Leather Lane, EC1.
Popular with Londoners, this market sells cheap household goods and clothes. Weekdays.

New Caledonian Market
Tower Bridge Road, Bermondsey, SE1.
Fascinating antiques market where many traders themselves arrive as early as 4am to buy their stock. Friday.

Petticoat Lane
Middlesex Street, E1.
Sunday market famous for clothes including designer fashion. Also household goods and food. Sunday only.

Portobello Market
Portobello Road, W11.
A walk down cheery Portobello Road starts at the top with the antique shops, takes you through the colourful vegetable market, on to the second-hand clothes and bric-a-brac and ends with a fascinating array of junk and treasures spread over the pavements of Golborne Road. Saturday.

Spitalfields Market
Commercial Street, E1.
Stalls in this elegant old market building specialise in organic meat and vegetables, as well as arts and crafts. Under the same management as Camden Lock. Mainly weekends.

Perfume

Floris
89 Jermyn Street, W1.
Expensive English flower perfumes.

Penhaligons
41 Wellington Street, WC2.
Old-fashioned and beautifully packaged traditional English toiletries.

Toys

Covent Garden Market
The market is good for unusual (if expensive) toys:
Cabaret Mechanical Theatre
33 the Market (£1 admission); **The Dolls House,** 29 the Market; **Bejamin Pollock's Toyshop**, 44 the Market.

Early Learning Centre
36 King's Road, SW3 and at branches throughout London.

Hamleys
188–196 Regent Street, W1.
Six floors of dolls and games and other fabulous toys.

Sport

Spectator

Boat Race One of London's most famous sporting events is the University Boat Race, during which rowers from Oxford and Cambridge universities race down the Thames from Putney to Mortlake.

Cricket is played in summer only, at the Oval, Kennington, SE11, tel Surrey County Cricket Club: 020-7582 6660, or at the Lord's Cricket Ground, St John's Wood, NW8, tel: 020 7289 1611. You should buy tickets well in advance for Test Matches but there's generally less competition for seats for one-day internationals.

The Dogs (greyhound racing) Going "down the dogs" is a popular night out, in the East End of London. At most tracks you can choose between standing by the track or watching from a table in the restaurant. Most tracks hold two meetings a week; the days vary so call ahead to check. Tracks: Catford, Hackney Wick, Romford, Walthamstow, Watford, Wembley, Wimbledon. The best is Walthamstow Race Track, Chingford Road, E4. Tel: 020-8498 3300.

Football (Soccer) The football season runs from August to May, with matches usually held on Saturday afternoons. The top football clubs in London are: Arsenal (Avenell Road, Highbury, N5, tel: 020-7704 4242), Chelsea (Stamford Bridge, Fulham Road, SW6, tel: 020-7385 5545) and Tottenham Hotspur (White Hart Lane, 748 High Road, N17, tel: 020-8365 5000).

Horse Racing The flat-racing season is March to November, while steeplechasing takes place virtually all year round. The nearest racetracks to London are: Ascot, tel: 01344-878555; United Race Courses (Kempton Park, Epsom and Sandown Park) tel: 01372-463072 and Windsor, tel: 01753-865234.

Rugby is played from September to April/May. Top Rugby Union games are played at Twickenham Rugby Football Ground (Whitton Road, Twickenham, Middlesex, tel: 020-8744 3111). The Rugby League holds its cup final matches at Wembley Stadium.

Tennis Wimbledon, on the district line of the Underground (Southfields), is the venue for the famous two-week tennis championship, which starts in the last week in June. Seats for the show courts – Centre Court and Courts 1 and 2 should be reserved six months in advance. However, you can queue on the day for outside court tickets, and you may be able to buy cheap return tickets in the afternoon. For information contact the All England Tennis Club, Church Road, Wimbledon, SW19 (tel: 020-8946 2244).

Participant

Horse Riding is available in Hyde Park. Hyde Park general enquiries tel: 020-7298 2100.

Tennis courts There are tennis courts all over London, many in public parks. Among the more central public courts are those at Regent's Park, Holland Park, Paddington Recreation Ground, Parliament Hill and Battersea Park.

Further Reading

Good Companions

The Concise Pepys by Samuel Pepys, Wordsworth. Read a first-hand account of the Great Fire of London and find out about daily life in 17th-century England
London Villages by John Wittich, Shire Publications. A walker's notes on his travels through village London. John Wittich has also written several other walker's guides to London, including **Walks in Haunted London**, and **Discovering London Curiosities.**
A Literary Companion: London by Peter Vansittart, John Murray. A journey around the capital with the literary luminaries.
The London Encyclopaedia by Ben Weinreb and Christopher Hibbert, Papermac/Dictionary of London. Detailed and interesting, but more of a reference book than a good read.
Secret London by Andrew Duncan, New Holland Publishers. Uncovers London's hidden landscape from abandoned tube stations to the gentlemen's club.
Dr Johnson's London by Liza Picard, Weindenfeld & Nicholson. Brings 18th-century London to life.
London: The Biography by Peter Ackroyd, Chatto & Windus. Anecdotal and entertaining history.
London Under London by Richard Trench, John Murray Publishers. Delves into London's hidden subterranean network of tunnels and rivers.
The London Blue Plaque Guide by Nick Rennison, Sutton Publishing. Details the lives of more than 700 individuals who have been commemorated with a blue plaque on their houses.
A Literary Guide to London by Ed Glinet, Penguin. A very detailed, street-by-street guide to the literary lives of London.

Other Insight Guides

Three types of Insight Guide are designed to meet the needs of every traveller.

The **Insight Guides** series includes books on *Great Britain, England, Scotland, Wales, Oxford, Glasgow, Edinburgh* and *The Channel Islands*.

The **Insight Pocket Guides** series offers personal recommendations and a full-size map; titles include *South-East England, London, Southwark and the South Bank* and *Scotland*.

The **Insight Compact Guides** series provides the ideal portable, fully illustrated guidebook to specific areas. Over 20 titles cover every tourist area in the UK, from Cornwall to the Scottish Highlands.

Feedback

We do our best to ensure the information in our books is as accurate and up-to-date as possible. The books are updated on a regular basis, using local contacts, who painstakingly add, amend and correct as required. However, some mistakes and omissions are inevitable and we are ultimately reliant on our readers to put us in the picture.

We would welcome your feedback on any details related to your experiences using the book "on the road". Maybe we recommended a hotel that you liked (or another that you didn't), as well as interesting new attractions, or facts and figures you have found out about the country itself. The more details you can give us (particularly with regard to addresses, e-mails and telephone numbers), the better.

We will acknowledge all contributions, and we'll offer an Insight Guide to the best letters received.

Please write to us at:

Insight Guides
PO Box 7910
London SE1 1XF
United Kingdom

Or send e-mail to: **insight@apaguide.demon.co.uk**

ART & PHOTO CREDITS

Philippe Achache 246
Ping Amranand 255
Apa 46, 73, 75, 85, 86, 87L, 91, 94, 95, 122T 128T, 129T 143T, 144T, 147T, 166, 141, 148T, 161L, 166, 167R, 168, 170 171L, 171R, 171T, 172, 178, 181T, 182T, 186, 187, 198, 204, 205T, 205R, 206T, 207T, 213T, 201, 213L, 213R, 213T, 214T, 214L, 215, 216R, 217R, 218T, 221T, 222T, 242, all small cover pictures except back cover left and back flap bottom
BBC Hulton Picture Library 33, 36, 38
Martin Black 82/83, 159
Nelly Boyd/Robert Harding 85
Ian Bradshaw 206
John Bulmer 163L
Julian Calder 126, 203
Mark Cator/Impact 127, 158, 183, 222/223
Conran Restaurants 93
Sulvia Cordaliy Photo Library/Mary Clark 239
Dewinters 77
Chris Donaghue 258/259
Andrew Eames 15, 174/175, 210, 211, 232
English Tourist Board 256
Sally Fear 162
Fortnum & Mason 158T
Lee Foster 205L
Fotomas 25
Nigel Francis/Robert Harding 72, 81
Glyn Genin 37, 43, 44, 45, 47L, 47R, 48, 49, 108, 109, 110, 114T, 139, 140 156T, 192, 193, 194T, 194, 196T, 196, 198T, 199T, 199, 214T, 216T, 217L, 220, back cover left and back flap bottom
Dennis Gilbert 74, 109
Tim Graham 62
David Gray 18, 55, 130, 195T, 210L, 234/235, 232, 244T,
Susan Griggs Agency 177
David Haiden 59
Robert Harding 84, 89, 92, 112T, 114, 226, 223, 233
Brian Harris 241, 218L
John Heseltine 179
Andy Hibbert/Collections 226/227
Geoff Howard/Collections 87R
Anthony Howarth 40, 219

Richard Kalina/Shakespeare's Globe 79
John Kegan 200/201
Landscape Only 134/135, 188, 250/251
Alain Le Garsmeur 8/9, 23, 34, 123, 145, 152/153, 164
Libera Design/Pawel Libera 146, 160R, 197
John Londei 41
London Docklands Development Corporation 231
Mike McQueen/Impact 100/101, 133, 184, 228
Neil Menneer 17, 50/51, 56, 57, 58, 65, 68, 108L, 132, 138, 119, 144, 147L, 147R, 173, 241, 244, 245
J. Miller/Robert Harding 96/97
Museum of London 18/19, 22, 28, 29, 30, 31, 35
Julian Nieman 163, 185
Richard T. Nowitz 10/11, 16, 54, 60, 61, 67, 69, 71, 120, 123, 125, 147L&R, 149, 151, 160L, 163L, 163R, 176, 177, 181, 182, 176, 179R, 221L, 221R, 250/251
Tony Page 247
David Reed 229
Brian Rybolt 218
Jürgen Schadeber 88
Ted Spiegel 189T
Mike St Maur 155
Liz Stares/Collections 239T
Tony Stone Worldwide 139, 131, 169, 245, 257
Homer Sykes 52/53, 219
Liba Taylor/Collections 180L, 260
Topham Picturepoint 39 , 41, 66, 80, 112, 116, 160T, 179, 183R

Cartographic Editor **Zoë Goodwin**
Production **Linton Donaldson**
Design Consultants
Klaus Geisler, Graham Mitchener
Picture Research **Hilary Genin**

Alex Wallerstein/Impact 110
Bill Wassman 42, 115, 141, 125L, 154, 240
Roger Williams 126T, 127T, 128, 129
Adam Woolfitt 64, 76, 156, 157L&R, 158R, 189, 180R, 202, 207, 216L, 212R, 218, 236,
Adam Woolfitt/Robert Harding 14, 12/13, 90, 102, 120, 118/119, 161R
Gregory Wrona 117
Ian Yeomans 167L

Picture Spreads

Pages 74/75: Clockwise from top: Collections/Brian Shuel; Mary Evans Picture Library; Libera Design Ltd; Collections/Bartholomew; Collections/Brian Shuel; Collections/Brian Shuel; Network/B. Hermann.
Pages 150/152: Top left: Glyn Genin. Paintings by courtesy of the National Gallery, London. Top right: Courtesy of the National Portrait Gallery, London
Pages 190/191: Clockwiase from top left: Mary Evans Picture Library; Apa; Collections/John Miller; Collections/Liba Taylor; Collections/Brian Shuel; Network/Sunil Gupta; Collections/Michael George
Pages 224/5: Clockwise from top left: Apa; London Aerial Photo Library; Apa; Apa; Apa; Collections/James Bartholomew; Apa; Collections/James Bartholomew;
Pages 240/241: Clockwise from left: Pictorial Press (Audrey Hepburn); Ben Edwards/Impact; Collections/ Michael St Maur Sheil; Rex Features; Piers Cavendish/ Impact; Johnathan Trapman/Ace (Wimbledon Cup) Collections/Liba Taylor; Collections/Geoff Howard

Map Production
Polyglott Kartographie

INDEX

a

b

c

m

n

o

p

q

r

s

t

u–v